MW00355434

The U.S. Navy and Its Cold War Alliances, 1945–1953

The U.S. Navy and Its Cold War Alliances, 1945–1953

Corbin Williamson

 University Press of Kansas

Published by the University Press of Kansas (Lawrence, Kansas 66045), which was
organized by the Kansas Board of Regents and is operated and funded by Emporia
State University, Fort Hays State University, Kansas State University, Pittsburg State
University, the University of Kansas, and Wichita State University

Library of Congress Cataloging-in-Publication Data

Names: Williamson, Corbin, author.
Title: The U.S. Navy and its Cold War alliances, 1945–1953 / Corbin Williamson.
Description: [Lawrence] : University Press of Kansas, [2020] | Series: Modern war
studies | Includes bibliographical references and index.
Identifiers: LCCN 2020007579
  ISBN 9780700629787 (cloth)
  ISBN 9780700629794 (epub)
Subjects: LCSH: United States. Navy—History—20th century. | United States—History,
Naval—20th century. | United States—Military relations—Canada. | United States—
Military relations—Great Britain. | United States—Military relations—Australia. |
Canada—Military relations—United States. | Great Britain—Military relations—United
States. | Australia—Military relations—United States.
Classification: LCC E746 .W56 2020 | DDC 359/.03097309044—dc23
LC record available at https://lccn.loc.gov/2020007579.

British Library Cataloguing-in-Publication Data is available.

Printed in the United States of America
10 9 8 7 6 5 4 3 2 1

The paper used in this publication is recycled and contains 30 percent postconsumer
waste. It is acid free and meets the minimum requirements of the American National
Standard for Permanence of Paper for Printed Library Materials Z39.48-1992.

CONTENTS

ACKNOWLEDGMENTS

This project would not have been possible without the support of a constellation of individuals who have contributed in a variety of ways. John Guilmartin was a strong supporter from the beginning, writing countless letters of recommendation and supporting numerous funding requests until his untimely passing. Peter Mansoor has provided invaluable support and helped me to think about book projects more clearly. Financial support for research trips has been provided by the Department of History and the Graduate School at Ohio State University, the Bradley Foundation, the Marine Corps Historical Foundation, and the English Speaking Union of Cincinnati. The archival and reference staff at the National Archives and Records Administration, Naval History and Heritage Command, U.S. Naval Institute Library, Hoover Institution Library, Library and Archives Canada, Directorate of History and Heritage, Naval Historical Branch, National Archives of the United Kingdom, Imperial War Museum, National Archives of Australia, Sea Power Centre—Australia, and Australian War Memorial all provided invaluable support. In particular, John Hodges, Nathaniel Patch, Dale Gordon, Laura Waayers, Michael Whitby, Isabel Campbell, Jenny Wraight, Jock Gardner, David Stevens, and John Berryman at these institutions were especially helpful. Thomas-Durell Young's excitement for the subject of American-Australian naval relations has been encouraging. Randy Papadopolous and Peter Swartz repeatedly expressed interest in the project and encouraged me to continue. James Levy helped by answering questions about the Royal Navy's Home Fleet. Laurence Maher shared his research on the information embargo on Australia. Andy Nicholson and Alannah Croom both helped photograph documents when I was unable to travel to archives. Ian Pfennigwerth and Chris Coulthard-Clark both shared information on the Royal Australian Navy that has been helpful. Isabel Campbell has helped clarify my thinking on the Royal Canadian Navy and been a source of encouragement. Colleagues at the Historical Office of the Office of the Secretary of Defense encouraged me to continue working on the project. Thanks to Erin Mahan, Glen Asner, Jon Hoffman, Edward Keefer, Ryan Carpenter, Ryan Peeks, Tony Crain, Marshall Yokell, Shannon Mohan, Rachel Levandoski, Sandra Doyle, Tom Christianson, Breck Walker, and Steven Phillips. My fellow faculty at Air War College have created a supportive atmosphere. Thanks to Ken Callahan, Mike Sierco, Douglas Peifer, Brian McNeill, Will Waddell, Alex Lassner, Xiaoming Zhang, David Palkki, Ron Gurantz, Roy Houchin, Douglas Drake, Lee Donaldson, Patrick Budjenska, Jeremy Weber, Andreas Wachowitz, Michelle Scott, and Howard Hensel. Thanks also to Peter Dean and Rhys Crawley for their friendship and support. Michael Whitby, Frank Blazich, Jessica Ricketts, Will Waddell, Brian McNeill, Ryan Wadle, and Heather Venable have all read draft chapters and provided insightful feedback that has significantly improved this book. Joe Panza at the Air University Foundation provided valuable financial support for the index. The English Speaking Union of Cincinnati generously supported an archival research trip for this project. Thanks to Joyce Harrison and the team at the University Press of Kansas for their support for this project.

My parents, Matt and Lauri, and my in-laws, Mike and Brenda, have supported my interest in history and my family in general. Thanks to John and Patty Mellinger for their hospitality. Members of our various churches have been encouraging and supportive throughout this project. Thanks to Micah and Heather Green, Laura and Sam Hohbein, Todd and Elise Walters, Jonathan and Erin Baker, Mike and Emma Juday, Danny and Janelle Jackson, TJ and Holly Wood, Keith and Amanda Robinette, Jay and Megan O'Brien, Cory and Karen Perkins, Mary Storie, Rob and Lina Lehner, Xris and Christina Vallianos, Tyler and Emily Anderson, Mark and Victoria Batey, Chad and Rachel Pack, Jeremiah and Emily Nichols, Nate and Molly Jaeger, Greg and Courtney Duke, Mike and Danni Donahue, Rusty and Kim Jacksland, Robert and Natie Mitchell, Alex and April Emanuel, Eric and Becky Collier, Cody and Kathleen Daughtry, Joe and Taylor Mills, Paul and Beth Dye, Keith Parsons, and Doug and Lori Hudgins. In particular the support and friendship of Rusty Jacksland, one of Prattville's finest, has been critical.

Our daughters provide encouragement to write in ways they do not understand. Finally, I could not have completed this project much less five years of graduate school without the support of my wife. She has put up with covering too many walls in too many apartments with bookshelves, five different jobs, five moves, and countless hours photographing documents in archives, including one research trip to Canada while she was pregnant with our first child. She has heard and learned more about early Cold War naval cooperation than she ever wanted and at various points has served as travel agent, librarian, research assistant, and cheerleader. The completion of this project is due to her support as much as anything. Thank you, Ashley.

The views expressed in this manuscript are those of the author and do not reflect the official policy or position of the U.S. government, the Department of Defense, or the Air War College.

ABBREVIATIONS AND ACRONYMS

1SL	First Sea Lord (U.K.)
ABC	American, British, Canadian
ABDA	American, British, Dutch, Australian .
ACNB	Australian Commonwealth Naval Board
ACP	Allied Communication Publication
AFMED	Allied Forces Mediterranean
AFPAC	Army Forces, Pacific (U.S.)
AFSOUTH	Allied Forces Southern Europe
AIO	Action Information Organization
ANZAM	Australia–New Zealand–Malaya
ANZUS	Australia–New Zealand–United States
ASIO	Australian Security Intelligence Organization
ASW	antisubmarine warfare
ATP	Allied Tactical Publication
AWM	Australian War Memorial
BAD	British Admiralty Delegation, Washington, D.C.
BJSM(W)	British Joint Staff Mission (Washington)/British Joint Services Mission (Washington)
BPF	British Pacific Fleet
BuAir	Bureau of Aeronautics (U.S.)
CANAVHED	Canadian Naval Headquarters
CANAVUS	naval member, Canadian Joint Staff (Washington)
CANCOMDESFE	Commander, Canadian Destroyers Far East
CANUKUS	Canada–United Kingdom–United States
CAP	combat air patrol
CAT	Canadian anti–acoustic torpedo
CCB	Combined Communications Board
CCS	Combined Chiefs of Staff
CIC	Combat Information Center (U.S.)
CINCFE	Commander in Chief, Far East Station (U.K.)
CINCHF	Commander in Chief, Home Fleet (U.K.)
CINCLANT	Commander in Chief, Atlantic (U.S.)

CINCLANTFLT	Commander in Chief, Atlantic Fleet (U.S.)
CINCNELM	Commander in Chief, Naval Forces, Eastern Atlantic and Mediterranean (U.S.)
CINCPAC	Commander in Chief, Pacific (U.S.)
CINCPACFLT	Commander in Chief, Pacific Fleet (U.S.)
CJS(W)	Canadian Joint Staff (Washington)
CNO	Chief of Naval Operations (U.S.)
CO	commanding officer
COM7THFLT	Commander, Seventh Fleet (U.S.)
COMAIRLANT	Commander, Naval Air Force, Atlantic Fleet (U.S.)
COMAIRPAC	Commander, Naval Air Force, Pacific Fleet (U.S.)
COMCARDIV	Commander, Carrier Division
COMNAVEU	Commander, Naval Forces, Europe (U.S.)
COMNAVFE	Commander, Naval Forces, Far East (U.S.)
COMNAVSWPAC	Commander, Naval Forces, South West Pacific (U.S.)
COMSUBLANT	Commander, Submarine Force, Atlantic Fleet (U.S.)
CTE	commander task element
CTF	commander task force
CTG	commander task group
DAW	Director of Air Warfare (U.K.)
DCNO	Deputy Chief of Naval Operations (U.S.)
DNAD	Director, Naval Air Division (Canada)
DNH	Director of Naval History (U.S.)
DNI	Director of Naval Intelligence (U.S., U.K., and Australia)
DNPI	Director of Naval Plans and Intelligence (Canada)
DOD	Director of Operations Division (U.K.)
DoP	Director of Plans (U.K.)
DSD	Director of Signal Division (U.K.)
DStand	Director of Standardization (U.K. and Canada)
DTASW	Director of Torpedo, Antisubmarine, and Mine Warfare (U.K.)
DTSD	Director of Tactical and Staff Duties (U.K.)
DWS	Director of Weapons and Tactics (Canada)
FAETU	Fleet Airborne Electronics Training Unit (U.S.)
FECOM	Far East Command (U.S.)

FO2FE	Flag Officer, Second-in-Command, Far East (U.K.)
FOAC	Flag Officer Atlantic Coast (Canada)
FOPC	Flag Officer Pacific Coast (Canada)
HIA	Hoover Institution Archives
HMAS	His/Her Majesty's Australian ship
HMCS	His/Her Majesty's Canadian ship
HMNLS	His/Her Majesty's Netherlands ship
HMS	His/Her Majesty's ship
HUK	hunter-killer
IEP	information exchange project
JASS	Joint Anti-Submarine School (U.K.)
JCEC	Joint Communications-Electronics Committee (U.S. and U.K.)
JCS	Joint Chiefs of Staff (U.S.)
JMWS	Joint Maritime Warfare School (Canada)
JSM(W)	Joint Staff Mission (Washington) (U.K.)
JTC	Joint Telecommunications Committee (Canada)
MAD	magnetic anomaly detection
MCC	Military Cooperation Committee (U.S. and Canada)
MIC	Military Information Control Subcommittee (U.S.)
NATO	North Atlantic Treaty Organization
NMCJS(W)	naval member, Canadian Joint Staff (Washington)
NSC	National Security Council (U.S.)
ONI	Office of Naval Intelligence (U.S.)
OPDEVFOR	Operational Development Force (U.S.)
OTC	officer in tactical command
PJBD	Permanent Joint Board on Defense
RAF	Royal Air Force
RAN	Royal Australian Navy
RCAF	Royal Canadian Air Force
RCN	Royal Canadian Navy
RG	record group
RN	Royal Navy
ROK	Republic of Korea
SACEUR	Supreme Allied Commander, Europe
SACLANT	Supreme Allied Commander, Atlantic

SANACC	State-Army-Navy-Air Force Coordinating Committee (U.S.)
SCAP	Supreme Commander for the Allied Powers
SWNCC	State-War-Navy Coordinating Committee (U.S.)
TAS	Torpedo Anti-Submarine Branch (U.K.)
TE	task element
TG	task group
TF	task force
UHF	ultrahigh frequency
UN	United Nations
UNO	United Nations Organization
USA	United States Army
USD	United States dollar
USN	United States Navy
USS	United States ship
VF	fighter squadron
VCNO	Vice Chief of Naval Operations (U.S.)
VHF	very high frequency

Introduction

Temperatures hovered in the low forties Fahrenheit as the Americans left on December 1, 1918.[1] A line of American battleships headed out of Rosyth, the home of the Royal Navy's Grand Fleet. In the final year of World War I, the U.S. Navy deployed a squadron of battleships to reinforce the British Grand Fleet guarding the North Sea. With the signing of an armistice on November 11, the American ships headed for home. During their time with the Grand Fleet, the U.S. Navy ships operated as integrated parts of British formations and adopted Royal Navy communications practices and tactical doctrine, an unprecedented amalgamation of Anglo-American naval forces for an extended period. Admiral Hugh Rodman, the American commander, said that the American squadron intended to maintain the ties of friendship that had grown up between the two sides "for all time."[2]

Despite Rodman's intentions, U.S. Navy relations with the Royal Navy became strained in the 1920s and early 1930s due to disagreements over disarmament, fleet size, interpretations of freedom of the seas, and general economic competition. The Americans made no effort to maintain the body of knowledge built up during World War I that gave them the ability to fight alongside the British. For instance, American ships operating with the Grand Fleet had used the Royal Navy's set of signal flags but reverted to American flags at the war's end. Cordial relations existed between individual ships and between personnel of the two nations who met in the course of their duties. However, the navies did not exercise together, did not develop shared procedures and tactics, did not exchange personnel, and did not share information for most of the interwar period. In the late 1930s, the growing danger of Nazi Germany and Imperial Japan gradually drew the two fleets together, though lingering suspicion still colored relations between the two sides at times. Growing cooperation from 1939 to 1941 turned into a coalition when the United States entered World War II in December 1941. The U.S. Navy fought alongside the British, Canadian, Australian, and other Allied navies throughout the war until Germany and then Japan surrendered in 1945.[3]

Twenty-six years and nine months after Rodman left Rosyth, another Anglo-American fleet broke up when the battleship *Duke of York* and two escorts left Tokyo Bay on September 9, 1945. *Duke of York* carried Admiral Bruce Fraser, commander in chief of the British Pacific Fleet.[4] From March until the end of the war against Japan, this force of British and Commonwealth ships and aircraft had fought alongside the U.S. Pacific Fleet. Japan's formal surrender on September 2, 1945, ended the combined operations of the two fleets.[5] The British departed amid messages calling for continued close relations, similar to those sent by Rodman in 1918. The question facing U.S. Navy leaders in 1945 was whether or not to follow the pattern of the years after World War I, during which wartime Anglo-American naval links decayed.

One strain of academic scholarship argues that in the early Cold War the U.S. Navy did in fact follow the pattern of the interwar years by turning away from its wartime allies. Lisle Rose states that American admirals in 1945 and 1946 were "even more pugnacious, suspicious, and antagonistic toward their supposed allies" than had been admirals in the immediate aftermath of World War I. He also portrays the Royal Navy of the late 1940s as a wasting asset to which the U.S. Navy needed to pay little attention.[6] Michael Isenberg's history of the early Cold War U.S. Navy concludes that partnering with foreign navies "cut squarely across the grain of American naval tradition and practice."[7] These authors portray the U.S. Navy as nationalistic, convinced of its own superiority, and therefore uninterested in cooperating with allies.

However, previously unused and recently declassified records detailing U.S. Navy relations with the British, Canadian, and Australian navies in the early Cold War reveal that, in fact, the U.S. Navy was far more internationalist than has been recognized. These archival sources demonstrate that the

American navy both valued and pursued close links with these allies in the late 1940s. The U.S. Navy, for example, regularly trained and exercised with the British, Canadian, and Australian fleets. American naval policy and planning was based on the assumption of cooperation with the Commonwealth. American officials created a web of organizational links with these navies, pursued standardized equipment and doctrine, and wrote the foundational manuals for multinational naval operations that are still in use today. Concerned about the danger of a war against the Soviet Union and the threat posed by Soviet submarines, the U.S. Navy worked to retain interoperability with its closest wartime allies. In short, the U.S. Navy began constructing informal alliances with these three navies before the North Atlantic Treaty Organization (NATO) came into existence. Even after NATO's establishment in 1949, this American-led informal naval alliance continued to exist beneath NATO.

This informal naval alliance consisted of deep and wide links between navies. Deep links gave a small number of officers intensive experience with another navy for an extended period, such as through a liaison assignment or attendance at a foreign professional military school. Wide links provided larger numbers of personnel with briefer contact with another navy, such as through a multinational exercise or a week of training at a foreign training station. The combination of deep and wide links created between 1945 and 1953 demonstrated the shared interest in retaining close relations between the U.S. Navy and its closest wartime allies.

The U.S. Navy's efforts to maintain wartime ties with its allies represented a break from America's traditional avoidance of peacetime military alliances. Ever since George Washington's 1796 charge to "steer clear of permanent alliances," American officials had prided themselves on standing apart from Europe's alliances.[8] The U.S. Navy's post–World War II combined exercises, information sharing, and personnel exchange programs constituted a turn away from this pattern of American foreign policy.

This change in the Navy's course after World War II remains largely unexamined, in contrast to the Navy's prewar and wartime links.[9] Many scholars have delved into U.S. Navy ties with the Royal Navy and Royal Canadian Navy in 1940 and 1941 as well as wartime relations between the U.S. Navy and its closest allies.[10] However, the question of what happened to these wartime naval links in the late 1940s is largely unanswered.[11]

The U.S. Navy's continued cooperation with its closest wartime allies reflected the wider national shift toward greater American international involvement in the early years of the Cold War. In September 1945, American citizens applauded the creation of the United Nations, a new international organization dedicated to preserving the peace. However, the end of World War II removed the common threat that had brought the Soviet Union, Britain, and America together. Tensions between the wartime allies grew in late 1945 and into 1946. For example, debates over occupation policy in Germany highlighted differences of opinion and interests between the Soviets on one hand and the British and Americans on the other. Many Americans viewed growing Soviet influence in Eastern Europe as a breach with agreements reached between the three allies at Yalta in February 1945. These tensions led to a growing break between the Soviets and the Western Allies in the late 1940s, resulting in the creation of NATO in 1949.[12]

At the end of World War II President Harry Truman had been in office for less than five months. Truman sought to carry on the policies of his predecessor, Franklin Roosevelt, who had led the nation throughout the Great Depression and for most of the war. Truman, a plain-speaking native of Missouri, recognized that after four years of war, the public looked forward to peace. Specifically, Americans wanted their massive military demobilized, their family members returned home, and their economy taken off its wartime footing. Truman recognized that reconfiguring the American economy while cutting military spending could lead to an economic recession. The demand for demobilization and cuts in military spending thus encouraged the U.S. Navy to look for partners to share the responsibility for patrolling the war's oceans.[13]

The story of how the U.S. Navy built peacetime informal alliances is significant for three reasons. First, the Navy's assumption of a larger role in international naval affairs after World War II was a microcosm of American society's coming to terms with an expanded role for the United States on the world stage. Navy leaders such as Secretary of the Navy James Forrestal often took steps to counter the Soviets before public or congressional opinion came around to supporting such steps.[14] For example, the navy began building an informal naval alliance with the British and Canadians in the summer of 1946, three years before Congress approved the North Atlantic Treaty. In this sense, navy officials adopted a Cold War mentality and began building ties with allies in advance of American society or even elements of the U.S. government. Second, the navy's cultivation of potential allies for a war with Russia emphasizes the role of common threats in U.S. relations with Britain, Canada, and Australia, rather than shared cultural values or language. A common language smoothed relations with the British, Canadians, and Australians, but it was the Soviet threat that led the Navy Department to build deep naval links. Finally, the navy's efforts to maintain links with these navies revealed that the U.S. Navy was unprepared in important respects for the challenges of leading a multinational naval alliance system in peacetime. In particular, the Navy lacked the administrative capacity for handling basic liaison work such as sharing information and arranging visits. The navy had to restructure its organizations such as the Office of Naval Intelligence to meet the demands of this new pattern of close peacetime relations with friendly navies.

The U.S. Navy's pursuit of continued close relations with the British, the Canadians, and, to a lesser degree, the Australians came about because of three factors. First and most important was the need to prepare for a third Battle of the Atlantic in which Soviet submarines, ships, and aircraft would seek to sever the North Atlantic and Pacific shipping lanes. While the Soviet navy of the 1940s operated primarily in coastal waters, the U.S. Navy knew that in 1945 the Soviets had acquired advanced German submarine technology.[15] Soviet submarines equipped with this technology would pose a significant danger in the future. To counter this growing Soviet naval threat, the U.S. Navy established an information-sharing program with the Royal Navy and the Royal Canadian Navy in the summer of 1946 and a standardization program in November of that year. Both of these efforts laid the foundations for sustaining wartime naval links. Concerns about Soviet power also led Admiral Louis Denfeld, commander in chief of the U.S. Pacific Fleet, to suggest staff talks between the U.S. Navy and the Royal Australian Navy in June 1947. These talks eventually led to the little-known 1951 Radford-Collins Agreement, which bound the two navies closer together. In addition to the Soviet threat, the successes of Anglo-American sea power in World War II against the Axis suggested the value of maintaining naval links in the postwar period. Finally, U.S. Navy postwar planning called for a global division of oceanic policing duties with the British, which would require a level of coordination and cooperation. In 1944, U.S. Navy planners assumed that the Royal Navy would patrol the Eastern Atlantic, Mediterranean, and Indian Ocean while the Americans handled the Western Atlantic and the Pacific.[16] These last two reasons might have led to friendly relations on their own. However, the focus on retaining interoperability, which led to standardization, combined planning, and multinational exercises, stemmed from concerns about the Soviet threat.[17]

In addition to these factors, Canada benefited from its unique geographic relationship with the United States. From the U.S. Navy's perspective, Canada was different from other nations because of shared interests in securing the seaborne approaches to the North American continent. Alone of the Commonwealth countries, Canada's proximity to the United States provided a secure foundation for continued postwar naval cooperation. While U.S. size and strength at times created concerns over Canadian sovereignty in Ottawa, coordination and cooperation made sense for both navies given shared North American interests. Canadian-American naval relations reflected both continental defense interests and concerns about the Soviet naval threat.

Understanding the U.S. Navy's early Cold War informal alliances requires a survey of Anglo-American naval relations from World War I through World War II. After World War II the organizations that would manage relations between the U.S. military and the British, Canadian, and Australian militaries gradually came into focus. With this background, it becomes possible to topically examine four elements of navy-to-navy links during the period from 1945 through the early 1950s. First, the U.S. Navy established planning links with its closest wartime allies to prepare for a war with the Soviet Union. Second, liaison officers such as attachés and exchange personnel deepened navy-to-navy links through their contacts and personal relationships. Third, the Americans, British, and Canadians pursued standardization, though with more success in the fields of doctrine, procedures, and communications than in equipment. Fourth, educational exchanges, training links, and combined exercises helped naval forces retain interoperability, especially in antisubmarine warfare. The outbreak of the Korean War in June 1950 provided a test of the U.S. Navy's efforts to retain the ability to effectively fight alongside the British, Canadians, and Australians on short notice. The naval war in Korean waters demonstrated the considerable progress made in retaining interoperability while also highlighting enduring differences in capabilities and skills between the Americans and their allies. Analysis of the organizational structure and these four fields of naval relations demonstrates the U.S. Navy's commitment to maintaining close links with the British, Canadians, and, to a lesser degree, Australians in the early Cold War.

Tracing the course of U.S. Navy relations with the British, Canadians, and Australians reveals three themes that influenced navy-to-navy ties. Personal relations between officers and officials at the working level proved critical to developing and sustaining these ties. Employing Paul Kennedy's concept of doing "history from the middle" helps illuminate these often overlooked midlevel ties. Kennedy argues that military history tends to focus on senior leaders or tactical engagements with insufficient attention to the midlevel personnel and organizations who translate policy into practice.[18] Midcareer officers (lieutenant commanders, commanders, and captains), in fact, profoundly shaped the ways in which navy-to-navy ties came together. These midlevel personnel benefited from support from key advocates for close naval relations in all four navies. In the U.S. Navy, Chester Nimitz, Arthur Radford, and Charles Styer worked to advance these ties, as did James Somerville and Bruce Fraser in the Royal Navy. The Royal Canadian Navy's Harold Grant (though often described as British-oriented) took important steps to bring the RCN closer to the U.S. Navy.[19] In Australia, John Collins pursued close links with the U.S. Navy throughout his leadership of the Royal Australian Navy.

Finally, domestic political concerns exerted a strong influence on naval relations in all four countries. In the United States, public support for the United Nations in 1946 and 1947 especially meant American admirals had to avoid taking public steps that might appear to undermine the UN, such as forming a peacetime naval alliance. As a result, many of the discussions and agreements involved in this effort were highly classified and purposefully kept out of the public eye because of their political sensitivity. In Britain, Winston Churchill politicized naval command arrangements for the Atlantic in 1951 as a means of attacking Prime Minister Clement Attlee's government, reopening an issue that British and American admirals had already settled. Canada's traditional ties with Britain and concerns over potential American intrusions into Canadian sovereignty made Ottawa cautious about entering into agreements with the U.S. military. In Australia, Prime Minister Ben Chifley's efforts to expand the role of the federal government in Canberra led some American officers such as Stephen Jurika, the U.S. naval attaché, to view Australia as overly subservient to communist pressure. The influence of political concerns led naval officers in all four nations to craft agreements and links that would be relatively immune from shifts in political opinion.

To trace these themes, this work draws on official government records, personal paper collections, and oral histories from the United States, the United Kingdom, Canada, and Australia. Recently declassified documents in both the United States and Canada reveal the depth of postwar cooperation between the American, British, and Canadian navies. The records of the Canadian naval mission in Washington, D.C., highlight Canada's creation of a network of liaison and exchange positions with the U.S. Navy. Stephen Jurika's papers at the Hoover Institution bring to light this officer's little-known role in cutting off Australian access to classified American information in the late 1940s. The records of Australian naval leaders at the National Archives of Australia demonstrate their continued interest in building ties with the U.S. Navy despite the information embargo. Using records from all four nations emphasizes the role that the British, Canadians, and Australians played in building postwar relationships with the U.S. Navy.

The U.S. Navy's interest in retaining interoperability with its closest wartime allies grew out of experiences in World War II. In the Battle of the Java Sea in 1942, a multinational formation thrown together with little opportunity to train together as a combined unit fared poorly in battle. More broadly, the development of practices and equipment to allow American ships to fight effectively with their allies took years. American planners assumed that in a war with the Soviet Union, the speed of Soviet advances would not give the U.S. Navy time to build interoperability once hostilities began. President Truman said in 1945 that the nation should not "count on the luxury of time" in a future conflict.[20] The solution was for the navy to be able to fight in multinational formations with little warning. To accomplish this goal required extensive peacetime coordination, planning, and training.

From World War I to the Cold War

Prior to World War I Anglo-American naval cooperation was sparse at best. In the decades before the American Civil War, American warships periodically cooperated with the Royal Navy's efforts in interdicting the slave trade off the African coast.[1] In 1859, American Commodore Josiah Tattnall supported an Anglo-French attack on Chinese forts during a treaty dispute.[2] However, prior to World War I, the two navies had never operated together for an extended period, which meant that in 1917 both were sailing into uncharted waters when American warships joined the British Grand Fleet. Although relations at the working level between the two navies were close during the war, the U.S. Navy made no effort to retain the ability to operate with the British after the war's end.

The lack of American interest in retaining naval interoperability with Britain reflected the growth in Anglo-American tensions after World War I. Throughout the 1920s and early 1930s, the two nations bickered over naval arms limitation treaties and financial arrangements stemming from World War I while British and American companies competed vigorously for business, especially in South America. Although the prospect of the two nations going to war was remote, military-to-military contacts lacked the critical features of ongoing close military relations: combined training to practice interoperability and regular personnel exchanges. In this strategic context, the U.S. Navy focused on internal improvements rather than preparing for a future coalition war.

As a result, when America entered World War II, the U.S. Navy had to improvise procedures for combined naval operations, sometimes with disastrous results. Still, throughout World War II, American, British, Canadian, and Australian ships operated together in mixed formations on a number of occasions in the Mediterranean and European theaters, culminating in the large-scale combined operations involving the U.S. Pacific Fleet and the British Pacific Fleet in 1945.

THE U.S. NAVY AND SCAPA FLOW, PART 1

When the United States joined World War I in April 1917, President Woodrow Wilson directed that the U.S. remain an associated, not allied, power. This distinction highlighted the administration's desire to defeat Germany and Austria-Hungary but without fully joining in the Allied cause.[3] Wilson also wanted to ensure a strong American role in crafting the terms of peace after the presumed Allied victory.

Within the U.S. Navy, however, Chief of Naval Operations Admiral William S. Benson and Secretary of the Navy Josephus Daniels recognized that the American naval effort must be coordinated with the existing Allied naval effort and in particular with the Royal Navy. Benson and Daniels sent Canadian-born Rear Admiral William S. Sims to London to coordinate with the British. Sims was later given responsibility for all U.S. naval forces in Europe and oversaw a steadily growing naval effort that, by the summer of 1918, included dozens of destroyers, naval aviation squadrons, submarine patrols, and a squadron of battleships deployed with the British Grand Fleet. In contrast to the U.S. Army and General Pershing, Sims regularly called for amalgamation, placing American and British warships in mixed formations. He once wrote, "Our destroyers! Your destroyers!—I am tired of hearing of it. We have one fleet and it ought be used as one."[4]

Sims's advocacy earned him praise in London and skepticism from Washington.[5] Benson, Daniels, and Wilson remained wary about becoming too closely associated with the Royal Navy throughout the war. For example, when the British offered to make Sims an honorary member of the Admiralty, Wilson and Daniels shot down the idea. Another request to promote Rear Admiral Hugh Rodman, the commander of American battleships operating with the Grand Fleet, to match the Grand Fleet's rank structure was similarly refused.[6] Still, despite Washington's wariness, relations between

Admiral David Beatty, RN, and Rear Admiral Hugh Rodman, USN, 1918. *Source*: 165-BO-0343, National Archives ID 16577855, National Archives at College Park, College Park, MD.

operational commanders in Europe proved to be quite close, as shown by the experience of Rodman's command, the Sixth Battle Squadron.

After several months of back and forth negotiations between Washington and London, a squadron of four American battleships under Rear Admiral Rodman joined the Grand Fleet at Scapa Flow in December 1917. The Americans never saw significant action, but their time with the Grand Fleet represented the first time that the two navies operated together on a regular basis. The American ships formed the Sixth Battle Squadron and quickly began adjusting their practices to match British methods. For example, the Americans adopted British signaling procedures to integrate into British formations and learned how to take on coal more rapidly so that the fleet could quickly return to sea after arriving in port. Gunfire practices quickly revealed that American battleship gunnery was not up to British standards. Part of the problem was that U.S. Navy gunfire practice took place under ideal weather conditions while the British practiced under wartime conditions, firing rapidly in bad weather. The Americans' gunnery slowly improved, though it took several months before Admiral David Beatty, the commander in chief of the Grand Fleet, was satisfied.[7] An internal Royal Navy memo concluded that based on the experience of the Sixth Battle Squadron, American warships needed four months working up before they could operate as full members of British formations.[8] The squadron's experience illustrated the extended familiarization period required for warships to develop interoperability without the aid of standing arrangements.

The American willingness to adopt British methods as well as Rodman's and Beatty's efforts to keep disagreements private helped maintain good relations between the Sixth Battle Squadron and the Grand Fleet.[9] In several instances, the crews of a British ship and an American ship even formed connections. For example, the battleship *Arkansas* had a number of skilled musicians on board but lacked a conductor, while the light cruiser *Southampton* had a conductor but no band, so the two ships pooled their resources.[10] Through these connections, British and American officers frequently visited one another's ships, leading each side to compare and contrast their organization and equipment.

Such comparisons highlighted differences in organization and equipment. American officers who went on board British battleships were surprised to find that the turret officer knew less about the mechanical details of the turret than the senior enlisted gunner. In the U.S. Navy, officers received extensive technical training and were expected to be experts in the operation of their equipment.[11] Technical differences aside, the Sixth Battle Squadron's time with the Grand Fleet built up a significant body of experience in combined naval operations within the U.S. Navy.

In addition to the battleship squadron, the U.S. Navy also deployed a force of destroyers for antisubmarine duty to Queenstown, Ireland. Secretary Daniels had Sims place the American ships under the control of Vice Admiral Lewis Bayly, the local British commander. Bayly, "the archetype of the crusty old seadog," was known for his brusque manner, and Sims recalled that at their first meeting, Bayly was "as rude to me as one man could well be to another."[12] However, Sims's efforts to develop a working relationship with Bayly paid off, and the two became close personal friends.[13] Bayly operated the British and American destroyers under his command as a single operational force, creating mixed operational formations while allowing the Americans to take care of their own internal administration.[14] Bayly also developed close relations with many of the young commanding officers of the American destroyers, referring to them as "my destroyers" and "my Americans."[15] The American destroyers also adopted British communications methods.[16] The U.S. Navy also sent a squadron to operate out of Gibraltar. Under Rear Admiral Albert Niblack, American escorts joined a multinational pool of warships to provide escorts for Allied convoys. Gibraltar's strategic location meant that a quarter of Allied shipping sailed past the base by the end of the war.[17]

On the whole, relations between the U.S. Navy and Royal Navy during World War I were positive. However, the armistice in November 1918 inaugurated a cooling-off period in navy-to-navy relations. As has often been the case, at the end of the war the American public demanded the rapid return of soldiers from overseas. The U.S. Army and Navy removed the bulk of their forces from Europe. The two fleets did not retain their combined communications methods, did not pursue standardization of equipment, and did not conduct combined training. The U.S. Navy made little effort to maintain its interoperability with the British, which reflected the friction that frequently marked Anglo-American naval relations during the 1920s.[18]

INTERWAR FRICTION

David Reynolds convincingly argues that despite fighting as allies in World War I, the British and Americans in the 1920s "were rivals as much as collaborators." The twin centers of this rivalry were naval power and finance, both areas in which Britain had traditionally been dominant but was now challenged by the growing strength of the United States.[19] This strength was certainly on display in 1919 when President Wilson arrived in Europe for the Versailles Peace Conference. Wilson's subsequent failure to bring the United States into the League of Nations, created at Versailles with his support, led many in London to conclude that the United States was quite capable of producing diplomatic communiques but rarely able to back up words with force.

The roots of the interwar naval rivalry between the two countries lay in 1916, when Wilson secured congressional approval for a massive expansion of the U.S. Navy. This 1916 building program was followed by approval for a second building program in 1918. During the war, the need for building anti-submarine escorts and merchant ships prevented much progress from being made on constructing the capital ships authorized by the two programs. However, with the defeat of the Central Powers, America appeared poised to build a fleet that would challenge and possibly surpass the Royal Navy's numerical supremacy.[20] The Admiralty and the Cabinet, determined to maintain Britain's position at sea, began planning for a naval building race.

In response to this looming arms race, President Warren Harding's new Republican administration called the 1921 Washington Naval Conference to limit naval armaments. On its opening day, November 12, 1921, Secretary of State Charles Evans Hughes dramatically proposed a cessation of capital ship construction and a massive program of scrapping older warships.[21] Hughes also suggested that the strength of British, American, and Japanese capital ships be set at the ratio of five to five to three respectively. The British government accepted, relieved that London would not have to compete with American industrial strength in shipbuilding. The British also agreed to an American diplomatic request. The U.S. Navy wanted the Anglo-Japanese alliance dissolved as the Navy Department viewed Japan as a likely future opponent and did not want the Royal Navy coming in on Japan's side. The British acquiesced, and the alliance was not renewed.[22]

However, naval construction, especially in cruisers, continued to create tension in Anglo-American naval relations after the Washington Naval Conference. Between 1922 and 1926, Britain laid down a number of new cruisers in accordance with the terms of the Washington conference. However, Congress and the administration of President Calvin Coolidge did not fund a corresponding American cruiser program. As a result, many American naval officers felt that the conniving British had taken advantage of the United States.[23]

Another naval disarmament conference in Geneva in June 1927 foundered over the issue of cruisers. The Americans wanted the major powers limited to building a smaller number of large long-range heavy cruisers, which were ideally suited for use in the Pacific. In contrast, the Royal Navy viewed smaller light cruisers as essential to protecting their overseas trade routes from raiders, a task that required more ships than the Americans had in mind. The British and Americans also disagreed over the use of blockades in a future war. The Admiralty wanted this traditional tool of British sea power preserved, while Washington insisted on freedom of the seas for neutral powers. The Geneva conference broke up in August 1927 after two months of failed negotiations. Subsequently, the 1930 London Naval Conference produced an agreement on cruisers and reaffirmed the Washington Conference's naval ratios, but in London "there was growing feeling that since 1919 Britain had appeased America too often for too little in return."[24]

As a result of these differences, relations between the Admiralty and the Navy Department in the 1920s and early 1930s were frequently marked more by friction than by cooperation. An important exception was relations between the U.S. Navy's Asiatic Squadron and the Royal Navy's China Squadron. David Kennedy has shown that during the 1930s the commanders of these two forces, as well as other British and American officials in East Asia, informally cooperated regularly. In 1933, the two squadrons developed a communications code for use in emergencies, though it was never implemented. In addition, the British shared information from their strategic planning conferences with the senior American naval commander in the area. Cooperation in East Asia became even closer after the Japanese invasion of China in 1937. Admiral Harry Yarnell and Admiral Charles Little, the respective American and British local commanders at the time of the invasion, shared information about their plans and policies and became close personal friends.[25]

Despite the friction of the 1920s and early 1930s, growing tensions in Europe and the Pacific gradually improved relations between the two navies. The close naval ties demonstrated in East Asia gave support to the view of Ronald Lindsay, the British ambassador in Washington from 1930 to 1939, who in October 1934 sought to temper British fears that in a future conflict

America would not come to Britain's aid: "Lay this maxim to heart; that in any war, in which America is destined to not remain neutral, she will be the last to come in . . . if ever America ceases to be neutral in a war . . . though she may postpone her decision until the eleventh hour and the fifty-fifth minute, she will in the end flop down on the English side."[26]

The new commander in chief of the Royal Navy's America and West Indies Station, Vice Admiral Sydney Meyrick, also found cause for optimism in April 1937 after a meeting with the new chief of naval operations, Admiral William Leahy: "Admiral Leahy the CNO was most forthcoming, and genuinely, I think pro-British. . . . There was a general feeling amongst all the Admirals that ours was a common cause with theirs in the Pacific—but not so in Europe, though even [so] some felt they might be with us 'before the end.'"[27]

The two navies also began a small information-sharing program in 1939. The naval attachés in Washington and London served as conduits for a limited flow of technical and planning information between the two navies.[28] A series of staff talks and meetings in 1938 resulted in little combined planning but gave each navy critical information about the other's intentions, plans, and capabilities. The British learned that the Americans planned to concentrate their fleet in the Pacific, while the Americans found that tensions with Germany and Italy reduced the likelihood that the Royal Navy could send a strong force to Singapore.[29] These improvements in Anglo-American naval relations paved the way for further cooperation after the outbreak of World War II.

OBSERVING EACH OTHER, 1939–1941

The German invasion of Poland in September 1939 opened hostilities in Europe, bringing the Royal Navy and the Commonwealth fleets into the war by September 10. From the American perspective, the war in Europe provided an opportunity to observe and learn from the Royal Navy's growing body of wartime experience. The American naval attaché in London, Captain Alan Kirk, found that the British were willing to provide some information, "but in no case was there what you might call wide-open exchange. Our side was very, very cautious, and so were they."[30] Kirk made friends with a number of British officers, especially Rear Admiral Bruce Fraser, the third sea lord and controller, responsible for procurement and equipment. Fraser proved to be a staunch advocate for closer Anglo-American relations throughout the 1940s. Kirk was joined by a growing number of junior American officers assigned as observers with the Royal Navy beginning in the fall of 1940.[31] These observers typically returned to the United States as advocates of closer collaboration with the British.

One observer, Commander James Fife, a submariner, made contact with Rear Admiral Max Horton, the head of the British submarine force. Fife later recalled a close relationship with Horton, who "practically made me a member of his staff." The American officer also found that British willingness to share information increased dramatically once Fife went on a wartime submarine patrol. Spending time with the Royal Navy led many of these observers to become admirers, with Fife as a prime example. He later recalled that the Royal Navy "had more of a warrior spirit than we had," and he thought that "the British submarine people were most friendly and most cooperative." Fife's positive experience with the Royal Navy gave the British a friend in high places when he became commander, Submarine Force Atlantic in 1947.[32]

The most senior observer was Vice Admiral Robert Ghormley, sent as part of a three-person team in August 1940 to evaluate Britain's position in the war. Ghormley became a conduit for information sharing between the Admiralty and the Navy Department. He benefited from the work of the Bailey Committee, a Royal Navy body established in June 1940. This committee studied how the United States could provide naval assistance and how to organize this aid. Many of their suggestions, such as the need for coordinated plans and improved Anglo-American communications capabilities, were ultimately adopted by the two navies.[33]

During the observation program, the United States gradually become increasingly involved in sustaining Britain's war effort against Germany. In September 1940, the Roosevelt administration exchanged fifty World War I–era American destroyers for leases on British bases on the Western Hemisphere. The destroyers helped bolster the Royal Navy's escort strength, contributing to the defense of British sea lines of communication. The two militaries participated in staff talks in the spring of 1941, which led to an agreement to prioritize the defeat of Germany if the United States entered the war. Britain's increasingly desperate financial situation also led Washington to pass the Lend-Lease Act in March 1941. Lend-Lease allowed the United States to supply the British war effort without requiring immediate payment, as had been the case under the prior "cash and carry" policy. Finally, in September 1941 the U.S. Navy began escorting transatlantic convoys to help the Royal Navy and the Royal Canadian Navy in their struggle against German U-boats. By this point, the U.S. Navy was in an undeclared naval war with Germany.[34]

While growing American aid helped Britain's war effort, many Royal Navy officers hoped for more active support from the Americans. Rear Admiral Victor Danckwerts, one of the British representatives in the 1941 staff talks, visited the U.S. Pacific Fleet at Pearl Harbor in April after the talks ended.[35] Danckwerts's visit was part of a program of British officers who were sent to observe the U.S. Navy in 1941. He described the fleet's "magnificent appearance" and "lines of cruisers and destroyers" as "enough to make one weep when one thinks of our terribly extended forces in the Atlantic and Mediterranean."[36] From his perspective, these American ships were desperately needed in the war against Germany.

The program that Danckwerts was part of involved visits by the naval attaché in Washington and his staff as well as officers sent on longer tours of duty with the Americans. The reports sent back by these observers revealed a decidedly mixed British opinion of American naval capabilities. A British officer who spent time with the Pacific Fleet in 1941 made an extensive report just before Pearl Harbor. The report cast doubt on the Americans' ability to fight in night actions, in bad weather, or in range of enemy shore-based aircraft. He listed a number of weaknesses: "defensive spirit and caution which dominates their strategy and planning . . . the tendency to count the odds before any operation and regard it as unsound if the odds are unfavorable . . . their lack of realistic operational experience; their inability to make up for it by their vision . . . [a] general lack of initiative through being tied down by detailed instructions."[37]

British reports such as these led one officer to recall: "At the time of Pearl Harbor, the average British naval officer's impression of the American Navy was not inspiring."[38] The British view of the U.S. Navy was not helped by their sense that the Americans thought they had little to learn from the British. Although the presence of American observers in Britain belied this as far as Navy Department leaders were concerned, the view persisted within the Royal Navy. As a junior Royal Navy officer, Patrick Bayly went to Philadelphia on the battleship *Resolution* for repair work in 1941. He recalled that whenever the *Resolution*'s officers tried to share what they had learned fighting in Europe, the Americans were dismissive, an attitude he found "very tiresome" and "extremely aggravating." As a result, when he heard about the attack on Pearl Harbor on December 7, 1941, Bayly's first reaction was "serves them right," though on reflection he decided this was a horrible attitude.[39]

Anglo-American naval relations in the years before Pearl Harbor have attracted the attention of a number of historians.[40] These scholars have highlighted elements of both cooperation and conflict, though the general trend in 1941 was toward closer cooperation, especially in the Atlantic.[41] The two navies gradually built up closer relations, which would prove beneficial once the United States formally entered the war. The scale of World War II precludes a comprehensive discussion of U.S Navy operations that involved allied navies. However, examining selected episodes where the U.S. Navy operated in combined formations with the Royal Navy highlights recurring issues of coalition naval warfare. These experiences set the stage for postwar efforts to retain interoperability.

ABDA

The December 1941 Japanese attack on Pearl Harbor brought the United States fully into the war. Within weeks of the attack, Japanese forces threatened the resource-rich regions of Southeast Asia, defended by the American, British, Dutch, Australian (ABDA) Command. ABDA's mission was to hold the Malay Barrier, a line running from Malaysia through Singapore to Borneo and Java in the Dutch East Indies and anchored by Burma on one end and Australia on the other. From the beginning, each nation viewed the ABDA Command's role differently. The British wanted to focus on defending Singapore and Burma, the Dutch prized Java and Borneo, the Americans felt that the Philippines should be reinforced, and the Australians worried about possible Japanese raids on their northern coast. The experience of the warships from all four navies attempting to stem the Japanese advance highlighted the difficulties of combined naval operations to American officers.[42]

Command and control problems plagued the ABDA naval forces from the start. Admiral Thomas C. Hart commanded the ABDA naval component but found that Dutch Vice Admiral Conrad E. L. Helfrich thought a Dutch officer should be in overall command.[43] Hart's operational commander was Admiral Karel Doorman, who failed to stop the Japanese from landing on Borneo in late January 1942. The fall of Singapore on February 15 and the Japanese air raid on Darwin, Australia, on February 19 underscored the worsening Allied situation. Meanwhile, Helfrich's behind-the-scenes efforts to get Hart relieved eventually bore fruit, and Helfrich replaced him as the overall naval commander. Throughout February, Doorman took his Combined Striking Force to sea several times, fruitlessly trying to intercept Japanese convoys carrying troops and supplies for the occupation of the Dutch East Indies. On February 27, the day that the Battle of the Java Sea began, Doorman's force consisted of five cruisers and nine destroyers from four different navies. The Dutch admiral sought to intercept Japanese invasion convoys bound for Java. The force included one British heavy cruiser, one American heavy cruiser, one Australian and two Dutch light cruisers, and three British, three Dutch, and four American destroyers. The Allied force was opposed by a Japanese force of approximately equal strength, but composed of ships and crew built, trained, and equipped to operate together as a single unit.[44]

In contrast, the Allied force lacked experience working together, effective tactical plans, shared doctrine, and communications procedures. The ABDA command had published a French/English code book, but for an unknown reason it was not issued to the warships of the Combined Striking Force. Most of the individual ship commanders met each other for the first time at a brief one-hour conference just prior to sailing, hardly sufficient time to build trust and confidence in each other.[45] Dorman issued only a single rudimentary tactical plan with little ability to respond to unanticipated tactical situations.[46] The system for relaying orders from Doorman on the Dutch light cruiser *De Ruyter* was cumbersome at best and prone to miscommunication. A British officer on *De Ruyter* would relay Doorman's orders to the largest British warship in the formation, the heavy cruiser *Exeter*. *Exeter* would then pass along the orders to the other English-speaking warships. However, *Exeter* was damaged early in the engagement, and there were no effective alternative communication arrangements other than signal flags.[47] The result, as one American captain wryly commented in his report, was that "the crystal ball was our only method of anticipating the intention[s]" of Doorman.[48] Furthermore, constant service for weeks had left ships and personnel worn out.[49]

During the action, the Allied ships repeatedly tried and failed to get past the Japanese escorts to attack the invasion convoys bound for Java. By the end of the battle, the Japanese sank the entire Allied surface force, except for four American destroyers, which escaped.[50] The Allies had forced the Japanese to delay their invasion of Java by "exactly one day," a serious defeat for ABDA.[51]

The experience of the Combined Striking Force in the Battle of the Java Sea highlighted the inherent difficulties of combined naval operations on short notice without adequate preparation.[52] With an inadequate communications and tactical system, no prior experience operating as a formation, and diverging national objectives, the ABDA navies had little chance of working together effectively. Instead of a unified formation, the Combined Striking Force was little more than a collection of ships that happened to be fighting in the same area.[53] A contemporary American report noted that "the practical difficulties of international cooperation are tremendous." The report concluded that the circumstances of the battle "gave little opportunity for planning and the polyglot character of our striking force made inapplicable the sort of tactical doctrines which would have prevailed had only a single navy been represented."[54] For Admiral Ernest King, commander in chief, U.S. Fleet, in February 1942, and other American officers, Java Sea highlighted the inherent flaws of mixed formations and the importance of avoiding them where possible. King told a group of American correspondents in November 1942: "We have had enough of 'mixed command.' It does not work."[55] King's views on multinational formations, in fact, had already influenced Allied naval deployments in the Battle of the Atlantic.

ESCORTING CONVOYS, 1941–1943

By 1941, the Royal Navy and Royal Canadian Navy had been fighting German submarines (U-boats) in the Atlantic for two years. In May 1941, the two Commonwealth navies were finally able to escort convoys all the way across the Atlantic. The U.S. Navy began escorting convoys to the mid-Atlantic in September 1941 in coordination with the British and Canadians. Admiral King, the U.S. Atlantic Fleet commander at the time, preferred that Canadian and American escorts operate in separate groups.[56] Accordingly, the Americans handled escorts for fast convoys while the Canadians covered slow convoys to a midocean meeting point where British escort groups coming from Iceland took over.[57] In November 1941, however, the Germans began redeploying U-boats from the North Atlantic into the Mediterranean and Norwegian Seas, which led to a sharp decline in merchant ship losses.[58]

After the attack on Pearl Harbor and Germany's declaration of war on the United States on December 11 the tide turned back in favor of the U-boats. German submarines savaged shipping off the U.S. East Coast for the six months of 1942. At night, lights from cities such as Miami and New York silhouetted merchant ships, making them easy targets for U-boat captains. Until the U.S. Navy implemented a coastal convoy system in May 1942, shipping sailed largely without effective protection. The coastal convoy system pushed the submarines south into the Gulf of Mexico and the Caribbean. To avoid the dangerous U.S. East Coast, the British rerouted critical oil tankers east to Africa, while Canada implemented its own tanker convoys in late April, independent of the U.S. Navy.[59] The battles off the American seaboard also pulled U.S. Navy assets away from escort duty in the northwest Atlantic.[60] However, convoys carrying U.S. troops to Europe still received heavy U.S. Navy escorts. In World War I, the U.S. Navy had safely escorted the American Expeditionary Force to France in 1917 and 1918, and it did not want to tarnish this reputation in World War II.[61] Therefore, by the summer of 1942 the Royal Navy and the Royal Canadian Navy provided 98 percent of the escorts for transatlantic trade convoys in the north Atlantic.[62]

Nevertheless, the U.S. Navy retained strategic direction over convoy operations in the Western Atlantic in 1942. Accordingly, the absence of a single overall Allied commander in the Atlantic allowed differences in doctrine to persist. Only in September 1942, a year after the U.S. Navy began escort operations, did the Allies introduce a common escorting instruction for transatlantic trade convoys. Previously, American escorts had used one set of instructions while British and Canadian ships used another.[63] At a Washington conference in March 1943, the Americans, British, and Canadians reorganized their convoy escort efforts. The Americans agreed to leave the North Atlantic trade convoys to the British and Canadians while the U.S. Navy handled the Central Atlantic convoys and troop convoys.[64] In the critical convoy battles of May 1943, the Royal Navy provided the bulk of the combat power that dealt serious blows to the German U-boat force.[65] In the Central Atlantic the U.S. Navy began to deploy escort carriers to hunt submarines. With the benefit of accurate radio intelligence, the Americans crippled the U-boat submarine tanker fleet by August 1943, reducing the German ability to conduct long-range operations.[66]

The debates over command arrangements and allocation of escorts from 1941 through 1943 shaped Anglo-American-Canadian naval relations well into the early Cold War. The Battle of the Atlantic also shaped British and American views of each other's navies. British officers struggled to understand the apparent American reluctance to adopt coastal convoys, especially in early 1942. For their part, American officers generally recognized the Royal Navy's experience and depth of knowledge in antisubmarine warfare. This perspective shaped the U.S. Navy's interest in retaining close relations with the Royal Navy after World War II. However, these decisions were still in the future in 1942.

THE U.S. NAVY AND SCAPA FLOW, PART 2

As a result of the Japanese advances in Southeast Asia, the destruction of the Royal Navy's presence east of Singapore, and the loss of the Singapore naval base, in early 1942 the Royal Navy rushed reinforcements to the Indian Ocean to counter further Japanese moves. In order to maintain British naval strength in home waters, the Admiralty requested that the U.S. Navy reinforce the Home Fleet, based at Scapa Flow north of Scotland, with a squadron of American warships. Admiral King, now the chief of naval operations, agreed and sent Task Force 99, comprising the aircraft carrier *Wasp*, the battleship *Washington*, the heavy cruisers *Wichita* and *Tuscaloosa*, and escorts. The American ships joined the Home Fleet on April 4, 1942.[67] The experience of Task force 99 highlighted the time required for multinational formations to build cohesion and familiarity with foreign publications.

The Americans adopted British signal books and tactical procedures during their time with the Home Fleet, as they had during World War I. One American destroyer captain remembered: "We were overwhelmed with a tremendous lot of British fleet regulations, signal books, and things."[68] To ease the American transition, the British provided each American ship with a liaison team to explain Royal Navy methods. This assistance helped U.S. Navy personnel gradually become more comfortable with using British publications.[69]

Over the following weeks and months, the British and American crews were able to compare their ships and approaches to naval warfare. The Americans thought that their ships performed better in antiaircraft drills, while the British thought the Americans were initially insufficiently concerned about German U-boats.[70] Often differences of opinion reflected the different threats faced by each navy during the war. At a postexercise critique in 1943 involving the Home Fleet and another American contingent including the carrier *Ranger*, Rear Admiral Alva Bernhard, the American commander, argued that the aircraft carrier should be placed in the center of a formation to provide maximum antiaircraft protection. Admiral Fraser, the Home Fleet commander, replied, effectively summarizing a point of difference between the two navies: "Admiral Bernhard has said that aircraft torpedoes have been the cause of all the sinkings of American carriers in the Pacific and the point is well taken. In the British Navy, however, all carriers lost, except one, have been sunk by submarine torpedoes. Aircraft torpedoes have been your principal enemy, submarine torpedoes ours. The area of operations must determine the defensive formation best suited to the conditions."[71]

Overall, the American warships operating with the Home Fleet in 1942 and 1943 worked effectively with their British counterparts. The focus on antiaircraft defense in the U.S. Navy and the British focus on antisubmarine warfare, however, proved to be enduring differences between the two fleets into the early Cold War.

EXCHANGING AIRCRAFT CARRIERS, 1943–1944

By December 1942 the U.S. Navy in the Pacific was down to one undamaged aircraft carrier, the *Saratoga*. The Battles of Coral Sea and Midway and the actions around Guadalcanal had damaged or destroyed the rest of the American carriers in the Pacific. As a result, the Americans requested and the British agreed to send the carrier *Victorious* to the Pacific to reinforce the U.S. Navy. The British carrier left the United Kingdom in December 1942, but was not ready for use in the Pacific until May 1943. The delay stemmed from the extensive preparations made for operating *Victorious* with the U.S. Navy. The Americans fitted the British carrier with VHF radios and more antiaircraft guns, exchanged the British aircraft for American aircraft, and retrained the British pilots to fly American aircraft and land on a carrier deck using American landing signals.[72] In May 1943, *Victorious* arrived in the South Pacific and joined up with the *Saratoga*.[73]

During the few weeks when the two carriers operated together, personnel from both ships visited one another's carriers, allowing them to compare and contrast the two ships. For a short period, all the fighter aircraft, both British and American, operated from *Victorious*, while *Saratoga* carried all the attack aircraft. This exchange gave pilots from both sides experience "cross-decking," or operating from another nation's carrier. John Fay, a British pilot, later remembered being impressed with *Saratoga*'s size and the size of the American Avenger torpedo planes, which he thought were designed for "six foot Texans."[74] Rupert Wilkinson, another British pilot, found American carrier aircraft more rugged and capable of flying further than British planes.[75] These equipment differences reflected the U.S. Navy's focus on and preparation for fighting in the long distances of the Pacific.

At the end of the period when the two carriers operated together, Captain Lachlan D. Mackintosh of *Victorious* sent home a report providing his assessment of the U.S. Navy in the Pacific. He commented on the dominant role of aircraft carriers in the U.S. Navy: "Aircraft carriers are the core of the Fleet and maneuvering is done on the principle that 'a carrier can do no wrong.'"[76] American refueling at sea techniques were impressive, as was the effectiveness of American antiaircraft gunnery. Mackintosh noted that on several occasions the American destroyers escorting *Victorious* had shot down airborne practice targets before *Victorious* had a chance to fire. As noted by American officers during World War I, Mackintosh found that "the United States Navy Officer is more highly educated in the general naval subjects and technicalities than ours."[77] Overall, the British captain was impressed with many elements of the U.S. Navy, concluding his report by stating that the Americans had "many features in their service, which, at times, give them an advantage over us."[78]

The British reinforcement of the U.S. Pacific Fleet demonstrated that American and British carriers could operate together effectively, albeit after months of preparations. In contrast to the Home Fleet, which accepted American carriers into its formations with minimal changes in equipment alterations, the U.S. Navy insisted on making *Victorious* more like an American carrier by using American aircraft and landing procedures in addition to making a number of alterations to the British ship. The challenge in the future for both fleets would be to determine whether carriers from each navy could operate together on short notice, without significant advance preparations.

THE BRITISH PACIFIC FLEET

One of the largest operations involving the U.S. Navy and the British and Commonwealth navies occurred in the summer of 1945 when the British Pacific Fleet reinforced the U.S. Navy's Pacific Fleet. By late 1943 and early 1944, the declining naval threat in Europe allowed a significant redeployment of British naval power to the Pacific.[79] The British considered a number of proposals on how best to utilize this increase in naval strength before deciding to send a fleet to participate in the U.S. Navy's operations against Japan.[80] After securing American approval at the Quadrant Conference in 1944, the British began moving ships, aircraft, personnel, and equipment to the Indian Ocean and Australia in late 1944.[81]

As a part of this redeployment, the commander in chief of the British Pacific Fleet (BPF), Admiral Fraser, flew to Hawaii in December to meet with Admiral Chester Nimitz, commander in chief, U.S. Pacific Fleet.[82] The two officers agreed that the British would operate in a separate formation from the U.S. Fifth Fleet under Admiral Raymond Spruance but would be under Spruance's operational command. The British made a number of changes to ease their transition into the Pacific war. They adopted American signal procedures and tactical formations, utilized the American task force organization system, and established an underway replenishment group to enable the BPF to stay at sea for long periods, as did the Americans.[83] These were significant changes that in many cases required British personnel to replace procedures they had used for years with new methods for operations in a new environment. One British officer later described the change as a "total revolution."[84] The transition was not helped by the fact that most of the British ships did not have good ventilation or air conditioning, which made sailing in the Central and South Pacific a warm experience at the very least.

To aid the British, the U.S. Navy provided more than two hundred officers and four hundred enlisted personnel to serve on the ships of the BPF as liaison personnel, primarily for communications. Captain Charles Wheeler served as the senior U.S. Navy liaison officer and was assigned to Fraser's headquarters in Sydney, Australia. Wheeler had served on an American destroyer based at Queenstown, Ireland, in World War I and later recalled that the British use of American signals "was exactly the reverse of what happened in World War I when I was at Queenstown in a destroyer and we used the British communications."[85] The experience of Petty Officer Paul Kincade, one of Wheeler's sailors on the Australian destroyer *Quickmatch*, illustrates the role performed by liaison personnel and some of the differences between the Australian and American navies.

Kincade's job was to help the ship's crew interpret and understand American signals and to coordinate with any American ships and personnel they encountered. Kincade's memoir repeatedly mentions the impact of food, specifically the superiority of the food provided by the U.S. Navy compared to the British and Commonwealth ships. During a rest period in between operations off the Philippine island of Leyte, Kincade and the two other American sailors stationed with him took several Australians to the American destroyer *Dixie* for a U.S. Navy–style meal. Kincade's description of the meal on the *Dixie* highlights the important role food can play in relations on an individual level:

We took trays and started down the serving line, stopping at every server. The Aussies couldn't believe their eyes, as they look at all of the food before them . . . the menu that day include roast beef, mashed potatoes and gravy, green peas, quarter head of lettuce, ice cream and cake. . . . As I moved my tray along the line, each server placed food onto it. When I came to those beautiful, snow white, fresh mashed potatoes, the server plopped a large spoonful into the indented compartment of the tray. I stood there waiting for him to put more on, when he told me to keep moving. I asked for more, but he just said, "You know the rules, Mac. One to a customer." When I told him I was from one of the British Fleet ships and was starved, he exclaimed, "You poor bastard!" and proceeded to construct a small version of the Swiss Alps on my tray. . . . The messcooks [*sic*] passed the word down the line and as we move [*sic*] along, each server heaped huge mounds of food on our trays. Our guests' eyes were bugging out of their heads, they were so amazed by the bounty of an American Navy messhall. Even as I write about this experience so many years later, tears come to my eye as I recall our emotions at the time. We certainly experienced equal parts of gratitude and pride, as we enjoyed the first decent meal in almost two months.[86]

Kincade had good relations overall with the *Quickmatch*'s crew but noticed that some of the British sailors "began to resent being out there [in the Pacific] fighting 'the Yank's war,'" particularly after the Germans surrendered in early May 1945.[87] However, the expressions of grief by the British and Australian sailors when news of President Roosevelt's death arrived made Kincade feel that "at that moment, we weren't foreigners to each other; we were like family, sharing a mutual loss of a great person."[88] Kincade summarized his interactions with the Australians and British as "playfully adversarial, needling each other about our national and naval differences," though he found that he missed his Commonwealth counterparts after serving together for three months.[89]

The BPF supported the April 1945 invasion of Okinawa by attacking airfields on islands off Taiwan used by the Japanese as staging areas for attacks on the American invasion fleet. After Okinawa, the BPF operated as a part of the American Third Fleet under Admiral William Halsey during the air and naval bombardment of Japan in July and August. The Japanese surrender revealed divergent opinions within the Royal Navy about communicating with the U.S. Navy in the Pacific. The Admiralty, led by First Sea Lord Admiral Andrew Cunningham, wanted the BPF to return to British communications as quickly as possible, while Fraser and the BPF staff believed that cooperation with the U.S. Navy during postsurrender operations would be improved by continuing to use American communications. The Admiralty won the debate. The physical links between the BPF and the USN were removed by the end of 1945. The U.S. Navy withdrew the bulk of its communication teams from the BPF by the end of August 1945, and by October the senior American liaison officer, Captain Wheeler, was in the process of leaving Fraser's staff.[90] On December 1, 1945, the BPF reverted to British communications, though in 1946 the Royal Navy began rewriting its signal publications to incorporate the experience gained in the Pacific.[91]

The Royal Navy's internal adjustments to better fit into the U.S. Navy's system in the Pacific, combined with the large-scale use of U.S. Navy liaison officers with the BPF, contributed significantly to the cooperative relationship between the two fleets. The BPF's experience also highlighted the fact that during the war against Japan, the U.S. Navy had gained substantially more experience in underway replenishment and extended carrier operations than the Royal Navy. The BPF's transition to American communications books underlined the value of developing common signals books that could be used in international naval formations.

U.S. Navy flyover of USS *Missouri*, September 2, 1945. *Source*: 80-G-421130, National Archives ID 520775, National Archives at College Park, College Park, MD.

COLD WAR

While prospects for continued relations between the U.S. Navy and the Royal Navy appeared relatively bright, the same could not be said for ties between the United States and the Soviet Union.[92] Despite cooperating to defeat Hitler's Germany and Imperial Japan, their experiences in World War II differed dramatically. The Soviet Union suffered ninety times as many casualties—civilian and military—as did the United States during the war, while the United States emerged from the war with the most advanced economy in the world. Their objectives for the postwar world diverged significantly. The Soviet leadership wanted to have security, provided by territories and lands currently on their borders, and to remain in power until the capitalist nations turned on each other. For Washington, especially President Roosevelt, postwar security lay in the creation of the United Nations organization. Financially, economically, and physically exhausted from two world wars, the United Kingdom wanted to retain close relations with the United States and to pursue a domestic program of social and welfare spending.[93] Disagreements over postwar issues further clouded relations between the former allies. Excluded from the occupations of Japan and Italy, the Soviet Union denied the British and Americans a role in occupying Romania, Bulgaria, and Hungary. Furthermore, American possession of the atomic bomb spurred the Soviets to launch an intensive effort to develop their own nuclear weapons, which they did by 1949.

Soviet efforts to obtain naval bases in former Italian North African colonies and reluctance to withdraw their troops from Iran—jointly occupied by the Allies during the war as a Lend-Lease corridor—led officials in London and Washington to search for the reasoning behind Soviet behavior. George Kennan's "long telegram" from the American embassy in Moscow in January 1946 provided a compelling answer. Kennan argued that the Soviet leaders had to treat their former allies as hostile in order to justify their continued dictatorship. The appropriate Western response was not war against the Soviet Union, but containment until the internal inconsistences within the Soviet system worked themselves out. This policy of containment became the foundation of American foreign policy during the Cold War. The Truman Doctrine and Marshall Plan, announced in March and June 1947 respectively, put the policy into practice. Truman requested congressional approval for an economic and military support program for Turkey and Greece to replace the withdrawal of British support. Truman argued that the United States should "support free peoples who are resisting attempted subjugation," casting the debate in the widest possible terms in an effort to gain the support of Congress. The Marshall Plan committed the United States to the economic reconstruction of Europe, whose economic and political future looked increasingly unstable.[94]

Stalin responded by creating in September 1947 the Cominform—an international communist organization committed to Soviet-led revolutionary activity—and approving the communist overthrow of the democratically elected government in Czechoslovakia in February 1948. The coup in Czechoslovakia helped convince Congress to approve the administration's plan for European economic recovery. The Berlin Blockade, Stalin's effort to starve the Western allies out of their occupation zones in Berlin, began in April

1948 and continued until May 1949. For the newly created United States Air Force, the blockade provided an opportunity to demonstrate the utility of American airpower by airlifting supplies into the city. For European nations concerned about their security needs, the blockade and the coup in Prague highlighted the need for a security agreement to supplement the American economic recovery agreement, leading to the creation of the North Atlantic Treaty Organization by April 1949. It was within this context of growing international tension that the U.S. Navy made decisions about its postwar relations with its closest World War II partners, Britain, Canada, and Australia.

Despite closely cooperating with the Royal Navy in World War I, the U.S. Navy made no effort to retain its wartime interoperability with the British. Disagreements over naval arms limitation caused friction between the two navies throughout the 1920s and early 1930s before increasing tensions led to a series of consultative meetings and limited information sharing. The U.S. Navy's observer program helped build on the information exchanges of the late 1930s with the Royal Navy. Many observers developed an appreciation and at times an admiration for the Royal Navy. They advocated closer relations with the Royal Navy, which in turn shaped the development of post–World War II relations when these officers became senior leaders.

World War II cemented the principle, established in World War I, that in a mixed formation, the smaller contingents adopted the operating procedures of the largest contingent. The war showed that with adequate advance preparations, American ships could effectively work with British and Commonwealth ships in combined formations. However, the Battle of Java Sea also highlighted the problems caused when multinational formations lacked prearranged procedures and doctrine. If the U.S. Navy wanted to be able to effectively operate with foreign nations on short notice, then peacetime collaboration to prepare such procedures and doctrine would be required. World War II also gave a large number of American personnel practical experience operating with foreign navies, mostly the British, the Canadians, and the Australians. The question facing the U.S. Navy at the end of the war was whether to build upon this body of knowledge by creating close peacetime relations with the British, Canadian, and Australian navies.

2

Postwar Partnerships

Gray clouds hung low in the Washington, D.C., sky as Colonel
Charles H. Deerwester, U.S. Army Air Forces, glanced up before
walking into the building. He entered the secure room where the
congressional committee would hold its hearing this morning and
took his seat. The date was June 18, 1947. After sitting quietly for
over two and a half hours while two three-star generals spoke, Deerwester finally began his testimony a little after 1 p.m. on the U.S.-
Canadian Permanent Joint Board on Defense (PJBD) on which
he served as the Army Air Forces member. With stomachs growl-
ing around him, the colonel described the board's role in U.S.-
Canadian military cooperation to the House Committee on International Relations. He emphasized that the board's charter stemmed
from an executive agreement, not a treaty. Therefore, the U.S. military had "not violated the warning of George Washington" to avoid
entangling alliances. He described a military subcommittee of the
board in similarly benign terms: "We do not consider it a treaty or
anything of the sort. We are merely two groups of military folks getting together and deciding. If you do this on this side of the border,
we will do the same thing independently on our side."[1]

Earlier that year in February, the Truman administration had
publicly announced that the cooperation with Canada that existed
during the war would continue. Just as Colonel Deerwester would
do in June, the administration's February announcement also
sought to avoid any hint of a military alliance. The statement specifically cast the relationship between the two nations as supportive

of the United Nations (UN), not an alternative to that body, which remained "the cornerstone of the foreign policy" of each nation.[2]

The State Department's announcement and Colonel Deerwester's June testimony both highlighted key themes in the U.S. military's postwar relations with Britain, Canada, and Australia. After fighting for four years together in an alliance unprecedented in its integration, the United States chose not to follow the pattern of the post–World War I years. During that period, the Americans allowed close wartime military relations to atrophy. However, in 1945 and 1946, the potential for confrontation and conflict with the Soviet Union made continued close relations between the English-speaking allies seem prudent. In the event of a war with the Russians, the American military would likely not have time to develop interoperability with its allies. The Allies would need to be able to fight together effectively from the start of the war. Accordingly, the U.S. military sought to maintain the links and interoperability created during World War II with the British, Canadians, and Australians on distinct levels.[3]

However, public opinion and American tradition shaped this effort in two ways. First, widespread American public support for the United Nations made U.S. military leaders wary of taking any action that might be construed as undermining the new international body. Second, the long-standing U.S. foreign policy tradition of not entering into formal peacetime alliances also constrained Washington's willingness to openly pursue close military relations with Britain, Canada, and Australia. Thus, even in a hearing closed to the public, Colonel Deerwester downplayed the importance of the joint board and explicitly invoked Washington's 1796 charge to "steer clear of permanent alliances" in his farewell address.[4] The challenge for the U.S. military was how to play favorites with the British and Canadians without appearing to do so publicly.

Concerns about the Soviet Union played a critical role in keeping the U.S. and British and Commonwealth militaries close after World War II. At the end of World War II, the Western Allies faced a change in the international strategic situation "more comparable indeed with that occasioned by the fall of Rome that with any other change occurring the succeeding fifteen hundred years" in the words of the Joint Chiefs of Staff (JCS). Though considerably diminished, the "relative military power of the British Empire" remained "superior to that of any nation" aside from the United States and the Soviet Union.[5] By the summer of 1945, British military planning assumed the Soviet Union would be a potential enemy, and in September 1945 the JCS labeled the Soviets as America's most likely potential enemy.[6]

In addition to the Soviet threat, shared interest in North American defense suggested the need for continuing cooperation between the U.S. and Canadian militaries. The two nations had established the Permanent Joint Board on Defense in 1940 to prepare plans for the defense of North America. As a result, Canada enjoyed a unique position in the eyes of American military officials. At times, geographic proximity to the United States gave Canada an inside track with the U.S. military, though not in all circumstances.[7]

Given fears of Soviet power and the demands of North American defense, American officials faced a challenge: what should be done with the wartime organizations that had enabled cooperation? Specifically, should the Permanent Joint Board on Defense, the Anglo-American Combined Chiefs of Staff (CCS), and the Combined Communications Board (CCB), a subsidiary to the CCS, remain in existence? In 1945, senior military leaders on both sides of the Atlantic wanted to maintain close relations, but the press of immediate postwar demands such as occupation duty and demobilization largely prevented these sentiments from becoming actions. The Royal Navy's Admiral James Somerville ran into this problem when he sought to firmly entrench Anglo-American naval relations in the fall of 1945.

By 1946, growing concerns about the Soviet Union led to more action, as shown in the chronology below in table 2.1. Consequently, in 1946, the joint board recommended principles for ongoing U.S.-Canadian military cooperation, and the CCS continued to function through 1949. At the same time, growing American concerns about Australian security undermined Commonwealth access to the Combined Communications Board. In 1948, the United States forced Canada, Australia, and New Zealand off the Combined Communications Board because of issues with access to classified information. By 1951, Canada fought its way back into the heart of Anglo-American military communication links. Ultimately, the story of how the U.S. military structured its postwar military ties with the British and individual Commonwealth countries reflected three themes: the pursuit of military interoperability, the desire to limit U.S. ties to trustworthy nations, and a wish to not be seen as playing favorites.

In the summer of 1945, most U.S. senior military leaders wanted to retain

Table 2.1. Timeline of Early Cold War and U.S. Military Relations, 1945–1950

1945	
July	Admiral Somerville calls for comparative U.S. Navy–Royal Navy study.
July–August	Potsdam Conference.
August	Japan surrenders, ending World War II.
September	Igor Gouzenko defects, revealing Soviet spy ring in Canada and the United States.
November	United States proposes Permanent Joint Board on Defense continue to function in peacetime.
December	Somerville Committee report completed, Somerville steps down from head of British naval mission in Washington.

1946	
February	Joint Chiefs tell British that Combined Chiefs must go underground.
	George Kennan writes Long Telegram, analyzing Soviet ideology and policy.
March	Winston Churchill gives Iron Curtain speech in Fulton, Missouri.
April	Permanent Joint Board on Defense recommends policies for U.S.-Canadian military relations.
May	State-War-Navy Coordinating Committee (SWNCC) requests Joint Chiefs' comments on draft information disclosure policy.
September	Bulgarian communist government cements power when monarchy is abolished.
November	SWNCC approves Joint Chiefs–inspired disclosure guidance. Australia and New Zealand's access to classified information reduced.
	Canada–United Kingdom–United States (CANUKUS) military standardization conference.

1947	
February	Italian peace treaty signed, ending a principal rationale for the Combined Chiefs of Staff's (CCS) continued existence.
March	Truman Doctrine announced, United States to support Greece and Turkey.
June	Marshall Plan economic aid for Europe announced.
July	U.K. decides CCS dissolution acceptable if British Joint Staff Mission (BJSM) remains in existence.
	Truman signs 1947 National Security Act, creating the secretary of defense position and the Department of the Air Force.
August	CANUKUS standardization program approved by all three governments.
December	Communist government established in Romania.

(*continued on the next page*)

Table 2.1. Continued

1948	
February	Communist-led coup in Czechoslovakia overthrows government.
March	Joint Chiefs ask British Chiefs to agree to removing Commonwealth observers from the Combined Communications Board (CCB).
June	Soviet blockade of Berlin begins.
	Australia loses access to all U.S. classified information.

1949	
April	North Atlantic Treaty signed, creating the North Atlantic Treaty Organization (NATO).
	U.K. agrees to remove Commonwealth from CCB, U.K. starts blocking CCB invitations to Canadians.
May	Federal Republic of Germany created from America, British, and French occupation areas.
	Initial Canadian effort to rejoin CCB fails.
	Soviets end blockade of Berlin.
June	Canadian civilians insist on reentry into CCB.
August	Soviets test first atomic bomb.
	Joint Chiefs secure British Chiefs' approval to end the CCS.
October	Chinese Communists establish People's Republic of China.
	CCS and CCB dissolved.

1950	
March	British make informal offer to Canada: Canada can attend all CCB meetings based on verbal commitment.
May	General Charles Foulkes gets Field Marshal William Slim to support Canada CCB membership.
June	North Korea invades South Korea, starting the Korean War.
July	Canada accepts written U.S. offer that Canada will attend all CCB meetings.

Source: Tony Judt, *Postwar: A History of Europe since 1945* (New York: Penguin Press, 2005), chaps. 4 and 5; J. P. Dunbabin, *The Cold War: The Great Powers and Their Allies* (Harlow, U.K.: Pearson, 2008), chaps. 3 and 4.

close ties with the British. In June, Chief of Naval Operations Fleet Admiral Ernest King and Secretary of the Navy James Forrestal told Admiral Somerville, the head of the British Admiralty Delegation (BAD) in Washington, that they wanted to maintain close Anglo-American naval relations after the war.[8] At the Potsdam conference, U.S. Army Chief of Staff General of the Army George Marshall privately informed Field Marshal Alan Brooke, the British army's chief of staff, that "some similar organization to the CCS should be kept alive after the war." Marshall wanted to avoid repeating the post–World War I collapse of military-to-military links.[9] Similarly, Truman's senior military advisor and military chief of staff, Fleet Admiral William Leahy, shared King's and Marshall's views.[10] However, the Americans were not yet willing to take concrete steps to pursue these goals. When the British chiefs pressed the JCS at Potsdam to preserve the Combined Chiefs of Staff after the war, the Americans demurred. President Harry Truman told Admiral Leahy that retaining the CCS postwar smacked of a military alliance to which he did not want to commit.[11] The Truman administration worried that a commitment to preserve the CCS might damage relations with Soviet leader Joseph Stalin, which in turn could undermine the possibility of continued postwar cooperation with the Soviets. Furthermore, the JCS wanted to ensure that the Red Army entered the war against Japan.[12]

One exception to American reluctance to commit to postwar military relations with the British was in the field of intelligence. By 1945 both navies were sharing intelligence on a regular basis, though the closest naval intelligence ties related to the Battle of the Atlantic in 1942 and 1943.[13] In the weeks before and after the Potsdam conference, military intelligence leaders on both sides of the Atlantic committed to continued cooperation against the Soviet Union. In June 1945 Admiral Hewlett Thebaud, the head of the U.S. Army-Navy Communications Intelligence Board, and Edward Travis, director of the British Government Code and Cipher School, had verbally agreed to "complete cooperation." Intelligence officers from both nations met in mid-August to flesh out this agreement, and their work was approved by Admiral King and General Marshall on August 18, two weeks after the Potsdam conference ended.[14]

Postwar intelligence cooperation took a further step with the signing of the British-U.S. Communications Intelligence Agreement on March 5, 1946. In this agreement both sides agreed to "unrestricted" exchange of communication intelligence products, with a few minor exceptions.[15] Further agreements in 1947 and 1948 codified these arrangements.[16] Intelligence cooperation was influenced by American concerns about public opinion to a lesser degree than navy-to-navy relations because intelligence matters were so highly classified and tightly controlled. Concerns about Soviet intentions and capabilities played a significant role in encouraging close Anglo-American intelligence cooperation as they did in navy-to-navy relations.

THE SOMERVILLE INITIATIVES

While intelligence officials took steps to continue relations into the postwar period in the summer of 1945, Admiral Somerville was also working to extend the Royal Navy's close links with the U.S. Navy beyond the end of the war.[17] Since 1944, Somerville had led the British Admiralty Delegation, a group of over 750 personnel responsible for liaison with the U.S. Navy.[18] Although ultimately his efforts produced few tangible results, Somerville's two initiatives highlighted issues in Anglo-American naval relations that became prominent in the coming years: information exchange and shared operating procedures. His advocacy for creating shared tactical and signal books foreshadowed the writing of Allied Tactical Publication 1 in 1949, which became the foundational document for Anglo-American and international naval operations during the Cold War.

Somerville's interest in these two topics stemmed from his experience in World War II. As head of the Gibraltar-based Force H from 1940 to early 1942, the admiral valued the reports and outside perspective provided by U.S. Navy observers who spent time with his force.[19] When Somerville took command of the Eastern Fleet in March 1942, he tried to gain access to more information about the American war in the Pacific. He sent his American liaison officer to Australia soon after taking command "to try to get the Americans to give us more news" and regularly pressed the Admiralty for help so that he could better coordinate his Indian Ocean operations with the Americans.[20]

The admiral also recognized the barriers created by a lack of common operating procedures. Twice in 1942, the U.S. Navy asked the Admiralty to send reinforcements from the Eastern Fleet to operate under American command in the Pacific. Somerville doubted the utility of these proposals, explaining in a letter to Admiral Dudley Pound that his ships lacked "the intimate knowledge of American methods which is essential for really close tactical cooperation."[21] As clearly shown in the 1942 Battle of the Java Sea, formations of ships from different navies thrown together without the opportunity to train together struggled to perform effectively in combat. This issue persisted in 1944 when the American carrier *Saratoga* briefly joined the Eastern Fleet.[22] Operations with the British carrier *Illustrious* revealed that the two ships' fighter aircraft did not have the right radio crystals to communicate with each other, even after three years of war together.[23] Command of Force H and the Eastern Fleet convinced Somerville of the need for information sharing and shared operating procedures. This belief guided his initiatives as head of the BAD in Washington, D.C., in 1944–1945.

Soon after arriving in Washington, Somerville began meeting with senior American naval officials to secure their support for continuing technical exchanges after the war. Through such exchanges, he believed the British would benefit from American superiority in engineering, aircraft, and anti-aircraft equipment while the Americans benefited from British strengths in radar, sonar, fighter direction, and carrier landing equipment.[24] He found a number of supporters for the initiative, including Secretary of the Navy Forrestal, Admiral King, and Rear Admiral Julius Furer, the Navy's coordinator of research and development.[25]

Eager to take advantage of this high-level support for information sharing, in July 1945 Somerville sought to establish a forum for such sharing. He called for the Royal Navy to study American ship design and naval engineering methods with an eye to improving British practices. The admiral considered British design and engineering techniques inferior to their American corollaries and wanted to know why. He argued that the U.S. Navy "have managed to get . . . rather more per ton out of their ships than we appear to have achieved."[26] He emphasized to the Admiralty the need for the British to take advantage of the currently favorable climate within the Navy Department: "Our present close relationship with the United States Navy provides such a unique and possibly fleeting opportunity to study American ships and equipment and the organization and methods of production behind them . . . before our own postwar policy crystallizes and before, too, many American doors which are still ajar become closed to us."[27]

Somerville's proposed study would require detailed analysis of the U.S. Navy, which in turn would involve a steady flow of American information across the Atlantic. The admiral wanted the British to learn from American practices, thus highlighting the benefits of sharing with the U.S. Navy to London while simultaneously extending information sharing for months to come. The study would serve as a bureaucratic doorstop, keeping the door of information sharing open for the immediate future until long-term policies were established.

The Admiralty replied to the proposal in August, telling Somerville that he was welcome to use Washington-based personnel to study American methods but should not expect additional staff due to the Royal Navy's ongoing demobilization.[28] The admiral did just that.

While the Somerville Committee conducted its work, the admiral launched a second effort to cement close Anglo-American naval ties. In the fall of 1945, he asked the U.S. Navy to agree to write common tactical and signal publications for use by both navies.[29] In World War II, formations involving ships from both navies—such as Task Force 99, which operated with the British Home Fleet—adopted the communication methods and books of the dominant navy. The disadvantage of this approach was that the ships using foreign publications could never become as proficient in their use as those with years of experience.[30] Becoming familiar with foreign books required time for personnel to study and practice, which hurt combat readiness. Furthermore, tactical publications reflected the unique doctrinal, organizational, and force structure characteristics of each navy and were therefore at best a mediocre fit for foreign ships. Somerville's proposed Anglo-American books would have removed a major barrier to effective multinational operations in World War II had they been available.

However, the Americans proved reluctant to agree to Somerville's idea, in large part because the U.S. military lacked a detailed postwar policy on sharing U.S. classified material, much less working with foreign nations to create new classified documents. Information-sharing policy became a serious issue in the early Cold War that exerted considerable influence on relations with foreign militaries, especially the Combined Communications Board. Instead, the Royal Navy began rewriting its own books in early 1946 and finished in late 1947 without substantial American input.[31]

Despite the initial failure of Somerville's proposal, two years later his idea became reality. In 1947, the British, Canadians, and Americans began writing the combined books Somerville had suggested two years earlier. The admiral recognized the value of such publications in 1945, but the strategic climate was not right.[32]

In the meantime, the Somerville committee finished its comparative Royal Navy–U.S. Navy study in December 1945.[33] The resulting report made a number of recommendations but languished in the Admiralty for several years before it was quietly shelved.[34] This dismissive bureaucratic reaction stemmed in part from the departure and absence of the report's original patron. Just as the committee finished its report in late 1945, Admiral Henry Moore replaced Somerville as head of the British naval mission, now merged with the army and air force missions in Washington into the British Joint Staff Mission (BJSM).[35] Moore lacked Somerville's level of wartime contact with the U.S. Navy, having spent most of the war in the Admiralty and then with the Home Fleet. This turnover removed one of the principal senior advocates for adopting American practices within the Royal Navy.

After being relieved by Moore, Somerville returned to London to share his views on military relations in Washington with the British Chiefs of Staff. At a meeting with the chiefs in early January 1946, he emphasized two points: first, that U.S. senior officers wished to continue cooperating and exchanging information with the British, and second that continuing such links must be done in a way that did not smack of favoritism in light of the new United Nations since the multilateral institution enjoyed strong support from the U.S. public.[36] This domestic political reality began casting a long shadow over discussions about the future of Anglo-American military relations in 1945 and 1946, specifically the Combined Chiefs of Staff (CCS).

GOING UNDERGROUND

The Combined Chiefs of Staff consisted of the U.S. Joint Chiefs of Staff and the British Chiefs of Staff, represented by senior British officers in Washington such as Somerville. The body and its subsidiary committees served as the focal point for coordinating Anglo-American strategy in World War II. In the immediate aftermath of Japan's defeat in August 1945, President Truman took two actions regarding the CCS that alarmed London. In September, the president approved a statement calling for the eventual dissolution of the CCS, which seemed at odds with General Marshall's private comments at Potsdam in support of continued close collaboration.[37] That same month, Truman also directed that the chiefs restrict their work to matters arising from wartime cooperation, such as occupation administration.[38] These actions, along with the abrupt ending of Lend-Lease aid on August 20, created doubts in the minds of British officials about the future of military collaboration with the United States.

For the remainder of the year, the British chose not to press the issue so as to avoid forcing the Truman administration to make a choice. The CCS retained a role, albeit a minor one, in postwar military policy.[39] Specifically, the Allied occupation forces in Italy and in Trieste between Italy and Yugoslavia remained under the direction of the CCS.[40] This occupation role provided political justification for the body for the moment.

In the winter of 1945–1946, the U.S. Joint Chiefs went through a period of significant change as the wartime leaders, George Marshall, Ernest King, and Hap Arnold, stepped aside for their replacements, Dwight Eisenhower, Chester Nimitz, and Carl Spaatz. Admiral Leahy provided the sole source of continuity and remained an advocate for close military links with the British and Canadians.[41] The new crop of American leaders shared their predecessors' belief that postwar Anglo-American military relations should remain close. They wanted to avoid a break in ties similar to the aftermath of World War I, though their thoughts on the organizational machinery to accomplish this were hazy at best.[42] Their commitment reflected growing concerns in the fall of 1945 within the Joint Chiefs organization about Soviet intentions and the consequent need for Anglo-American solidarity.[43] However, the British felt uneasy about simply trusting the attitudes of current American leaders as the basis for long-term military collaboration. From their perspective, an agreement with the Americans, preferably a written one, would provide a more secure foundation.

In early 1946, the head of the British Joint Staff Mission in Washington, Field Marshal Henry "Jumbo" Wilson, opened a series of talks with the American service chiefs about the future of Anglo-American military links.[44] The nascent UN, created in October 1945, played a critical role in these conversations. The new international organization included a military staff committee, which appeared to some observers to be the natural successor to the CCS. The UN Military Staff Committee might coordinate the military activities of the wartime allies that were now on the Security Council.[45] The Committee met for the first time in February 1946 and reflected the Combined Chiefs of Staff model: each member of the Security Council appointed representatives of their Chiefs of Staff to the body.[46] Wilson sought to clarify the future of the CCS, especially in the context of the UN and the Military Staff Committee.

Wilson argued that continued Anglo-American military collaboration should rest on two principles: that it was "unthinkable" that the two nations should ever have "any grave misunderstanding" and that transatlantic collaboration "must support and not prejudice" making the UN "an effective power in the world."[47] Wilson and the British Chiefs of Staff believed that even after the UN Military Staff became operational, some form of the CCS could be maintained.[48]

In further discussions on February 8, both sides affirmed their desire for continued close relations "on exactly the same scale" as during the war. However, the U.S. Joint Chiefs ruled out any agreement on indefinite collaboration. The Americans told Wilson that "so much has been said about UNO [the United Nations Organization] and the need for collaboration with everyone on an equal footing, that the American people would not understand" openly giving the British special treatment. The Joint Chiefs explained that in the United States retaining the CCS would be seen as "incompatible" with the United Nations. As a result, the Combined Chiefs, as an expression of ongoing special treatment for Britain, "would therefore have to go underground." For domestic political reasons, the Americans wanted to avoid publicly admitting their close military relations with the British, while public acknowledgment was precisely what the British themselves wanted. Wilson reported the conversation back to London, urging that Britain push back against the assumption that the Combined Chiefs must go underground.[49]

THE IRON CURTAIN SPEECH

A month after the February discussions, former prime minister Winston Churchill gave a lecture at Westminster College in Fulton, Missouri, on March 5, 1946, with President Truman seated on stage. Churchill famously described Soviet domination of Eastern Europe as an "iron curtain" and called for continued close military relations, a "fraternal association" between the United States and the British Commonwealth. Specifically, he wanted combined war plans, officer exchanges, and the standardization of weaponry. He addressed implicit critiques of his proposal, arguing that such a "special relationship" was the best way to build up the UN.[50] Although Truman denied it, he had read a copy of the address in advance and encouraged

Churchill to make the speech, saying it was "admirable and would do nothing but good though it would make a stir."[51]

The president was right. The speech drew heavy criticism in the United States from conservatives wary of entangling foreign alliances and from liberal anti-imperialists who wanted the British Empire dissolved, not bolstered by the U.S. military.[52] Newspaper editorial opinions ranged from strong criticism in the *Chicago Daily Tribune* to a mixed review in the *Wall Street Journal* that supported certain elements while rejecting a fraternal association.[53] To many Americans, Churchill's proposal and his critical comments on Russia appeared to undermine the United Nations. Senator George Aiken (R-VT) spoke for many in Congress when he declared: "I'm not ready to enter a military alliance with anyone. Britain, the United States, and Russia should pull together to make the United Nations work."[54] The *Washington Post* declared Churchill's proposal "anathema to the American people because it means only a partial association of nations."[55] Though Churchill later denied that he sought a formal military alliance, Americans generally interpreted his fraternal association proposal as calling for such an alliance.[56]

The public reaction to Churchill's speech also illustrated the accuracy of the Joint Chiefs' comments to Wilson about the political dangers of any formal agreement to retain the CCS. In a national poll in early April 1946, 40 percent of Americans disagreed with Churchill's proposed association, while only 18 percent approved.[57] In contrast, 49 percent expressed satisfaction with the work done by the United Nations, with only 20 percent dissatisfied.[58] Later that year, a November poll found 55 percent of the country wanted the United States to support the UN, while only 10 percent wanted to abandon the international organization.[59] Support for the United Nations spanned American political and regional divisions, which explained the Pentagon's insistence that the Combined Chiefs "go underground."[60]

The public response to the speech highlighted the difference between attitudes inside and outside the administration. The month before Churchill spoke, George Kennan, U.S. chargé d'affaires in Moscow, sent his Long Telegram. Kennan argued that the Soviets had rejected the possibility of peaceful coexistence with the United States.[61] In March, the Joint Chiefs assessed that the Soviets were intent on dominating the Middle East and the Eastern Mediterranean.[62] In light of such assessments, American officials such as Admiral Leahy wanted to continue close collaboration with the British.

Leahy, the chief of staff to the president and nominal chairman of the Joint Chiefs, privately approved of Churchill's Fulton speech. Days after the address, Leahy met with Wilson to discuss ways "to continue in peacetime the present cooperation between the British and American Chiefs of Staff," according to Leahy's diary.[63] A JCS subcommittee recommended on March 13 that the CCS remain in operation "as long as possible."[64] Both sides valued their relationship and felt no immediate pressure to disband the Combined Chiefs. At the same time, the U.S. chiefs recognized the political impossibility of permanently retaining the organization. The question from their perspective was when and how to wind up the CCS, not whether.

TIES WITH CANADA

While the British faced an uphill battle to preserve the Combined Chiefs in 1945 and 1946, the Canadians and Americans both agreed that the U.S.-Canadian Permanent Joint Board on Defense should remain in existence. President Franklin Roosevelt and Prime Minister Mackenzie King created the board in August 1940 to coordinate the defense of North America.[65] At the time, the fall of France and the seemingly imminent German invasion of Britain led both nations to give more attention to the security of the Western Hemisphere. Shared Canadian and American interest in postwar continental defense provided a clear rationale for making the board permanent. Geographic proximity with Canada made retaining the board less politically charged than keeping the Combined Chiefs in existence.

The board consisted of senior American and Canadian civilian officials and military officers. As a consultative body, the organization lacked the authority to establish policy. Instead, the board issued joint recommendations to each nation's leaders.[66] In contrast to the Combined Chiefs, whose staffs met continuously, the board came together only a few times each year. The American military representatives to the board were not as tightly integrated with the U.S. military as the Joint Chiefs, who represented the United States on the Combined Chiefs. However, the Canadian service representatives each held high-ranking staff positions in Ottawa.[67]

In November 1945, the U.S. members of the board proposed continued military collaboration, and in January 1946 the Canadians agreed.[68] As an initial step in February 1946, the board created the Military Cooperation Committee (MCC) to update the 1941 plan for defending North America.[69] This committee established a link between the Canadian Chiefs of Staff and the U.S. Joint Chiefs of Staff and gave the Canadian military insight into U.S. strategic thinking.[70] More controversially, the board also prepared a draft list of five policies to guide U.S.-Canadian military to military relations, shown below:

1. Free exchange of military information
2. Exchanges of personnel
3. Standardization of equipment and procedures
4. Combined training exercises and exchanges of exercise observers
5. Reciprocal access to ports, airfields, and military bases.[71]

In April, the board wrote a draft recommendation, the thirty-fourth in the board's history, incorporating these principles.[72] However, concerns about other nations requesting similar access to U.S. military information led the board to separate the last four recommendations into a separate thirty-fifth recommendation.[73] While the thirty-fifth recommendation eventually became public in 1947, the information exchange provision and the existence of the MCC were classified top secret.[74] President Truman immediately approved both recommendations, but Ottawa assented only to the information exchange provision, deferring final agreement on the thirty-fifth recommendation for the moment.[75]

Canadian hesitation stemmed from an effort to balance multiple competing pressures in 1946 in the field of Canadian national security. Militarily, the closest possible standardization and integration with the American armed forces made sense. However, to some Canadians, such intermingling threatened Canada's status as an independent international entity and potentially Canadian sovereignty.[76] Ottawa wanted assurances that the United States did not seek to deploy vast American forces to Canada to guard against a Soviet attack, subsuming Canada and its sovereignty in the process.[77] For Canadian officials, America's greater size and strength fostered feelings both of security and anxiety. In the 1940s, the population of all of English-speaking Canada was equal to that of New York City.[78] Prime Minister Elliott Trudeau would capture this sentiment by later comparing living next door to the United States to "sleeping with an elephant."[79]

In addition to its concerns about American size and intentions, the Mackenzie King government strongly supported the UN and multilateral institutions.[80] Pursuing close bilateral ties with the Americans could be seen as running counter to the UN. Furthermore, many Canadians placed a high value on their close ties with the British and viewed overly close links with the United States warily, as such ties might weaken Anglo-Canadian relations.[81] At the same time, discoveries about Soviet espionage in North America suggested the need for close security cooperation with the United States. In February 1946, defector Igor Gouzenko's revelations about Soviet spy rings in Canada became public. Balancing these concerns, which involved central issues of Canadian national identity and policy, represented a difficult challenge at best.

Ultimately after further talks with the Americans and revisions to safeguard Canadian sovereignty, Ottawa approved the thirty-fifth recommendation in late 1946.[82] The two nations publicly announced the thirty-fifth recommendation as policy in February 1947. Both governments took care to frame their military cooperation as supporting the UN, to which they reaffirmed their commitment, as mentioned earlier in the chapter.[83] The approval of these two recommendations established the foundation for postwar U.S.-Canadian military relations, demonstrating that the Permanent Joint Board on Defense truly would be permanent.

INFORMATION EXCHANGE

In the aftermath of World War II, many members of the anti-Axis coalition wanted to continue to receive classified U.S. military information. In theory, by 1946, a subcommittee of the State-War-Navy Coordinating Committee (SWNCC) held responsibility for approving or disapproving requests to release material to foreign governments.[84] The committee, created in 1944 to handle political-military issues such as occupation duties, consisted of senior representatives from the State, War, and Navy Departments. By the end of World War II, the committee held policy-making authority and acted in the collective name of the secretaries of the three departments.[85] The committee's principal members in November 1945 are shown below. In some respects the SWNCC served as a prototype for the National Security Council (NSC).[86]

Member	Department
Assistant Secretary of State	State Department (Chairman)
James C. Dunn	
Assistant Secretary of War	War Department
John J. McCloy	
Under Secretary of the Navy	Navy Department[87]
Artemus L. Gates	

The small SWNCC subcommittee on information release had fewer than twenty members who all had other responsibilities. They could not handle every request for information from foreign nations. The military and the State Department needed guidance so that they could handle the majority of requests on their own without constant referral to the subcommittee, which became known as the Military Information Control Subcommittee (MIC or SWNCC-MIC).[88] At the time the U.S. government had four levels of classification, from highest to lowest grade:

Top secret
Secret
Confidential
Restricted.[89]

The MIC prepared draft guidance on disclosing classified information in May 1946 and sent the draft to the Joint Chiefs for their comments. The draft established five categories for disclosure, as shown in table 2.2 below. The military could release most classified information up to top secret to the first two groups without referring requests to the MIC, while Latin American nations could receive nothing higher than confidential and that only in specific circumstances. The fourth category could receive only restricted information, with the exception that confidential material was allowed but only for equipment they already possessed.[90] As drafted in May, the guidance would give Commonwealth nations such as Australia and South Africa access to a wide array of information.

The Joint Chiefs found themselves pressed by a number of high-priority issues in the spring of 1946, including the nature of post–World War II relations with the British and Soviets. Historically, the army and navy in-

Table 2.2. Proposed Categories for Access to U.S. Classified Information, May 1946

Nations	Access
Canada	Up to top secret, with caveats. Greater access to U.S. research and development (R&D) projects.
United Kingdom, Australia, India, New Zealand, South Africa	Up to top secret, with caveats. More restricted access to U.S. R&D projects.
Argentina, Bolivia, Brazil, Chile, Colombia, Costa Rice, Cuba, Dominican Republic, Ecuador, El Salvador, Guatemala, Haiti, Honduras, Iran, Mexico, Nicaragua, Panama, Paraguay, Peru, Uruguay, Venezuela	Up to restricted when requested by the nation, though up to confidential when certified as mission essential.
France, Belgium, Holland, Norway, Denmark, Sweden, Turkey, Luxembourg, China	Up to restricted, though up to confidential for equipment already held by the nation.
Abyssinia, Afghanistan, Czechoslovakia, Egypt, Eire, Finland, Greece, Iraq, Italy, Lebanon, Portugal, Saudi Arabia, Siam, Switzerland, Syria, Transjordan	Up to restricted.

Source: "SWNCC 206/16," May 23, 1946, Folder CCS 350.05 (3–16–44), Sec. 8, Box 76, Entry UD 3, Central Decimal Files, 1946–1947, Records of the U.S. Joint Chiefs of Staff, Record Group 218, National Archives at College Park, College Park, MD.

Note: "Access" means information releasable by the War and Navy Departments without reference to the SWNCC-MIC. Requests outside of the defined level of access required SWNCC-MIC approval.

telligence agencies handled requests for U.S. military information from foreign militaries, so U.S. military leaders tended to view disclosure policy as a matter for intelligence personnel.[91] As a result, the Joint Chiefs assigned the MIC's request for comments on their draft to a JCS subcommittee on intelligence.[92] Overburdened with work, the intelligence subcommittee took more than three months to provide their comments, despite pressure from the SWNCC and then the Joint Chiefs.[93] The intelligence officers believed the draft gave too much authority to the War and Navy Departments to share information with too many nations—specifically mentioning India and South Africa—without reference to the SWNCC or the JCS.[94]

Eventually, on September 5, the intelligence subcommittee settled on a revised draft with two major changes. First, the subcommittee removed Australia, New Zealand, India, and South Africa from their initial position in the second category as equal to the United Kingdom. However, they failed to add these four nations back into one of the existing categories. Second, the subcommittee added some restrictions on sharing technical information with Canada and the United Kingdom, requiring greater SWNCC review.[95] These additional restrictions may have stemmed from Igor Gouzenko's revelations about Soviet espionage in Canada as well as the Venona project's disclosures on Soviet spies in the United States, Britain, and Australia.[96] By now, the MIC's initial request for comments on their draft guidance had languished in the JCS intelligence subcommittee for three and a half months. The delay eventually caused problems for Australia and New Zealand.

After they took so long to reply, bureaucratic and administrative pressure pushed the intelligence officers to complete their work quickly. However, they needed to address the glaring problem with their draft response: Australia, New Zealand, India, and South Africa were not in any of the authorized categories, which would mean all requests for material from those nations would require SWNCC-MIC review. The intelligence personnel felt the press of time to respond before a fourth month passed. On September 9, the intelligence subcommittee simply added the four Commonwealth nations into the fourth category, which also included France, Belgium, Norway, and Turkey.[97] For some reason, the subcommittee's members chose not to create a separate category for these Commonwealth nations—which arguably warranted greater access than Turkey, though less than Britain. The JCS had already noted that the disclosure policy would require adjustments after being approved.[98] Adding a new category for these Commonwealth nations would simply have become one of these necessary changes which would have been handled by the Military Information Control Subcommittee.

As written on September 9, 1946, the draft policy allowed the War and Navy Departments to release confidential material to Australia and New Zealand only for equipment already held by these nations. Otherwise, Australia and New Zealand could receive only restricted information. All other requests for information, such as secret or top secret material release, required MIC approval.[99] In theory this provision for MIC review could allow the two South Pacific nations to continue to receive a broader array of confidential data as well as selected secret and top secret material. However, requests for MIC release required a burdensome and extensive process, which in practice meant that the level of release authority given to the War and Navy Departments generally became the level of access for any given nation. Ultimately, the hurried work of the Joint Chiefs intelligence subcommittee became official U.S. policy in November 1946 when the JCS and then the SWNCC approved the revised disclosure guidance.[100] Australia's and New Zealand's access to U.S. information had been significantly narrowed.

The new November 1946 disclosure guidance soon began to impact U.S.-British-Commonwealth military cooperation in the signals field, specifically through the Combined Communications Board (CCB). The American and British Chiefs of Staff had created the CCB in July 1942 in order to standardize American, British, and Commonwealth signaling. The CCB consisted of senior American and British communicators who were supported by a large staff and observers from Canada, Australia, and New Zealand.[101] The American members also served on the Joint Communications Board (JCB), which reported to the Joint Chiefs of Staff, while the British members represented their equivalent body, which reported to the British Chiefs of Staff.[102]

The CCB handled communication electronics policy, including frequency allocation, call signs, and navigational aids for aircraft. The early years of World War II highlighted the need for such a body as Allied forces repeatedly struggled to effectively talk with each other.[103] By the end of World War II, the Combined Communications Board had substantially improved the interoperability of the Western Allies. The question facing British, American, and Commonwealth planners in 1945 was what to do with the CCB and more broadly the whole Combined Chiefs structure after the end of hostilities.

In the months immediately after the end of the war, the CCB continued to function, more from bureaucratic inertia as neither London nor Washington wanted to be the first to propose closing down the Combined Chiefs or the CCB. By the spring of 1946 growing concerns about the Soviet Union put the CCB's future on a more secure footing and made the board "one of the most active" of all the combined Anglo-American organizations still in existence.[104] Anglo-American strategists assumed that a war with the Soviet Union would involve widespread, high-intensity operations from the very start. Any chance of successfully defending Britain as a base for future operations in such a war depended on the ability of British and American forces to fight and operate together at the outset of hostilities.[105] Planners believed the Soviets would not allow the Allies the time required in World War II to become familiar with each other's equipment and methods. Retaining wartime interoperability depended on peacetime standardization of communications, which in turn depended on the work of the CCB. Without the ability to talk to one another, British and American forces could not fight together effectively.[106]

However, American information-sharing policies began to inhibit the work of the CCB after the SWNCC issued the November 1946 disclosure guidance. In practice, the new disclosure rules prevented Australia and New Zealand from participating in the CCB. In early 1947, the American Joint Communications Board proposed ejecting Australia and New Zealand from the CCB to resolve the problem, though this idea was not pursued for the moment. In the interim, the Joint Chiefs in January 1947 authorized continuing communications coordination with the British and Canadians through the CCB despite the problems with Australia and New Zealand.[107]

THE IRRITATING COMBINED CHIEFS

The problems with the Combined Communications Board were matched by the unwelcome publicity created by the continued existence of the Combined Chiefs in the second half of 1946. A series of articles in the *Chicago Daily Tribune* in August and September of 1946 had cast the CCS's existence in a nefarious light. The conservative paper, a strong critic of the Truman administration, suggested that the British used the CCS to exercise control and influence over the postwar U.S. military, specifically in Europe.[108] Then, a September 1946 visit by British Field Marshal Bernard Montgomery to Canada and the United States focused editorial and press attention on Anglo-American military relations, including the continued existence of the CCS.[109] During a White House visit, Montgomery deflected questions about the CCS when asked by reporters, who then pressed Truman to comment.[110] The president merely noted that the organization would remain until the official peace treaties ending World War II were signed.[111] In the wake of Montgomery's visit, the *Tribune* attacked the CCS as a tool to "subordinate American arms to British command . . . a conspiracy . . . utterly to enslave the American people" to British interests.[112] While the *Tribune* represented an extreme position on this issue, in October 1946 the more mainstream *Boston Globe* asked why the CCS had not yet been dissolved and called for the president to give the order.[113]

President Harry Truman (*left*) and Field Marshal Bernard Montgomery (*right*), September 11, 1946. *Source*: Accession 73–2273, Abbie Rower, National Park Service, Harry S. Truman Library & Museum.

However, the Joint Chiefs did not want to propose formally closing down the body for fear of appearing to drive a wedge between the two nations.

For their part, 1947 found the British chiefs also unwilling to broach the subject of the organization's future. In May 1947 the new head of the British Joint Staff Mission, Admiral Henry Moore, warned London of a growing suspicion among senior American officers of any British actions or decisions that could be interpreted as "flirting" with the Soviets.[114] Moore's warning created a reluctance in London to propose revising or replacing the chiefs out of concern that American officials might view such a proposal as a weakening of Britain's resolve. Part of the problem was that the democratic socialist policies pursued by Prime Minister Clement Attlee's government led many American officers in the late 1940s to view the British government as overly left-leaning. For example, a British officer at the U.S. Naval War College in 1949 was asked by an American student when Britain would "return to a democratic form of government."[115] The summer 1947 decision to offer a second set of Rolls-Royce jet engines to the U.S.S.R. for sale only contributed to these suspicions.[116] The growing revelations about Soviet spies in British Commonwealth circles, such as those reported by defector Igor Gouzenko, simply fanned American fears.[117] In this climate the British chiefs were reluctant to do anything that might upset the status quo regarding the CCS.

The warning from Admiral Moore led to a round of internal British deliberations about the position London should take regarding the Combined Chiefs.[118] Ultimately, on June 11, 1947, Attlee and Foreign Minister Ernest Bevin approved a recommendation from the British Chiefs of Staff: Britain could accept the unpalatable dissolution of the Combined Chiefs so long as the Joint Staff Mission remained in place.[119] However, British officials would not propose ending the CCS. By 1947, most of the active coordination between the two militaries took place through the work of the Joint Staff Mission, which maintained office space in the Pentagon and served as the umbrella organization for the individual service missions in Washington such as the British Admiralty Delegation.[120]

Growing Cold War tensions underlined the need for solidarity with the Americans, especially as Washington embraced containing the Soviets. In March 1947, President Truman announced that the United States would support nations threatened by communism, specifically in this case Greece and Turkey. Three months later in June, Secretary of State George Marshall called for a large program of economic aid for Europe, which became known as the Marshall Plan. Subsequent events in Europe seemed to highlight the need for such measures. In December 1947, Romania's king abdicated under pressure from communists who then announced the formation of the Socialist Republic of Romania. Then in late February 1948, Soviet-backed communists overthrew the democratically elected government of Czechoslovakia in a coup that rocked Western European officials.

FRENCH PRESSURE

British reluctance to raise the Combined Chiefs issue meant the subject remained largely dormant in the fall of 1947. However, the Czech coup in February 1948 alarmed French leaders, who in response sought closer collaboration with the British and Americans.[121] Throughout 1948, French military and diplomatic officials pressed American representatives to accept France into the Combined Chiefs. General Pierre Billotte, the head of the French military mission to the UN, regularly proposed U.S.-French staff talks and French participation in the Combined Chiefs to U.S. Army General Albert Wedemeyer.[122] In August 1948, the French ambassador made similar requests to Secretary of State George Marshall, who replied that the CCS no longer functioned.[123] The French had good reasons for doubting Marshall as the publicly available *Official Congressional Directory* published the CCS membership and address once or twice a year from 1946 through 1949.[124] Undaunted, in September, Lieutenant General Maurice M. Mathenet, the French military attaché in Washington, formally requested a report on the activities of the CCS both during and after World War II.[125] The Anglo-Americans dragged their feet in replying, sending a response in late December 1948 with a vague statement that since World War II, the Combined Chiefs organization was "discharging its continuing military responsibilities."[126] The question of French participation in the CCS reflected fundamentally diverging views between Paris on the one hand and London and Washington on the other concerning Western strategy and internal security.

From Paris's perspective, France stood in the direct path of any Soviet assault on Western Europe, and in the late 1940s French officials expected to provide the bulk of the initial Western ground force to resist such an attack.[127] Under the March 1947 Treaty of Dunkirk, the French expected British support and hoped for American assistance as well in the event of war. In such a scenario, the French assumed that the CCS would play a leading role in directing Western forces and wanted to be a part of such deliberations. The French also believed that the CCS handled global strategic planning for a war with Russia and wanted to be consulted.[128] Finally, participation in the CCS would demonstrate that France had regained great power status.

In contrast, the British and Americans wanted France kept off the CCS for security and strategic reasons. British officials doubted the integrity of French security due to reports from British intelligence about leaks of classified information to the press and to the Soviets. In particular the British distrusted the French air force and air ministry.[129] These concerns were in part justified since in 1945 and 1946 Soviet intelligence received reports from several sources within the French intelligence services, though the Soviets struggled to recruit sources in the French military.[130] American officers shared these concerns about French security since they also worried about the possibility that the French Communist Party might overthrow the government. Recent scholarship shows that U.S. military intelligence tended to rely on reports from French conservatives and military personnel, who played on American fears to encourage greater American financial support for France.[131] Finally, the U.S. Joint Chiefs viewed France as having "only European and North African responsibilities," in contrast to the United States and Britain, which had global commitments.[132] Thus France need not be involved in global strategic planning nor the CCS.

While the Soviets did enjoy several sources inside French intelligence, the British and Americans tended to overstate the influence of communists on French national security. After the February 1948 coup in Prague by Czech communists, the French government launched a purge of communists and suspected communists within the military and civil service.[133] A British liaison officer's report on his time at the French army's staff college in the 1950s captures the French military's antipathy toward communism in the early Cold War. The officer described how the commanding general of the college specifically told the junior officer students, "If the communists ever get into power, it will be the duty of the army to overthrow them."[134] In addition, British and American concerns appear even more overdrawn in light of Soviet penetration of their security apparatus through agents such as the Cambridge Five, Klaus Fuchs, and Julius Rosenberg.

THE COMMONWEALTH AND THE COMBINED COMMUNICATIONS BOARD

In the Pacific, growing American concerns about Australian security in 1948 matched similar concerns about France on the other side of the world. Distrust of Australia led the Joint Chiefs to push for the removal of the Commonwealth observers from the Combined Communications Board. American anxiety flowed from three sources: revelations about Soviet spies in the Australian Foreign Ministry, wariness about Australia's future under Prime Minister Ben Chifley's democratic socialist policies, and the critical reports on communism in Australia from the U.S. naval attaché, Commander Stephen Jurika (discussed in chapter 4).[135] Furthermore, under the American disclosure policy established in November 1946, Australia and New Zealand lacked access to most of the material discussed by the Combined Communications Board.

As a result, in March 1948, the Joint Chiefs asked their British counterparts to agree to remove Canada, Australia, and New Zealand from the CCB, citing Australia's and New Zealand's lack of access. Although the Canadians enjoyed sufficient access, the Americans did not want to be seen as playing favorites, writing that while "Canada is acceptable from a security standpoint, the retention of Canada while eliminating Australia and New Zealand would appear discriminatory."[136]

The American proposal put Britain in the difficult position of having to choose between Canada and the Pacific Dominions. The British sat on the letter from the JCS for a whole year, from March 1948 to March 1949. The British chiefs did not want to agree to remove the Dominions from the CCB as this would damage inter-Commonwealth military relations.[137] However, the prospect of keeping Australia on the CCB became increasingly remote in June 1948 when the U.S. military cut off all Australian access to classified information (discussed in chapter 4).[138] Beginning in the fall of 1948, the U.S. military put pressure on Britain to respond to the U.S. proposal. The Americans began refusing to attend CCB meetings, thus effectively ending Anglo-American military communications cooperation at the working level.[139] The embargo on Australia and the refusal to attend CCB meetings illustrated American assertiveness in military-to-military relations where security issues were concerned.

THE END OF THE COMBINED CHIEFS

The issues of what to do with the Combined Chiefs and what role the Commonwealth nations should have on the Combined Communications Board merged in March 1949. U.S. Air Force Chief of Staff General Hoyt Vandenberg raised both issues with the British chiefs at a meeting in London on March 7. Vandenberg reminded the British that the U.S. chiefs "still awaited" their reply to the U.S. proposal to remove Commonwealth from the CCB. He raised the negative effects on interoperability caused by the current standstill in CCB work. Marshal of the Royal Air Force Arthur Tedder, Vandenberg's British counterpart, replied that the British were still considering the American proposal. This was a thin excuse since the JCS letter had arrived a year ago.[140] While the British found the pressure regarding the CCB unwelcome, the subsequent discussion of the Combined Chiefs came across as even more troublesome.

Vandenberg brought a thunderbolt from the Pentagon. Due to growing French pressure, the Joint Chiefs wanted the CCB disbanded soon, though with the understanding that "its work [would] . . . continue under some other guise." Tedder countered by proposing that the CCB become the unofficial governing body of NATO, an effort to retain Britain's World War II level of authority in the new Western alliance. Vandenberg rejected this suggestion, noting that the French would never agree. The British asked for time to study the issue. Vandenberg agreed, though he did not consent to a British request for a full meeting of the American and British service chiefs. In doing so, he implicitly demonstrated that British intransigence on this issue could negatively impact other areas of Anglo-American military relations. In the fall of 1948, the Americans had already demonstrated their willingness to cut back on Anglo-American military links to get what they wanted.[141] The lapse in coordination beginning in the fall of 1948 had led to certain elements of U.S. military communications falling out of sync with their British counterparts, underlining the need for constant efforts to keep systems compatible.[142] Breaks in Anglo-American military links threatened the ability of the two nations' forces to operate together effectively with little warning, a critical capability from London's perspective.

Hesitant to resist the Joint Chiefs on two fronts, the British chiefs gave way on the Commonwealth in the CCB issue while focusing their attention on the CCS. The CCB resumed meetings in late April after a revised charter restricting Canadian, Australian, and New Zealand access came into effect on April 1.[143] The new charter did allow the three Commonwealth nations to attend CCB meetings, but only when both the British and Americans agreed to extend an invitation.[144] The tacit understanding was that "Canada would be present more often than not" at CCB meetings.[145] However, in practice whenever the American members proposed inviting the Canadians, the British members objected so as to avoid treating Canada differently than Australia or New Zealand.[146] As one British report explained, "We have to keep the peace between the Dominions," and bringing Canadian representatives into CCB meetings would "annoy the other Dominions."[147] Thus, British concerns about Commonwealth military relations kept Canada out of the CCB throughout 1949.

As far as the CCS were concerned, London found itself in a difficult situation. The Americans had made their position clear and in a rare move had taken the initiative to raise a topic typically broached by British officials over the past four years. Concerns about NATO increasingly shaped American thinking about the CCS. As an American report later in March noted, for the proposed North Atlantic alliance to succeed, France must be included in the alliance's highest command structure; otherwise "the political purpose of this Pact would be destroyed."[148] As an exclusive Anglo-American body, the CCS cut against the grain of the broader, more multilateral North Atlantic Treaty, which was signed on April 4.

Vandenberg's shot across London's bow initiated a transatlantic essay contest that stretched into the summer of 1949.[149] On April 27, the British chiefs refused to approve the American dissolution proposal until the Joint Chiefs clarified the future of U.S.-U.K. military relations.[150] Concerned about future American leaders cutting back on military-to-military ties, the British sought assurances. Part of the problem stemmed from the fact that the Joint Chiefs apparently gave little serious thought to how the two militaries would cooperate if the CCS was dissolved. At the March talks in London, Vandenberg had suggested a number of alternate methods but admitted that the Joint Chiefs did not have clear ideas on post-CCS machinery. The American general's proposal that the Combined Munitions Committee, which had handled equipment distribution, might serve as a replacement for the Combined Chiefs seemed far-fetched. Earlier American proposals, such as a 1946 suggestion that the Canadian-American PJBD serve as a cover for Anglo-American military exchanges, also strained credulity.[151]

In contrast, over the previous four years, British officials had regularly prepared detailed analyses of possible alternatives to the CCS for maintaining links with the U.S. military.[152] As a result of these efforts, the British had settled on the Joint Services Mission as the best method of maintaining close relations post-CCS; hence their commitment to the Mission's survival. Having given such laborious attention to the subject, the British generally found the American proposals cavalier at best and at worst reflective of an underlying lack of commitment to Anglo-American military relations.[153]

Meanwhile in Ottawa, Canadian officials decided to push back against their ejection from the CCB. The same day that the British declined to support dissolving the Combined Chiefs (April 27, 1949), the Canadian representatives in Washington informed their British counterparts that Canada refused to accept its removal from the Combined Communications Board. Based on the Canadian chiefs' view that Canadian membership on the board was "essential," the Canadian Joint Staff Mission (Washington) argued that Canada must have "full membership in any board or agency which might replace . . . the Combined Communications Board."[154] The Canadian message reflected their knowledge of ongoing Anglo-American talks about closing down the Combined Chiefs and subordinate bodies such as the CCB. Also, on April 27, the Canadians sent a similar letter to the American Joint Chiefs, emphasizing that as signatories of the North Atlantic Treaty (NAT) and as close partners of the United States they wanted full CCB membership.[155]

While the Canadians launched their campaign to rejoin the Communications Board, the Joint Chiefs sought to assuage British concerns about transatlantic collaboration after the Combined Chiefs organization ended. British anxiety stemmed in part from the haphazard American proposals about how the two militaries would share information without the structure of the Combined Chiefs. On May 20, 1949, the Joint Chiefs reiterated their continued commitment to close military relations with the British. They proposed replacing the Combined Chiefs with a steering group within NATO on which the United States would insist on "strong U.S.-U.K. participation." This idea did little to demonstrate serious American military thought on post-CCS machinery. First, such a steering group (which looked like what became NATO's Standing Group) would hardly be the place for sharing exclusive Anglo-American information as even "strong U.S.-U.K. participation" would not fully exclude other nations. Second, the British preferred to keep their links with the U.S. military outside of NATO channels, a goal that a NATO steering group would clearly not satisfy. More helpfully from a British perspective, the Joint Chiefs also proposed a July meeting to discuss the issue.[156] The British accepted the proposed meeting (which eventually took place on August 3) and refocused the discussion on the Joint Services Mission by insisting on the mission's post-CCS retention.[157]

While the British and American chiefs struggled to agree on the exact structure of their military relations after the Combined Chiefs, they both turned down Canada's first attempt to regain admittance to the Combined Communications Board.[158] When Canadian officials met on June 27 to consider their next step, civilian leaders voiced the strongest opposition to anything less than full Canadian participation in the CCB. Deputy Minister of National Defence Charles "Bud" Drury, a former soldier, insisted that "the necessity of tripartite arrangements should be made clear" to the British and Americans. Deputy Under Secretary of State for External Affairs Escott Reid, a rising diplomat, suggested that "certain pressure might be brought to bear" on the United States through the State Department to encourage the Joint Chiefs to accept Canada's position. Reid wanted Canada to chart its own course in international affairs, writing in 1943 that "we have not won from London complete freedom to make our own decisions on every issue—including that of peace and war—in order to become a colony of Washington."[159]

In contrast, Canada's military leaders did not feel the need to press for full CCB membership as strongly as their civilian counterparts. General Charles Foulkes, the senior officer in the Canadian Army, noted that Canada still received notice of CCB decisions informally in spite of formal exclusion. Vice Admiral Harold Grant, the chief of the naval staff, argued that if Canada continued to pursue the issue, the British or Americans might restrict this existing flow of information.[160] The admiral recognized the importance of information sharing and was wary of courses of action that might damage this critical feature of relations with the U.S. military. At another Chiefs of Staff meeting on July 19, Reid again advocated that Canada take a hard line, asserting that "Canada should continue to press vigorously for full Canadian participation in the Combined Communications Board." Again, Admiral Grant demurred, though Air Marshal Wilfred Curtis, the head of the Royal Canadian Air Force, supported Reid.[161] Despite the initial rejections from both the United States and the U.K., the Canadians, led by Reid and Drury, decided to continue their campaign to rejoin the CCB.

However, the Canadians then shifted their line of argument in response to the initial British and American rejections. Beginning in July, Canadian correspondence on the CCB issue focused on Canada's membership in the tripartite CANUKUS standardization program rather than Canada's participation in NATO.[162] In August 1947, the three nations had agreed to a broad program of military standardization (discussed in chapter 5). This change in tactics strengthened Canada's case in two ways. First, as one of three members of the standardization program, logically Canada should be a part of the

The U.S. Joint Chiefs of Staff, November 22, 1949. *Left to right*: General Omar N. Bradley, USA, chairman; General Hoyt S. Vandenberg, USAF; General J. Lawton Collins, USA; and Admiral Forrest P. Sherman, USN. *Source*: Accession 97–1883, United States Army, Harry S. Truman Library & Museum.

body that handled communications standardization for the three militaries. Second, deemphasizing the North Atlantic Treaty angle assuaged British and American fears of other nations also trying to join the CCB. The Americans especially wanted to prevent a parade of petitions from European nations— especially France—eager to follow Canada's path onto the CCB. The U.S. insistence on closing down the CCS because of France's concerns shows the significant French impact on Anglo-American military relations. While the Americans were willing to end the Combined Chiefs to avoid French pressure, they still did not want France to enter into the deepest realms of U.S.-U.K. military links. These twin perspectives shaped the outcome of the August 1949 meeting that decided the future of the Combined Chiefs of Staff organization.

Ultimately, at the August 3 meeting in London, the British agreed to the American demand to dissolve the Combined Chiefs of Staff. In exchange, the Americans agreed to preserve the Joint Services Mission's level of access, though they insisted that the mission move out of its Pentagon offices so as to allay French concerns. The two sides also agreed to preserve the functions of the Combined Chiefs "in fact, if not in name."[163] Through subsequent communications in September and October, the two sides agreed to substitute regular informal meetings between British and American staff officers for the various combined subcommittees that made up the Combined Chiefs organization such as the Combined Communications Board.[164] With these arrangements in place, the Combined Chiefs officially ceased to exist on October 14, 1949.[165]

The end of the Combined Chiefs did not change British and American commitments to excluding France from global planning for a war with the Soviet Union. This attitude extended to NATO as well. The need for such planning appeared even clearer after the Soviets tested their first atomic bomb on August 29, 1949. In the preparations for the August meeting in London, the U.S. chiefs assured their British counterparts that they did not view NATO as the highest authority in a global war with the Soviets.[166] Exclusive Anglo-American planning sessions continued to occur regularly to refine plans for a global war after the Combined Chiefs ended.[167] The two sides reaffirmed this position at a meeting in April 1950 and again in October.[168] At the October meeting, the service chiefs from both nations agreed that in a global war the Anglo-Americans would "meet in the back room for the global business and let the French continue in NATO" as Vandenberg put it. They also agreed that no printed organization chart would show an Anglo-American body above NATO, though such a group would be formed to coordinate a Western war with Russia.[169] French pressure could help dissolve the Combined Chiefs but could not break the French military into Anglo-American global war planning. Behind closed doors, the Americans were perfectly willing to give the British special treatment when there was no danger of public disclosure.

CANADA'S CAMPAIGN FOR
COMMUNICATIONS COOPERATION

When the Combined Chiefs ceased to exist on October 14, 1949, the British and Americans agreed that the groups and personnel on the Combined Communications Board would continue to meet, even though the body itself no longer existed.[170] The end of the CCB as an organization complicated Canadian efforts to regain access to a body that no longer existed. Canada had been excluded from the CCB since April 1949 because British officials rejected American efforts to invite the Canadians to board meetings.

Despite British opposition, American elements within the CCB pushed for Canadian participation throughout the fall of 1949. As early as September 1949, a CCB report proposed that when the CCB dissolved "complete Canadian participation" should be the basis for the CCB's successor.[171] As one British report explained, "The Americans still wish to admit Canada to most of their inner councils, simply because of her geographical association."[172] Shared American-Canadian interest in North American continental defense gave Canada a unique status in the eyes of many American officers. In November 1949, the Americans asked their British counterparts to agree to immediately begin inviting the Canadians to their combined meetings.[173] The British turned down this idea in mid-November, suggesting U.S.-U.K. meetings only, with separate Canadian-U.S. meetings as required.[174] Ultimately, in early 1950, the two sides agreed to return to the previous arrangement where Canada could attend U.S.-U.K. communications meetings when invited.[175]

In March 1950, the British tried to end the Canadian campaign to regain access to the CCB's replacement. British representatives in Washington offered a two-part proposal to the Canadians. The Canadians would accept the "attend when invited" standard in exchange for an informal promise to invite Canada to all U.S.-U.K. communications meetings.[176] However, the British refused to put this promise in writing "because of the United Kingdom policy respecting equality of treatment for all Commonwealth countries."[177]

Canadian officials in Washington and Ottawa disliked the idea of returning to the "attend when invited" standard. British objections to American attempts to invite Canada to CCB meetings since 1949 were the source of Canada's exclusion from the Board in the first place. In mid-April, Canadian officers stationed in Washington encouraged Ottawa to continue to take a hard line and insist on full formal membership instead of informal assurances. They also encouraged Ottawa to continue arguing for Canadian membership on the basis of their place in the tripartite CANUKUS standardization program.[178] Canadian membership in CANUKUS reflected shared interest in North American continental defense, and arguing on this basis might create additional American support. The Canadians believed that the Americans refrained from fully adopting their position because "the matter is regarded politically as a Commonwealth issue" on which the United States remained reluctant to override the British.[179]

By late May 1950, the Canadian chiefs decided to focus their efforts on the British chiefs, who might override those officials who had been blocking Canadian participation for most of 1949. The Canadian chiefs all wrote to their British counterparts, explaining the problem and asking for their help.[180] In addition, General Foulkes met personally with Field Marshal William Slim, his British Army counterpart, on May 12, explaining that "Canada must be represented [on the CCB] as a right."[181] Slim agreed with Foulkes, and in early July, the British chiefs instructed the British Joint Staff Mission in Washington to support full Canadian participation.[182] Having cleared the way with the British, on July 13 the Canadians asked the U.S. Joint Chiefs to agree to full Canadian membership.[183]

The Americans agreed that Canada should participate in meetings with the United States and U.K. "where the subject matters is of concern to all three nations . . . on a coequal basis."[184] This was a broader standard than the British-proposed "Canada alone of the Commonwealth" standard. The onset of the Korean War in June underlined the need for standardized communications between the three militaries. Furthermore, the Americans stated in writing that Canada would attend "meetings such as occurred under the former Combined Communications Board and that Canada should receive all associated papers."[185] The Canadian chiefs found this assurance acceptable since it was in writing and from the Americans as opposed to verbal British promises.[186] In January 1951, Canada essentially gained full membership to the "informal agency" that replaced the CCB.[187] Canada finally achieved its goal through "considerable correspondence," in the understated words of one Canadian assessment.[188]

By 1951, the U.S. military had settled on the organizations that would manage day-to-day relations with the British and Canadians. After Admiral Somerville's mostly failed 1945 efforts to embed wartime naval cooperation, in 1946, the Joint Chiefs spent considerable time and energy orchestrating America's postwar military relations. Links with the British Joint Staff Mission replaced most of the functions performed by the Combined Chiefs of Staff, while the CANUKUS standardization program took over from the Combined Communications Board. The Permanent Joint Board on Defense remained in operation, giving Canada a unique forum for interacting with the U.S. military. Canada's shared interest in continental defense provided a strong foundation for continued Canadian-American military relations. In contrast, Australia found itself distrusted, ejected from the Combined Communications Board, and under an American classified information embargo. Canberra's position improved in 1951 with the signing of the 1951 Australia–New Zealand–United States (ANZUS) Treaty. The story of how these structures were established, embedded, and adjusted reveals three themes in the U.S. military's postwar relations with the British and Canadians.

First, all three nations wanted to retain their wartime interoperability, specifically, the ability of their forces to operate effectively together with little warning. Aware of the time required to build this capability in World War II, officers from all three nations wanted to avoid repeating the getting-to-know-one-another phase of the last war. They also believed that in a war with the Soviets, they would have little or no time for such preparations, hence the need for instant readiness. Working communications between their armed forces represented the indispensable foundation of this ability.

Consequently, membership in the Combined Communications Board and later the CANUKUS standardization program became critically important. The Joint Chiefs demonstrated that they understood the importance of interoperability, especially to their British allies, when they stopped attending CCB meetings to pressure the British. For their part, the Canadians recognized that without a presence on the CCB or its successor, they would have limited ability to influence communications harmonization efforts. The emphasis on retaining wartime interoperability particularly shaped naval cooperation. The CCB's work on shared communications equipment and procedures allowed the allied navies to focus on creating common doctrine and operational procedures (discussed in chapter 5).

Second, while the U.S. military wanted to pursue close relations with the British and Canadians, the Pentagon did not intend to treat all nations equally. U.S.-U.K.-Canadian military ties were to be exclusive and not open to other less trustworthy nations such as Australia and France. Australia suffered under an American information embargo for more than two years.

American distrust of France ran so deep that a British report concluded that if France gained access to the CANUKUS program, the Americans would likely establish a separate U.S.-U.K.-only body simply to keep the French out.[189] While the UN might appear to make all nations equal, for the U.S. military, some nations were "more equal than others."[190] Within the U.S. Navy concerns about French security made the Navy reluctant to allow French naval officers to attend the U.S. Naval War College (discussed in chapter 6).

Third, as the Americans pursued exclusivity, they did not want to appear to be doing so. The Joint Chiefs clearly recognized the political danger of publicly treating one nation better than others—with the exception of Canada—in an era of strong domestic support for the United Nations. Concerns about the UN kept the Combined Chiefs in a hazy existence until 1949, when the combination of an imminent North Atlantic Treaty and the need for French involvement led to the CCS's dissolution. This desire to avoid being seen as playing favorites also led the Joint Chiefs to eject all three Commonwealth nations, not just Australia and New Zealand, from the CCB. Similarly, it took Canada almost two years to overcome Britain's commitment to equal treatment of the Commonwealth on the CCB. Concerns about public favoritism ultimately led the U.S. Navy to evict Canadian and British officers from the U.S. Naval War College in June 1951 (discussed in chapter 6).

The U.S. military in 1945 expressed interest in ongoing collaboration with the British and Canadians, but it was not until 1946 that the growth of the Soviet threat led to serious discussions about how to continue cooperation. Information sharing proved to be a critical factor in military relations, as Australia and Canada found out. Both of these characteristics of cooperative military links would influence the development of U.S. naval planning with the British, Canadians, and Australians for a potential third world war with the Soviets.

3

Global Naval Planning

In the two decades before World War II, U.S. Navy planning gave
little attention to how to fight alongside allies. The various iterations
of War Plan Orange, which covered a war with Japan, focused on
how American forces would fight their way across the Pacific.[1] The
coalition warfare experience of the Second World War and the postwar threat of advanced Soviet submarines led the U.S. Navy to turn
away from this prewar planning style. In the late 1940s, navy planners worked with their British, Canadian, and Australian counterparts to coordinate planning for a possible third world war against
the Soviet Union. This coordination represented a shift from the
navy's and America's traditional practice of avoiding entangling
military alliances.

Combined naval planning also provided a foundation for cooperation in other arenas such as exercises, personnel exchanges, and
standardization. Since the U.S Navy planned to fight with allies, the
fleet needed to practice doing so in peacetime. A summer 1946 decision to share antisubmarine warfare information with the British
and Canadians paved the way for expanding navy-to-navy links. In
a military organization where access to classified information was
tightly controlled, giving classified access to foreign navies highlighted the depth of American interest in naval cooperation.

The U.S. Navy's shift toward cooperative planning began in the
final years of World War II as the navy prepared its first postwar
demobilization plans. Demobilization at the war's end involved a
massive reduction in the fleet's size, which in turn highlighted the

value of working with allies who could bolster the U.S. Navy's strength. In early 1946, a series of exercises highlighted the potential threat of advanced Soviet submarines, which in turn spurred the Navy to prioritize antisubmarine warfare. As part of this effort Chief of Naval Operations Fleet Admiral Chester Nimitz authorized information sharing with the British and Canadians, cementing wartime sharing policy. Expanded naval staff links were followed by growing ties between operational commands, especially in the Mediterranean.

Cooperative naval planning naturally raised issues of command and control. The U.S. Navy and Royal Navy struggled to agree on a command structure for the Atlantic and Mediterranean from 1945 through 1952. Despite these debates, shared planning continued to move down the organization chart, creating deeper and wider naval links. In contrast to the Atlantic, in the Pacific naval planning grew out of the initiative of regional commanders, not the actions of Washington or London. A series of American commanders in chief of the U.S. Pacific Fleet worked to expand relations with the Royal Australian Navy (RAN) through navy-to-navy, not national, channels. Admiral John Collins, the head of the RAN from 1948 to 1955, played a critical role in deepening ties with the U.S. Navy in the Pacific. The relatively unknown story of these Pacific agreements highlights the value of personal relationships in combined naval planning.

American global naval planning helped extend the close wartime relationships between the U.S. Navy and its allies into the postwar era. However, the story of U.S. Navy planning with the British in the Atlantic and Mediterranean on the one hand and the Australians in the Pacific on the other highlights two different models of navy-to-navy relations.

ALLIES AND U.S. NAVY PLANS

In the final years of World War II, U.S. Navy officials sought to prepare for the coming postwar environment. Within the Navy Department, Chief of Naval Operations Admiral King's attention focused on managing the global war with the Axis. Therefore, administrative tasks such as postwar planning fell primarily on Vice Chief of Naval Operations Admiral Frederick Horne. A critical issue for postwar plans was the degree to which the Navy should expect to work with other navies, in particular the British. In a late 1943 memo,

Horne argued that "Great Britain will be a strong commercial rival with the attendant possibility of future differences."[2] Horne's position echoed a lingering attitude prominent within the interwar U.S. Navy, where economic and naval competition with Great Britain strained transatlantic relations, especially in the 1920s.[3] Horne also channeled the Navy's "traditional emphasis on the disadvantages of alliances."[4]

However, Secretary of the Navy Frank Knox cast a different vision at a speech in Chicago on December 6, 1943. Knox called for continuing the global division of labor between the British and American navies. Knox argued that under this plan, "when the ships of either nation pass into the control area of the other, they [would] pass into the command of the controlling Navy." Together, the two fleets would comprise a "postwar naval police force."[5] A fervent advocate for closer Anglo-American relations, in 1940 and 1941 Knox had pressed President Roosevelt to do as much as possible to aid Britain.[6]

Knox's vision gradually gained currency within the Navy Department, though Knox himself died in late April 1944. By late 1943 the navy's General Board, an advisory body to the secretary, assumed the two fleets would police the world's oceans.[7] Navy Basic Demobilization Plan No. 2, issued on June 9, 1944, called for an Anglo-American division of the world's oceans and continued postwar collaboration.[8] Horne's head of the Special Planning Section, retired admiral Harry Yarnell, sent a memo to Horne in mid-June 1944 that called for maintaining close relations with the British, in part as a means of limiting postwar American involvement in Europe.[9] Under Plan No. 2, the United States would maintain naval supremacy in the Western Hemisphere and the Pacific while the Royal Navy handled the Eastern Atlantic, the Mediterranean, and the Indian Ocean. Although the Americans would eventually establish a strong presence in the Mediterranean in the late 1940s, in 1944 American naval thinking tended to view Europe as Britain's area of responsibility.[10]

James Forrestal, Knox's successor as secretary of the navy, cemented this assumption of peacetime cooperation with the Royal Navy throughout 1944 and 1945. Forrestal had served in the navy in World War I before becoming wealthy on Madison Avenue in the advertising business in the interwar period. President Roosevelt appointed him as under secretary of the navy in 1940.[11] By late 1944, Forrestal was convinced that the Soviet Union would be America's principal adversary in the postwar world.[12] As such, the U.S. needed allies like Britain.[13]

Forrestal's assessment mirrored that of planners within the British and American militaries. By the summer of 1944, British military planners regularly cast the Soviets as their most likely potential enemy.[14] In September 1945, the Joint Chiefs of Staff identified the Soviet Union as the nation's most likely enemy, and formal war planning began that December.[15] The September report, JCS 1518, also called for deploying U.S. air and naval assets at a distance from the United States. New technological developments such as jet aircraft, guided missiles, and the atomic bomb made devastating surprise attacks a serious possibility to Pentagon planners. Forward deployment, as this pattern became known, would serve both to deter the Soviets and to prevent a repeat of a Pearl Harbor–style attack on the United States.[16] In 1947 and 1948, in fact, the U.S. Navy would adopt a forward-deployed posture based on two regional stations: the Mediterranean and the Western Pacific.[17] American ships in these waters regularly cooperated with the Royal Navy, as Knox and Forrestal intended. Concerned about a future conflict with the Soviets, the U.S. Navy increasingly viewed the British and the Commonwealth as a potential ally. The reality was that in 1945 and 1946, the American and British navies (particularly the latter) both needed allies to meet widespread commitments with rapidly diminishing resources.

ECONOMICS AND NAVAL STRENGTH

In the wake of World War II both the American and British fleets fell in size. Political leaders prioritized economic recovery over military and naval spending. The resulting cuts in naval strength had two impacts on naval planning. First, British and American admirals had to make hard choices about where to deploy scarce ships and sailors and which capabilities to retain. Second, declining naval strength made allied warships appear ever more attractive as potential partners. Securing the sea lines of communication would be easier if other navies shared the burden.

In the fall of 1945, navy leaders focused on demobilization and transportation of U.S. military personnel back to the United States from overseas. As American forces returned home, the navy's strength simultaneously fell rapidly. From 1945 through 1947, the navy dramatically reduced its size from a wartime high of more than 3.5 million men and women to its congressionally authorized postwar strength of just over 550,000, a reduction of over 80 per-

Table 3.1. U.S. Navy Personnel Strength, 1945–1950

	Officers	Enlisted	Total
1945	323,755	3,005,534	3,329,289
1946	233,035	1,832,896	2,065,931
1947	58,689	464,501	523,190
1948	45,298	396,204	441,502
1949	46,158	397,655	· 443,813
1950	54,423	498,954	553,377

Source: Naval History and Heritage Command, https://history.navy.mil/research/library/online -reading-room/title-list-alphabetically/u/usn-personnel-strength.html, accessed July 5, 2018.

cent.[18] The Navy Department matched these cuts in personnel with reductions in the active-duty strength of the fleet as shown in table 3.1 and table 3.2. To meet commitments in both the Atlantic and Pacific, the U.S. Navy would need to find partners who could share the load.

In Britain, the end of World War II also resulted in political pressure to cut military spending, which in turn highlighted the importance of continuing close relations with the United States. Prime Minister Clement Attlee came into office in July 1945 facing serious economic challenges. For example, rations on food in Britain remained in effect into the early 1950s to limit reliance on food imports that soaked up scarce foreign-currency reserves.[19] After six years of an all-consuming focus on wartime production, the Brit-

Table 3.2. U.S. Navy Ship Strength, 1945–1950

	Fleet Carriers	Destroyers	Submarines	Total Active Ships*
August 1945	28	377	232	6,768
June 1946	15	145	85	1,248
June 1947	14	138	80	842
June 1948	13	134	74	737
June 1949	11	143	79	690
June 1950	11	137	72	634

Source: Naval History and Heritage Command, accessed July 5, 2018, https://history.navy.mil /research/histories/ship-histories/us-ship-force-levels.html#1945.
*Includes other categories.

ish economy needed to convert back to civilian production. On August 21, 1945, President Truman unexpectedly ended American aid through the Lend-Lease program, which London had assumed would be available to help economic reconversion.[20] Furthermore, Attlee campaigned and was elected on the promise of expanding social welfare programs, which would require additional government spending.[21] Without Lend-Lease, economic reconversion and expansion of Britain's social safety net would be difficult tasks.

The nation's massive debt hung over these challenges like a dark cloud. In 1945, the British debt of 21 billion pounds equaled 215 percent of the nation's GDP.[22] Paying down this debt would be hard given the resources expended during World War II. Defeating the Axis powers cost the United Kingdom 28 percent of the nation's total wealth.[23] Facing this storm of economic and fiscal pressure, Attlee insisted on major cuts in the size of the British military and defense spending.[24]

However, Britain struggled to remain an imperial power with military commitments around the globe, including troops stationed in Germany, Palestine, Egypt, India, and Malaya. The cost of maintaining this global presence meant that in 1947 British military spending came to just over 16 percent of national GDP, compared to 5.4 percent in the United States.[25] Britain's defense burden was simply unsustainable given the nation's economic and fiscal balance sheet.

In January 1946, the Attlee government established three principles for British defense policy that sought to balance maintenance of Britain's international presence with financial realities. Defense spending would be guided by the assumption that the nation would not fight a major war in the next two or three years, that the United States "will probably" be Britain's ally in a crisis, and that in the immediate future no fleet (aside from the U.S. Navy) would be capable of threatening British security.[26] Under these principles, spending fell, forcing the military to make hard choices. The British Chiefs of Staff prioritized the defense of the United Kingdom and the Middle East over Southeast Asia.[27] From a naval perspective, this policy involved defending the sea lines of communication in the Eastern Atlantic Ocean and the Mediterranean Sea from Soviet air and submarine attack. These shipping lanes connected Britain to the Middle East—which held 40 percent of the world's oil reserves—and to the strategic minerals in Malaya as well as to Australia and New Zealand.[28] When the U.S. and Royal Navies began to plan

Table 3.3. Royal Navy Active Duty Strength, 1945–1950

Year	Active Duty Personnel
1944	790,000
1945	788,800
1946	350,000
1947	189,600
1948	135,300
1949	136,900
1950	129,400

Source: Central Statistical Office, *Annual Abstract of Statistics No. 90* (London: Her Majesty's Stationery Office, 1953), 95.
Note: Personnel strength listed as of June 30 each year.

for a war with Russia, much of the debate therefore centered on who would command forces in the Eastern Atlantic and Mediterranean, regions of crucial importance to Britain.

The challenge facing the dwindling Royal Navy was how to carry out these tasks in the event of a war with the Soviet Union. In accordance with his government's defense principles, Attlee ordered major cuts to the personnel strength of each of the services in early 1946. He wanted the Royal Navy down to 175,000 personnel by December 1946, compared to over 780,000 in mid-1945.[29] While subsequent discussions raised this figure slightly, the fleet's size fell dramatically, as shown in table 3.3.

COUNTERING SOVIET SUBMARINES

Such reductions forced British naval leaders to pick which capabilities they wanted to prioritize. During World War II, the Royal Navy had executed the full range of naval missions, including long-range carrier air strikes, surface warfare, amphibious warfare, minesweeping, and trade protection. This last role, defending merchant shipping at sea, became the Royal Navy's principal focus in the late 1940s. Both British and American officials feared a third Battle of the Atlantic in which advanced Soviet submarines would cut the shipping lanes that linked together their key strategic regions: North America, the British Isles, Western Europe, and the Middle East.

In 1944 and 1945, U.S. Navy planners had generally viewed cooperation with the British in terms of global naval policing of the seas. However in 1946, concerns about Soviet submarine capabilities shifted the rationale for cooperation. Increasingly, American officers wanted close ties with the Royal Navy to help combat the Soviet submarine threat. In July 1946 Chief of Naval Operations Admiral Nimitz recommended that one of the basic elements of American naval policy should be "formulation of a coordinated naval policy with appropriate members of the British Commonwealth" along with securing the sea-lanes to Britain, the Far East, and the Mediterranean.[30] While the two navies developed different plans for how best to secure the sea, both were concerned about the Soviet threat to sea-lanes.

Anglo-American officers with experience in antisubmarine warfare worried about the Soviets taking advantage of German submarines that fell into Soviet hands at the end of World War II in Europe, specifically the Type XXI. In contrast to the majority of German wartime designs, the Type XXI was primarily designed to operate submerged and could travel underwater at higher speeds than older U-boats. Such capabilities made the Type XXIs much more difficult for antisubmarine ships and aircraft to detect, track, and attack.[31] The new submarines were coming into service just as the Allies conquered Germany, and the British, Americans, and Russians all gained access to the design and several captured submarines.[32] The U.S. Atlantic Fleet conducted a series of tests with a captured Type XXI in early 1946 and found that the submarine's capabilities negated the strengths of most of America's and Britain's existing antisubmarine warfare (ASW) forces.[33]

The potential challenge posed by Soviet submarines in combination with aircraft and surface ships led the British and American navies to consider how best to counter these threats at sea. While both navies planned on employing a combination of offensive- and defensive-oriented measures, the Americans tended to give more weight to offensive strikes on Soviet naval and air facilities while the British prioritized direct defense of merchant ships organized into convoys.[34] These overlapping though distinct responses reflected each navy's unique historical context. For the U.S. Navy, the prominent role played by aircraft carriers in the Pacific in World War II seemed to encourage continued reliance on this offensive capability.[35]

Three events in June 1946 demonstrated the growing priority the U.S. Navy placed on countering the Soviet submarine threat at its source. In early June, Nimitz assigned ASW the highest priority within the U.S. Navy, equal only to the coming atomic bomb tests in the Pacific, Operation Crossroads. Nimitz backed his policy directive with an organizational change by assigning Rear Admiral Charles Styer duty as the new coordinator of undersea warfare to draw together the navy's disparate ASW efforts.[36] A June 17, 1946, conference on antisubmarine warfare crystalized American thinking on how to counter the Soviet submarine threat. Vice Admiral Forrest Sherman, one of the navy's foremost strategic thinkers and one of the deputy chiefs of naval operations, opened the conference by noting the high priority placed on antisubmarine warfare. After Sherman's opening remarks at the 1946 conference, subsequent presentations showed that if the Soviets deployed copies of German Type XXI submarines, then existing American antisubmarine forces would struggle to effectively respond, as highlighted in the Atlantic Fleet's exercises earlier that year.[37] Furthermore, due to demobilization, by 1946 the U.S. Navy simply lacked the escorts and aircraft needed to protect Atlantic convoys on the scale required. In his concluding remarks, Sherman said, "As you know the strategic counter to this sort of thing is high emphasis on attack at the sources of the trouble."[38]

From the U.S. Navy's perspective, a shortage of escorts, limited ASW capabilities, and a proven naval air arm all pointed toward an offensive-oriented strategy. Sherman's approach of "attack[ing] at the source" became a critical component of U.S. Navy planning.[39] According to this concept, strikes by carrier aircraft on Soviet submarine bases would destroy both submarines and their logistical support facilities, degrading the Soviet ability to interdict shipping at sea. "Attack at the source" reflected American confidence that carrier task forces could effectively strike land-based targets even in the face of formidable sea and air defenses, as the Pacific Fleet had done against Japan in 1944 and 1945. Sherman's concept also provided a strategic rationale for maintaining the navy's carrier forces, which navy officials perceived as under threat from land-based-airpower advocates who believed that strategic bombing could meet the nation's security requirements at the expense of land and sea power.[40]

The Royal Navy viewed offensive-oriented measures such as "attack at the source" as complementary to defensive approaches like convoy escort.[41] However, British planners recognized that they lacked the offensive carrier capabilities for sustained strikes on Soviet bases, especially early in a conflict.[42] Escorting convoys, on the other hand, appeared attractive to the Royal

Navy for a number of reasons. Convoy escorts had destroyed a significant number of German submarines in World War II and thus could be seen as an offensive measure.[43] Furthermore, Britain depended on secure sea lines of communication.[44] While attacking Soviet facilities could reduce the submarine threat in the middle stages of a war, in the meantime Britain needed supplies to arrive in British ports unharmed. Finally, escorting convoys drew on the fleet's extensive experience in this area, gained at great cost during World War II. As Admiral Fraser told the fifth sea lord in 1948, "planning can only proceed on something we know we must do; escort safely our convoys."[45]

Faced with declining fleets, by 1946, the British and Americans viewed continued cooperation as a way to counter Soviet submarines. The methods each navy prioritized for winning a third Battle of the Atlantic reflected each service's unique historical, strategic, and national context. Despite these differences, American officials began to expand links with the British and Canadians in 1946.

COORDINATED PLANNING BEGINS

Although the U.S. Navy planned to rely on offensive carrier operations conducted largely by all-American task forces, the Americans recognized the value of coordinating with the British and Canadian navies. At the June 1946 ASW conference where Sherman called for "attack at the source,'" Rear Admiral Jerauld Wright told the assembled American officers that "the British are much more anti-submarine conscious than we are."[46] Wright, the director of the CNO's Fleet Operational Readiness Section, recognized that Britain's geographic position and experience fighting submarines led the Royal Navy to focus on ASW. The U.S. Navy could benefit from British expertise and vice versa. Wright proposed "swapping information with them [the Royal Navy] in its entirety," a policy Nimitz implemented in late July.[47] Nimitz expanded this program in September to include the Royal Canadian Navy.[48] Wright and Nimitz's sharing policy provided a crucial foundation for continued close relations with the British and Canadians. While King had discussed such an arrangement with Somerville in the summer of 1945, no agreements came out of their talks. By 1946, the potential danger of Soviet submarines provided a rationale for information exchange that had been lacking in 1945.

The U.S. Navy classified the new information exchange policy due to its political sensitivity. Six days before Nimitz expanded the policy to include the Canadians, Secretary of State Henry Wallace gave a speech in New York calling for a more conciliatory policy toward the Soviet Union. Wallace, who had served as President Franklin Roosevelt's vice president from 1941 to 1945, represented those within the Truman administration who criticized Washington's increasingly confrontational approach to the Soviets. The speech forced Wallace out of the administration by the end of the month.[49] While Wallace's proposal drew broad criticism, public opinion would nevertheless likely have reacted strongly against information sharing that laid the foundation for a military alliance with the British and Canadians. Churchill's call for such an alliance six months earlier in March 1946 had drawn a storm of condemnation.[50]

Nimitz's approval to share information led to increased contacts between officers on the navy staff level in all three nations. However, for the three navies to operate effectively together on short notice, operational commands such as fleet commanders needed to develop links with their counterparts. These fleet-to-fleet contacts began to blossom in 1946–1947 due to three events that signified deepening ties between the three navies.

First, on September 30, 1946, Secretary of the Navy Forrestal announced an expanded U.S. Navy presence in the Mediterranean, a reversal of recent practice.[51] The U.S. Navy's Mediterranean presence had dwindled in late 1945 and early 1946. For example, in January 1946, the senior U.S. Navy officer in the Mediterranean was working to reduce the American naval presence "just as fast as possible."[52] American ships became an increasingly common sight in Mediterranean waters after Forrestal's September announcement. The Americans used British facilities at Gibraltar and Malta for logistical support, which naturally increased contact with Royal Navy officers, especially the commander in chief, Mediterranean Fleet, and his staff on Malta. Second, links between operational commands also expanded in 1947 after an American-British-Canadian standardization conference was held in Washington, D.C., in November 1946. Finally in early 1947, the Canadian government approved the recommendations of the Permanent Joint Board on Defense for closer U.S.-Canadian defense collaboration (discussed in chapter 2).[53]

The November 1946 conference focused on American-British-Canadian strategy in a war with the Soviets and the resulting need for standardization.[54] (The standardization discussions are covered in chapter 5.) Planners

from all three militaries discussed contingency plans, a continuation of Anglo-American discussions held throughout 1946 on war planning in great
secrecy.[55] American political concerns led the U.S. representatives to be wary
of overly formal agreements with the British and Canadians, which might
prove to be politically embarrassing given the Truman administration's publicly stated support for the UN. Therefore, the Americans broke with normal
practice and did not record the November conference agreement with the
Joint Chiefs of Staff but handled the document "more anonymously."[56] The
Americans wanted to avoid "embarrassing queries," likely from Congress,
about why the U.S. was standardizing weaponry and practices with the British and Canadians.[57] The planners recognized that their meeting could be
politically damaging because military level links were preceding formal political commitments.

However, the attendees believed that military requirements demanded
closer coordination now. The conference report from late 1946 argued that
their forces needed to be capable of operating effectively together with little
notice: "Our ability to win the 'last battle' can no longer be regarded as a valid
defense, since the first battle may be the last. To cope with the new danger
of a very powerful onslaught delivered with little warning or as a complete
surprise, we must arrange for greater preparedness in peacetime."[58] Standardizing equipment, doctrine, and procedures would improve the ability
of the three militaries to fight together "with little warning." Once such interoperability was established, retaining it required regular contact between
subordinate commands in order to synchronize planning efforts, rather
than relying solely on naval staffs in capitals. Combined Canadian-British-
American military planning on the national level therefore provided a framework for planning efforts at the operational level.[59]

The frequency of these contacts between operational commands and
midlevel officials picked up steam in 1947. Rear Admiral Styer, the U.S. Navy's ASW coordinator, proved to be a strong advocate for closer cooperation
with the British, especially after a January 1947 trip to the United Kingdom.[60]
Styer reported that the first sea lord, Admiral John Cunningham, insisted
that the Americans "be briefed on everything available" during their visit.[61]
At a meeting with Admiralty officers, Styer agreed to arrange regular visits
to Britain by American personnel working on specific ASW projects.[62] Styer
returned the favor in May by including British officers who were stationed

in Washington in internal U.S. Navy deliberations on antisubmarine warfare policy, though he reminded the attendees that the policy of exchanging
information with the British was classified.[63] The Americans sought to avoid
the public stigma if their policy of favoritism was revealed.

The U.S. Navy also improved operational links with the Canadians. In
January 1947, the Americans invited the Royal Canadian Navy to send observers to upcoming exercises in both the Atlantic and the Pacific.[64] In June,
the Canadians assigned a communications officer to the Atlantic Fleet staff,
both to work for the U.S. Navy and also to expand Canada's contacts within
the service.[65] The next month Nimitz ordered that Canadian ships exercising
with the Atlantic Fleet be given access to U.S. Navy publications to enable
them to fully benefit from the training.[66] However, Nimitz ordered "for political reasons" to keep the existence of such exercises classified.[67]

THE ATLANTIC AND MEDITERRANEAN COMMANDS

Growing contacts between midlevel officials and operational commands
naturally raised an important question: Who would command all these
naval forces in the event of a war, specifically in the Atlantic and Mediterranean? During World War II, the British and Americans had established
single naval commanders who generally held operational control of units assigned to their area. Nimitz, the Pacific Fleet commander, led both the U.S.
Pacific Fleet and the British Pacific Fleet when the two formations operated
together in the spring and summer of 1945. A notable exception to this policy
was in the Atlantic. The Allies chose not to establish a single overall Atlantic
command to protect convoys because of organizational and doctrinal differences and because neither the British nor the Americans were willing to
entirely turn over the Atlantic to the other.[68] In part because of this legacy,
early Anglo-Americans plans for war with the Russians like the 1946 Pincher
plans did not propose detailed command arrangements.[69]

In April 1948, the British Joint Planning Staff, a subsidiary of the Chiefs of
Staff Committee, proposed a command structure for the Atlantic and Mediterranean as part of an overall contingency plan code-named Doublequick.[70]
An American admiral would command the Central and South Atlantic while
a British officer oversaw the North Atlantic, with each admiral reporting to
his respective chief of staff. Initially, a British supreme commander would

be responsible for the Mediterranean and Middle East, though an American would take over once the United States enjoyed a preponderance of forces in the area. In November 1948, the Americans countered by adding an American supreme commander for the Atlantic while keeping the British model of a north/south split. In their response, British planners retained the north/south split from the American proposal but sought to reduce American influence by suggesting that the Chief of Naval Operations (CNO) provide overall direction, but not control, of Atlantic operations. The CNO, who would have global responsibilities in wartime, would have a combined British-American-Canadian staff, further diluting American influence.[71] For the rest of the winter of 1948–1949, this growing Atlantic command debate stayed in limbo as attention focused on the shape of the coming North Atlantic Treaty Organization.

Each side came to the Atlantic debate with a different perspective. The British were reluctant to give the U.S. Navy control over the sea-lanes that fueled Britain's economy and that the Royal Navy had guarded for decades. Furthermore, Royal Navy officers worried that the U.S. Navy did not place the same priority on convoy defense as they did. In 1948, the head of Britain's Home Fleet, Admiral Rhoderick McGrigor, visited the commander of the U.S. Atlantic Fleet, Admiral Lynde McCormick. To McGrigor's horror, the American admiral outlined a plan for protecting Atlantic shipping that relied on merchant ships sailing individually until sufficient escorts for convoys became available. McGrigor wrote to the first sea lord that "it seems difficult to believe that the USN have not learned this lesson from their experiences on their east coast in 1942."[72] British fears that McCormick's views were widespread in U.S. Navy circles made Royal Navy admirals hesitant to fully turn over the Atlantic to the Americans.

In contrast to these doctrinal and historical concerns, American admirals focused on numbers, U.S. law, and British weaknesses. They argued that since the U.S. Navy would be providing the majority of the ships, aircraft, and submarines in the Atlantic and the Mediterranean, logically an American officer should be in overall command of these areas. Additionally, the U.S. Navy wanted its offensive antisubmarine warfare operations under a single unified American commander to maintain their effectiveness.[73] Furthermore, the August 1946 McMahon Act placed strict controls on sharing nuclear information with foreign nations. Since in wartime U.S. carriers would likely carry nuclear weapons for use against the Soviet Union, American officers insisted that these ships remain under U.S. command.[74] Finally, elements within the U.S. naval aviation community doubted the Royal Navy's ability to effectively employ carrier aviation. Captain Herbert Riley expressed this perspective several years later in 1952 when he told Vice Admiral William Andrewes, the deputy supreme Allied commander, Atlantic, "I don't think that there's anything that the Royal Navy or the Fleet Air Arm can teach American naval aviators about operations in combat."[75] These diverging British and American attitudes ensured the Atlantic command problem remained deadlocked throughout 1949 and well into 1950.

The signing of the North Atlantic Treaty on April 4, 1949, and the end of the Berlin blockade in May illustrated the hardening Cold War, which in turn highlighted the importance of establishing command structures. Such commands could allocate scarce ASW forces. Cuts in naval budgets since 1945 meant that the Western Allies' assets to guard the Atlantic were limited. For example, an April 1949 study found that the U.S. needed 216 long-range maritime patrol planes to guard convoys in the Atlantic and Mediterranean. However, only 144 aircraft were on hand.[76] Establishing a consolidated command structure could help deploy these limited assets efficiently.

Several months later, in September, the U.S. Navy decisively rejected the earlier British idea of giving the CNO direction but not control over Atlantic operations. The Americans insisted that the head of the Atlantic Fleet serve as the supreme Atlantic commander with two subordinates: an American over the Western Atlantic and a British deputy over the Eastern Atlantic.[77] Ultimately by August 1950, the British military accepted an American Atlantic supreme commander with a western American deputy and an eastern British deputy. The NATO Council approved this agreement in October.[78]

Britain's acceptance stemmed in part from events in East Asia. The outbreak of the Korean War in June 1950 was drawing to Northeast Asia American forces that could have reinforced Europe in a crisis or conflict. Supporting an American commander for the Atlantic could tie the U.S. more firmly to the defense of Europe. The Korean conflict also highlighted the need for NATO to become a military alliance to demonstrate Western resolve in the face of communist aggression, but such resolve would be suspect if NATO lacked a command structure for the Atlantic.[79]

In the spring of 1951, however, Winston Churchill began to use the Atlantic command structure as a political weapon to attack the Attlee government's defense policy. Churchill believed that under Attlee British officials too frequently gave in to the Americans.[80] He criticized the government for agreeing to place an American admiral in overall command of the sea-lanes that were critical to Britain's survival. A steady drumbeat of such criticism continued throughout 1951 until Churchill became prime minister on October 26, 1951. As prime minister, Churchill wanted to improve Anglo-American relations, specifically by conveying to Washington that the United States ought not to assume British support. He wanted Britain viewed as a partner by the Americans and not a supplicant to them. In pursuit of this goal he traveled to North America in January 1952 for a series of meetings with Truman and U.S. officials where he tried to revise Atlantic command agreements.[81]

Churchill sought a joint U.S.-U.K. naval command for the Atlantic that would report jointly to the chief of naval operations and the first sea lord. In contrast, Truman was committed to the principle of a single unified Atlantic commander, similar to Supreme Allied Commander, Europe (SACEUR).[82] Admiral William Fechteler, now the CNO, recognized that Churchill's preferred structure would "mean the re-establishment of a section of the combined chiefs of staff, and this would not be in harmony with the concept of NATO."[83] The U.S. military strongly opposed any formal revival of the Combined Chiefs (for reasons outlined in chapter 2). Canadian officials supported the American position, though they also underscored the value of giving Churchill a face-saving concession.[84] Canadian support highlighted its national willingness to take a position apart from Britain in military affairs.

On the specific issue of the Atlantic command, Churchill failed to achieve his goal, and Britain remained committed to the October 1950 NATO Council decision. However, the Americans did agree to expand the boundaries of the Royal Navy's Home Station and to give the British Eastern Atlantic commander the authority to send additional forces into these home waters in an emergency. The Americans insisted that the second concession remain confidential for British and American consumption only.[85] Accordingly, on January 30, 1952, the North Atlantic Defense Committee approved Admiral Lynde McCormick, commander in chief of the Atlantic Fleet, as the first Supreme Allied Commander, Atlantic (SACLANT).[86] The SACLANT saga once again illustrated that while the U.S. military was willing to give Britain

President Harry Truman (*left*) and Admiral Lynde McCormick, USN (*right*), February 1, 1952, at the White House. *Source*: 80-G-438919, National Archives at College Park, College Park, MD.

special treatment, this willingness extended only to private matters, not to public, formal agreements.

The Atlantic command debate also showed how preexisting U.S.-U.K. arrangements and discussions were brought into NATO. These Anglo-American ties lay beneath NATO's formal structures. For U.S. admirals, Churchill's attempt to reopen the Combined Chiefs of Staff and Atlantic command issues in January 1952 highlighted the pitfalls of allowing naval ties to become political issues. Churchill's intervention changed little in terms of the accepted naval command structure and caused unnecessary strain from the U.S. Navy's perspective. The episode likely reinforced the commitment of American naval officials to keep navy-to-navy links out of the political and public spheres wherever possible.

While McCormick's appointment resolved one NATO naval command dispute, the British and Americans were also at odds over command in the

Mediterranean. By January 1952, General of the Army Dwight Eisenhower had been SACEUR since April 1951. Admiral Robert Carney served as one of Eisenhower's subordinate commanders as Commander in Chief, Allied Forces Southern Europe (CINCAFSOUTH). In addition to this NATO command position, Carney also held a U.S. Navy command, Commander in Chief, Naval Forces Eastern Atlantic and Mediterranean (CINCNELM). The USN's Sixth Fleet, the most powerful naval force in the Mediterranean, reported to Carney, but AFSOUTH's relationship with the British Mediterranean Fleet based at Malta remained unclear.[87] The stage was set for another debate over naval command arrangements.

The British wanted the head of their Mediterranean Fleet to command all NATO naval forces, including the Sixth Fleet, which would continue the arrangement used during World War II. From London's perspective, the Royal Navy had been the dominant naval power in the region for many years, and command of the Mediterranean would help protect the sea lines of communication to the Suez Canal and the oil of the Persian Gulf. Furthermore, some British officials felt that between Eisenhower, McCormick, and now possibly Carney, the Americans were getting too many of the top command slots in NATO.[88]

American attitudes were similar to those expressed during the Atlantic command debate. Since the U.S. Navy would contribute more resources to the Mediterranean than any other nation, an American admiral should be in overall command. Furthermore, the Sixth Fleet's aircraft carriers and their nuclear weapons must remain in American hands. Eisenhower as SACEUR also wanted to ensure that he received sufficient air and naval support for his right flank from AFSOUTH in general and the Sixth Fleet in particular.[89] The most straightforward way to ensure this support was for the senior U.S. Navy admiral in Europe to be placed directly under Eisenhower with control of the Sixth Fleet, similar to Eisenhower's assumption of operational control of Allied strategic bombers prior to the Normandy invasion.

Ultimately, in November 1952, after numerous proposals and counterproposals, the first sea lord, Admiral McGrigor, and Admiral Fechteler, the CNO, reached an agreement. As approved later in November by NATO's Standing Group, the agreement established a separate naval command, Allied Forces Mediterranean (AFMED), which would be equal in position to AFSOUTH, both of which reported to SACEUR. Admiral Louis Mountbatten, the head of the Mediterranean Fleet, became the new organization's first commander in chief (CINCAFMED).[90] When finalized in December, Carney commanded the Sixth Fleet and Italian coastal waters, while Mountbatten oversaw the rest of the Mediterranean.[91] Although the debate over command caused tension in Anglo-American naval relations, planning between the Mediterranean Fleet and the Sixth Fleet continued, and the two fleets exercised together regularly, often using U.S. Navy signal and tactical books.[92]

From 1945 to 1952, the debate over who should command the Atlantic and Mediterranean was the most divisive issue in Anglo-American naval relations. Both navies wanted to work together to defeat the Soviet submarine threat, but they differed over how to organize that effort. National pride, historical precedent, numerical strength, domestic politics, and doctrinal differences all shaped the struggle. Churchill's decision to make the Atlantic command explicitly political only reinforced the desire of senior officers on both sides to keep naval matters under wraps where possible.

Still, planning to fight the third Battle of the Atlantic continued through the command struggle. The threat of advanced Soviet submarines stalking convoy routes spurred the U.S. Navy to establish information-sharing arrangements with the British and Canadians. Furthermore, planning contacts steadily extended down the organization chart to the fleet level, creating deeper and wider naval links. In contrast, naval planning in the Pacific between the Americans and the Australians began with contacts at the fleet level before rising to the national level. This difference reflected tension in American-Australian relations over Pacific security and military base rights in 1945 and 1946.

PACIFIC POLICIES

In the wake of Japan's formal surrender on September 2, 1945, the United States sought to balance a number of competing priorities, including occupying Japan, demobilizing the U.S. military, supporting the Nationalist government under Chiang Kai-Shek in China, and guarding against a potential future attack from the west across the Pacific. To achieve this last goal the U.S. military worked to establish a system of postwar military bases. Britain and Australia were also involved in occupying Japan, but were reducing their wartime military forces to focus on their domestic economies.

As in the Atlantic, shrinking fleet sizes suggested the need for closer American-Australian naval ties. However, regional naval commanders took the initiative in developing these ties, as opposed to the Atlantic, where national figures played a more direct role. These Pacific planning efforts are far less well known than the SACLANT debates.

In Canberra, London, and Washington, officials tended to view their security interests in the Pacific through the lens of their recent history. The Australians recognized their need for a powerful ally, though each of their two choices, Britain and the United States, posed problems. Many Australians felt abandoned by Britain's failure to come to their defense against Japanese expansion in the spring of 1942. While the United States did come to Australia's aid in that moment of crisis, the Americans had remained neutral for over two years from September 1939 through December 1941. In a future conflict involving the British Commonwealth, the U.S. might remain neutral again, leaving the Dominions and Britain to stand alone.[93] In the end, historic ties to Britain led Canberra to pursue a Commonwealth-oriented security policy after World War II, though Australia still sought close relations with the United States.[94] In 1945, Frederick Shedden, the senior civil servant in the Australian Department of Defence, believed that Australian security should be based on three pillars: Commonwealth cooperation, collective security through the United Nations, and local defense. Cooperation with the United States, though important, was not one of these pillars.[95]

British leaders also worried about a future neutralist America, hence the priority they gave to Anglo-American relations. However, the British Chiefs of Staff assessed the danger to Southeast Asia and the South Pacific from the Soviets or Communist Chinese as well below that faced by Western Europe and the Middle East. Accordingly, British plans assumed the virtual withdrawal of British naval power from East Asia in wartime and the United States providing for the defense of Australia and New Zealand, as the Americans had in World War II. This American shield would allow the two Pacific Dominions to contribute to the defense of the Middle East and the Mediterranean as they had done in the previous conflict. However, Royal Navy leaders such as Admiral Andrew Cunningham, the first sea lord, and Albert Alexander, the first lord of the Admiralty, wanted to retain a peacetime Pacific naval presence. The presence of British warships in the Western Pacific

Table 3.4. Pacific Naval Commanders, 1946–1950

	1946	1947	1948	1949	1950
Commander in Chief, Pacific Fleet (U.S.)					
Admiral John Towers[a]	Feb 46–Feb 47				
Admiral Louis Denfeld		Feb–Dec 47			
Admiral DeWitt Ramsey			Dec 47–Apr 49		
Admiral Arthur Radford				Apr 49–Jul 53	
Commander in Chief, British Pacific Fleet/Far East Station (U.K.)[b]	Dec 44–Mar 46				
Admiral Bruce Fraser					
Vice Admiral Denis Boyd[c]		Mar 46–Jan 49			
Vice Admiral Patrick Brind				Jan 49–Feb 51	
Chief of Naval Staff (Australia)					
Admiral Louis Hamilton	Jun 45–Feb 48				
Rear Admiral John Collins[d]			Feb 48–Feb 55		

Sources: David Hobbs, "The Royal Navy's Pacific Strike Force," *Naval History Magazine* 27, no. 1 (February 2013): 24–32; U.S. Indo-Pacific Command, "Previous Commanders, United States Indo-Pacific Command," accessed January 3, 2019, http://www.pacom.mil/About-USPACOM /USPACOM-Previous-Commanders/; Royal Australian Navy, "Professional Heads of the Australian Navy," accessed January 3, 2019, http://www.navy.gov.au/professional-heads-australian-navy-o.
[a] Admiral Raymond Spruance served as commander in chief, U.S. Pacific Fleet, before Towers, from November 1945 to February 1946.
[b] Commander in chief, British Pacific Fleet, became commander in chief, Far East Station, on September 14, 1948.
[c] Vice Admiral Boyd was promoted to admiral in January 1948.
[d] Rear Admiral Collins was promoted to vice admiral in May 1950.

would support British commercial interests while demonstrating that the United States was not the only power in the region.[96]

While the British sought to ensure Dominion support for their Mediterranean war effort, American leaders wanted to prevent another Pearl Harbor–like attack across the Pacific. In their minds, the Pacific ought to become an American lake in which the United States controlled key island chains while mobile sea and air forces prevented any enemy from crossing the ocean. Rejecting the multilateralism of the 1920s' naval arms limitation treaties, the Americans pursued unilateral control of the Pacific based on a system of mobile forces and fortified bases.[97]

To oversee these bases the U.S. military relied on two separate Pacific commands. General of the Army Douglas MacArthur oversaw Japan's occupation as Supreme Commander for the Allied Powers (SCAP) while the majority of the Pacific fell under Fleet Admiral Chester Nimitz, commander in chief, U.S. Pacific Fleet and Pacific Ocean Areas. Nimitz's command, however, experienced considerable turnover in the late 1940s, as shown in table 3.4 below. In contrast, MacArthur remained in his post until April 1951. MacArthur also headed up U.S. Army Forces, Pacific (AFPAC) which was replaced by Far East Command (FECOM) in January 1947.[98] FECOM covered Japan, southern Korea, the Ryukyu Islands, the Philippines, and the Mariana Islands.[99] This divided command structure reflected the World War II division of the Pacific theater into area commands under MacArthur and Nimitz as well as the Southeast Asia Command under Britain's Admiral Mountbatten.

PACIFIC NAVAL PLANNING

The great distances between Pacific naval commanders and their superiors in Washington or London led these Pacific leaders to regularly exercise their initiative by making agreements with foreign counterparts. The U.S. Navy's Asiatic Fleet and the Royal Navy's China Squadron cooperated informally throughout the 1930s and in 1933 prepared a joint code for combined use.[100] When Japan invaded China in 1937 the senior American and British naval officers in the Western Pacific shared information and plans to improve cooperation between their forces.[101] In 1941 the Asiatic Fleet was preparing combined plans and procedures with local British and Dutch commanders before the Japanese attacked in December.[102] In 1944 Admiral Nimitz and Admiral Fraser reached a written agreement detailing how the British Pacific Fleet (BPF) would operate with the U.S. Pacific Fleet.[103] These arrangements involved local U.S. commanders exercising their judgement, often in advance of political commitments from Washington. Pacific planning in the early Cold War would continue to reflect this pattern of behavior.

In the final months of the war in the Pacific, the Royal Navy's British Pacific Fleet reinforced the U.S. Pacific Fleet's final campaigns against Japan. The BPF included ships and aircraft from Australia and New Zealand and operated from bases in Australia and the island of Manus, the latter of which became a source of contention in American-Australian relations in 1946.

The BPF's commander, Admiral Fraser, was a strong advocate for close An-glo-American naval relations. Fraser pressed the Admiralty to incorporate U.S. Navy communication practices into the Royal Navy's signal books.[104] Acting on Fraser's proposal, the Admiralty issued new signal books that re-flected wartime experience and American methods in early 1948.[105] Under Fraser and his successor, Vice Admiral Denis Boyd, the BPF regularly exer-cised with American units in the Western Pacific. For example, in February 1946, the battleship *Duke of York* trained with the heavy cruiser *Los Angeles*.[106] Later, in June 1947 ships from the two fleets exercised together off Japan.[107] These types of exercises helped both navies maintain their interoperability.

However, the Attlee government's military cuts beginning in early 1946 steadily reduced the Royal Navy's presence in the Western Pacific. By the end of 1947 only a few cruisers and a handful of destroyers remained.[108] British officials sought to counter this slide in Britain's strength through increased cooperation with the Dominions. Throughout late 1945 and 1946, Foreign Secretary Ernest Bevin and the British Chiefs of Staff argued for the policy of imperial defense—a pooling of the British Empire's security resources—as a way to retain Britain's great-power status while sharing the military burden of a global presence with the Dominions.[109] Specifically, Australia and New Zealand could support Britain in Southeast Asia and the Middle East.[110]

The cuts in the Royal Navy's strength in the Pacific paved the way for the Royal Australian Navy (RAN) to take a more prominent role in regional na-val planning. However, little planning occurred between the Australians and Americans before 1948 because of tensions over military bases, especially Ma-nus. This island, the largest in the Admiralty Islands, was located just north-east of New Guinea and by 1945 housed a major U.S. Navy base, including some of the most extensive repair facilities in the Pacific west of Pearl Har-bor.[111] The Americans retained control of the base after the war, though the island fell within the territory of New Guinea and was governed by Australia as a mandate. In late 1945, the U.S. military wanted access to a wide range of bases in the Pacific, including Manus. However, such long-term American access would require Canberra's assent. Dr. Herbert Evatt, the Australian minister for external affairs, sought to use the need for Australian approval as a bargaining chip to obtain American participation in regional defense planning involving Australia, New Zealand, the U.K., and the United States.

British leaders welcomed the prospect of greater American involvement in defending the Commonwealth in the Pacific, though London viewed America's role as freeing up Australia and New Zealand to commit to the Middle East. As the British Chiefs of Staff expressed in early 1946, it was "to our advantage to involve the United States to the maximum extent in the defence of the British Commonwealth in the southwest Pacific."[112] Furthermore, the British and Australians wanted to obtain base rights to American facilities elsewhere in the Pacific in exchange for American rights to use Manus. Officials such as Admiral Louis Hamilton, first naval member of the Australian Commonwealth Naval Board and professional head of the RAN, wanted to ensure that if the United States remained neutral in a future conflict, British Commonwealth forces might still use American facilities.[113] Australian efforts to obtain such American assurances came to a head in the spring of 1946.

At a Council of Foreign Ministers meeting in Paris in April 1946, Foreign Secretary Bevin told U.S. Secretary of State James Byrnes that the Dominions wanted to link American access to South Pacific bases such as Manus with American agreement to participate in a regional defense plan. In early May, Byrnes categorically rejected the idea, arguing that the United States had only limited interests in the South Pacific.[114] From Washington's perspective Manus's status was not worth becoming entangled in an Australian regional defense plan. American leaders such as Byrnes and John Hickerson, a senior State Department official, were determined to avoid being drawn into multinational arrangements in the Pacific.[115] In the summer of 1946, Evatt continued to press for such an arrangement in exchange for American use of Manus even after Truman himself rejected the idea.[116] Evatt's efforts only caused tension in Australian-American relations. Ultimately in June 1947 Admiral Louis Denfeld, head of the Pacific Fleet, personally went to Australia to explain that the United States was not interested in Manus.[117] The year after Denfeld's trip to Australia, Manus was returned to Australian control.[118]

The Manus episode highlighted Washington's reluctance to agree to any arrangements for Southwest Pacific defense on a national level. From the Joint Chiefs' perspective in 1946 the rapidly shrinking U.S. military already struggled to meet existing commitments: the occupations of Japan, Germany, Austria, and South Korea, the U.S. Marine presence in North China, and the growing naval presence in the Mediterranean. The chiefs wanted to avoid making additional commitments that would further spread American military strength, especially in a region with no immediate military threat. However, American Pacific commanders at Pearl Harbor saw value in developing links with Australia and began to take steps to build these ties.

While Denfeld's June 1947 trip to Australia signaled the end of American interest in Manus, the admiral did raise the possibility of Australian-American naval staff talks. On June 9, Denfeld met with Admiral Hamilton. At his meeting with Hamilton, Denfeld shared an outline of American military plans for Pacific defense and told Hamilton that he believed American and Australian plans should be coordinated.[119] However, Denfeld insisted on clear limits to such planning, as Hamilton recorded days after the meeting:

He [Denfeld] made it quite clear that neither he nor his government wanted anything to do with agreements on a high level. On the other hand he was very much in favor of *staff discussions* [emphasis in the original] on a Service level, and volunteered to send officers down here every 6 months if necessary . . . he said that as long as the remarks of his officers were regarded as confidential and remained on the Service level he was happy. He stressed that he never mentioned Service subjects to members of Congress for fear of publication.[120]

Denfeld's desire for secrecy mirrored the concerns of navy officials in Washington who insisted that U.S. Navy exercises and planning meetings with the British and Canadians remain classified. U.S. Navy leaders recognized the political damage that could be caused by public knowledge of deepening navy-to-navy ties. As noted above, revealing such ties would undermine the Truman administration's support for the United Nations and cut against a general American reluctance in 1946 and 1947 to agree to formal military alliances.

Denfeld took the next step by proposing USN-RAN staff talks because of growing concerns about the Soviet Union, which by early 1947 had replaced a resurgent Japan as the presumed threat to U.S. security in the Pacific.[121] He recognized that Australian forces could augment his much-reduced Pacific Fleet in protecting the extended sea lines of communication between Japan, the United States, and the Southwest Pacific. A 1947 U.S. Pacific Fleet intelligence report sent out by Denfeld estimated Soviet submarine strength in the Pacific at seventy-nine, though only three were oceangoing submarines. The report emphasized that Soviet aerial attacks, submarine attacks, and submarine-laid mines could threaten Allied shipping in the Pacific.[122] Coordinated

Table 3.5. U.S. Navy Ship Visits to Australia, 1947–1948

Ships	Date of Visit
USS *Currituck*, USS *Henderson*, USS *Cacapon*	March 1947
USS *Shangri-La*, USS *Antietam*, USS *Duluth*, USS *Atlanta*, USS *Robert K. Huntington*, USS *Ingraham*, USS *Laffey*, USS *Lowry*, USS *Moale*, USS *O'Brien*, USS *Allen M. Summer*, USS *Walke*, USS *Mattaponi*, USS *Chikaskia*	May 1947
USS *Sterlet*	December 1947
USS *Valley Forge*, USS *William C. Lawe*, USS *Keppler*, USS *Lloyd Thomas*, USS *William W. Wood*, USS *Mispillion*	January–February 1948
USS *Navasota*	March 1948
USS *Bugara*	June 1948
USS *Greenwich Bay*	August–September 1948
USS *Bergall*	December 1948

Sources: "Byrd's Warships," *West Australian*, February 20, 1947; "For Goodwill Visit Here," *Herald* (Melbourne), April 24, 1947; Commander Stephen Jurika, U.S. Naval Attaché, Australia to Captain Paul D. Stroop, USN, July 10, 1948, 1948, Folder June-1948-December, Box 3, Stephen Jurika Jr. Papers, Hoover Institution Archives; "U.S.S. Valley Forge World Cruise, 1947–48" (1948), 1948, USS Valley Forge (CV-45), V, Navy Cruise Books, 1918–2009, Fold3.com, https://www.fold3.com /image/1/301476460.

plans with the Royal Australian Navy could free up American ships to counter Soviet submarines operating in and around Japan. American warships therefore began to visit Australia regularly beginning in 1947, as shown in table 3.5, both to show the flag and to help build navy-to-navy ties.

The Americans used the January–February 1948 visit of Task Force 38 to advance Denfeld's proposed staff talks. Commanded by Rear Admiral Harold Martin and built around the carrier *Valley Forge*, Task Force 38 arrived in Australia on January 30.[123] Martin met with Hamilton on February 2 and suggested that Hamilton visit Pearl Harbor for navy-to-navy talks with Admiral DeWitt Ramsey, who had replaced Denfeld as commander in chief, Pacific Fleet, in January 1948.[124] After the task force left Australia, Martin recommended further exchanges and contacts between the two navies and Ramsey approved, though both admirals sought to avoid the impression that the U.S. Navy wanted to supplant the Royal Navy's relationship with the RAN.[125] Given Australia's historic ties with Britain, such an impression would cause unnecessary tension in relations with Australia.

USS *Valley Forge* enters Sydney Harbor, February 1948. *Source*: NH 96950, Naval History and Heritage Command, Washington, D.C.

Admiral Hamilton himself was relieved as head of the RAN by Rear Admiral John Collins at the end of February 1948. Collins became the first Australian to hold this position; previous heads of the RAN had all been provided by the British. Collins served with the U.S. Seventh Fleet in the Pacific in 1943 and 1944, making connections with numerous American naval officers.[126] One of the most experienced RAN officers of the era, Collins remained a staunch advocate for closer relations with the United States throughout his career.[127]

Collins followed Martin's suggestion to visit Pearl Harbor and obtained approval from the Australian Council of Defense for such a visit in April 1948.[128] By making contact with the U.S. Navy's regional commander, the Australians acted in accordance with the American preference to avoid national-level agreements. In July, Collins began to lay the groundwork for his trip to Hawaii through the U.S. naval attaché in Australia, Commander Stephen Jurika.[129] A potential obstacle arose when the United States cut off Australian access to classified U.S. military information in the summer of 1948 (described in chapter 4). Collins learned of the decision, but chose to press ahead.[130] He arrived at Pearl Harbor on November 16, 1948, for talks with Admiral Ramsey and his staff.[131] The preparations for the visit reflected a developing pattern in Pacific naval planning: regional commanders took the initiative while keeping their superiors informed.

Collins shared Australian capabilities with the Americans and asked for their assistance in antisubmarine warfare training. He emphasized to Ramsey's staff that "the Australian Government is very conscious of its sovereignty" and valued being consulted on regional security matters. Collins asked whether the Americans would agree to a line dividing the Pacific into areas of Australian and American responsibility for naval tasks such as convoy routing, antisubmarine warfare, and reconnaissance. Ramsey's staff agreed that Collins's proposed boundary line should be a "possible guide in any future discussions" with the Australians.[132] While the Americans likely intended to give only provisional approval, the boundary quickly became known as the Ramsey-Collins line. This agreement between regional Pacific commanders reflected the willingness of Denfeld, Collins, and Ramsey to take the initiative, in advance of any formal political commitments between the two nations.

Thereafter, the context changed. In the winter of 1948–1949, the growing success of Mao Zedong's People's Liberation Army (PLA) over the Nationalists in the Chinese civil war presented a mounting threat to American, Australian, and British security interests in the Western Pacific. By the summer of 1948 the PLA had achieved military parity with Chiang's Nationalist forces, which suffered a series of crushing defeats in early 1949, including the loss of Beijing.[133]

As Communist victory in the Chinese Civil War appeared more and more likely, Australian officials struggled to balance competing planning priorities. On the one hand, Britain wanted Australian forces committed to the Middle East in wartime. However, Chifley and Minister for External Affairs Evatt resisted such British pressure, preferring to focus on the defense of the Australia–New Zealand–Malaya (ANZAM) region.[134] In August 1949, a British planning team met with Australian and New Zealand representatives in Melbourne to begin planning for the defense of Southeast Asia under what become known as the ANZAM arrangement.[135] The October 1949 establishment of the Communist People's Republic of China by Mao Zedong's forces only highlighted the need for greater Commonwealth defense coordination.

The Australian Chiefs of Staff took the lead in ANZAM planning, supported by British and New Zealand representatives. Such planning initially focused on the defense of sea and air communications in the Southwest Pacific. In wartime the three nations agreed that the Australian chiefs, again with British and Kiwi representatives, would command the region.[136] However, the ANZAM Agreement could not paper over persistent differences in strategic priorities.

British officials assessed the threat to the Middle East in a war as greater than the danger in the Pacific. They encouraged Australia and New Zealand to commit to reinforcing the Middle East in a conflict and to help combat the growing communist insurgency in Malaya, which had begun in June 1948. Britain prized Malaya for its rubber industry, which provided more exports to the United States than the British economy did.[137] Field Marshal William Slim, the head of the British army, pressed this point of view in March 1950 when he met with the Australian Defence Council, now chaired by Prime Minister Robert Menzies. Menzies, whose Liberal-Country coalition defeated Chifley's Labor Party in December 1949, was more willing to consider a commitment to the Middle East than Chifley's government. However, the March meeting resulted in only an Australian decision to plan for deployments both to the Middle East and Malaya in wartime.[138] The struggle in Malaya, known as the Malayan Emergency, raised the prospect of further instability in the Southwest Pacific, which in turn increased the risk of a large Australian deployment to the Middle East. The emergency also forced Britain to deploy more forces to the region, and by early 1950 London had the equivalent of two divisions in Malaya.[139] British leaders therefore sought greater commitments from Australia and New Zealand to help share the growing demands for fighting the counterinsurgency.

In Canberra, the Malayan Emergency called to mind the national experience in the winter of 1941–1942. Having sent the bulk of its combat power to the Mediterranean to help the British, Australia was caught flat-footed by the Japanese attack in December 1941. In the moment of crisis, Britain proved unable to provide for Australian security, leading to strategic anxiety for officials in Canberra. Before Canberra committed to the Middle East in the late 1940s, it wanted assurances that the Americans would guard Australia. Australia had no wish to repeat the anxious months of the winter of 1941–1942 if its forces deployed to the Middle East in a future war with Russia. Instead, they insisted that someone "bolt the back door."[140]

British officers such as Admiral Fraser, now the first sea lord, understood Australian concerns and pressed the United States to commit to Australia's defense or at least coordinate planning. During an address to the U.S. Naval War College in Newport, Rhode Island, in April 1950, Fraser noted that "the Pacific is an area of U.S. interest and responsibility." He explained that "Australia and New Zealand will not commit any forces to assist the U.K. until they know what U.S. intentions are. The U.S. should inform the Anzacs regarding [American] plans."[141] In a July 1950 meeting with Prime Minister Menzies, Fraser reiterated the importance of Australia coordinating with U.S. plans for the Pacific.[142] As Fraser had said at Newport, closer coordination with the Americans could help Britain if Australia felt secure enough to commit forces to the Middle East.

A memo written by the U.S. Navy's director of strategic plans, Rear Admiral Stuart Ingersoll, that same month showed the gap between Fraser's views and those of the U.S. Navy. Ingersoll wrote that U.S. officials meeting with Menzies—who was traveling to Washington after meetings in London—should impress "upon him the urgent need" for Australia to contribute forces to the Middle East in wartime. However, in the same document, Ingersoll urged that the United States not enter into "any agreements on the JCS [Joint Chiefs of Staff] or governmental levels" with Australia on regional defense planning.[143] The Ingersoll memo illustrated the need for Fraser's efforts, as senior U.S. Navy officers in Washington appeared unaware of the connection between Australian commitments to the Middle East and coordinated Australian-American plans.

This disconnect extended beyond the U.S. Navy. General Omar Bradley, the chairman of the Joint Chiefs, wanted to know about Australian plans for countering possible Chinese communist aggression in Southeast Asia.[144] At the same time, the Joint Chiefs wanted to avoid any action that might be interpreted as approving or joining the ANZAM Agreement, thus encumbering the United States with "pre-established combined commands."[145] For example, later in September 1950, the Australians offered the U.S. naval attaché, Commander Adrian Perry, Jurika's successor, the opportunity to sit in on ANZAM planning meetings. Perry was told to refuse the offer.[146] Navy officials feared that Perry's attendance might be a prelude to further American commitments to the region. The U.S. military wanted Australia to be able to support both the Middle East and Southeast Asia in wartime but without the assurance of formal commitments from Washington.

Given the Pentagon's noncommittal attitude toward regional defense planning in the Pacific, local officials continued to take the initiative in coordinating plans. In May 1950, Admiral Arthur Radford, Ramsey's replacement as CINCPAC, visited Australia for talks with Australian officials on Pacific defense.[147] Radford, a naval aviator, went on to become the chairman of the Joint Chiefs in 1953.[148] In Australia, Radford met with Prime Minister Menzies and attended a meeting of the Australian Chiefs of Staff.[149] The visit highlighted Collins's American connections as he personally knew Captain Charles Adair, one of Radford's staff officers, from World War II.[150] Following Radford's visit, the RAN passed their plans to Radford in writing through Commander Perry in Melbourne.[151] These fleet-level ties preceded formal U.S. political commitments to Australia.

The outbreak of the Korean War in June 1950 dramatically increased tensions in the Pacific. The Truman administration's decision to support South Korea with ground forces days after the North Korean invasion committed the United States to a major conflict on the other side of the world from Europe, which nevertheless remained America's priority. British officials worried that Australia might now become more reluctant to send forces to the Middle East and encouraged Canberra to continue contingency planning for such a deployment. Both Britain and Australia sent troops, ships, and aircraft to support the Americans and South Koreans (discussed in chapter 7). The potential for conflict to spread beyond the Korean Peninsula highlighted the need for closer coordination of Pacific plans, a subject raised at an important meeting on October 23, 1950, between the British and American service chiefs.

At this conference, Admiral Forrest Sherman, now the CNO, opened a discussion of Pacific security by approving the 1948 Ramsey-Collins boundary as the basis for future planning. The British likewise agreed. Admiral Fraser, the first sea lord, then asked how Pacific planning should proceed. Fraser's question was insightful, as it called for the Americans to resolve the tension between their desire for further coordination in the Pacific and their reluctance to enter into formal arrangements with the Australians. Sherman replied that Radford should work directly with the Australians and New Zealanders, thus avoiding chiefs of staff–level commitments. Furthermore, shared plans should be based on the assumption that "we will commit enough forces in that ocean to ensure the security of Australia and New Zealand." Sherman's commitment was an important concession designed to meet Australia's desire to "bolt the back door," a recognition that the Joint Chiefs now understood Canberra's concerns about its national security. Fraser may have smiled to himself as the Americans recognized what he had been emphasizing for months. The British admiral remained focused on the process and asked in reply who should take the next step. Air Marshal John Slessor, chief of staff of the Royal Air Force (RAF), suggested, and General Bradley agreed, that the Australian Chiefs of Staff should contact Radford, who in turn would receive instructions from the Joint Chiefs.[152] Pacific naval planning would remain principally in the hands of the Pacific commanders.

In the wake of the October 1950 meeting Collins contacted Radford and set up a meeting to finalize the naval boundary between the two commands. When Collins traveled to Pearl Harbor in late February 1951 his party included the head of the Royal New Zealand Navy, Commodore F. A. Balance, RN, and representatives from the Royal Navy's Far East Station command.[153] This collection of representatives from Commonwealth countries highlighted the multilateral nature of Pacific naval planning, which concerned Britain, America, Australia, and New Zealand.

The resulting conference lasted from February 26 to March 2, and at its conclusion Radford and Collins agreed on a naval boundary between their respective commands. Furthermore, the two admirals approved ongoing contact through the British liaison officer on Radford's staff as well as an exchange of communication publications.[154] In contrast to the informal 1948 Ramsey-Collins agreement, at Radford's suggestion both men signed the conference report as representatives of their nations.[155] The agreement was ratified by both nations and became known as the Radford-Collins Agreement.[156] Collins described the meeting as "very fruitful and enjoyable" in a letter to Admiral Fraser. The Australian also highlighted the benefits of his connections with the U.S. Navy: "Knowing Radford well personally helped me a lot."[157]

The Radford-Collins Agreement provided the foundation for operational Australian-American naval relations, even after the Australia–New Zealand–

United States (ANZUS) Treaty was signed in September 1951. ANZUS did not develop the integrated military command structure and multinational staff organization of the NATO alliance. Instead, Radford-Collins provided for ongoing contacts and exchanges between the U.S. Pacific Fleet and the RAN.

While the Australians had hoped for a voice in American strategic planning, this goal turned out to be a bridge too far. Given the Royal Australian Navy's likely wartime role—defending sea lines of communication—U.S. Navy policy called for coordination at the fleet commander, not national, level.[158] According to a 1947 Navy Department memo, the Atlantic and Pacific Fleets were charged with liaising "with commanders of contiguous areas outside of U.S. responsibility for the coordination of anti-submarine operations."[159] Fleet commanders were responsible for coordinating convoy protection measures with neighboring unified commands such as Far East Command or European Command. From this perspective, the U.S. Navy treated the Royal Australian Navy as another unified command in both the 1948 Ramsey-Collins and the 1951 Radford-Collins Agreements, though only for specific naval tasks, not overall control of military operations in the region.

Still, the two navies established operational planning links that allowed regional commanders to coordinate and share information. In contrast to the Atlantic and Mediterranean, in the Pacific Fleet commanders in both the RAN and the USN took the initiative to build closer American-Australian naval relations. The meetings and agreements between Collins and his American counterparts in Hawaii helped to overcome the trans-Pacific tension caused by the Manus base dispute and the American embargo on Australian access to U.S. secrets.

Pacific planning was simply a lower priority for Washington than a third Battle of the Atlantic. However, from the American headquarters at Pearl Harbor coordination with potential allies was an urgent requirement. U.S. Navy admirals in the Pacific had already established a tradition of taking the initiative in talks with friendly navies that extended back into the 1930s. From that perspective, Denfeld, Ramsey, and Radford were all acting in accordance with U.S. Navy tradition.

In the final years of World War II, American officials such as Knox, Sherman, and Forrestal advocated continued cooperation with the Royal Navy. The

Royal Navy's Admiral Fraser and Australia's Rear Admiral Collins shared this desire to extend wartime links into the postwar period. The perceived threat posed by the Soviet Union and later Communist China encouraged U.S. Navy planners to coordinate with presumed allies. Budget cuts and demobilization meant that no single fleet remained large enough to patrol or secure the world's oceans. Cooperative naval planning could therefore help allocate scarce naval resources.

While these influences established a framework for planners, the course of cooperative naval planning depended heavily on the geographical and strategic context. During 1946–1947, the U.S. Navy shifted its principal strategic focus from the Pacific to Europe, specifically the Mediterranean. In a war with the Soviets, control of the Mediterranean could support strategic bombers based in Egypt or North Africa and protect the shipping lanes connecting Britain and Western Europe to the resources of the Middle East. The establishment of NATO in 1949 highlighted the growing priority that the Truman administration placed on containing Soviet influence in Europe.

Accordingly, planning links between the Americans and British began at the national naval staff level before extending down to the fleet level, especially between the U.S. Sixth Fleet and the British Mediterranean Fleet. As established at the November 1946 standardization conference, the goal of such connections was to maintain interoperability. American and British planners believed that in a war, the speed of Soviet offensives would demand that the Anglo-American militaries be able to effectively fight together with little warning. Combined planning at the fleet level blossomed in 1947, as did regular Anglo-American naval exercises, first in the Mediterranean and later in the Atlantic. (These exercises are discussed in chapter 6.)

Although from 1948 through 1952 the two navies fought over who would command the Atlantic and Mediterranean in wartime, at the naval staff and operational levels planning and information sharing continued. Such ties were in many respects designed to continue to operate beneath the turbulent waters of political concerns. Churchill's decision to use the Atlantic command debate as a political weapon against Attlee did delay the final agreement over the supreme Allied commander, Atlantic. However, the episode only convinced senior British and American admirals of the importance of keeping navy-to-navy ties separate from politics as much as possible.

While political priorities delayed command structure planning in the Atlantic, in the Pacific such priorities limited the scope of international naval planning. Australia, New Zealand, and the South Pacific were not high on the Truman administration's list of priorities. Furthermore, the Joint Chiefs wanted to avoid committing their dwindling forces to regions with little apparent military threat. As a result, Australian efforts in 1946 to draw the United States into regional defense planning for the Southwest Pacific fell flat.

However, a series of U.S. commanders at Pearl Harbor wanted to coordinate their planning with Australia. Admirals Denfeld, Ramsey, and Radford all pursued closer ties with the Royal Australian Navy by using navy-to-navy channels. They recognized that Washington would not approve a regional command structure similar to SACLANT, but they decided on their own initiative to develop naval ties with less ambitious goals. The Americans found ready partners in both Admiral Hamilton and Admiral Collins, the two professional heads of the RAN in this period. Collins in particular benefited from the personal relationships he made during his wartime service with the U.S. Seventh Fleet in the Pacific.

The resulting 1948 Ramsey-Collins and 1951 Radford-Collins Agreements established boundaries for antisubmarine warfare and convoy operations in the Pacific between the Americans and Australians. In these agreements the U.S. Pacific Command was in some respects treating the Royal Australian Navy as simply a neighboring U.S. military command. The two commands worked out boundaries and responsibilities similar to the way that Pacific Command coordinated with U.S. Far East Command. Radford-Collins also set up channels for ongoing cooperative planning and liaison. In contrast to the Atlantic, these agreements owed much to the initiative of regional commanders, highlighting the value of personal relationships between naval officers. These relationships were important not only at the highest levels but also between midlevel officials in exchange, liaison, and attaché positions.

4

Personnel

"The U.S. Navy is simply boring," Lieutenant Lygo thought to himself one morning in the fall of 1949. As a new exchange pilot in VF-172, an American fighter squadron, Raymond Lygo found his initial practice flights restricted to very elementary maneuvers. Unlike his native Royal Navy squadron where pilots were encouraged to test the capabilities and limits of their aircraft, the Americans allowed only pilots in special experimental squadrons to fly aircraft to their physical limits. Lygo decided that it was high time he found out for himself what his Banshee jet fighter could really do. He took off and practiced flying with one of the plane's two engines shut down, then the other, then landed on only one engine, after asking permission to do so from the control tower. After taxiing off the runway, Lygo found the squadron operations officer, the squadron commanding officer, and the base commander all waiting for him. The Americans assumed he had had a problem; why else would he land with only one engine? Lygo explained there was no problem, he was just practicing. Lieutenant Commander Vince Paul de Poix, the squadron commander, took Lygo inside his office before exploding: "Do you know how much that airplane costs? If you had damaged that plane you would be on your way back to England right now." Lygo replied, "But I didn't sir." "Well we don't do that," de Poix said with finality. Lygo decided to leave the matter at that.[1]

At some point in officer exchanges such as Lieutenant Lygo's time with the U.S. Navy, different practices and procedures inevitably caused friction. However, they also provided unparalleled opportunities for officers from each navy to get to know their counterparts over the course of a year or longer. The creation of U.S. Navy exchange programs with the British and Canadians in the late 1940s complemented the growing planning links between these navies at the staff and fleet level. Exchange programs gave junior and midcareer officers relationships and experience with an allied navy that would benefit them throughout their career. Two other types of officers also worked to improve connections between these four navies: liaison officers and naval attachés. In addition, ships and aircraft from these fleets regularly visited each other's nations, which also allowed personnel to meet each other. These positions and visits all helped create and sustain relationships between personnel, contributing to personnel interoperability. Exchanges and visits allowed officers to build new ties with allied personnel and in some cases renew friendships from World War II. However, attachés could also damage navy-to-navy relations, as seen in the story of Commander Stephen Jurika, the U.S. naval attaché to Australia in the late 1940s.

Personal relationships between naval officers were not new in 1945. Neither were warships visiting other countries. For instance, Admiral Sims, as head of U.S. naval forces in Europe in World War I, benefited from connections he made in 1910 when as captain of the battleship *Minnesota* he visited Britain. However, the post–World War II network of exchange and liaison programs the U.S. Navy built up with the British and Canadians represented a shift from past practice. The resulting expanding web of personal relationships reflected the U.S. Navy's interest in retaining close relations with its closest wartime partners as well as British and Canadian initiative. Both navies devoted time and money to build exchange and liaison links with the Americans. These links included professional educational exchanges (discussed in chapter 6).

ATTACHÉS, STAFF MISSIONS, AND LIAISON OFFICERS

The fundamental links between the U.S. Navy and the British, Canadian, and Australian fleets consisted of relationships between people. Three types of officers handled most of the day-to-day contact between these navies in the early Cold War: naval attachés, staff missions, and liaison officers. Attachés held diplomatic positions as formal representatives of their navy and reported to their ambassador at the embassy.[2] In addition to their attachés, the British, Canadians, and Australians established military staff missions in Washington that reported directly to their respective chiefs of staff, not through diplomatic channels. The U.S. Navy had a similar arrangement in London, though structured differently. While attaches dealt with a wide range of issues, liaison officers focused their efforts on a specific organization or office. For example, the Royal Canadian Navy established a liaison officer at the U.S. Naval Base at Key West, Florida, to report on American antisubmarine warfare (ASW) developments. Liaison officers typically reported to the military staff mission, if one existed, or to the attaché.

The British Joint Staff Mission consisted of officers from all three services and stood apart from the attaché system in order to facilitate information sharing with the U.S. military. As explained by the British Chiefs of Staff: "The Americans for their part, would not permit military attachés access to intelligence and technical information to the extent necessary, as by so doing, a precedent would be stablished for similar functions being given to military attachés of other countries."[3] The U.S. military was willing to share information with the staff missions but wanted the sharing to stay outside diplomatic attaché channels.

The Australian and Canadian missions in Washington functioned similarly, though with less direct contact with the U.S. Joint Chiefs. For both Canada and Britain the military staff mission was larger than the attaché's staff at the embassy.[4] Exchanging information and managing its flow occupied a significant portion of the time of officers assigned to these staff missions.

During World War II, the British and American militaries exchanged information freely regarding research and development. At the end of the war, the U.S. military adopted the position that collaboration with the British could continue on projects launched prior to Japan's surrender but that sharing data from projects started after September 1945 would require individual approval. This position shifted American information-sharing policy from wartime openness toward the prewar position, in which the intelligence agency of each service controlled foreign access to information on a case-by-case basis. In the spring of 1946 the British staff mission in Washington expressed concern about this trend—most noticeable with the U.S. Army Air Force—to the U.S. Joint Chiefs, who told the British that they were in favor of continued collaboration "on exactly the same scale" as during World War II. However, neither the British nor the JCS wanted to press the White

House for a broad statement of information-sharing policy as this would involve the State Department and might raise unwelcome political questions, such as why the United States was sharing information with Britain but not the Soviet Union. The U.S. chiefs believed that "so much has been said about UNO [the United Nations Organization] and the need for collaboration with everyone on an equal footing, that the American people simply would not understand discrimination" in favor of Britain.[5] In late 1945 and 1946, the U.S. government remained hopeful that the United Nations would eliminate the need for alliance blocs, though this quickly turned out not to be the case.

During late 1945 and 1946, the Canadian military missions also adjusted to peacetime relations with the U.S. military. During World War II, the Canadian naval mission wanted to develop its own relations with the U.S. Navy rather than rely on British connections. However, the Office of the Chief of Naval Operations initially opposed the establishment of an RCN mission in Washington in 1941 and agreed only in July 1942.[6] At the 1943 Washington Convoy Conference, Canadian representatives successfully pressed for the creation of an independent Canadian command in the Northwest Atlantic. In 1945 and 1946, the RCN wanted to ensure the continued existence of Canadian-American channels of communication and liaison.[7]

Canadian interest in maintaining these links shaped national postwar attitudes about their military representation in America. The Canadian Chiefs of Staff rejected a British proposal in the fall of 1945 to combine the Dominion military missions in Washington under the umbrella of the British mission. The chiefs noted that frequently during the war when the British represented the Canadians on combined boards and committees, "Canadian interests were perhaps not adequately protected." As a result, the Canadian chiefs chose to retain separate military missions in Washington after the war as a way of avoiding dependence on Anglo-American channels.[8]

In addition to its military mission, Canada had another link to the United States through the Permanent Joint Board on Defense (discussed in chapter 2). The board, established in 1940 to coordinate the defense of the Western Hemisphere, consisted of diplomatic, political, and military representatives from each country and met twice a year.

In contrast to Canada's exclusive military link, the Permanent Joint Board on Defense, Australia struggled to build similar ties with the U.S. military. Australia's first ambassador to the United States only arrived in 1940. The lack of diplomatic representation before 1940 reflected Australia's close ties with Britain and concern that establishing a separate mission would undermine British Empire unity.[9] During World War II, an Australian military mission handled relations with the U.S. military in Washington. The Australians maintained this mission after the war but ran into resistance when they attempted to create new, formal links. The Americans turned down an Australian request in 1948 to have their mission accredited to the U.S. secretary of defense, arguing that this would encourage other countries to do the same.[10] Formal accreditation would have allowed easier communication with the Joint Chiefs of Staff and possibly established the basis for future accreditation to the Combined Chiefs of Staff. A similar Australian request in 1949 was also rejected.[11] The request led the director of the U.S. Office of Naval Intelligence to conclude that the Australians were attempting to "set themselves up on the same level as the Canadians in Washington."[12] The Joint Chiefs wanted to avoid such an outcome. A JCS report in 1950 argued that the British Chiefs of Staff already represented Australia's military interests to the United States, an opinion the British chiefs would have been encouraged to hear. The Joint Chiefs also feared that formal links with an Australian mission would lead to an implied American guarantee of Australian security. The JCS thought that America's military was already overcommitted and did not want to undertake additional commitments.[13] While the Australian Joint Services Mission and the naval attaché in Washington gave Australia a level of access to the U.S. Navy, the RAN did not enjoy the preferential treatment accorded the Canadians and British.

Day-to-day relations between all four navies relied primarily on military staff missions and the attachés. The size in personnel and the physical location of these offices were crucial considerations, as is the case in most bureaucracies. The size of the British, Canadian, and Australian missions fell after World War II due to budget cuts until the Korean War and NATO launched a period of growth in representation in America. For example, the Canadian naval staff in Washington consisted of seventeen officers in July 1945, nine in April 1946, seven in 1949, and eighteen in 1953.[14]

Strategic locations and extensive access tended to compensate for the size reductions for the Canadians and British. Australian access to American information depended less on the size or location of the mission in Washington than on the reports coming from the U.S. Navy attaché in Australia. The

Canadians enjoyed day-to-day access to the Navy Department's offices—located in a building known as Main Navy—and regularly attended meetings in the Pentagon. One Canadian officer assigned to the naval member's staff remembered spending most of his time in the Main Navy building, freely going in and out of offices, and frequently playing golf with his American counterparts.[15] In addition, the U.S. Navy regularly invited British and Canadian staff officers to observe trials and exercises, invitations not extended to other nations.[16]

The British enjoyed even better access as their offices were initially physically inside Main Navy and the Pentagon. For example, the U.S. Navy's Bureau of Aeronautics gave the British Naval Air Service Liaison Office two rooms within Main Navy until 1952, when the office was disbanded. As an indication of the Royal Navy's privileged position, a 1951 directory shows that three non-USN organizations had offices inside the Bureau of Aeronautics: the Patent Office, the U.S. Air Force, and the Royal Navy.[17] Office space within Main Navy and the Pentagon gave the Royal Navy better access to the U.S. Navy than any other navy had.

When British commander Edmund Poland went to Washington in 1952, he remembered having an office in Main Navy as "an extraordinary thing, no other foreign navy was there, but there we were, the British naval staff in our own offices all in amongst the Americans and very much a part of the whole thing." Although later in the 1950s the U.S. Navy placed some restrictions on British staff officers visiting American offices at will, in the early 1950s the British could go where they liked, a period Poland described as "the Open Door."[18]

In April 1947, the British Joint Staff Mission moved into offices in the Pentagon provided by General of the Army Dwight Eisenhower, then chief of staff of the U.S. Army.[19] This move facilitated regular meetings between senior British representatives and the Joint Chiefs. However, in keeping with the American desire for Anglo-American military cooperation to be kept out of the public eye, Admiral Leahy and Admiral Moore agreed that the meetings should be informal, with no agenda and no official minutes.[20] Two years later, the Americans took away the British office space in the Pentagon as part of closing down the Combined Chiefs of Staff. The U.S. military worried that the European members of the newly formed NATO alliance might accuse the British and Americans of "forming an Anglo-American bloc."[21]

Still, even with offices outside the Pentagon, the Royal Navy maintained close relations with the U.S. Navy's senior leadership. In November 1952, Vice Admiral Cecil Hughes-Hallett, the senior British naval officer in Washington, wrote to the first sea lord about a dinner he attended at the invitation of the chief of naval operations, Admiral William Fechteler. Other guests included the secretary of the navy, every senior member of the CNO's office, several assistant chiefs of naval operations, and the commander in chief, U.S. Naval Forces Eastern Atlantic and Mediterranean. Hughes-Hallett was the only foreigner, and he reported that Fechteler told him that "it was a good thing for me to hear what they had to say when they 'let their hair down.'"[22]

Despite losing their privileged place in the Pentagon, the British still enjoyed office space in Main Navy. These offices helped the British keep abreast of U.S. Navy technical developments and plans while making the British staff readily available to meet with American officers. Hughes-Hallett described the importance of office location in getting the Americans to buy three pieces of British equipment:

In the case of the latter two items, and to some extent in the case of the first, this [the sales] would never have arisen if the appropriate British staff officers were not permanently over here. By being here they were able to inject the idea at the psychological moment; an officer sent over here for a few days visit would never have been lucky enough to be at the right meeting at the right time.[23]

However, the British and Canadians did not rely solely on their office location to develop contacts with the U.S. Navy. Officers on both the Canadian and British naval staffs frequently visited American establishments around the country. RAN representatives in Washington also visited American bases, though the smaller size of their staffs limited the scale of such trips. These visits provided three primary benefits. First, the British and Canadians formed relationships with American officers in operational squadrons, ships, and bases, rather than interacting only with the headquarters staff in Washington. Commander Poland later recalled that "the really good staff officers got around and made as many friends as you possibly could" by visiting USN bases. In the mostly informal meetings that took place during these visits, Poland remembered, "we never viewed ourselves as US Navy, Royal Navy, we were just naval officers talking about the same thing together."[24] Poland made friends with the American captain in charge of developing ASW tactics at Key West and in return received a desk in the unit office for use during his visits.[25]

In addition to forming relationships, these visits to American naval bases allowed British and Canadian officers to get reports and documents directly from frontline American officers instead of waiting months for the documents to work their way through the Office of Naval Intelligence (ONI) bureaucracy. Finally, during these visits, the British and Canadians would share with the Americans the progress of projects in their home countries. Often this sharing created American advocates for further information exchange. In turn, internal supporters of information sharing within the U.S. Navy proved critical to getting around ONI.

THE U.S. NAVY'S STATE DEPARTMENT

ONI functionally served as the State Department for the U.S. Navy by managing relations with foreign navies in addition to its more obvious intelligence roles. The office handled attaché assignments and reporting in addition to controlling the flow of information from the U.S. Navy to foreign navies. In fact, the British and Canadian missions in Washington often found ONI to be an overly effective gatekeeper, inhibiting their access to the rest of the U.S. Navy. For instance, in peacetime, all visits to American naval bases by foreign officers required ONI's approval, as did all requests for copies of U.S. Navy documents and publications.

During World War II, ONI had largely lifted these restrictions to meet the urgencies of war. However, by 1946, the office began to reassert its role as gatekeeper. A 1947 decision by the U.S. government gave the British and Canadians access to a wide array of information in peacetime, up to and including top secret information, except for information related to atomic energy and a few other minor restrictions.[26] Even so, in the immediate postwar years, all correspondence and visit requests from both the British and Canadian staffs to U.S. Navy offices required ONI review and approval.[27] Unfortunately for the British and Canadians, ONI's Foreign Liaison Section could not keep up with all this review work. British and Canadian officers repeatedly complained about delays of weeks or months before ONI cleared their requests for documents or visits. Part of the problem stemmed from an increase in the volume of requests in the postwar years, a pattern that only intensified after the Korean War started. For example, between May and November 1950 the number of Canadian personnel—mostly RCN—visiting

American bases for liaison, observation, and training purposes increased 300 percent.[28] Canadian Commodore Morson Medland glumly noted in December 1952 that "there is still no alleviation of the shortage of staff in the office of the Director of Naval Intelligence (USN)."[29] That same month, the Canadian ordnance officer on Medland's staff pleaded with Ottawa to understand that delays in receiving American documents stemmed from "a considerable increase in the volume of correspondence and a shortage of staff" at ONI.[30] ONI personnel shortages impacted American attachés as well as foreigners. As early as 1947, Rear Admiral Tully Shelley, the naval attaché in London, complained about delays in correspondence to the head of ONI:

Many letters are written from this office to the Chief of Naval Intelligence but very few acknowledgements or replies are received. In one case in point a request was made for a nomination for an officer to attend the last class of the Royal Naval Staff College, Greenwich. No reply was received until too late to arrange naval representation in this course. . . . It is realized that a shortage of personnel exists throughout the Navy, but it would be most helpful to those of us in the field to receive at least a post card acknowledgment of a letter to which an answer is ultimately expected.[31]

By May 1950, ONI recognized it had a problem and proposed a solution at a conference in Washington, D.C., of British, Canadian, and American officers. The three navies would create a series of information exchange projects (IEPs), formal navy-to-navy agreements that would facilitate the flow of information. Each IEP would cover a specific topic, such as carrier landing operations, and would identify offices and organizations within each of the three navies that would participate in the project. These offices would agree to respect the classification of each other's documents and not to distribute information without the permission of the other two navies. Within these guidelines, the offices could exchange information without going through ONI up to a certain classification level, often secret. Top secret information would still need to be reviewed by ONI. Within the scope of the IEP's topic, visits to American facilities could be arranged and documents could be shared without going through ONI, though in both instances ONI needed to be notified.[32]

ONI's hopes that this new program would ease its workload proved to be short lived. The three navies agreed to the procedure in May 1950. The Royal

Navy, eager to establish written agreements for information exchange, submitted sixty proposed IEP agreements by the end of the year, completely overwhelming ONI's ability to respond. By December 1950, ONI rejected thirteen of the proposals as too broad or insufficiently detailed, redrafted five, and failed to respond to forty two.[33] The increased demands for intelligence brought about by the Korean War certainly did not ease ONI's workload. By spring 1952, ONI began to catch up on the backlog and finalize some of the IEP proposals with the British and Canadians.[34] However, the delays in processing information through ONI continued. As a result, in the winter of 1952–1953, the U.S. Navy decided the IEP system required revision and gradually reduced the need for British and Canadian visits and requests for documents to go through ONI. In March 1953, the U.S. Navy placed the entire IEP program on hold in an effort to find a "suitable means of releasing information on a subject without the delay and formality of an IEP."[35] By April, the British and Canadian naval missions in Washington could correspond directly with U.S. Navy organizations without ONI's supervision, a privilege not granted to other navies.[36] ONI's efforts to establish a formal program to smooth the flow of information with the British and Canadian navies ultimately did not accomplish that goal. The Americans found that removing ONI from the process proved to be a much more satisfactory solution for all concerned. The IEP experience reveals a U.S. Navy that knew it wanted to share information with the British and Canadians on a regular basis but was still feeling its way to determine the best means of accomplishing that goal.

CANADA'S LIAISON AND EXCHANGE PROGRAM

While a number of nations stationed attachés in Washington, the U.S. Navy exchanged officers with or loaned officers to only a select few allies. In the aftermath of World War II, both the British and Canadians pursued officer exchanges with the U.S. Navy in an effort to maintain close ties. While attachés and officers assigned to staff missions had to keep up with American developments across a range of topics, exchange officers could study the USN more narrowly and more intensively. Combining the wide approach of attachés and the deep immersion of exchange officers provided the British and Canadians with a more balanced perspective on American naval trends and developments. The RCN's creation of an exchange program with the U.S. Navy in the years after World War II clearly illustrates these themes.

Less than six weeks after Japan's surrender, the Canadian Joint Staff Mission in Washington proposed creating a program of officer exchanges between the American and Canadian militaries. Such exchanges would create operational, technical, and education links in addition to "creating better mutual understanding and knowledge within those respective services." The Joint Staff Mission proposed exchanging six RCN officers with six USN officers, with each country continuing to pay the exchanged personnel.[37] When the Naval Staff in Ottawa examined the issue in January 1946 they increased the proposed number of exchange positions to ten. The Naval Staff's proposed distribution illustrates the fields in which Ottawa was most interested when it came to collaboration with the Americans. Of the ten officers, three would attend or teach at the Army-Navy Staff College, three would reside in the Bureau of Ships, one would be with the deputy chief of naval operations (air), one would be at sea, and two would have additional appointments. This proposal emphasized staff exchanges, ship design, and naval equipment, with a secondary interest in American naval aviation.[38] In 1946, the Canadians considered a pilot exchange program but decided that they did not want to send their naval aviation pilots to the USN until their own experience in carrier operations was greater.[39]

The U.S. Joint Chiefs approved officer exchanges with Canada in February 1946 with the goal of "continuing collaboration and to assist in coordinating the armed forces of the two nations" and the Canadian chiefs gave their blessing in October.[40] The exchange program began in earnest in May 1947 after the RCN and USN both agreed on the details of the arrangement.[41] Each side would pay its own officers and provide additional funds for their travel. Exchanged officers would report to the local commanding officer and would follow the host navy's regulations. The RCN decided that USN officers, known as integrated officers in Canadian parlance, would have virtually unlimited access to Canadian information.[42] The U.S. Navy's Office of Naval Intelligence insisted that the subject of exchange and liaison officers be classified confidential "to preclude possible embarrassment requests from other countries."[43]

The initial exchanges between the two navies focused on the communications field since the RCN was gradually adopting American communication procedures and publications. In June and July 1947, the RCN sent one lieu-tenant commander to the communications staffs of the Second Task Fleet and a lieutenant to commander, Submarine Force Atlantic. In return, the Americans sent one lieutenant to naval headquarters in Ottawa to serve on the director of naval communication's staff and another to the RCN's Signal School as an instructor.[44]

Lieutenant Commander Robert Murdoch served as the Canadian officer assigned to the Second Task Fleet in Norfolk, Virginia, and arrived in July 1947. He was one of the first Canadian naval officers to be exchanged with the U.S. Navy. Murdoch later recalled that he was the assistant communications officer for the fleet and was the first foreign officer to serve in a regular staff position in the fleet, as opposed to a liaison position. Having served with the Royal Navy during World War II, Murdoch found that the British, Ameri-can, and Canadian navies were trying to solve the same problems, but doing so in slightly different ways. He described the differences between the three as the differences between three universities "devoted to the same problem in the same environment."[45] Murdoch's time in Norfolk gave him a wealth of U.S. Navy experience, which he took back to the RCN when the exchange was complete.

The RCN's growing use of USN communications steadily increased inter-est in officer exchanges in the Canadian fleet. In particular, the ships on the Canadian West Coast had used American communications since Novem-ber 1946. After over a year and a half of using American methods, the Pacific squadron reported on its experiences in the summer of 1948. Rear Admi-ral Edmond Rollo Mainguy, flag officer Pacific Coast, wrote that American publications were used successfully and argued in favor of the entire Cana-dian fleet adopting USN methods in order to increase personnel exchanges. Mainguy noted that the "interchange of personnel with the U.S. Navy for technical instruction and service afloat would be most beneficial."[46] Two of Mainguy's subordinates agreed. Commodore John Edwards, who com-manded the naval base at Esquimalt, British Columbia, suggested appointing an RCN gunnery officer to an American cruiser for a period of two months in order to improve Canadian understanding of American fire-control pro-cedure.[47] The skipper of the cruiser *Ontario*, Captain James Hibbard, had pared down an early proposal for officer exchanges with the USN when he served as deputy director of naval personnel in 1946. However, as a cruiser commander, Hibbard viewed the issue somewhat differently, writing: "It is recommended that Officers and Men of the RCN be exchanged on loan with Officers and Enlisted Personnel of the US Navy so that American Communication Nomenclature and Methods may be indoctrinated into the RCN by experience afloat."[48]

Initially, the RCN-USN exchange program focused on communications officers. However, in 1948, the Canadians asked for two American naval aviators to fill senior positions in their new naval aviation branch, in part due to the efforts of the American naval attaché in Ottawa, Captain Benjamin Custer. Commander J. J. Hilston became the deputy director of naval aviation in Ottawa in February 1949 and served under a British officer who was the director. Captain Herschel A. House, also American, became director of air logistics in August 1949.[49] The U.S. Navy continued to provide an aviator to serve as deputy director of naval aviation until 1953, when a Canadian officer took over.[50] The presence of British and American officers in the RCN's naval air office illustrated the Canadian navy's interest in retaining close ties with both navies.

Canadian interest in expanding the exchange program with the Americans continued in 1951. In March 1951, Commodore Horatio N. Lay, the naval member of the Canadian Joint Staff (Washington), reviewed the liaison work performed by his staff during the previous year. Lay emphasized that while his staff enjoyed positive relations with the Americans, "the RCN is at a disadvantage vis-à-vis the other two services [the RCAF and the Canadian Army] because of the absence of liaison or integrated officers in the Navy Department." Lay argued for expanding the RCN's placement of officers within the U.S. Navy. The commodore concluded that establishing these arrangements with the Americans would "greatly assist . . . in maintaining the favored position that the RCN presently holds vis-à-vis other foreign navies."[51]

The American responses to another Canadian effort illustrate the range of attitudes within the USN toward cooperation with foreign navies. In July 1951, the RCN asked for an American submariner to teach at the Canadian Maritime Warfare School and work with the staff of flag officer Atlantic Coast, the senior Canadian naval officer on the East Coast.[52] The RCN did not have its own submarines and could benefit from American experience. In December 1951, the U.S. Navy agreed.[53] In contrast, in August 1951, the Canadian staff

Acting Captain Horatio Nelson Lay, RCN, and Mrs. Lay at Government House, Ottawa, ca. 1943. As the head of the Canadian naval mission in Washington from 1949 to 1952, Lay was the senior RCN representative to the U.S. Navy. Previously he had served in senior RCN staff positions in Ottawa that also involved regular liaison with the U.S. Navy, such as director of naval plans and intelligence. *Source*: Royal Montreal Regiment Museum, Montreal, Canada, https://commons.wikimedia.org/wiki /File:Horatio_Nelson_Lay_and_Mrs._Lay.tif.

complained of security officers at the U.S. Navy's Bureau of Aeronautics rejecting Canadian requests to discuss experimental American aircraft that the RCN might purchase.[54] Problems with the Bureau of Aeronautics continued, and in November Commodore Lay wrote that "the interpretation of USN security regulations by the Security Officers of BuAer have, for some time, been more rigid than in the other Bureaus."[55] This attitude was in stark contrast to the Bureau of Ships, where "a very gratifying spirit of co-operation has been displayed" and "there is evidence to believe that Canada is the most favored nation in obtaining classified information."[56] In December 1951, the Canadians asked the Americans for permission to station an RCN liaison officer at the U.S. Navy bases at Key West, Florida, and Patuxent River, Maryland, centers of ASW and naval aviation development, respectively.[57] The Canadians also proposed a pilot exchange program, which began in March 1952 with two Canadian pilots exchanged for two American pilots.[58] In April 1952, the USN agreed to the proposal, and Lieutenant Commander John W. Roberts was appointed as Canadian liaison officer to Key West. By July Canadian officers held liaison posts at both Key West and Patuxent River.[59] The U.S. Navy also provided the Canadians with a naval aviator to serve as a staff officer with flag officer Atlantic Coast, beginning in 1952.[60] Despite some difficulties with the Bureau of Aeronautics, by the summer of 1952 the Canadians succeeded in creating a series of exchange and liaison appointments within the U.S. Navy.

However, two events in the fall of 1952 highlighted the continuing difference between the views within U.S. naval aviation and the rest of the U.S. Navy on the liaison and exchange program. First, in September, the U.S. Navy's communications branch agreed to replace the American communications officer at the RCN's Signal School with another officer to continue the position. At Key West, the Americans gave the RCN liaison officer expanded access that same month.[61] In the communication and ASW fields the Americans were expanding or sustaining their links with the Canadians. However, a month later, in October, the Bureau of Aeronautics kicked all foreign pilots out of Naval Air Station Patuxent River. Security officers at the bureau decided that the increasing number of projects at the air base involving restricted atomic information meant that no foreign aviators could be in units stationed there. For example, units at the base were developing a version of the Banshee jet fighter that could carry a nuclear bomb.[62]

In contrast to the Bureau of Aeronautics's approach, the U.S. Navy Supply Corps welcomed closer relations with the Canadians. Back in 1947, the RCN had arranged for an American supply specialist, Commander M. A. Peel, to analyze their supply system and make recommendations. The resulting Peel Report led the Canadians to adopt a modified version of the U.S. Navy's supply system in 1949 and to begin sending supply officers to the U.S. Navy's Supply School in Bayonne, New Jersey. By 1953 an exchange program swapped two Canadian supply officers for two American supply officers.[63] One officer, in particular, in this exchange program discovered that professional competence was not the only path to good relations with the Americans. Lieutenant Robert Darlington found his relations with American supply officers at the Aviation Supply Office in Philadelphia lukewarm upon arriving. However, Darlington's stock rose rapidly when the Americans found that he was "the best baseball player" at the office, according to a visiting Canadian officer.[64]

The Canadian experience establishing a liaison and exchange officer program in the United States illustrates two facets of relations between the British, American, Canadian, and Australian navies. First, the U.S. Navy's antisubmarine, communications, and logistics branches encouraged and expanded connections with the British and Canadians more readily than the Bureau of Aeronautics. The bureau proved to be more than willing to send officers to Canada to help RCN naval aviation, but it took a more guarded view of giving the Canadians access to the latest aircraft designs. Second, personal relationships undergirded navy-to-navy relations by providing a day-to-day connection between fleets. However, these personal relationships could sometimes seriously undermine relations, as the Royal Australian Navy painfully discovered.

ATTACHÉ INFLUENCE: HELPFUL AND HURTFUL

Commander Stephen Jurika Jr. became the U.S. naval attaché to Australia on July 17, 1947, and held the position until July 1949.[65] Commander Jurika grew up in the Philippines before attending the U.S. Naval Academy and becoming a naval aviator. From March 1946 to May 1947 Jurika served on a subcommittee of the State-War-Navy Coordinating Committee (SWNCC), which gave him personal contacts on this body, which was responsible for setting U.S. information disclosure policy as discussed in Chapter 2.[66] In May

1947, Jurika received orders to report to Melbourne as the U.S. naval attaché. Although the Australian federal government was located at Canberra, the Department of the Navy's and Department of the Army's offices were still in Melbourne in the 1940s. Before Jurika left, Captain Stanley Spurgeon, the Australian naval attaché in Washington, gave Jurika a list of contacts in each Australian city who could help him make connections.[67] He also received lists of friendly contacts from the Australian embassy staff, and he remembered later that "these contacts from the Australians [proved] to be far more worthwhile and very effective on first meetings than anything I got in the Office of Naval Intelligence."[68] Spurgeon's efforts and those of the Australian embassy reflected Australia's interest in good relations with the United States, especially in the aftermath of the disagreements over the Manus island base (discussed in chapter 3).

When Jurika reached Australia, he became close friends with Rear Admiral John Collins, the Australian chief of naval staff, an advocate for closer relations between the U.S. Navy and the RAN. In contrast to ONI's insistence on approving visits by British and Commonwealth officers, Collins ensured that Jurika had "literally blanket authority" to arrange visits and request information on his own.[69] Jurika's reports and correspondence indicated he thought very highly of the RAN. In October 1947, he reported that "The Aussie Navy . . . are a group of highly qualified, gentlemanly officers, professionally capable."[70] The American officer even coordinated several visits by U.S. Navy ships to Australia and helped Admiral Collins establish connections with commander in chief, U.S. Pacific Fleet at Pearl Harbor.[71]

However, Jurika's positive impression of the RAN did not extend to all aspects of Australian society and certainly not to the Australian government. He found the strict Australian trade union rules frustrating, complaining once to a friend about "a complete indifference here concerning when something is to be accomplished. Tomorrow, or next week, or even next month is as good a time to do something as today."[72] Jurika saved his harshest criticism for Prime Minister Ben Chifley's Labor Party. Chifley became prime minister in July 1945. Chifley and the Labor Party believed that the federal government should play a more active role in the Australian economy.[73] Under Chifley, Australia expanded government-provided health care and unemployment, widow, and maternity benefits and solidified Canberra's authority over income taxes.[74] Jurika strongly disapproved of the Labor Party's approach. Several months after arriving, he wrote to a friend: "Free enterprise is being driven from the country by the socialism fostered and encouraged by the Federal Labor Government." From his perspective, "the Trade Unions control the Government (Labor) and the spineless bunch at Canberra jump when the Commies [communists] crack the whip."[75] He deplored the annual losses posted by government monopolies such as Qantas Airlines, noting that "all lose heavily each year—but what the hell? It's the taxpayer's money, and the Prime Minister and Treasurer, Mr. Ben Chifley, cares little for the people."[76] Jurika's view that Chifley and the Labor government leaned dangerously close to communism regularly surfaced in his reports to ONI back in Washington. The reports helped cloud the view of Australia within ONI. A note on one of Jurika's reports by ONI in 1949 stated, "The reports of NA [naval attaché] Melbourne on Communism and security in Australia have been excellent and one of the best sources on this subject."[77]

Attaché commentary on national politics was a long-standing feature of the attaché system. After observing the new administration of President Dwight D. Eisenhower for several months, Canadian commodore Morson A. Medland wrote approvingly of the "understanding and support" for the U.S. military provided by the new administration, which he thought could lead to "the greatest armed forces sustained by . . . any democratic nation throughout history."[78] However, Commander Jurika's reports created a narrative in ONI that Australia was not as trustworthy an ally as had been the case during World War II. This narrative also gained support in the State Department through the reports of the American ambassador to Australia in 1948 and 1949, Myron Cowen, who also cast the Chifley government as overly left-wing.[79]

Jurika's concerns were in part validated by the discovery of Soviet espionage efforts in Australia and the West in general through the Venona Project. Venona involved the interception and decryption of Soviet diplomatic cables, an intelligence coup not revealed until 1995.[80] In 1945, American security agencies began decrypting some of these cables, which by late 1946 revealed the existence of numerous Soviet spies in the United States, Great Britain, and Canada. Venona confirmed the presence of large Soviet spy rings in the West suggested first by Igor Gouzenko, a code clerk at the Soviet embassy in Ottawa who defected in September 1945.[81] By April 1947, Venona revealed Soviet sources in Australia, including several officials in the Department of

External Affairs, who had passed top secret British documents to the Soviets.[82] The Americans allowed the British to tell the Australians about the leak but not the Venona Project, and the Australian government began an investigation in January 1948.[83]

At the same time that Venona was revealing Soviet spies, American political leaders were becoming increasingly concerned about the loyalty of their own government officials. In March 1947, President Truman created a loyalty program designed to weed out communists within the federal government. In December 1947, the Civil Service Loyalty Review Board began assessing the loyalty of federal workers. [84] The February 1948 communist coup in Czechoslovakia only made the international arena appear even more threatening. In light of growing American apprehension over communist infiltration and influence, Jurika's cables and the Venona reports of Soviet spies in Australia laid the foundation within the Office of Naval Intelligence for an information embargo directed against Australia.

Australia's investigation into the spies reported by Venona did not calm American fears that were fanned by Commander Jurika's reports. These fears came to a head in early June 1948, when the U.S. Navy representative on the State-Army-Navy-Air Force Coordinating Committee (SANACC), the successor to the State-War-Navy Coordinating Committee, demanded that Australia lose its access to classified American information, arguing that Australia was "a poor security risk."[85] Prior to June 1948, the Australians had enjoyed regular access to information up to the secret level, though not research and development projects.[86] Captain Spurgeon, the Australian naval attaché, even received top secret material informally from American officers such as Captain Arleigh Burke.[87] However, a SANACC subcommittee went along with the U.S. Navy's wishes.[88] The U.S. Navy representative's position during the SANACC deliberations was largely shaped by the reports received in ONI from Commander Jurika.[89] Jurika's service on the predecessor to SANACC and the contacts he developed during that period likely increased the consideration given to his reports.

Jurika's reports not only played a central role in Australia's losing access to American classified information, they also undermined Australia's subsequent efforts to convince Washington that it could be trusted. In March 1949, Prime Minister Chifley created an Australian security service, which became the Australian Security Intelligence Organization (ASIO). ASIO was modeled on MI5, which provided a liaison officer to assist the Australians in what they called "the Case," the search for the Soviet spies revealed by Venona.[90] ASIO reported to Herbert V. Evatt, the attorney-general and the minister for external affairs, which compromised the new security organization in Jurika's view. Jurika's reports to ONI stated that Evatt based much of Australia's foreign policy on "trivial personal antagonisms" and "unrelated whims," a pattern that would soon force the United States "to make a choice either to rescue Australia or let some 'colored' country take over," an apparent reference to Southeast Asia nations.[91] As a result of his anti-Evatt views, Jurika reported in March 1949 that the new Australian security organization would "be used for political purposes as well as security" since Evatt still "holds the reins on Australian security."[92] Jurika's reports pulled the rug from under Frederick Shedden, a senior Australian civil servant, who visited Washington in April 1949 in an attempt to restore the flow of classified information to Australia. Shedden—whose position was similar to the chairman of the Joint Chiefs in the United States—impressed American officials but was told that the United States would not give Australia access until a new government was elected. Specifically, the Americans wanted Robert Menzies and his Liberal Party, the conservatives currently in opposition, in power, not Chifley and Labor.[93]

Menzies won the December 1949 election, and the next month Washington promptly authorized the individual services to release information to Australia up to the confidential level. Two months, later in March 1950, the United States proposed a security agreement that would formally restore Australia's access, and this was signed in August 1950, giving Australia access to information up to top secret.[94]

Commander Jurika played a prominent role in the United States embargo on classified information toward Australia.[95] His reports turned the Office of Naval Intelligence into an advocate for cutting off Australia. In combination with the Venona revelations and Ambassador Cowen's reports, Jurika's views on the Chifley government ultimately led to the embargo. Jurika illustrated the potential power of an attaché to damage relations between the Australian and American militaries. Canada and Britain both had Soviet spies in important positions in the late 1940s, including Kim Philby, who worked as the head of counterintelligence for MI6 and was the senior British intelligence officer in Washington. However, neither country had Commander Jurika as an attaché, and neither lost access to classified America information. Both

Canada and Britain benefited from a larger scale of cooperation with the U.S. Navy across a number of fields, which meant that relations were less susceptible to the influence of one officer.[96] Ultimately Australia fell victim to Jurika's inability to see that the Chifley government's policies, while politically left-wing to an American, were not communist.

In contrast to Commander Jurika in Australia, Captain Benjamin Custer's time as naval attaché to Ottawa demonstrated the power of an attaché to positively influence military-to-military relations. In 1949, the Canadians began examining replacements for their British-built Fairey Firefly antisubmarine aircraft and considered purchasing surplus U.S. Navy Avengers or a more advanced version of the Firefly.[97] Canadian comparisons of the two revealed that the Firefly as an ASW platform was a "singularly useless new aircraft" according to the staff officer for ASW at Halifax. The Avenger was a more mature design, was less susceptible to frequent modifications, and reflected the assumption that in the future the RCN would operate more with the USN than with the RN.[98] The RCN made initial inquiries with the Americans in August and September 1949 about purchasing seventy-five Avengers.[99]

In 1949, Captain Custer took an interest in the RCN's effort to acquire American Avengers. Custer became the naval attaché to Canada on July 28, 1948, and served there until July 29, 1950.[100] Early in his time in Ottawa, Custer met the RCN's chief of the naval staff, Vice Admiral Harold Grant, to talk about Custer's recent cruise with the Canadian carrier *Magnificent.* Custer recalled bluntly telling Grant, when Grant asked for Custer's evaluation, as an aviator, of *Magnificent*'s flight operations, "It's terrible. This is no way to operate an aircraft carrier." Custer suggested to Grant that the RCN ask the USN for some aviators to come up to Canada to help the RCN's naval aviation program, and a few days later Grant approved.[101]

A naval aviator himself, Custer viewed helping Canadian naval aviation as his personal project. Custer flew to Washington to get approval for the USN to loan the RCN the requested naval aviators. He was banking on an important conversation he had with the vice chief of naval operations, Admiral Arthur Radford, to get what he wanted. Custer later recalled that before he left for Canada, Radford told him, "I'd like for you to know, from me—this is from the Secretary of the Navy and the Chief of Naval Operations—you are to inform the Canadian Navy that they can have anything they want from us. They can send anybody they want to any of our schools. All you have to do is found out [*sic*] and let me know. We must work closely with them."[102] Custer used this verbal authority and his connections in the American naval aviation community to get several USN aviators assigned to the RCN.

The American officer continued to work to build ties between the two navies when he found out that pending budget cuts threatened the RCN's ability to buy new antisubmarine aircraft. Custer's acquisition of this information reveals the value of the personal connections he made in Canada. When he arrived in Ottawa, Custer joined the Rideau Club, the social gathering place for Ottawa's political and business elite. There he met Brooke Claxton and Charles Drury, the minister and deputy minister for national defense respectively, as well as Douglas Abbott, minister for the treasury, who told Custer about the pending cuts. Custer went to see Admiral Grant and suggested that the RCN ask for seventy-five American Avengers as a cheaper alternative to the Fireflies. Once again Grant agreed, and the two navies opened talks about a potential sale.[103]

Custer's efforts helped smooth the RCN's talks with the Americans. Throughout the Avenger negotiations, Commodore Lay, the senior Canadian naval officer in Washington, felt that "USN officers showed excellent cooperation and understanding and did everything possible to facilitate the acquisition of the aircraft by the RCN."[104] In early March 1950 Claxton approved the Avenger purchase over the opposition of the RCAF, and by the end of the month the deal was completed. The first planes arrived from the United States in May. The Avengers cost $405,000 USD all together, less than a third of the cost of new Fireflies, and Ottawa recovered the money by selling retired Fireflies and spare engines to foreign countries.[105]

During the final Avenger negotiations, Custer continued to do what he thought necessary to support the RCN's naval air arm. When *Magnificent* ran aground in June 1949, Custer suggested to Grant that the RCN send its pilots down to the United States so that they could continue to practice carrier landings on an American carrier. Grant agreed, and Custer again flew to Washington, where he secured the approval of fellow aviator Vice Admiral John D. Price, who had replaced Radford as the vice chief of naval operations in May 1949. With Price's blessing, Custer arranged the transfer in ten days. At this point, Custer's activities got him in trouble with his immediate superior, Rear Admiral Thomas B. Inglis, the director of ONI. Custer later recalled that Inglis angrily complained that Custer was "acting like you're the chief of a naval mission!" "I've been involved in trying to save Canadian Naval Aviation," Custer retorted. Inglis replied, "That's not your job. Your job's intelligence." Custer responded, "Well Admiral, there isn't anything we need to know about the Canadians that they won't tell us. There are other things that are needed," before again bringing up Admiral Radford's instructions. Custer clearly relied heavily on the support of fellow highly ranked naval aviators (Radford and Price) to accomplish his goals. He concluded by telling Admiral Inglis that if he had gone through normal ONI channels, the Canadians would have received approval to come to the United States about the time *Magnificent*'s repairs were completed. Custer shared the frustration of British and Canadian attachés with ONI's slow processes.[106]

With Custer's help, the RCN secured seventy-five Avengers. The Canadians went on to purchase fifty more Avengers in 1952, again with the support of key American officers. Commodore Horatio Lay, the senior Canadian naval officer in Washington, reported that during the 1952 negotiations, "Vice Admiral J. [John] Cassady DCNO (Air) [deputy chief of naval operations (air)] has proved himself again, a very true friend to the Canadian Navy."[107] Lay described Cassady's assistance and motivations at a conference in Ottawa in March 1952:

The fact that we got the last 50 Avengers after having had them more or less on ice for over nine months was the essence of good will, not only of the USN as a whole, but to individual people, mainly Admiral Cassady, who is the DCNO for Air. He was on our side and keen on keeping the RCN in naval aviation. We got them at 10 per cent of their original cost and to do that they had to be declared surplus by the CNO. . . . We have had a tremendous amount of moral support and every other kind of actual support in the USN because they appreciate that if we went to the wall in naval aviation it would be an argument that would be used by their own air force, to try to cut down on [American] naval aviation.[108]

In contrast to the admirals and commodores that the British and Canadians sent to Washington, the USN attachés to Ottawa or Canberra were captains and commanders, midcareer officers. Both the Canadian and Australian naval chiefs of staff recognized the outsized influence these midcareer officers might exert on their relations with the Americans, and both made a special effort to build relationships with the American naval attaché. Admiral Grant regularly met with Custer in Ottawa to ask for Custer's advice and opinion.

RCN 881 Antisubmarine Squadron Grumman Avenger in flight, 1952. © Government of Canada. Reproduced with the permission of Library and Archives Canada (2019). *Source*: Library and Archives Canada/Department of National Defence fonds /e010777699.

Down under, Admiral Collins and his wife, Phyllis, both became close friends with Jurika and his wife, Lillian.[109] Collins also liked to ask Jurika for rides in Jurika's official plane when Collins needed to go up to Canberra from Melbourne.[110] In return, both Custer and Jurika clearly thought of these senior officers as friends. However, in Jurika's case, this friendship was not enough to prevent Australia from losing access to U.S. classified information.

SHIP VISITS

Ships from each of these navies frequently visited each other's ports in the course of their normal operations. Diplomatically, these visits tended to generate positive press and serve as a physical demonstration of good relations, which explains their popularity with ambassadors and consuls. Visits also gave personnel from one navy the chance to observe the visiting ship's equipment and practices. Furthermore, visits gave officers an opportunity to meet their counterparts and form relationships. From the U.S. Navy's perspective, visits to Australian, British, and Canadian ports required less administrative work since these visits did not have to be cleared with the Department of State like visits to other ports.[111] The worldwide cruise of Task Force 38 in 1947–1948 illustrates the potential significance and impact of ship visits.

Task Force 38 left San Diego on October 9, 1947. The force consisted of the carrier *Valley Forge* and several destroyers and was commanded by Rear Admiral Harold Martin. After training for several months in Hawaii, Martin and his force departed for Sydney, Australia, on January 16, 1948. The RAN flew six officers to Pearl Harbor to observe USN air operations during the *Valley Forge*'s voyage to Australia.[112] Captain Wilfred Harrington, the group leader, reported that according to Admiral Martin "there were no security restrictions and that any information which we might desire would be made available to us," a stark contrast to the American position later taken in the summer of 1948, when Washington cut off Australia's access.[113] Captain Harrington took the opportunity to discuss cooperation between British-built and American-built ships with the *Valley Forge*'s captain, Captain Richard Ruble, noting that American technical developments increasingly could easily hinder communication between USN ships and other allied navies, an ongoing problem in USN relations with the British, Canadians, and Australians.[114] The long voyage to Australia provided the visitors with the chance to observe every aspect of American carrier operations, and one RAN officer concluded that "all United States Naval Officers and men co-operated to the fullest possible extent."[115] At the time, the RAN was establishing its own carrier air arm and sought to learn from British and American experience operating carriers.[116]

Upon arriving in Australian waters, the Americans conducted basic training exercises with the Royal Australian Navy and the Royal Australian Air Force in early February. Ashore, Admiral Martin took part in staff talks with the RAN's senior leaders on planning for the defense of Pacific sea lines of communication.[117] Martin later remembered that these talks "gave us reason to believe that we would have close friends and a navy oriented to the same concepts of naval warfare in our Australian allies."[118] The U.S. naval attaché, Commander Jurika, reported that the task force visit "was exemplary in every way."[119] After leaving Australia and heading for Hong Kong and the Chinese coast, Task Force 38 received orders to return to the West Coast via the Atlantic Ocean. Martin and his ships sailed to Singapore, Saudi Arabia, the Suez Canal, Britain, and eventually the Panama Canal before returning to San Diego.[120]

In addition to giving American personnel a broader perspective, ship visits served to create connections and relationships that could prove useful later in an officer's career. Admiral Arthur Struble took part in a U.S. Pacific Fleet cruise in 1925 to Australia and later remembered:

There's no doubt about the fact that our '25 cruise was valuable to us when we went to war out there in the Southwest Pacific. . . . We were there [in Australia] long enough on the '25 cruise so that we got to know each other and we kind of trusted each other. The people that were youngsters and got drunk in '25 were the people that were up in positions of more authority when we got into the real war. That's good stuff, no doubt about it.[121]

While British, Canadian, and Australian attachés, staff officers, and exchange officers spent extended periods of time with the U.S. Navy, their numbers were never very large. All together the British and Canadians did not have more than a hundred naval officers stationed in the United States in 1950. In contrast, ship visits brought much larger numbers of officers into contact with each other, albeit for shorter, structured periods of time.

In the wake of World War II, the Royal Navy sought to solidify its access to American technical information. To that end the Admiralty established or strengthened a variety of personal links with the U.S. Navy. If American information was a gold mine, guarded by the Office of Naval Intelligence, then by 1953 the British had dug eight distinct shafts to access the gold. These shafts consisted of the various RN links with the USN: naval attachés, the naval staff mission, liaison officers, ship visits, exchange officers, standardization programs (discussed in the next chapter), personnel attending USN schools, and contact between ships operating off Korea. Once in place, these links tended to reinforce themselves through feedback loops. For example, if the British liaison officer with the Atlantic Fleet's submarine force had access to experimental designs, he could share this information with British naval architects, who could in turn share how their designs complemented the American designs. The liaison officer could then pass this information along to the Americans. This return flow of information came back to the Americans who were the most interested in receiving it, solidifying the value of the liaison officer to the USN submarine community and creating a precedent for future sharing.

If the postwar Royal Navy focused on retaining access, the Canadians sought to expand their access, building their own shafts rather than relying on the Royal Navy's. In particular, in Washington, D.C., the Canadian naval member and his staff slowly built up a web of liaison and exchange officers in the United States in the years after World War II. Overall, the Canadians found that most of the U.S. Navy welcomed closer ties with the RCN, with the exception of portions of the Bureau of Aeronautics.

In general the British and Canadians found the U.S. Navy interested and willing to expand personnel links through liaison and exchange officers, so long as the links remained out of the eyes of the public and the press. This same concern for secrecy shaped American attitudes toward the Canadian and British staff missions in Washington. So long as the public and other navies were unaware of the privileged access enjoyed by the British and Canadians, the Americans went along willingly. When the U.S. Navy felt this blanket of secrecy was being lifted, the Americans were quite willing to take dramatic steps to avoid answering awkward questions, such as forcing the British out of their offices in the Pentagon and Main Navy.

For the British and Canadians, exchange officers and liaison officers with the U.S. Navy gave them better access to American naval thinking and technical developments. Interactions between American officers and these exchange and liaison officers tended to produce advocates for further cooperation. These advocates proved useful to the RN and RCN as they sought to get around ONI's bureaucratic logjam. For its part, ONI seemed to recognize the need to remove obstructions in the flow of information between these navies but floundered in its initial attempts. Ultimately, the solution adopted by ONI was to largely remove itself from the management of day-to-day relations with the British and Canadians.

Australia, like Britain and Canada, enjoyed missions and attachés in Washington. However, the Australians did not develop similar levels of access with the U.S. Navy for several reasons. Australia's distance from the

United States made the South Pacific a tertiary theater for the Truman administration. The U.S. Joint Chiefs' desire to avoid overcommitting their dwindling forces hindered Australia's efforts to build formal links with the American military. The 1948–1950 embargo on Australian access to classified information reflected both Commander Jurika's reporting and growing American concerns about security. However, the December 1949 election in Australia along with Australia's involvement in the Korean War rapidly repaired the damage done to USN-RAN relations. In general, the RAN found more interest in close Australian-American naval relations among Pacific Fleet commanders in Pearl Harbor than in Washington, D.C. In the middle of the information embargo in November 1948, for instance, Admiral Collins and Admiral Ramsey agreed to the Ramsey-Collins line, which set the stage for the 1951 Radford-Collins Agreement.

5

Standardization

On November 8, 1941, the British battleship *Warspite* arrived at the U.S. Navy Yard in Bremerton, Washington, to undergo repair work after being damaged in the Mediterranean. As part of the repair work, the battleship's primary guns, fifteen inches in diameter, needed to be replaced. However, the U.S. Navy did not make fifteen-inch guns because American battleships at the time carried fourteen-inch or sixteen-inch weapons. As a result, the British had to ship replacement guns across the Atlantic Ocean in multiple transports, load them onto railcars in Norfolk, Virginia, and move them all the way across America by rail.[1] As Britain received more and more material assistance from the United States during World War II, this type of mismatch between American and British specifications repeatedly caused headaches for British planners. For example, the threads on metal screws used in British shipyards were not compatible with American screws and fasteners, so the Royal Navy had to send a large quantity of nuts, bolts, and screws to those American shipyards repairing British warships.[2]

These technical differences caused delays in using American equipment. Often, before the British could use American equipment, they had to spend weeks or months modifying the equipment to meet their specifications. After the war, British planners anticipated relying heavily on American products in any future conflict. To avoid some of the delays experienced in World War II, they began investigating the possibility of standardizing British and American specifications and equipment. Inquiries to Ottawa and

Washington revealed considerable interest in standardization between Britain, Canada, and the United States.

Efforts to achieve standardization between these three nations became known as tripartite standardization and led to a Canadian-British-American 1947 agreement. The U.S. military's decision to pursue commonality reflected its interest in retaining close links with the British and Canadians. In contrast to the view that the post–World War II U.S. Navy was uninterested in cooperating with allies, the tripartite program demonstrated the navy's commitment to working closely with the British and Canadians. Technical standardization complemented the personal relationships built through the liaison and exchange efforts of the three navies. The tripartite program represented a break with past U.S. Navy practice, which had not previously pursued standardization with other navies over a sustained period of time. Like combined naval planning, interest in standardization stemmed from concerns about a war with the Soviet Union. The Soviet threat provided much of the impetus for the tripartite agreement. Political factors also played a significant role. Worries over attracting publicity, appearing to undermine the United Nations, or being seen as forming an anti-Soviet military alliance shaped the course of the standardization talks in 1946 and 1947.

In the wake of the 1947 agreement, two realities of technical standardization quickly became apparent. First, creating standard pieces of equipment proved extremely difficult, if not impossible, over the course of the next five years. Economic considerations, national pride, and incompatible tactics combined to thwart efforts to create a standard sonobuoy, for instance. Second, officers from the tripartite navies discovered that creating common doctrine and communications could be accomplished far more rapidly than agreeing on common weapon designs. In fact, aligning doctrine and tactics removed one of the stumbling blocks to equipment standardization, leading to a "concepts before calibers" approach.

THE PROSPECT OF STANDARDIZATION

In November 1945, the British Deputy Chiefs of Staff Committee began examining the prospect of standardizing equipment between the United Kingdom, Canada, and the United States at the request of the Royal Navy.[3] The committee's initial report on the subject focused on equipment, rather than procedures, a theme that ran throughout British discussions of the topic in 1945 and 1946. The report clearly expressed dissatisfaction with the need during World War II to modify American equipment before British forces could employ it. In a future war, the British assumed that they would have to again rely heavily on equipment produced in the United States, and they wanted to avoid this time-consuming modification work. The solution, according to the report, was to pursue standardization of equipment with the United States in peacetime. This work should initially involve "common maximum dimensions, common fixing details, and perhaps identical weights" before advancing to the more difficult challenge of agreement on common gun calibers, ammunition, and radio equipment.[4]

The British Chiefs of Staff also feared that Soviet air attacks on Britain in a future war would damage or destroy many of their industrial facilities. Even without losses to Soviet attacks, the chiefs concluded that Britain had insufficient industrial capacity to support a future war. The chiefs wanted to encourage the Dominions of Canada, Australia, New Zealand, and South Africa to expand their industrial bases and standardize equipment with the United States so that British forces could obtain American equipment from the Commonwealth even if British factories were destroyed.[5] Attlee's government approved the chiefs' views on standardization on September 19, 1946.

While the British Chiefs of Staff were still preparing their initial report on standardization, they sought out their American counterparts on a range of postwar collaboration issues, including the Combined Chiefs of Staff (discussed in chapter 2). American concerns about being seen to undermine the UN meant any Anglo-American military standardization effort would have to be covert and classified.

The British Chiefs of Staff wanted standardization for industrial and operational reasons. In contrast, Foreign Secretary Ernest Bevin viewed the project as the first step on the road to arms reductions.[6] In a letter to the chiefs of staff in spring 1946, the Foreign Office proposed a four-step plan that would bring about international regulation of weapons sales and trade. The first step in the plan involved integrating the American and British arms industries by standardizing the equipment produced by each country. This integration would form the basis for an agreement between the two countries to avoid competition in selling weapons to foreign nations. The Foreign Office feared that such competition would damage Anglo-American relations and that if small countries such as Portugal, Egypt, Turkey, and Norway purchased American weapons it would damage British industry. The solution was to divide sales by equipment type. For example, only Britain would sell aircraft to Latin America, while only America would sell small arms. After Anglo-American weapons markets had been divided, both governments would take legal control of patents for weapons, giving the government the ability to regulate weapons sales. The Foreign Office hoped that by setting an example, the British and Americans could get other countries to take control of their weapons sales, leading eventually to the international control of armaments.[7]

The Foreign Office plan was overly optimistic at best. Given that the U.S. military had spent the first half of the 1940s encouraging Latin American militaries to buy American weapons, it was highly unlikely that the Pentagon would reverse course and suddenly encourage Latin America to buy British. Furthermore, in 1946, the U.S. Congress was pushing the administration to *lessen* federal authority over the economy, not to increase this authority through greater regulation of arms manufacturers. Still, the Foreign Office plan did show that both British diplomats and military leaders supported standardization with the United States, though for different reasons.

The British Chiefs of Staff set forth goals and initial steps for a standardization program in a late May 1946 report to the Cabinet Defense Committee. The report noted that while there were great advantages to creating common equipment, "on a large scale [doing so] would be so costly that it could only be regarded as a long term policy" due to the need to replace current stocks with new standardized items. Tellingly, the report declared that collaboration between the United Kingdom and Canada during World War II in research and development as well as weapons production was the ideal model for standardization. If this model were followed, Britain would have a considerable level of influence in handing out research and production projects. However, the chiefs recommended a more manageable goal instead of full standardization, with "interchangeability" of weapons and supplies to be achieved by adopting common industrial standards, similar calibers, communications, power supplies, and tire sizes. The chiefs requested approval for this lower standard and for permission to approach the Canadians about making a joint proposition to the United States.[8] Coordinating with the Canadians first would give the British proposal added weight when the time came for talks with the Americans. Furthermore, Canadian participation in standardization would tend to dilute American influence in selecting the equipment to be used.[9]

On September 19, 1946, the Attlee government approved the chiefs' May 1946 report on standardization and authorized the chiefs to contact their Canadian and American counterparts on the subject.[10] When approached, the Canadians agreed in principle with the British approach, but thought it that was "optimistic" to expect official support from the Truman administration for any standardization project. Ottawa felt that the best path forward lay in direct talks with the U.S. military.[11]

THE CANADIAN DILEMMA

In these upcoming talks, the Canadian government sought to balance a desire for closer relations with the United States with a commitment to retaining Commonwealth ties. Postwar Canadian-American defense cooperation reflected the legacy of 1940. In August 1940, Prime Minister Mackenzie King and President Franklin Roosevelt met in Ogdensburg, New York, and created the Permanent Joint Board on Defense, which was composed of military and civilian representatives from both nations. The plans drawn up by the board were suited for the wartime strategic situation, but the end of the war raised the question of what plans, if any, should now be adopted. Canadian planners recognized that the experience of World War II and the ever-increasing range of aircraft meant that the Atlantic and Pacific Oceans no longer protected North America as they once did. One Canadian planner described the change as a shift from a Mercator projection of the world that overemphasized the size of regions near the poles to a polar projection of the world that highlighted the proximity of Canada and Russia.[12] As a result, Ottawa recognized that the United States would want, and might demand, close cooperation between the U.S. and Canadian militaries in order to protect America from aerial attack.

The board met in November 1945 and proposed general principles of Canadian-American military cooperation, which were toned down in March 1946 due to Canadian concerns that the original proposals veered too close to a military alliance. The March 1946 proposals called for exchanges of personnel between the two militaries, standardization of equipment and training, combined exercises, and the reciprocal use of air and naval facilities. President Truman approved the board's proposals by the end of May.[13] Although Ottawa did not give its immediate blessing to the proposals, in practice the Canadian government allowed its military to begin implementing the board's recommendations.[14] Ottawa's decision to support cooperation in practice while not yet in policy reflected Canadian political concerns.

The Canadian government was reluctant to approve the recommendations for two reasons. First, in spite of February 1946 revelations about Soviet espionage in Canada, Prime Minister Mackenzie King remained wary of taking steps that could be interpreted by Stalin as the formation of an anti-Soviet coalition. Second, Canada found itself "on the horns of a dilemma," according to an August 1946 letter from the American ambassador in Ottawa. Members of King's cabinet "realize the necessity for joining with the United States in defense of this continent, yet they fear such action may lead eventually to withdrawal of Canada from the Commonwealth."[15] Political and public support for Canada's position in the Commonwealth made overly exclusive links with the United States a delicate matter as well.[16]

Still, there was strong support for the recommendations in the Canadian military. Minister of National Defense Douglas Abbott announced in Parliament in August 1946 that it was the government's policy to pursue "standardizing equipment as far as possible" with the United States and Britain and that the Royal Canadian Navy should be "capable of operating in close cooperation, if needed, with either the British Navy or the Navy of the United States."[17] Eventually, after receiving additional assurances from Truman about American respect for Canadian sovereignty, King's government approved the board's recommendations, announcing this decision in February 1947.[18]

THE 1946 STANDARDIZATION TALKS

In contrast with the King government's leisurely deliberations on standardization policy, Field Marshal Bernard L. Montgomery, head of the British army, thought that standardization talks could not begin too soon. In mid-September 1946, the British Defense Committee authorized the British Chiefs of Staff to approach the Canadian and American chiefs on the topic of standardization. However, the British chiefs had only just begun this process when one of their members, Field Marshal Montgomery, decided to take matters into his own hands. In June 1946, Montgomery left command of the British occupation forces in Germany to become the senior officer in the British Army. Montgomery's time in Germany convinced him of the need for close relations between Britain and America in the face of Soviet pressure. Montgomery felt that the committee-based, deliberative process used in the cabinet and the chiefs of staff was indecisive, and he decided to personally advance the cause of Anglo-American military cooperation.[19]

The opportunity to do so came in August and September 1946 when Montgomery went on a trip to Canada and the United States. Before Montgomery left Britain, the other chiefs warned him not to make commitments without cabinet approval and under no circumstances to meet with American politicians. In part because of the poor personal relations between Montgomery and the other chiefs and in part because he had already made up his mind, Montgomery ignored their advice, meeting with Prime Minister King on September 9 and President Truman on September 11.[20]

The British general wanted to get King and Truman to agree to the policy of standardization while leaving the details of implementation to the military. As General Foulkes, the head of the Canadian army, recorded, Montgomery asked King for approval to discuss standardization, after which "the soldiers could work the thing out very easily." Montgomery secured King's support and then headed for Washington, all before the Attlee government had approved the chiefs' standardization proposal.[21]

On September 11 Montgomery told Truman that he had raised the issue of standardization of weapons and combined military planning with a supportive Prime Minister King and that General Eisenhower also recommended tripartite talks. When Montgomery suggested that the three governments "leave it to the Military Staff to get on with the job," Truman replied, "That is quite O.K. by me, go straight ahead."[22] On September 16, Montgomery then met with the U.S. Joint Chiefs, who were "anxious that discussions on standardization should begin."[23] A conference was scheduled for November 1946 in Washington for planning officers from all three countries to meet.[24] In October, Truman reaffirmed his support for the talks to Mackenzie King.[25] The British wanted the November standardization talks to take place using exclusively military channels such as through the British Joint Staff Mission in order to minimize the potential for State Department involvement and to minimize publicity. The British Chiefs of

Staff feared that diplomatic involvement and the resulting publicity would "endanger the whole scheme."[26]

The British succeeded in limiting the talks to military officers, who met from November 12 to 25 at the Pentagon. These talks were the first time since the war that representatives from all three militaries gathered with government support to discuss standardization and combined military planning. The discussions focused on two separate issues: the general strategic situation facing Britain, the United States, and Canada and the issue of standardization. The talks identified many of the issues that would shape the standardization efforts of the three nations in the coming years. In terms of creating common equipment, the planners determined that "the achievement of absolutely identical equipment between the three nations was impractical and not necessarily desirable." Instead the objective would be the ability to use another nation's equipment "without extensive conversion" as well as use common articles such as tools, screws, and other basic parts. The planners also determined that standardizing procedures, doctrine, and communications was of "considerable importance" and that in these three fields, the "least difficulties would be encountered."[27]

The conference attendees established a separate committee to address the issue of standardization, and as a result most of the meetings focused on broad strategic issues. The standardization committee presented an initial draft of its report on November 19. The planners generally approved of the paper but wanted it to explicitly describe the organizational structure that should be used (the "machinery") to implement standardization.[28] A revised version was discussed two days later with the American planners recommending that parallel standardization agencies be established in each country rather than a single "formal, interlocking combined control agency." The Canadians accepted this suggestion, as did the British, who then noted that "any indication that overall standardization was taking place should be top secret." This suggestion was also accepted.[29] The final standardization report was approved on November 22, 1946, by all the planners, though the American planners "indicated that for security reasons the [standardization] paper may not be published as a formal US Joint Chiefs of Staff paper but may be handled more anonymously."[30]

The American position at the talks on the standardization "machinery" represented a compromise between two competing desires. On the one hand, the U.S. military wanted to continue close cooperation with the British and Canadians. On the other hand, the Americans feared that if these cooperative arrangements became public knowledge, the U.S. could be accused of undermining the United Nations and establishing an anti-Soviet coalition.[31] The American officers' preference for independent agencies rather than a single, multinational body reflected their political awareness of the problems caused by the Combined Chiefs of Staff (discussed in chapter 2). The continued existence of the Combined Chiefs was already causing political problems for the Truman administration, and a multinational standardization agency could easily lead to more of the same.

The November 1946 talks produced three reports that the representatives agreed would be submitted to their governments for approval. The most important report was entitled "British-Canadian-United States Standardization, Pertinent Facts and Considerations Bearing on the Problem."[32] This report began by noting the limits of standardization. Initially, most of the equipment in each military would not be fully compatible with equipment from other nations, but over time the goal was to gradually increase the interchangeability of equipment. Further, standardization programs were to be "subservient" to the political and economic policies of each country, recognition that, in a democracy, political considerations such as jobs in the arms industry must be taken into account when purchasing equipment.[33] The ultimate objective of standardization was that "the Army, Navy, and Air Forces of each country should be able to operate with the services of the others and in certain cases as integrated forces."[34] With these objectives in mind, the report broke the standardization effort into four categories.

The first category was collaboration in research and development. The idea was that each nation would focus its military research programs in fields that were not emphasized by the other two nations. For example, if the United States focused on developing more advanced sonar equipment for surface ships, the British should focus their efforts on a related field such as sonar for helicopters but should not duplicate the American research program.[35] This process of avoiding duplication was referred to as rationalization and in practice proved difficult at best. The greater level of funding available to the U.S. military meant that American research programs were typically significantly larger in scope and scale than the other two nations. As a result, there were few, if any, areas of military research in which the

U.S. military was not involved. As a result, most British and Canadian projects were at least partially duplicating American projects. A strict adherence to the principle of collaboration would have meant a virtual end to British and Canadian scientific research. This outcome was unacceptable for at least two reasons. First, British and Canadian scientists and project managers were confident that they had important contributions to make and that the Americans did not have a monopoly on scientific development. Second, it was inconceivable that London and Ottawa would shut down their research and development programs and simply follow Washington's lead. To do so would mean that the British and Canadian military research programs would have little of interest to offer the Americans and would quickly find the Americans unwilling to share their research, since the United States would have nothing to gain. For all these reasons, collaboration in research and development tended to involve sharing test results, ideas, and progress, rather than strict efforts to avoid duplication. Edmund Poland, a British naval officer stationed in Washington in the early 1950s, later recalled that the two navies never reached any agreement on rationalizing research projects, even though the idea was the subject of "an amazing number of meetings."[36]

In addition to collaboration in research and development, the report discussed the potential for standardization in three other areas. The second field of standardization in the report was interchangeable weapons. The document called for forces from one nation to be able to use another nation's ammunition, fuel, power, and other basic supplies. Achieving this outcome involved changes in future systems rather than modification of existing weapons.

Progress in this second area of standardization would inevitably lead to progress in the third area: common doctrine and tactics. As equipment became more interchangeable, the tactics governing employment would necessarily become more standardized. The planners called for the services to create common doctrine by exchanging observers and holding combined exercises.

The fourth field of standardization was procedures and organization. The report emphasized uniformity in terminology, map markings, charts, manuals, and communication procedures.[37] The final section of the report dealt with the bureaucracy of standardization. The report recommended that the each nation establish a standardization steering committee in Washington that would meet regularly with the other two committees to coordinate the work of standardization. Although the planners were united in this goal, in the end it would be only partially adopted.

The American delegates insisted that each nation individually submit the conference reports to their respective chiefs of staff instead of presenting the conference reports to the Combined Chiefs of Staff for approval, which would involve filing them with the United Nations.[38] The U.S. Joint Chiefs would later report that standardization was "fraught with practical, political, and industrial difficulties" since "such a program might be attacked as constituting a military agreement of a type contrary to the spirit and intent of the United Nations Charter."[39] Thus, political concerns even shaped the administrative steps in submitting the report.

The November 1946 standardization talks represented an important step in creating peacetime standardization programs in Canada, the United States, and the United Kingdom. By the early 1950s, the combined standardization program of these three nations became known as Canadian–United Kingdom–United States (CANUKUS) standardization. The November 1946 meetings also revealed most of the recurring standardization problems that faced these three nations in the years to come. The Americans in particular remained concerned about any publicity related to standardization, initially over concerns related to the United Nations. By 1949, however, the United States was less concerned about antagonizing the United Nations and more worried about embarrassing NATO allies who were not a part of the inner CANUKUS club.

The planners clearly recognized the difficulty of standardizing equipment or even of making equipment interchangeable. Efforts over the next several years to develop standardized equipment, such as sonobuoys and antiaircraft guns, demonstrated the difficulty of this goal. Adopting equipment developed elsewhere proved challenging for all three nations, for cultural reasons as well as economic and political ones. A senior officer in the Admiralty highlighted this fact in a report on standardization with the U.S. Navy in July 1948, concluding that "progress [in standardization] has been made with many items, but over a considerable field standardization is hindered by national character and tradition. A crisis graver than May 1940 would be needed to get our seamen into American caps; a reversal of the War of Independence would be required to get American seamen into ours."[40]

When the planners returned to their respective countries from the November standardization talks, they presented their reports to their respective chiefs of staff. Political concerns weighed heavily on the resulting discussions on how to handle the recommendations. In mid-December, the British Chiefs of Staff recommended that their government approve the standardization report, which would formally create the standardization program and establish the steering committees in Washington.[41] The Defence Committee considered the chiefs' recommendation in mid-January and approved the report in principle, but decided that creating a new committee in Washington would require the Attlee government to make a public announcement.[42] Foreign Minister Bevin proposed formally publishing the standardization agreement but the chiefs of staff objected, arguing that to do so would seriously damage relations with the United States. The Defence Committee approved the standardization report on January 31, 1947, establishing the standardization program, but it then decided that a new committee in Washington would not be created and the agreement not be published.[43] The business of standardization would instead be handled through existing military communication channels, namely the British Joint Staff Mission in Washington.[44] This decision was communicated to the Americans through the British military mission in Washington in late May.[45]

In contrast, the Canadian chiefs approved the standardization report in early February 1947 and began making preparations to set up their new standardization committee in Washington.[46] The U.S. Chiefs of Staff had the report approved by the War and Navy Departments by late July but did not officially present the report to the State Department, though State had "been kept in touch informally."[47] Thus, by August 1947, Canada, the United States, and the United Kingdom had all decided, as a matter of policy, to standardize their military forces. The standardization program's focus now shifted from overall government policy to the individual military services.

NAVAL STANDARDIZATION

As senior civilian and military leaders on both sides of the Atlantic discussed and debated national standardization policy in 1946 and 1947, elements of the Canadian, American, and British navies worked to retain and even strengthen the close relations they enjoyed with each other during World War II. In particular, officers working in the fields of communications and antisubmarine warfare (ASW) reached out to their American, Canadian, and British counterparts as early as late 1945 and early 1946 to foster cooperation. These efforts were initially made through ad hoc organizations and groups that over time became more formal as national policies on standardization caught up with the work already occurring at a lower level. In the immediate years after World War II the Royal Navy and the U.S. Navy pursued several formal standardization projects. The three most important dealt with sono-buoys and antisubmarine warfare doctrine, and later an effort to standardize operating procedures in a combined tactical manual. The standardization work done in the three areas of sonobuoys, ASW doctrine, and tactical pro-cedures highlighted the challenges of standardizing equipment and the rela-tive speed with which concepts and procedures could be standardized.

The first sonobuoys were initially used by U.S. Navy blimps in 1942 that were hunting German submarines off the East Coast of the United States. The buoys consisted of a long cylindrical tube just over four feet long and six and one-quarter inches in diameter. The buoy would be dropped out of an aircraft or blimp, and a parachute would slow its descent to the water. Once in the water, the bottom of the tube would open and listening devices called hydrophones would slide out of the tube into the water. The hydrophones picked up sounds from nearby submarines and transmitted these sounds to the aircraft using a radio inside the tube.[48] These early buoys allowed air crews to hear the sound made by nearby submarines but could not deter-mine the bearing to the submarine from the buoy. Since these buoys received sound from all directions without differentiating azimuth, they were known as omnidirectional buoys.[49] During World War II, the U.S. Navy ordered more than fifty-nine thousand of these early expendable sonobuoys, which meant the navy had a large supply left over at the end of the war.[50] By Janu-ary 1945, the British and Americans were testing directional buoys that could provide a bearing to the submarine from the buoy. However, this directional buoy did not enter service before the war was over.[51]

At the end of the war, the U.S. Navy largely abandoned the directional buoy project. Most of the technical experts returned to civilian life, and the navy disbanded the scientific team overseeing buoy development.[52] One of the engineers who worked on the buoys during World War II, Russell Mason, later described the late 1940s as "a black era in airborne ASW."[53] The lesser priority given to sonobuoy development reflected the U.S. Navy's focus on finding another method of detecting submarines, such as radar, magnetic anomaly detection (MAD), or infrared detectors.[54] In addition, responsibility for sonobuoys lay with the Naval Research Laboratory, which at the time did not specialize in airborne research.[55] The sonobuoy situation, however, improved in 1950 when the navy transferred responsibility for the program to the Naval Air Development Center in Warminster, Pennsylvania, which specialized in research on airborne weapons.[56]

In early 1947, the Royal Navy received a supply of directional sonobuoys from the U.S. Navy that had been produced during the final months of World War II for use in exercises. The British modified the buoys to meet their technical requirements, but realized that the supply would be exhausted within two years. As a result, the British began to study the possibility of researching and developing in conjunction with the Americans a sonobuoy that could be built in both countries. In particular, the British were interested in building the new AN/SSQ-1 directional buoy that the U.S. Navy began developing in June 1947. The British raised this possibility with a U.S. Navy team that visited Britain in August and September 1947, but were told that the new directional buoy would probably not be ready by 1949.[57] However, the visiting team was in favor of sharing progress reports about the development of AN/SSQ-1, the new directional buoy, and these reports were duly provided.[58]

In addition to providing Britain with development reports, the U.S. Navy also provided the British with surplus World War II–era sonobuoys. In order to ensure a supply of sonobuoys for exercises and to conserve their scarce research and development funds, for instance, the Royal Navy acquired a supply of American omnidirectional sonobuoys in 1947.[59] The Admiralty's view was that these less than optimal buoys bought the Royal Navy time. By early 1948, the British began developing a specifically British directional buoy, called the Mark I, which was to be for use when their American-built supplies of directional buoys ran out.[60]

Despite launching a separate buoy program, the British still wanted to eventually standardize their sonobuoys with the Americans. In any future war, British buoy production might be curtailed by Soviet air and missile attacks on the United Kingdom. Prudence suggested developing a buoy that could be produced in America and used by both British and American forces in wartime. In pursuit of this goal, the Royal Navy approached the U.S. Navy in 1948 to discuss forming a combined Anglo-American committee to standardize this equipment.[61]

While preliminary discussions about such a committee were underway, in July 1948 the U.S. Navy suggested to the British that they abandon their efforts to develop the Mark I directional sonobuoy and concentrate their resources on creating a standardized model. The Sea/Air Warfare Committee, which oversaw British antisubmarine policy for the Admiralty and the Air Ministry, responded negatively. The committee was wary of halting development of their Mark I buoy simply for the purpose of standardizing with the Americans. Royal Air Force representatives pointed out that the British already had a working early prototype and that halting Mark I development in favor of a standardized buoy would impose a delay of eighteen months before the standardized buoy entered production. The committee admitted that "compared with the U.S. our experience of this equipment is limited, but our scientists are confident that they can produce as good a system as America."[62] In addition, the American proposal reminded the British of one of their ongoing concerns about standardization: that for the U.S. Navy, standardization meant buying American. The Americans offered to supply the British with additional sonobuoys in the interim, but the Royal Navy had already taken one delivery of American buoys and was anxious to avoid becoming dependent on American supplies. Furthermore, the British did not want to depend on an unproven American design without at least having the Mark I as a backup.[63] In fact, the success of the British Mark I buoy and the later troubles encountered by the American buoy demonstrated the wisdom of this approach.

By April 1949, the British had completed development of their new Mark I directional sonobuoy and placed orders for a thousand buoys to be delivered by February 1950. The Admiralty's limited financial resources meant the British concentrated their efforts on the more advanced directional buoy instead of the omnidirectional buoy.[64] As a result, the Royal Navy had to wait until August 1951 for a new British omnidirectional buoy, but it did have a workable directional buoy by early 1950.[65]

The American prediction that their directional buoy would not be ready by 1949 proved to be accurate, largely because of the U.S. Navy's own failings. In 1947, the navy tasked a contractor with developing a new directional buoy but did not provide the company with the research done on directional buoys in the closing months of World War II. Tests in June 1952 indicated that the new buoys performed well below expectations and that the internal components had an alarming tendency to break upon impact with the water.[66] As a result, the first attempt to develop the new AN/SSQ-1 sonobuoy failed, as did a subsequent attempt with a new contractor. The continued failure of American contractors to produce a functional directional buoy, the AN/SSQ-1, led U.S. Atlantic Fleet commanders to recommend buying the British Mark I directional buoy for American use.[67] The sale was completed in 1953.[68] Ironically, by 1954 the U.S. Navy had two failed contracts and was reliant on British directional sonobuoys. A new American directional buoy would not come into service until the late 1950s, by which time the design was overtaken by new technical advances.[69]

In light of the false starts made by the American sonobuoy program in the late 1940s and early 1950s, the British decision to develop a buoy independent of the Americans proved to be prudent. In addition, this decision represented diverging British and American approaches to sonobuoy development. Despite the free exchange of information resulting from the 1947 visits, the two sides failed to develop compatible technical standards for their sonobuoys. This failure to standardize technical requirements in 1947 and 1948 laid the foundation for the serious setbacks in sonobuoy standardization that occurred in 1950 and 1951.

For example, in 1950 the British and American navies agreed to establish the Sonobuoy Working Party in an effort to standardize their sonobuoys.[70] However, this move toward standardization was overcome by the Korean War and fundamental technical differences between the two navies' sonobuoys. The working party had no sooner scheduled combined trials of the British Mark I and American AN/SSQ-1 directional buoys than the Korean War forced the Americans to withdraw from the trials and begin full-scale production of the AN/SSQ-1 immediately.[71]

The two directional sonobuoys in question differed from one another in two fundamental respects: the radio frequencies used to transmit sound and the method used to keep track of buoy locations once they were deployed.[72] Operators on ships and aircraft with equipment designed to receive signals from a British buoy could not pick up signals from an American buoy and vice versa.[73] The American directional buoy used FM radio while the British buoy used AM radio, and according to Canadian observers, "on both sides scientific thought appears to be unwilling to change."[74] Furthermore, each navy had a different approach to using sonobuoys in combat. The American concept called for two aircraft to hunt a single submarine simultaneously, with one plane carrying detection equipment including sonobuoys and the other carrying antisubmarine weapons. This approach was not feasible for the British or Canadians since it required large numbers of aircraft, a financial burden that those two nations could not afford.[75] The two navies also used different methods of plotting where buoys had been dropped. In the U.S. Navy, all buoys included a small radar responder beacon that allowed aircraft to track their locations using the more advanced aerial radar deployed on U.S. Navy patrol planes.[76] British aircraft dropped a separate buoy that served as a beacon, marking the location of a pattern of sonobuoys. Aircraft dropped the buoys in one of several preset patterns and the beacon buoy would be dropped near the center of the pattern.[77] These basic technical differences between the sonobuoys were the result of a failure to standardize requirements. By the end of 1950, both navies were committed to their own directional buoys, which could not be used by the other nation.

In the midst of these technical differences, the Sonobuoy Working Party meeting in May 1951 fell into disarray when the American representatives accused the British of reneging on an earlier commitment regarding sonobuoy radio frequencies. The working party's talks broke down, requiring a six-month cooling-off period before talks could resume.[78] After the collapse of the talks, U.S. naval officers involved in sonobuoy standardization became increasingly anxious about the lack of progress.[79] The solution adopted by both sides when the working party's talks resumed in October 1951 was to invite the Canadians to join the talks.[80]

The inability of the Anglo-American Sonobuoy Committee to standardize a design impacted not only the two navies on the committee, but also the Canadians. In December 1948, the Canadian Naval Board had bought three hundred British sonobuoys for use in training and exercises.[81] By November 1950, Canadian naval officers were recommending buying American sonobuoys, in particular the AN/SSQ-2 omnidirectional buoy.[82] In May 1951, the RCAF took the initial step in moving from British to American sonobuoys by purchasing the AN/SSQ-2 buoy, and the RCN followed suit in December of that year.[83] Canadian officers sought an end to the difficulties of procuring equipment from two sources, and their efforts received a substantial boost when Canada joined the Sonobuoy Working Party in October 1951.[84] Membership in this group allowed the Royal Canadian Navy to lobby for one of their goals in naval standardization: creating common designs that would remove the need for Ottawa to choose between American and British equipment. The Canadians also wanted to standardize procedures, as RCAF and RCN aircraft laying sonobuoys used different patterns.[85]

Eventually, the Canadians got their wish. The resumption of Sonobuoy Working Party talks in late 1951 led to agreement on the technical details of a standardized sonobuoy by 1957.[86] The six years between the resumption of talks and the final agreement highlight the challenges of rapidly standardizing equipment, even between navies with close ties. Throughout the late 1940s and early 1950s, the three navies exchanged antisubmarine information and equipment freely, as demonstrated by the British procurement of American buoys in 1947, the Canadian purchase of American buoys in 1951, and the sale of British buoys to the Americans in 1953. However, these exchanges could not overcome the doctrinal, technical, and bureaucratic challenges of standardizing equipment.

Sonobuoy standardization was one of the two most significant standardization projects launched by the U.S. and Royal Navies in the late 1940s.[87] The ability to draw on each other's supplies of buoys in a crisis would provide both navies with greater logistical flexibility. However, despite the priority accorded to the project, the road to standardized buoys proved to be full of bumps and detours. Knowledge of the other side's plans could not bring technical requirements into line. Standardization of equipment came about only through lengthy negotiations.

COMMON DOCTRINE AND COMMUNICATIONS

In contrast to the troubled sonobuoy saga, the Canadian, British, and American navies found that developing a common doctrine for antisubmarine warfare and standardizing communications procedures could be accomplished relatively quickly. During World War II, warships escorting convoys in the Atlantic Ocean developed a variety of techniques to counter the threat posed by German submarines. The antisubmarine warfare tactics utilized by the three navies during the war overlapped but were not identical. During 1944 and 1945, the Germans began to deploy more advanced submarines equipped with devices called snorkels, which allowed the U-boats to remain underwater for longer periods of time while traveling at higher speeds. These technological developments challenged the prevailing ASW tactics then in use in the three navies. Convinced that the Soviet Union would seek to replicate the late wartime German advances in submarine technology, officers in all three navies struggled to determine how best to challenge the new threat posed by faster submarines equipped with snorkels. Planners on both sides of the Atlantic wanted to ensure that in a future war with the Soviet Union, all three navies used the same ASW doctrine. As a result, in December 1948, the British and Americans formed a working group to prepare common ASW doctrine and promptly invited the RCN to join.[88]

The full title of the group was the Joint Canadian-British-United States Anti-Submarine Warfare Doctrine Working Group.[89] In preparation for writing the common doctrine, the group reviewed several Admiralty papers on antisubmarine tactics.[90] After working for several months, the working group members completed the initial draft of the common doctrine in late April 1949.[91]

The draft doctrine declared that the goal of antisubmarine operations at sea was "to deny the enemy the effective use of his submarines," a direct quote from U.S. Navy doctrine.[92] Noticeably, the overall objective was *not* the Royal Navy's standard ASW goal: the safe and timely arrival of the convoy. The American approach gauged success by submarine activity while the British approach focused on completed convoy voyages. The draft explained that the overall goal would be achieved using five principles of ASW: restriction of submarine movement, operational control of shipping, convoy and task force antisubmarine defense, torpedo countermeasures, and coastal defenses.[93] The first principle, restricting submarine movement, emphasized preventing submarines from moving through certain areas through the use of barriers of ships, aircraft, and mines. The second and third principles both prioritized "the safe and timely arrival" of convoys and groups of warships, respectively. The fourth principle, torpedo countermeasures, was less a principle and more a technical issue of how to divert, confuse, or intercept homing torpedoes. The final principle, coastal defense, focused on making harbors and bases safe havens from enemy submarines.[94] The principles did not go into as much detail as the four papers that the Admiralty had provided to the working group since the U.S. Navy wanted agreement to be reached on broad principles before delving into the details of tactics.[95]

Taken together, the five principles in the draft doctrine represented a subtle, but significant shift away from the wartime British approach to ASW, which emphasized the arrival of the convoy at its destination. The U.S. Navy also focused on convoy protection during World War II but at the same time devoted substantial resources to killing German submarines through offensive operations, particularly in the last two years of the war. The Americans sent small escort carriers with escorts into the North Atlantic with the mission of finding German submarines and hunting them to exhaustion. This approach involved remaining in the submarine's operating area for an extended period and was therefore not well suited to defending a moving convoy.[96] The British approach also sought to destroy submarines but emphasized other tactics such as diverting convoys around known submarine locations and forcing submarines to retreat from attacks on convoys. These tactics prioritized protecting the convoy over killing submarines. Canadian tactics reflected an offensive orientation, similar to that of the Americans, though with innovative tactics designed to compensate for limited access to the most up-to-date equipment. For example, the RCN developed tactics using offensive illumination to drive off U-boats at night for escorts that lacked advanced surface search radar.[97] A U.S. Navy report in 1947 described the difference between the British and American approaches: "They place emphasis on convoy protection versus our emphasis on 'hunter-killer' group operations."[98] The combined principles drafted by the working group retained the Royal Navy's phrasing, "safe and timely arrival," but this phrase was no longer the overarching principle of ASW.

Once the working group completed a draft of the common ASW doctrine, the draft principles were sent to each nation for review and comment. Canadian officers reviewing the draft were reminded that "the existence of the tripartite standardization program and the contents of this particular agreement" were not to be released to any country other than Canada, Britain, and America.[99] The Canadians approved the draft as it stood in May 1949.[100]

Within the U.S. Navy, the first principle of restricting submarine usage received the most attention, a reflection of the offensive orientation in American antisubmarine doctrine. For example, an officer describing the doctrine at a conference in August 1949 listed eight principles of ASW, the first four of which consisted of offensive actions against submarines.[101] The Americans provided their comments on the doctrine by the end of August.[102] The British comments arrived in October, and at a meeting on October 27, 1949, the group reviewed the comments received from the operational commands and headquarters. [103] The group adopted a number of recommended changes to the doctrine provided by the British and Americans. The two most significant changes involved the first principle, restricting the movements of enemy submarines. The name of the principle became "offensive action against submarines," a change suggested by the U.S. Navy. The Americans also got the group to agree to expand one of the methods used in the offensive action principle. The "attack at source" method now explicitly called for bombing attacks on submarines and submarines bases, a major role envisioned by the U.S. naval aviation community and supported by Britain's Fleet Air Arm.[104] The group then sent the revised doctrine back to the three naval headquarters for approval, which came by early February 1950.[105]

At the October 1949 meeting, the working group also assigned each of the five principles to a sponsoring country, which would further develop the principle into specific recommendations with input from the other two countries through principle-specific committees.[106] The British recommended that the U.S. Navy chair the subcommittee on the offensive action principle because the U.S. Navy "has carried out more tactical exercises at sea" on this subject than the other two navies. Since the task force and convoy defense task was the "biggest problem of all," the British also suggested that the Americans take the lead in drafting the paper on this subject. As "the lifeline of the U.K. depends on the success" of operational control of shipping, the British sought to chair this subcommittee as well as the coastal defense subcommittee, the field with the lowest profile. The Admiralty recommended that Canada chair the torpedo countermeasures panel because "it is highly desirable that Canada" should chair at least one of the panels.[107] British interest in Commonwealth harmony aside, Canada's wartime experience developing Canadian anti–acoustic torpedo (CAT) gear gave the RCN the technical experience needed to tackle torpedo countermeasures.[108]

The group then discussed the instructions to be given to each subcommittee. The British representatives envisioned each subcommittee amplifying one of the principles without developing specific common tactics and then producing a book of the amplified principles that could facilitate combined operations. This approach would not force the British or the Americans to choose between differing approaches, choices that would have to be made if the goal was a detailed combined publication.[109] In contrast, the Canadian members strongly advocated, as they had throughout the process, "for common tactical books to be held on the bridge" of ships from all three navies. The Canadians wanted a common set of tactics and a single book so that the RCN could stop having to be familiar with different British and American books.[110] The U.S. Navy representatives did not hold a strong view at the meeting, and so each subcommittee was allowed to determine what form its final paper should take. However, Captain Archibald McFadden, the American head of the subcommittee on convoy and task force antisubmarine defense, told the Canadians that there was no point in "writing a book which would only go half way towards what is required." He intended for his subcommittee to write a common tactical book that would replace existing British and American publications, exactly what the Canadians wanted.[111]

Although the working group created subcommittees to expand each of the principles, the subcommittee on convoy and task force defense appears to have been the only one to produce a substantial product. Two pieces of evidence suggest that the members of this group began the discussions that eventually led to the three navies writing common tactical and communications books. First, the subcommittee was formed at a working group meeting on October 27, 1949, and the Canadian naval attaché in Washington reported that preliminary discussions about writing a common signal book were taking place in September and October.[112] Second, the American chairman, Captain Archibald McFadden, told the subcommittee that he intended for the group to produce a combined tactical book.[113] At the very least, the idea of writing common tactical and signal books was probably shared between the working group subcommittee and the group that would write the new tactical book since the same Canadian officer, Lieutenant Commander T. C. Mackay, participated in both groups.

Regardless of the immediate source, the more general impetus for writing common books came from recent wartime experience. When British and American warships operated together during the war, the nation with the smaller number of ships adopted the tactical books and signal publications of the larger fleet. This pattern of adopting the dominant fleet's books extended all the way back to the American battleships that operated with the Grand Fleet during World War I. In the final months of fighting against Japan in the Pacific, the Royal Navy's British Pacific Fleet (BPF) operated closely with the U.S. Navy. As a result of this experience, many British officers who served with the BPF, including Admiral Fraser, the fleet commander, concluded that the Royal Navy ought to revise its tactical and signal books to bring these books more in line with American practice.[114] In response, the Admiralty established a committee that rewrote the British signal books and adopted many of the U.S. Navy's practices by 1948.[115]

While the Royal Navy was revising its communications publications, officers in both navies struggled to determine the best methods and techniques for countering newer, faster submarines. Uncertainty about the effectiveness of new technical developments and the exact scale of the Soviet submarine threat meant that antisubmarine doctrine and tactics were "in a fluid state" in both navies, according to a June 1948 Admiralty report. The report noted that the two navies were aware of tactical developments made by the other and concluded optimistically that "there is every chance that the final tactical doctrine of the two navies will be similar if not identical."[116] ASW doctrinal links deepened in January 1948 when the U.S. Navy placed copies of American publications in London and Guam for use by Royal Navy warships operating with American ships and the Royal Navy did the same.[117] Later in 1948, arrangements were made between the two navies to regularly exchange communications books and tactical publications.[118]

This pattern of exchanges and information sharing culminated in September 1949 when preliminary discussions took place in Washington between American, British, and Canadian naval officers about writing a combined signal book that would enable allied warships to easily work together.[119] The senior Canadian naval officer in Washington, Commodore Horatio N. Lay, wrote to Ottawa that the discussions initially focused on standardizing the signal flags used by the British and American fleets. Furthermore, the proposed book was "to be made available to all allied nations for use in controlling ships of different nationalities when in company."[120] The Canadian Naval Board responded in late October, telling Lay that Ottawa was in favor of producing such a book, which "would fill a long-felt need and contribute to inter-naval cooperation."[121] Canada's intense interest in creating this signals book stemmed from the government's policy that the RCN be "capable of operating in close cooperation if need be with either the British navy or the navy of the United States."[122]

In practice, the RCN suffered from a split communications policy. RCN units on the Pacific coast converted to American signals and books in late 1945 with the support of Rear Admiral Victor Brodeur, who was flag officer Pacific Coast at the time.[123] East Coast units continued to use Royal Navy books and signals.[124] As Rear Admiral John A. Charles later remembered, "at the end of the war we were in a very difficult position vis a vis the two navies [the RN and the USN] . . . operating with both and communicating with both on two different systems."[125]

This unique challenge of trying to operate in two different systems led RCN communications officers to recommend adopting U.S. Navy signals and formations, a recommendation supported in 1947 by Vice Admiral Harold T. W. Grant, the chief of the Naval Staff.[126] However, during the transition, RCN communications personnel would have to become familiar with both the USN and RN systems.[127] Furthermore, adopting American signals and books did not overcome the fact that almost all of the RCN's mid-level and senior officers had vastly more experience with British than with American books. An Anglo-American set of signal and tactical books would eliminate the need for these choices to be made. The challenge of managing national naval communications in the late 1940s made Canadian representatives strong advocates for a combined signal book.

In late October 1949, the Americans turned the preliminary discussions about a combined signal book into action. Rear Admiral John R. Redman, the chief of naval communications for the U.S. Navy, sent a study to the senior Canadian and British naval officers in Washington, setting forth the American perspective on writing a combined signal book. Redman's cover letter asked the Canadians and British to nominate representatives for a working group to draft it.[128] The navy's study noted that the signal flags used by the RN and USN were largely the same, though the RN used several additional British-only flags. However, the focus of the study was on the signals themselves, not the flags used to send the signals: "a common signal book makes a common set of signal flags automatic."[129] The Americans eventually planned to distribute the new signal book to Western Hemisphere nations, NATO countries, Turkey, Greece, and the Commonwealth. However, the initial focus should be on writing "a limited combined (USN, RN, RCN) Naval Allied Signal Book" that would later be provided to the countries listed above.[130] This last point clearly demonstrates the way the Navy Department viewed relations with foreign navies in the late 1940s. The Americans wanted to be able to easily coordinate and operate with a significant number of navies and were prepared to develop publications that would make that possible. However, the actual writing of the book should be done by an inner circle of navies, the Canadians and the British, which had the closest relations with the U.S. Navy.

Despite taking the lead in proposing to write a new signal book, the U.S. Navy made an abortive effort in October 1949 to circumvent the whole writing process. The U.S. Navy observer to the Western Union, the precursor to the Western European Union, offered two U.S. Navy communications publications to the navies of the Union. The Canadian naval attaché in Washington, Commodore Lay, wrote to Ottawa that "it is understood that the USN hopes these books will be adopted by the Western Union countries, including the United Kingdom."[131] By December 1949, the Western Union talks revealed "that neither the UK nor the US appear willing to scrap their entire systems and accept the others in lieu."[132] This failed American attempt to have U.S. Navy publications accepted wholesale by the Europeans did serve to advance the discussions about a new combined signal book. The British indicated they would be prepared to accept the U.S. Navy's communications publication, the General Signal Book, as the basis for the new combined signal book. In return, the British wanted the Americans to agree to write a new combined book of tactical instructions based on the Royal Navy's tactical book, Conduct of the Fleet. The RCN supported the British in advocating for a new tactical book in addition to the proposed new signal book, though they wanted some of the U.S. Navy methods incorporated into the new tactical book.[133]

Discussions between the three navies on the proposed signal book and tactical book continued in both London and Washington during the first two months of 1950. The U.S. chief of naval operations, Admiral Forrest Sherman, took a personal interest in the new books, and by March, a tentative agreement was reached between the British and the Americans.[134] The two navies agreed to compromise: the new signal book would be built on the American General Signal Book and the new tactical book would be built on the British Conduct of the Fleet. Both books were to be written under the assumption that they would be used by the navies of NATO.[135] At a meeting on March 24, 1950, Sherman and the British first sea lord, Admiral Fraser, gave their approval to the agreement, clearing the way for drafting to begin.[136]

With approval to begin writing in hand, British and Canadian officers detailed to the writing groups headed to Washington in May 1950. At the same time, planners in Washington pondered whether to get approval from NATO's Standing Group for writing the two new books, especially since the plan adopted by the three navies was to draft the two new books with NATO in mind.[137] Commodore Lay, the senior Canadian naval officer in Washington, noted that seeking Standing Group approval might cause tensions with the French military since "it is known that the French have some objection to the UK-US short term agreement for Naval communications, but there is no doubt that these books will be produced."[138]

Despite this expression of confidence, British and American representatives on the Standing Group decided not to seek NATO's blessing at the outset. Instead, the signal and tactical books "will be written by ABC [American, British, and Canadian] Communicators [communications officers] outside, repeat, outside Standing Group organization" as relayed in a radio message from Commodore Lay to Ottawa. After the books had been written, they would be offered to the Standing Group for NATO's use but not ownership. The one concession made by the Anglo-Saxon navies was that the French navy would be allowed to send an observer to sit in on the committees writing the two books.[139]

The decision to keep authorship of the two books within the CANUKUS sphere reflected the way the three navies viewed NATO's role in the larger issue of Western defense. In 1950, British and American senior naval officers viewed NATO in many respects as one level down from CANUKUS. They rejected any suggestion, typically made by French representatives, that the Standing Group should oversee Western strategy worldwide (discussed in chapter 2). At the March 1950 meeting between Sherman and Fraser, the Americans emphasized that they viewed the Standing Group as a NATO-only body and "would not agree to the Standing Group being connected in any way with global planning." Fraser agreed that they should "not accept NATO as a world-wide authority." Both sides also agreed "that if the United States and United Kingdom took a strong line, the French would have to conform" to their position.[140]

The working group of British, Canadian, and American officers began writing the new tactical book in June and completed a draft of the first eight chapters by September 1950. This first set of chapters dealt with basic maneuvering and, taken together, would allow units from different navies to sail together.[141] Once written, the first eight chapters were sent out to operational commands within all three navies, such as the British Home Fleet, the American Sixth Fleet, and the Canadian flag officer Pacific Coast, for comments.[142]

The Chief of Naval Operations' (CNO) cover letter highlighted several features of the writing process for American officers reviewing the chapters. The CNO intended for the new tactical books to replace existing tactical publications like United States Fleet [Manual] 2 and the British Conduct of the Fleet. In addition, each navy committed to update its existing books to conform to the new tactical book in the interim period before the book became effective.[143] The content of the new tactical book came from both existing American and British books, while the format followed the British book. The authors prioritized clear, concise language that avoided ambiguity, an important consideration since the book would be translated into several different languages once adopted by NATO. The British members "leaned over backwards," according to the U.S. Navy, by accepting American spellings of words such as maneuver, defense, and center and by agreeing to avoid British expressions such as whilst and asdic (the British term for sonar). Furthermore, the Royal Navy accepted American organizational terms such as Officer in Tactical Command (OTC) and Combat Information Center (CIC) instead of the British Action Information Organization. All of these choices represented major British concessions. During the drafting process both the British and the Americans had made numerous concessions to each other to resolve points of difference in their tactical procedures. For example, a group of ships sailing one behind the other was a "column" in Britain but a "line" in America. Line was chosen over column. The British command for ships to "wheel" (turn) was accepted over the American command "change course."[144]

The comments received from officers in all three navies were mostly positive, though some bristled at giving up their national procedure. One officer in the U.S. Second Fleet commented on one passage that followed British procedure by writing, "This might work but I doubt it." More common were comments such as those by American Captain Frederick V. H. Hilles: "In general, I like the simple, clear uncomplicated language in which written. I think it is an excellent piece of work." Another officer on the Second Fleet staff found the new manual "easier to understand than USF-2."[145] Vice Ad-

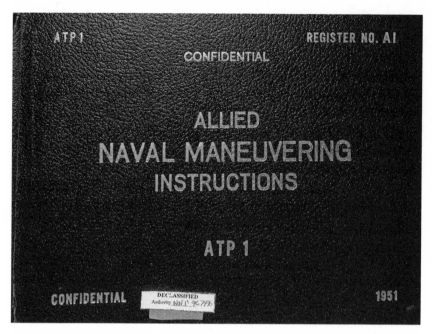

Allied Tactical Publication 1 Cover, January 1952. *Source*: Folder ATP 1 Change 1, Jan 1952, Box 3, Entry A1 337-A, Operational, Tactical, and Instructional Publications, 1947–1970, Records of the Office of the Chief of Naval Operations, Record Group 38, National Archives at College Park, College Park, Maryland.

miral Matthias B. Gardner, the commander of Second Fleet, concluded that the draft instructions "would be entirely adequate for maneuvering combined naval forces" and were "commendably well written in simple, direct style."[146]

By October 1950, the working group was revising the first eight chapters based on comments received.[147] While the operational commands were reviewing the drafts, the working group pressed on and began preparing drafts of the remaining twelve chapters, which dealt with antisubmarine warfare, replenishment at sea, and aircraft carrier operations.[148] The group completed the drafts of these additional chapters by April 1951.[149] After they received comments and revised these additional chapters, the book was published in January 1952. The new tactical book was entitled *Allied Naval Maneuvering Instructions, Allied Tactical Publication 1*, known as ATP 1 for short. By July 1952, ATP 1 had been adopted by all three navies and was being translated into NATO languages.[150]

At the same time that ATP 1 was being drafted, another working group of British, Canadian, and American naval officers were drafting a new signal book, based on the U.S. Navy's General Signal Book. The new book, which became known as *Allied Communications Publication 175* (ACP 175), was completed in March 1951.[151] The three navies approved releasing ACP 175 to NATO navies in August, and the new signal book was the first in a series of new communications publications, some written by CANUKUS and some by NATO.[152]

After the U.S. offered ATP 1 to NATO, the navies of the alliance rapidly adopted the new book as their tactical manual. The RCN quickly adopted ATP 1 for its own use, as reflected by a note by the Joint Maritime Warfare School in October 1951 that it was "the policy of this school [to] adhere strictly to instructions laid down in ATP 1."[153] The U.S. Sixth Fleet used ATP 1 and the new communications publication, ACP 175, for the first time in combined exercises with other NATO ships in October 1952.[154] The American commander of a destroyer division in these exercises remembered later that ATP 1 "worked extremely well" and quickly became "the Bible of the Sixth Fleet."[155] The reports from exercises relying on ATP 1 repeated comments made by reviewers that the book was well written and suitable for combined fleet operations.[156]

Although the United States provided NATO with access to ATP 1, the U.S. Navy retained ownership of the manual.[157] As a result, when Exercise Mainbrace in 1952 revealed the need for some changes to the administrative section of ATP 1, the U.S. Navy drafted the change and then sent the draft to British, American, and Canadian commanders for comment. The Americans did not include other NATO countries in the revision process.[158] The U.S. Navy's view was that the agreements reached by CANUKUS were not NATO-specific publications and were in fact intended for worldwide use.[159] This attitude was reflected in the names of the books: *Allied* Tactical Publication instead of *NATO* Tactical Publication.[160] An American captain voiced this position at a 1954 conference with British and Canadian officers during a discussion about changes suggested to ATP 2, the Allied Tactical Publication that laid down procedures for merchant ships to follow in wartime. The Canadians and British suggested changes to ATP 2 that would tailor the book for use by NATO and reflected NATO-specific concerns. The American captain replied, "It must be borne in mind that ATP is intended for worldwide

Allied usage. . . . If it is found necessary deviate from ATP 2 to accommodate peculiarities of a particular region such requirements should be promulgated in local commander orders or a supplement to ATP 2."[161] Supplements to Allied Tactical Publications, in fact, were issued by navies when the books did not fully meet national requirements. This practice was common; the Canadians had created a number of supplements to U.S. Navy publications in 1947 and 1948 when the RCN was adopting American communications procedures but the Allied Communication Publications were not yet written.[162]

By 1953, the Canadian, British, and American navies had invested considerable time and effort into standardizing their procedures and communications. However, all three navies were also a part of the NATO Alliance, which had its own standardization program that was run by NATO's Military Standardization Agency. This NATO agency oversaw standardization projects for navies, air forces, and armies. The tendency of the three English-speaking navies was to prepare standardization projects among themselves and then present these projects to NATO, as was the case with ATP 1 and ACP 175. However, the manner in which tripartite projects were presented to NATO could cause tension, a fact highlighted in 1952, when the Canadian director of naval standardization, Commander James V. Steele, addressed a Canadian naval aviation conference on the subject. Steele noted that there were two standardization programs, tripartite and NATO, and that the tripartite program was "more important as NATO leans heavily on Tripartite." In particular, the Army, Navy, and Air Force Boards of NATO's Military Agency for Standardization "lean very heavily on tripartite accomplishments." Steele tried to make light of the French attitude toward tripartite standardization: "There were cases [during Military Agency for Standardization meetings] of a gentleman having said, 'Honneur patrie [Honor Fatherland, part of the French navy's motto], regardless of what you have written on the subject I feel that my country must make a contribution,'" but "usually these officers were delayed with rich luncheons and by mid-afternoon the Tripartite program was found acceptable." Steele hastened to add that in reality obtaining European agreement to tripartite standards was not that easy and that "the Military Agency for Standardization had to go very cannily lest European nations stood up and declared the existence of a tripartite block against them, thus defeating the whole aim of NATO."[163]

Britain, Canada, and the United States all approached the process of tripartite standardization with different objectives and perspectives. For the British, standardization would remove the time-consuming World War II practice of modifying American equipment to meet British standards. Canada, in particular the RCN, sought to end the need to choose between British and American methods and equipment. For the American military, standardization represented a new era, one in which close peacetime cooperation with allied militaries would be the rule, rather than the exception.

While military requirements suggested the need for standardization, political concerns shaped the talks that ultimately led to the 1947 tripartite CANUKUS standardization agreement. The British wanted to pre-coordinate their views with the Canadians prior to the November 1946 conference. The Americans wanted to avoid public agreements that could be seen as undermining the UN. The Truman administration also insisted that the work of standardization proceed through independent national bodies, rejecting the idea of anything that smelled of the Combined Chiefs, whose existence caused political problems for the U.S. military. While Canadian-American defense relations caused few political issues in Washington, this was not the case in Ottawa. Prime Minister King's government wanted to ensure adequate protections for Canadian sovereignty before agreeing to Permanent Joint Board proposals for closer ties with the U.S. military.

Standardization as an ideal appealed to officers in all three navies; however, the process of standardization revealed that procedures and methods were more easily and rapidly standardized than equipment was. Efforts to develop a common sonobuoy initially floundered on technical differences as well as different methods for employing sonobuoys against submarines. These doctrinal differences highlighted the need to agree on procedures and methods before developing common pieces of equipment, the "concepts before calibers" approach. A British review of the progress of standardization in 1948, a year after the initial agreement between the tripartite nations, concluded: "It would seem standardization of techniques and tactics will be more important than standardization of equipment."[164] However, even after the three navies developed common procedures, creating standardized weapons remained a challenge, especially when the standardized weapon was to be produced in another country. As one Canadian officer later commented, standardized NATO equipment "is great so long as it is all manufactured in Toronto."[165]

The tactical and communications publications prepared by the tripartite navies in the late 1940s and 1950s would later become known as NATO publications. NATO publications, in particular ATP 1, are used by dozens of navies throughout the world today. These books allow navies with different traditions and different languages to work together in operations such as antipiracy patrols conducted off the east coast of Africa. While ATP 1 has become associated with NATO, the impetus and authors of the book came from the navies of Canada, Britain, and the United States in the aftermath of World War II. In contradiction to authors who claim the post–World War II U.S. Navy was not inclined to partner with allied navies, the creation of ATP 1 demonstrates the navy's commitment to continued close relations with the British and Canadians.

6

Training and Education

William Martin saw his opportunity. In the final war game of the U.S. Naval War College 1950–1951 class, Martin, a Royal Navy commander, played the deputy air commander on the team acting as the United States. As he examined the map of the Middle East laid out on the table, Martin's eye settled on a small city label in Iraq halfway between Baghdad and Basra, Samawah. Ten years ago, in May 1941, Martin and his squadron of aircraft had received orders to destroy the main bridge over the Euphrates, which cut Samawah in two. They had failed. Martin saw a chance to at least partially redeem that failure. He convinced the overall air commander on the American team that the bridge at Samawah must be destroyed with a nuclear bomb. At the postgame critique, Martin was invited up to the stage to explain why he wanted the bridge destroyed. He explained his history with the bridge from 1941, noting, "It is very rare in war that one gets a second chance." Martin concluded dramatically, "Today I had a second chance to destroy it, so I did." The assembled crowd of officers burst into loud cheers, and Martin returned to his seat, enjoying the acclaim.[1]

Two months later, in early June 1951, the U.S. Navy kicked the British and Canadians out of the Naval War College, though not because of Commander Martin's effort at atomic redemption. The Americans did not want to allow officers from certain NATO nations, France in particular, to attend the college and decided they could not very well tell the French no while telling the Canadians and British yes. This decision ended five years of British and Canadian officers attending the

Naval War College and reflected the two patterns of U.S. Navy relations with the RN and RCN: First, a willingness and desire in most instances to cooperate with the British and Canadians more closely than with other navies (and sometimes more closely than with the U.S. Army and Air Force), particularly in the fields of education and training. This cooperation in training and education demonstrates the U.S. Navy's pursuit of close peacetime relations with its closest allies after World War II, in contrast to those who argue that in this period the U.S. Navy was uninterested in allies. Second, an insistence that this cooperation remain secret and out of the public's eye. This second consideration reflected American political pressure: specifically, the Truman administration's desire not to be seen playing favorites and interest in not undermining the UN by creating military alliances. These twin themes shaped U.S. Navy relations with the British and Canadian navies regarding professional military education for officers, exchanges between antisubmarine training schools, and combined exercises at sea. Ties in training and education created both deep and wide naval links between the U.S. Navy and the British and Canadians. Educational exchanges gave individual officers deep experience with another navy, while combined training gave large numbers of personnel insight, though not deep knowledge, into how allied navies operated.

WAR COLLEGE EXCHANGES

In 1946, the U.S. military's education system for officers consisted of two distinct tiers of schools beyond the service academies. The lower tier consisted of staff colleges such as the Army-Navy Staff College and the Command and General Staff College, which prepared junior officers to serve on the staffs of headquarters and eventually command their own units. On the upper tier, the Army and Naval War Colleges taught midcareer officers a combination of strategic theory, American government, history, international affairs, and national security policy as preparation for further staff work or senior leadership positions. The National War College, created in 1946 in Washington, D.C., covered similar material but with a more diverse student body than either the service-centric Army or Naval War Colleges. While some army officers attended the Naval War College and vice versa, foreign officers at American war colleges were extremely rare prior to World War II. However, this pattern changed in the spring of 1946.[2]

In February 1946, the British Chiefs of Staff invited the U.S. Joint Chiefs of Staff to send American officers to attend the Imperial Defence College, the National War College's counterpart in London. The British school's student body included members of the Commonwealth but not Americans at the time. American attendance would help sustain the close relations with the U.S. military that the British chiefs wanted. The Americans recognized that accepting this invitation would lead to British officers being admitted into the National War College. The U.S. chiefs decided to accept the invitation, and by September 1946 an American presence at the Imperial Defence College was established.[3] The Joint Chiefs reasoned that they could justify British and Canadian students attending U.S. schools since the United States already had formal military relations with those countries, through the Combined Chiefs of Staff organization and the Permanent Joint Board on Defense respectively.[4]

In contrast to the National War College, the British and Canadian presence at the Naval War College extended back into the final years of World War II. In 1943, the U.S. military established the Army-Navy Staff College to prepare officers for duty on joint staffs. The college consisted of a sequence of courses held in Orlando, Florida; Newport, Rhode Island; Fort Leavenworth, Kansas; and Washington, D.C.[5] In 1945, one Royal Navy officer and one Royal Canadian Navy officer came to Newport as a part of the Army-Navy Staff College student body. The two students were British Commander Royston H. Wright and Canadian Commodore Horatio N. Lay.[6] The president of the Naval War College, Admiral Raymond Spruance, wrote to Admiral Nimitz in June 1946 to express his desire to have British officers attend the Naval War College.[7] When British officers arrived in Newport as students in 1947, they were the "first and only non-American officers to attend this course since two Swedes and a Dane had come to the College in 1894–95."[8] Wright and Lay inaugurated a five-year period from 1946 to 1951 during which British and Canadian officers attended American war colleges as the only foreign students allowed.[9] While other nations such as Australia could send officers to staff colleges and the Industrial College of the Armed Forces, only the British and Canadians were invited to attend the war colleges.[10]

The Royal Navy viewed the presence of British officers at American war colleges as an essential component of Anglo-American relations. British officers at Newport or at the National War College in Washington made connections with fellow students who often went on to senior command positions. These connections and friendships could play important roles in smoothing relations between the two navies. In 1951, for example, Commander Alexander B. Fraser-Harris became the senior Canadian naval officer in Korea and found that several of his friends from the 1950 class at the Naval War College were also in positions of leadership. Canadian Captain James C. Hibbard recalled that attending the National War College from 1949 to 1950 was a "wonderful experience" because he met so many of the people he saw during his later inspection trip to Korea.[11] Similar to attachés and liaison positions, educational exchanges built personal relationships that smoothed navy-to-navy relations.

The Admiralty and the Royal Canadian Navy also used the American schools to give their officers a foundation for future assignments involving close contact with the United States. For example, Commodore Lay, who attended the Army-Navy Staff College in 1945–1946, later served as the Canadian naval attaché from 1949 to 1952. Commander John Bush went to the newly renamed Armed Forces Staff College in Norfolk during 1948–1949 and returned to the United States in 1963 as the British naval attaché.[12]

In addition to preparing officers for future contact with the Americans, the Admiralty viewed attendance at war colleges as a means of bringing British and American strategic and operational thinking into alignment through personal relationships. Admiral Philip Vian, the deputy chief of the Naval Staff, noted that through officer exchanges at war colleges "we may expect to achieve some degree of standardization in the strategical and tactical spheres."[13] Finally, the Royal Navy wanted British officers to serve as ambassadors who were "capable of presenting the British idea to an American audience" as one report noted.[14] To accomplish this last goal, the British took pains to send only "really high caliber" officers, an approach strongly supported by the British staff mission in Washington.[15]

The British and Canadian students at American colleges received a warm welcome and reported positively about their experiences, both privately and through official channels. Three British officers attended the 1946–1947 course at the Armed Forces Staff College, where the commandant and faculty "went out of their way" to explain the facilities, the student body social life, and the school.[16] Initially, the British students were not allowed to see classified material, but early in the course the War Department ordered that they be given access to documents classified up to secret, which covered the vast majority of the material used at the school.[17] According to the British officers' final report, the school's administration went even further, making "every attempt to give complete freedom [of access] without deliberately transgressing official rules" and even turning "a blind eye on occasions; for British students are permitted to make use of publications theoretically banned from them provided they did not personally sign for them in the Library."[18] At one of the war games at the Naval War College in early 1947, British Commander T. V. Briggs served as the fleet commander during the game. This was a rare honor and "was very liberal when one remembers that a very large number of other officers in the course have not had similar opportunities."[19] Briggs reported, "I have been given the run of everything with no restrictions, and in fact treated like a brother."[20] At the working level, the British and Canadian students found school staffs and faculty supportive of their presence.

In addition to commenting on American kindness, British and Canadian officers noted in their reports how frequently they were called upon to speak on behalf of their native country. The American students tended to view their foreign counterparts as walking encyclopedias on their home nation. One report noted that "the subjects upon which opinions have to be expressed are most diverse," ranging from government policy to military affairs to economics. As a result, the course led "the British officer to give detailed thought upon many matters connected with his own country which he would normally take for granted."[21] The British students, however, sometimes felt they lacked the breadth of knowledge to handle the range of American questions, and as a result the British services arranged for special briefings in both London and Washington for students attending American schools.[22] Such briefings also proved useful for liaison personnel, who benefited from being able to answer an array of questions.

Reports from British officers who had finished courses at these American schools glowed with praise. Commander Briggs concluded that "I have made many friends and have a lasting friendship and high respect for the U.S. Navy."[23] Commander Martin later wrote that "this course at the U.S. Naval War College was the most fascinating experience in my whole career . . . and was in many ways superior to the R.N. Staff Course I attended in 1945."[24] American officers at British schools did notice that U.S. schools had longer working hours, a view shared by Vice Admiral Hill, the commandant of the National War College.[25] One officer who attended the National War College and then the Imperial Defence College later remembered: "I felt that in American fashion, if we had a spare 15 minutes in Washington, we had to do something. Whereas in London it was much more leisurely, but [as] you came along, you realized that you were learning a lot just the same."[26]

In addition to supplying students for the American war colleges, the British and Canadians sent senior officers to speak and answer questions. Both naval attachés in Washington spoke at Newport at least once a year, as did the Royal Navy's first sea lord or the Canadian chief of Naval Staff whenever they visited America.

These visits by senior officers also gave the British and Canadians a window into American naval thinking. The head of the Canadian naval mission in Washington, Commodore Morson Medland, went to Newport in March 1953 for five days to attend lectures and speak. He later reported to Ottawa that "on one occasion a self-appointed spokesman for some seventeen USAF [U.S. Air Force] students differed sharply with the lectures on a question of air power and it appeared from nearby commentary that the lecturer had the support of the majority of students; an indication that there is still a curtain between some elements of Air Force and Navy thinking regarding air power." Medland also suggested in his report that two of the American admirals at Newport seemed inclined to take for granted Canadian support for American foreign policy.[27] By the summer of 1951, seventeen British and Canadian officers had completed a course at the Naval War College. However, their access to American war colleges was already in jeopardy.

In April 1950, the French representatives on NATO's Standing Group asked permission for French officers to attend British and American military schools, specifically the Imperial Defence College and the National War College.[28] The British and American Chiefs of Staff did not want French officers at these schools due to security concerns. One senior American naval officer later recalled: "We knew that anything secret or confidential that the French knew or heard about, the Russians had it right away."[29] While the British were willing to reject the French request, the U.S. Joint Chiefs decided they could not allow British and Canadian officers to attend while keeping out French officers. As a result, the Americans decided to no longer allow any foreign students at the National War College in Washington, D.C., or the Industrial

College of the Armed Forces and to withdraw the American students from the Imperial Defence College in London.[30] The British protested this decision unsuccessfully, and a British Chiefs of Staff report concluded that the Americans had "imposed upon themselves a self-denying ordinance merely to please the French."[31] Anxious to avoid charges of favoritism, the U.S. military chose to curtail the most visible educational links: those in national capitals.

The next year, the news from America got worse. In early June 1951, the British Naval Staff in Washington received a letter from Admiral Forrest Sherman, the chief of naval operations, stating that the U.S. Navy had just decided "to forbid attendance at the [Naval War] College of all foreign nations."[32] Sherman's letter explained that under the 1946 McMahon Act, the U.S. government could not release atomic energy information to foreigners and that the courses at the Naval War College frequently referenced restricted nuclear information.[33] Efforts to change the U.S. Navy's position revealed that the decision applied to all the senior military schools, including the Army War College. The British could still send officers to the lower-level Army-Navy Staff College as could other NATO nations, but they would not be allowed at the institutions teaching strategy and national policy.

Royal Navy leaders were furious. One officer angrily noted, "We welcome them to everything we have to offer here; they treat us as acquaintances rather than close friends."[34] The British went out of their way to send only high-caliber officers to the American schools and now they were being tossed aside. The American argument about restricted atomic energy information seemed to be just an "excuse," especially after the Americans refused a British offer to have their students withdraw from discussions involving restricted atomic information.[35] The law prohibiting foreign access to this information, the McMahon Act, had been in force for five years, and during that time British officers at American war colleges had accessed classified data including war plans and sometimes nuclear information.[36] The British concluded that the decision stemmed from American concerns about being seen to show favoritism. Oliver Franks, the British ambassador to the United States from 1948 to 1952, wrote to a fellow diplomat in London that there was nothing to be done about the decision to exclude British officers. Franks accurately summarized the situation: "The position is that the Americans are willing and, for the most part, anxious to do all sorts of things with us which recognize the special relations between Britain and the United States, on one condition: these activities must be covert. Overtly they are not prepared to differentiate between the various NATO countries and in this context they always have the French particularly in mind."[37]

The American decisions to allow British and Canadian officers into their war colleges and then to remove them illustrates both sides of the U.S. Navy's cooperative approach with the British and Canadians. The U.S. Navy's leadership valued close ties with the British and Canadians but sought to avoid the public criticism and possible damage to relations with other navies of appearing to play favorites. In particular, American and British naval officers tended to view the French military as overly sensitive and insecure during this period.[38] As a result, the Americans were loath to take actions that could be seen as slights to France.[39]

Similar concerns about being seen to play favorites led the Joint Chiefs to insist in 1948 on the removal of Canada along with Australia and New Zealand from the Combined Communications Board (discussed in chapter 2). As noted above, Canada had to wage a twenty-month campaign to overturn this decision against largely British resistance. For their part, the British did not want to be seen as favoring one Dominion over another in military communication matters.

ANTISUBMARINE SCHOOLS

In contrast to the British and Canadian experience at American war colleges, antisubmarine warfare (ASW) training schools in all three navies created an interconnected network beginning in 1946. These connections steadily expanded throughout the late 1940s and came to include instructor exchanges as well as visits by ships and aircraft for operational training. The exchanges between schools allowed officers to see how the other two navies approached the problem of antisubmarine warfare. Links in ASW training reflected both the influence of the Soviet naval threat and the U.S. Navy's postwar interest in retaining links with the British and Canadians. The Americans were very impressed with the British approach to training, and observers called for the U.S. Navy to replicate the Royal Navy's ASW school. The British and Canadians, however, often concluded that the U.S. Navy's approach to hunting submarines emphasized the role of equipment without sufficient attention to how best to use it.

During World War II, the Royal Navy trained ships and escort groups in ASW through a sea-and-air Anti-Submarine School in Northern Ireland and through the Western Approaches Tactical Unit at Liverpool, which also developed new tactics. In September 1945, the Admiralty transferred the tactical development function to the school while renaming the facility the Joint Anti-Submarine School (JASS), located at Londonderry in Northern Ireland.[40] A Royal Navy captain and a Royal Air Force group captain jointly ran the school, reporting to the Joint Sea/Air Warfare Committee, composed of both Admiralty and Air Ministry representatives.[41] This administrative structure reflected the allocation of aerial assets in the British military. In Britain, the Royal Air Force controlled land-based antisubmarine planes, while the Royal Navy commanded carrier aviation. In contrast, the U.S. Navy controlled both land-based and carrier-based ASW planes.

The primary course offered at the Londonderry antisubmarine school, the joint unit course, ran for six weeks. The course provided basic and advanced training in ASW tactics for ships and aircraft that had already completed their basic unit training. Several surface ships were assigned to the school to participate in the training exercises along with submarines that rotated in and out of the school.[42] The presence of ships, aircraft, and submarines in JASS exercises brought together all the assets and personnel involved in hunting submarines. At the time, officers tended to divide antisubmarine operations into two categories: operations before the escorts and aircraft made contact with the submarine and efforts to drive off or destroy the submarine once contact was made. The instruction and exercises at JASS focused primarily on the first category.[43] In the Royal Navy's training system ship and aircraft crews learned how to employ their weapons and sensors to attack submarines prior to attending JASS.[44]

When the Canadian navy and air force established their ASW school in October 1950 in Halifax, Nova Scotia, they modeled their Joint Maritime Warfare School (JMWS) after the British school at Londonderry.[45] The origins of the Canadian school lay in a training center established in Halifax in 1944 to provide training in antisubmarine warfare.[46] The curriculum and tactics taught in Halifax were the same as in Londonderry, though the Canadian school benefited from being colocated in Halifax with the Canadian Atlantic squadron. As a result the school enjoyed regular access to the ships and personnel of the squadron.[47] By 1951, the Canadians had secured the appointment of an American commander with submarine experience to their school as well as British personnel to provide additional technical expertise.[48] Both the British JASS and the Canadian JMWS provided ASW training and developed tactics.[49]

In contrast to the British and Canadian approach, the U.S. Navy did not have one centralized location to conduct ASW training and develop tactical doctrine. The navy spread these functions over several different organizations. At the U.S. Navy base at Norfolk, Virginia, the Fleet Airborne Electronics Training Unit (FAETU) taught aircrews about airborne ASW equipment while the Operational Development Force (OPDEVFOR) developed ASW tactics. At Key West, Florida, a detachment of OPDEVFOR tested new ASW equipment for surface ships and also worked on new tactics. New airborne ASW equipment was evaluated and tested by a special aviation squadron also located at Key West. Finally, the Atlantic Fleet Sonar School at Key West trained ship crews in sonar equipment, while the Pacific Fleet Sonar School performed the same function at San Diego, California.[50] In order to keep all these various organizations informed of each other's work, the U.S. Navy held annual conferences in Washington, D.C., beginning in June 1946.[51] British and Canadian officers were routinely invited to attend and address these antisubmarine warfare conferences, a reflection on how the Soviet submarine threat drew the ASW communities of the three navies together.[52]

At the first of these conferences in June 1946, senior U.S. Navy officers discussed the current status of antisubmarine warfare, including cooperation with the British. Rear Admiral Jerauld Wright told the attendees that "it is an accepted principle that the British are much more anti-submarine conscious than we are," and representatives from the Bureau of Ordnance spoke out in support of closer ASW cooperation with the Royal Navy.[53] Based on the conference's recommendation, Admiral Nimitz requested and received authority from the secretary of the navy to freely exchange with the Royal Navy "all anti-submarine information, including material, research and development, training and tactics."[54] Two months later Nimitz secured approval to include the Canadians in this exchange.[55] The navy classified the existence of these exchanges in order to prevent other navies from asking for similar treatment.[56] These information-sharing agreements demonstrated the U.S. Navy's willingness to take formal steps to maintain close relations with the British and Canadians as early as the summer of 1946.

However, the matter of closer cooperation in training lay dormant until 1947, when two groups of American officers visited the United Kingdom to discuss cooperation in undersea warfare. The first group, led by Rear Admiral Charles Styer, toured Royal Navy facilities in January and February.[57] This first visit focused on establishing connections between officers performing similar functions on both sides of the Atlantic.[58] The group visited the Joint Anti-Submarine School at Londonderry and concluded that the British "facilities for tactical development are far superior to those employed by our own service."[59]

The second visit, which occurred in August and September 1947, also included a trip to JASS at Londonderry and extensive talks with the school's staff. The U.S. Navy representatives also came away from their visit very impressed.[60] They praised the school's program for acquainting air, surface, and submarine personnel with each other's equipment and capabilities and then building on this foundation through exercises at sea. The Americans also applauded the school's practice of holding postexercise conferences immediately after the exercise while the experience was still fresh for the participants.[61] Captain Elton Grenfell, the group leader, wrote that "I consider this to be an outstanding school" and that it "should be copied as soon as a similar school can be established within our own Navy."[62] The second group's final report, widely circulated throughout the U.S. Navy, concluded that "too much cannot be said" for JASS and recommended that the U.S. Navy establish its own school "using the curriculum" of JASS as a guide.[63] These two visits to Britain created advocates for closer Anglo-American naval relations within the U.S. Navy staff in Washington, D.C.

In the aftermath of these two visits, the U.S. Navy's interest in JASS steadily grew. By March 1948 American aircraft and destroyers regularly visited JASS for training.[64] A short visit to the school in April 1948 by the naval attaché in London generated another widely read report that praised the instruction as "well planned" and the exercises as "very thoroughly worked out."[65] In June 1948, the two navies finalized arrangements creating a liaison position for a U.S. Navy officer on the staff of JASS. Lieutenant Commander Gordon W. Smith, a naval aviator who had flown antisubmarine aircraft out of England during World War II, was the first American officer assigned to this position.[66] American officers began attending JASS as students in the summer of 1948 for the two-week joint tactical course, which emphasized

ASW tactics, tabletop war games, and exercises.[67] Beginning in the summer of 1948, the U.S. Navy sent one to three officers to almost every joint tactical course, where they learned alongside British, Canadian, and Australian students.[68]

Reports from American personnel who visited Londonderry regularly praised the course and often requested more time at the school to improve their ASW skills.[69] A U.S. Navy pilot on exchange duty with the Royal Navy, Lieutenant Commander Ernest H. Leggett, thought the course at JASS was "well organized, extremely interesting, and all in all perhaps the best course I have ever attended."[70] Another American pilot attended JASS and found the course "a logical follow-up of the Key West course," a reference to the U.S. Navy's ASW training course in Key West, Florida.[71] He appreciated the school's emphasis on realistic exercises based on equipment currently in use, rather than "dreaming about future developments." His report noted that the instruction "was uniformly excellent" and that the instructors and students focused on their work, in contrast to the "'breeze' attitude sometimes displayed in similar schools of our own."[72] Captain George P. Unmacht of the American destroyer *Waldron* found that "the liaison [at JASS] between RAF, RN, and US surface vessels was as close as that which normally exists in a similar all-US Force."[73] The regular American presence at Londonderry created within the U.S. Navy ASW community a growing body of advocates of continuing ties with the British.

For their part, the Royal Navy found the steady American presence at JASS beneficial. The directors reported that "the exchange of ideas with these American officers has been of immense value," noting that "American thought, though in many cases different from British, is usually complementary."[74] Visits by American ships and aircraft also gave the Royal Navy opportunities to observe the capabilities of the latest U.S. Navy hardware and vice versa.[75] In May and June 1948, the *Trumpetfish*, one of the first American submarines to be modified using German technology from World War II, came to Londonderry to exercise with the escorts assigned to JASS. The exercises with *Trumpetfish* clearly demonstrated the challenge posed by high-speed submarines, as in one exercise *Trumpetfish* attacked and sank all of the British escorts.[76] During 1949 and 1950, fast American submarines visited Londonderry twice for exercises, including one visit in 1949 by four USN submarines. [77] The British clearly demonstrated the importance they placed on having the U.S. Navy at JASS when expanding RAF training needs threatened to overwhelm the school's facilities. As the Admiralty and the Air Ministry worked to solve this problem, they decided that RAF training slots at Londonderry would be sacrificed in order to continue to offer slots to U.S. Navy aircraft.[78] This commitment to prioritize the American presence at JASS over British training needs illustrated the importance the British placed on training cooperation with the U.S. Navy.

One of the more important American visits to JASS took place in May 1953, when a U.S. Navy task force visited the school. The group consisted of the escort aircraft carrier *Block Island*, three destroyers, and a submarine, all commanded by Rear Admiral Ira E. Hobbs. The purpose of the visit was to demonstrate American hunter-killer (HUK) techniques, but the exercises turned into a broader exchange of ideas. For their part, the JASS staff welcomed visits by aircraft carriers from Canada or the United States since Royal Navy carriers were in high demand and short supply.[79]

The visit began with two days of instruction and introductory lectures by the JASS staff on the Royal Navy's approach to ASW as well as demonstrations by British ships and aircraft. In the first exercise, one American and two British submarines tried to attack a convoy defended by the *Block Island*, three American destroyers, and four British frigates. The escorts achieved some success as the submarines only made one attack on the convoy and that was from a long distance and therefore less accurate. Patrols by *Block Island*'s Avenger aircraft equipped with airborne radar located the British submarines on several occasions, leading to successful attacks by aircraft or surface escorts. Admiral Hobbs found the postexercise critique "most instructive" since the school staff laid out the actual movements of all the ships and submarines on the floor for all to see. Hobbs concluded that "the idea of a critique is a good one" and recommended the U.S. Navy adopt this approach "instead of writing these long reports."[80]

After this first exercise, which was prepared by the JASS staff, two further exercises took place, both prepared by Admiral Hobbs's staff. In the second exercise the three submarines were lined up on a starting line with twenty miles separation between them and then ordered to move to a much shorter finishing line, which had the effect of gradually drawing the submarines closer together. The *Block Island* and the escorts started the exercise on the starting line and were provided with the location of the finishing line. As a result, the American aircraft easily detected the British submarines. The captain of the *Block Island* reported, "We beat the hell out of the subs," but the British were not impressed.[81] A JASS observer on *Block Island* commented that "as an exercise its conception was so elementary that it gave the command very little cause for thought."[82] From the British perspective, the carrier and escorts had all the advantages in this second exercise, and a failure to find the submarines would have been embarrassing. In the final exercise, *Block Island* and the escorts were not given the location of the submarines, and this lack of intelligence, combined with rougher seas that limited the effectiveness of airborne radar, resulted in all of the submarines avoiding detection.

After observing the American performance in these exercises, the JASS staff found the American approach to ASW wanting. In their confidential report sent only to British and Canadian officers, the British observers concluded that the Americans "place complete reliance on the detecting devices," namely their airborne radar. As a result, the Americans had done little to prepare "a sound tactical approach to the problem" and failed to alter their plans to suit changing conditions, such as the weather. Observers on *Block Island* found that Admiral Hobbs "was primarily interested in the mechanics of the flying operations" instead of providing direction to the escorts. The observer's report concluded, "In brief, the carrier resembled the excellent coca-cola machine reposing in crimson splendor in the wardroom. Provided one inserted a nickel, the appropriate measure of aircraft would be delivered at the right time on the designated patrol and the screen would be oriented to cover the course of the carrier. A bent coin upset the whole works." The observers found American equipment "first class," but viewed the performance of the Americans as an indication of insufficient thinking about how to employ their material. "Instead of mastering what they have, they are rapidly becoming mastered by the material." American officers' informal discussions with the JASS staff shared this interpretation: "We have the equipment but you have the know how."[83]

The American reaction to the exercises varied. The *Block Island*'s captain, James Flatley, concluded that the American performance "has been little short of perfection."[84] In contrast, Admiral Hobbs saw more to criticize. He found the command centers of the American ships much noisier than British ships and American radio discipline quite poor.[85] Hobbs decided that "the Royal Navy has done a great deal more thinking about the overall ASW problem" compared with the U.S. Navy. He also found the JASS focus on antisubmarine operations *prior* to contact impressive and lamented the lack of a "similar institution in our own Navy."[86] In his most damning assessment of the American performance in hunter killer operations, Hobbs found that "while examining the British concept of H/K [hunter-killer] it was found that our own concept was not clear to me." "This is quite a statement," as one Canadian officer wrote in the margin.[87] The admiral commanding one of the U.S. Navy's hunter killer groups admitted that his navy had not clearly defined the fundamentals of his group's operations. As a result of increasing American interest in JASS and consistent British efforts to open the school to the Americans, the U.S. Navy's presence in Londonderry steadily increased from 1947 to 1953. In addition to being exposed to the school's renowned mixing of air, surface, and subsurface personnel, the Americans in attendance praised the school's approach to antisubmarine warfare, especially the focus on operations before contact. Furthermore, veterans of JASS frequently left Londonderry with a new commitment to greater cooperation with the Royal Navy. Their reports called for greater contact and cooperation with the British while also recommending that the U.S. Navy create its own version of JASS.

While the primary benefit of JASS to the U.S. Navy lay in tactics and doctrine, the British clearly valued learning about American thinking in ASW. However, in terms of tactics, the JASS staff generally felt that they had more to offer to and less to gain from the Americans. The roles in the realm of equipment were reversed. U.S. Navy visitors to JASS often brought along newly installed sonar gear or radar that the Royal Navy eagerly wanted to examine. This British focus on keeping up with American material developments also shaped the Royal Navy's relationship with ASW schools in the United States, such as the Fleet Sonar School in Key West, Florida.

The Royal Navy's presence at Key West dated back to 1942, when a British section of the Fleet Sound School opened with a British instructor on the school staff. By the end of World War II the renamed Fleet Sonar School had adopted many of the Royal Navy's procedures for escorting convoys and attacking submarines.[88] Postwar, the Royal Navy's interest in American ASW at Key West, Florida, focused on keeping abreast of advances in American equipment.[89]

By 1948, the U.S. Navy had modified several submarines to take advantage of equipment and designs drawn from captured German U-boats.[90] The Royal Navy's limited funds had so far precluded such modifications to British submarines. In an effort to gain some experience operating against these high-speed submarines, in late 1947 the British naval staff in Washington asked the U.S. Navy if two British escorts could be sent to Key West to exercise with one of the upgraded American submarines. The British appreciated the American willingness to place one of their rare modified submarines at the Royal Navy's disposal, noting that the American decision "represents a considerable concession on their part."[91] British destroyers *Battleaxe* and *Crossbow* exercised with several American submarines and destroyers in July 1948, and the British commander was pleased with the results, which allowed the British to compare their new sonar equipment with the American equivalent.[92]

In addition to testing their new equipment, the British also used Key West to provide basic ASW training for their frigates and destroyers that were assigned to the America and West Indies Station.[93] This arrangement mirrored the ASW training provided to U.S. Navy destroyers assigned to northern Europe by the Joint Anti-Submarine School. To facilitate links between ASW schools, the British requested and received approval for the Londonderry, Halifax, and Key West school staffs to write directly to each other on technical subjects without going through their respective Offices of Naval Intelligence.[94] In the summer of 1949, the British also established an exchange project for instructors at ASW schools. An American officer joined the staff of the Royal Navy's sonar school, and one British officer became part of the staff at each of the Fleet Sonar Schools, Key West and San Diego.[95] The British, Canadians, and Americans even discussed creating a combined ASW school for the use of all three navies, but talks broke down in August 1950 over the location of the new school. The British proposed Maine due to its proximity to North Atlantic convoy routes, while the Americans wanted southern Florida because of their existing facilities there.[96]

While British relations with U.S. Navy ASW schools emphasized equipment testing over tactical development, the Canadians sought both training and technical information from the Americans. Canadian officers regularly visited Key West to stay abreast of American technological innovations in torpedoes, sonobuoys, sonar, radar, and other antisubmarine equipment.[97] The RCN also made extensive use of the training facilities at Key West. The superior acoustic conditions in the Caribbean waters off Key West gave the Canadians the opportunity to train sonar operators away from the poor conditions prevailing off Halifax. Accordingly, Canadian sonar personnel honed their skills tracking U.S. submarines on Canadian escorts that visited Key West several times a year.[98] The RCN also received permission from the U.S. Navy in late 1951 to station a liaison officer at Key West year round.[99] As the Canadians established a more permanent presence at Key West, they learned more about U.S. Navy training practices. For example, the Fleet Sonar School provided only six hours of at-sea time for U.S. Navy sonar operators in training compared to ten days at sea in the Royal Canadian Navy.[100] Additionally, the Canadian officer exchange program expanded in 1953 to include Canadian officers at the Fleet Sonar School in San Diego and an American officer at the Joint Maritime Warfare School in Halifax.[101]

In addition to building a presence at Key West, the Canadians also worked to establish a relationship with the Fleet Airborne Electronics Training Unit (FAETU) at Norfolk, Virginia, beginning in 1950. In March, the Canadians concluded an agreement with the Americans to buy seventy-five U.S. Navy Avenger antisubmarine planes at a steep discount (discussed in chapter 4).[102] Since FAETU tested new equipment and trained operators on its use in airborne ASW planes, a connection with this organization would give the Canadians advance information about new American equipment that might be purchased for their recently acquired Avengers.[103] Visits to FAETU therefore allowed Canadian personnel to identify equipment, observe tests and evaluations, and then make an informed decision about whether to make a purchase.[104]

Unfortunately, Canadian officers who attended the FAETU course for pilots and observers found it wanting in several respects. First, the course was designed for junior officers with limited flying experience. A significant portion of the course covered basic flight instruction such as navigation and aerology.[105] As a result, students only began to learn about ASW tactics late in the course and had limited opportunities to practice these tactics while airborne.[106] Canadian students reported that the technical instruction in the equipment given by enlisted personnel was "very good" but that the officers who taught tactics simply read out of the ASW books in response to questions.[107] The school's access to "a vast supply of ground training equipment" aided instruction, but the tactical training was "something of a cinderella" that received insufficient support from the unit's leadership.[108] One officer who took the FAETU course concluded:

The United States Navy and in particular FAETU reminds me of a 1950 "Golden Jubilee" Packard with ultramatic drive. It is an extremely fine piece of machinery with loads of power under the hood. With a mighty bellow, gears whirring, lights flashing, and bells ringing it is away at a slow crawl. There seems to be just a bit of trouble in getting all that power to the wheels. The USN has a generous supply of the latest and in most cases the best equipment but the training given is most elementary.[109]

Overall, Canadian visitors to FAETU recommended that Canadian aircrews not come to Norfolk for tactical training in antisubmarine warfare but that the RCN should purchase American equipment.[110] These recommendations stemmed in part from the deficiencies the Canadians saw in the FAETU coursework but also from an appreciation for the British approach to ASW training. Canadian officers with experience in both British and American ASW training consistently recommended that the RCN continue to send its personnel to Londonderry, not America, for ASW training.[111] One Canadian officer compared each navy's approach to ASW training as follows: "A comparison between UK and US methods regarding policy may be derived from the saying 'Give us the tools to do the job.' Whereas the UK, places emphasis on the 'job' the US discusses the 'tools' at great length. For example, where it would be sufficient to discuss say the capabilities, limitations, and tactical use of MAD, hours were spent delving into the intricate electrical circuits."[112]

The relationships created between the Canadian, British, and American ASW training establishments between 1945 and 1953 naturally led officers in each navy to make comparisons. In particular, Canadian officers often found themselves well positioned to make comparisons between the two large navies on either side of the Atlantic. Canadian and American officers praised the well-defined British approach to antisubmarine warfare backed by a practical and effective training program at Londonderry. In contrast, the U.S. Navy lacked such a school. The RCN followed the Londonderry model, though resource limitations reduced the scale and frequency of at-sea exercises. Both the Canadians and the British valued their access to American technological developments and used the Americans' progress as a means of gauging the effectiveness of their own projects. The exchanges and visits to each other's training establishments allowed officers from all three navies to meet their counterparts and build relationships. Often, the officers who visited foreign schools returned to their fleet as strong advocates for closer cooperation between the three navies.

These three navies provided each other a level of access to ASW training schools not afforded to other allied fleets, even those in the NATO alliance. In mid-1951, for instance, the Royal Navy decided to allow NATO ships to take part in JASS exercises but excluded them from the coursework due to security concerns. A British report on this topic concluded with a short note: "There are, of course, no security restrictions on American, British, and Canadian units exercising at Londonderry."[113]

COMBINED EXERCISES

Just as exchanges and visits between ASW schools created relationships between counterparts, so did combined exercises, though on a much larger scale. When the two U.S. Navy destroyers typically assigned to northern Europe visited Londonderry, approximately forty officers and just under five hundred sailors could observe British ASW methods. When British, American, and Canadian task forces operated together, thousands of officers and sailors gained experience working with another navy.

Prior to World War II, U.S. Navy exercises did not involve foreign nations. The navy's most important annual exercise in the interwar years, the Fleet Problems, consisted of only American units.[114] In the aftermath of World War II and in light of the navy's extensive wartime operations in conjunction with allied navies, the U.S. Navy began exercising with foreign navies on a regular basis, in particular the British and Canadian navies.

Ideally, the ships participating in operational exercises would be manned by personnel fully trained in their respective tasks and welded together as a fighting unit through significant basic training and experience operating together. This happy ideal was rarely reflected in reality. High personnel turnover, insufficient time and money allotted for training, and regular deployments all reduced the skill levels of warship crews. As a result, few if any group of warships in the British, Canadian, and American navies could reach and maintain proficiency in all the fields of naval warfare. Crews in warships needed to practice basic skills constantly, and so operational exercises frequently involved some level of scripted maneuvers, which made them less realistic.

Combined naval exercises slowly grew in frequency in the second half of the 1940s. The demands of demobilization, the movement of large portions of the fleet into reserve, and the need to bring the troops home occupied the attention of all three navies in 1945 and well into 1946. British and American ships occasionally trained together in the Mediterranean beginning in 1946. Naval forces from all three navies assigned to the occupation of Japan took part in a few small exercises in the summer of 1947, and by 1948 Canadian surface ships on the west coast of Canada exercised regularly with U.S. Navy units stationed in the state of Washington.[115] By November 1947, Washington and Ottawa granted their respective fleet commanders the authority to arrange basic training exercises without reference to higher authority.[116] Anglo-American exercises began to occur with increasing frequency after June 1948 when the chief of naval operations gave American fleet commanders the authority to work directly with their British counterparts to plan and conduct "minor combined exercises."[117] The letter granting the additional authority also noted that the existence of this authority was classified top secret and that "no publicity is desired" regarding combined exercises.[118] Delegating authority to fleet commanders to arrange exercises with their counterparts helped reduce the potential for political concerns to upset combined training opportunities. Delegation also eased the process of setting up combined exercises since fleet commanders did not have to wait for approval from their national naval headquarters.

Concerns over publicity remained a constant theme for American naval commanders. American officers feared that if information about their increasingly frequent exercises with British and Canadian forces became public the U.S. Navy could be accused of forming a de facto peacetime military alliance. As early as December 1946, senior American commanders in Europe complained that the press tended to "discover and over-emphasize" any coordination or combined exercises involving British and American ships in the Mediterranean.[119] Visits by American ships to British or Canadian ports could be announced since the U.S. Navy visited ports in a number of countries, but the U.S. Navy classified combined exercises as confidential information.[120] The Canadian navy took these American restrictions very seriously and strongly complained when the Department for External Affairs in

October 1948 issued an unauthorized press release announcing an upcoming exercise in the Pacific:

The recent press release giving an outline of the exercises taking place between USN and RCN units in the Pacific has served to establish with both press and public, the fact that exercises on a noticeable scale, including anti-submarine exercise, are being carried out jointly by the two navies. Hitherto every care has been taken to prevent any publicity appearing regarding such joint efforts, in particular the periodical anti-submarine exercises in eastern and western coastal waters.[121]

British commanders shared American concerns about exercise publicity. The commander in chief of the Mediterranean Fleet expressed his relief in 1949 when U.S. Navy exercises around Malta became so commonplace that they no longer made the news.[122]

The establishment of NATO in 1949 only cemented the special status of the British and Canadian navies in American eyes. The chief of naval operations established exercise policy regarding NATO in May 1950. The Americans expected "numerous requests" from NATO navies for combined exercises with U.S. naval forces but suspected that the "frequency and extent of such operations" could reduce American naval readiness. As a result, the CNO decided that his office must review all requests from NATO navies for combined exercises. Furthermore, exercises would be granted only if they were in support of NATO plans and were not an "unwarranted expense," a broad statement designed to give the CNO maximum discretion in reviewing exercise requests. The two exceptions to this new rule were the Royal Navy and Royal Canadian Navy, where fleet commanders could still schedule minor training exercises on their own. The policy itself was classified secret and marked as "U.S. Eyes Only."[123] This policy clearly established two tiers of foreign navies. NATO navies required permission from the Navy Department to hold exercises with American forces, while fleet commanders could arrange exercises on their own with the British and Canadians. In practice, exercises with the RN and RCN were frequently arranged at an even lower level since both the Atlantic and Pacific Fleets authorized their subordinates to make exercise arrangements. Clearly, U.S. Navy exercise policy favored exercises with the British and Canadians, though the Americans made sure that this favoritism remained out of the public eye.

The large number of U.S. Navy exercises with the British and Canadians precludes discussion of more than a handful: Caribex 50, Mainbrace in 1952, and an exercise in the Pacific in March 1950. Exercise Caribex 50 took place in the spring of 1950 in the Caribbean Sea and off the American eastern seaboard. The Canadian carrier *Magnificent* escorted by one Canadian destroyer and several ships from the Royal Navy's America and West Indies Squadron opposed an American task force composed of the carriers *Philippine Sea* and *Wright*, the battleship *Missouri*, and several escorting cruisers and destroyers. The Canadian naval presence in the Caribbean for winter exercises dated back to the 1930s as part of an effort to train in better weather conditions.[124]

The exercise began on March 16, 1950, with each force searching for the other. A reconnaissance flight from *Magnificent* found the American force and avoided being detected by American radar by flying at very low altitude. The Canadian force launched an air strike of seven attack aircraft and successfully avoided the American Combat Air Patrol (CAP). While *Magnificent* launched a second air strike, the fighter direction officer, a Lieutenant John R. Doull, on the Canadian carrier discovered that he could pick up the transmissions of the American fighter direction officer on the *Philippine Sea*. Doull had spent the day before the exercise listening to the American task force's radio procedures and call signs. As the second Canadian strike approached the American force, Doull began issuing orders to the American Bearcat fighters, directing them to head off in a direction that took them away from the approaching Canadian aircraft. The senior American fighter pilot requested clarifying instructions as he was receiving contradictory instructions from Doull and the officer on the *Philippine Sea*. Doull firmly ordered that his instructions be obeyed and one of the pilots in the Canadian strike later remembered the result: "As our force approached the US fleet, we were very surprised to see a large swarm of Bearcats turning away from us." The umpires ruled that the resulting Canadian attack damaged the three largest American warships, *Philippine Sea*, *Wright*, and *Missouri*.[125] An American report on this portion of the exercise simply noted "confusion on the air control frequency."[126]

After these initial Canadian successes, the American force responded with a large air strike of fifty aircraft, more than twice the size of *Magnificent*'s air group. Although Doull provided the defending Canadian fighters with a good vector to intercept the Americans, the U.S. Navy aircraft were significantly faster than the Canadian aircraft and breezed past the defenders. The Americans then carried out a "very well timed and executed" dive-bombing attack, according to a Canadian report, damaging if not sinking *Magnificent*.[127]

After this exchange of air strikes, the two task forces merged into a single unit and the next day launched a combined air strike on the American base at Guantanamo Bay. The Americans and Canadians then allowed their fighter direction officers to control the other nation's fighters in interception exercises.[128] The combined force then headed north along the U.S. East Coast opposed by eleven USN submarines. Continuous patrols by carrier and land-based aircraft kept the submarines submerged for most of the exercise, and as a result the submariners made only one successful attack, on the British and Canadian carrier group.[129] After this antisubmarine phase of the exercise, the British and Canadian ships departed.[130]

In Caribex 50, the Americans, British, and Canadians practiced basic skills required to effectively operate aircraft at sea: flying search missions, attacking warship targets, and defending a task force against air attack. The exercise scenario resembled several of the naval battles of World War II in the Pacific where carrier forces used their aircraft to first find and then attack each other, such as at the Battle of the Coral Sea or the Battle of the Philippine Sea. The Canadians thought the exercise provided "great value" since their ships could operate with and against a large fleet, an opportunity they did not regularly enjoy.[131] The Americans valued the opportunity to practice communications with British and Canadian units, concluding that "the similarity of carrier task force procedure enabled our ships to operate effectively with the British-Canadian units with a minimum of preliminary instruction."[132] The British and Canadians attended a preliminary conference in Norfolk before the exercise in order to sort out procedural issues, such as which set of communications and tactical books to use. The British and Canadians used American books, which they already had on board due to earlier book exchange agreements. If the planners for NATO's Exercise Mainbrace in 1952 had been at this planning conference, they would have turned green with envy over the ease with which the three sides planned the earlier exercise.

Although NATO came into existence in 1949, the alliance's military command structure remained ill-defined until the outbreak of the Korean War in June 1950. The war stirred the alliance into creating the position of Supreme Allied Commander, Europe (SACEUR), first occupied by General of the Army Dwight Eisenhower in April 1951. SACEUR's naval counterpart, Supreme Allied Commander, Atlantic (SACLANT), took longer to establish due to the reluctance of some British leaders to place an American admiral over the new command (described in chapter 3).[133] Eventually the British gave in and the first SACLANT, Admiral Lynde McCormick took office in January 1952. Nine months later, after a frenzied planning effort, Exercise Mainbrace began in September 1952. Mainbrace was the largest international naval exercise ever held to date and employed more than two hundred ships, one thousand aircraft, and eighty thousand personnel.[134] The exercise took place in the North and Norwegian Seas with three primary objectives. Militarily, NATO commanders sought to test their command and control system while simultaneously providing advanced training for the forces involved.[135] In particular, could the naval-based SACLANT command structure provide support to Allied Command North in Norway and Denmark, which reported to the land-based SACEUR? Politically, NATO sought to reassure its northern members, Norway and Denmark, that military power could be deployed in their defense rapidly and effectively and that they were not simply NATO's northern appendages.[136]

According to the exercise scenario, Orange, a large continental power, launched a surprise attack on Blue, a coalition of nations in Western Europe and North America. Blue forces planned to respond to these Orange attacks by using several groups of warships. A strong group of aircraft carriers, the Carrier Strike Force, would sail from northwest England to northern Norway, along the way intercepting an Orange warship trying to reach the North Atlantic to attack Blue convoys. A Hunter Killer Force would attack submarines near the Carrier Strike Force, and both of these groups would refuel from the Logistic Support Force. After launching air strikes in support of Blue ground forces near Trondheim in Norway, the Carrier Strike Force would refuel at sea and then head south to provide air support for Blue forces in Denmark. While all these operations were taking place, a Carrier Support Force would protect convoys sailing between Britain and Norway from submarine attack. Twelve Orange submarines and several dozen Orange aircraft would attack the Blue forces throughout the exercise.[137]

The exercise began on September 13, 1952, when the Carrier Strike Force (the solid line on the Mainbrace map) left England heading for northern

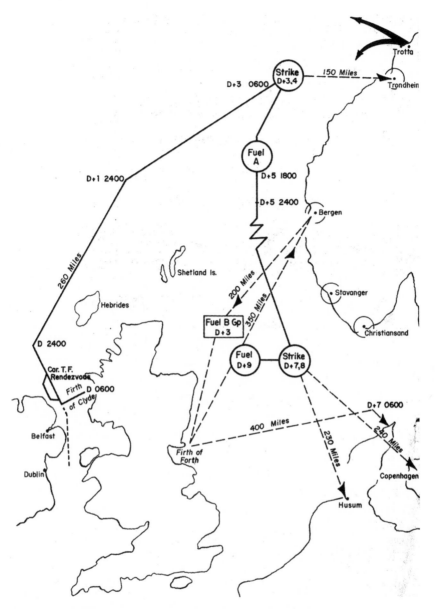

Exercise Mainbrace Map, 1952. © Government of Canada. Reproduced with the permission of Library and Archives Canada (2019). *Source*: Enclosure to Exercise Planning Group to SACEUR and SACLANT, "Exercise Ping Pong," February 28, 1952, File 1640–21–14, Part 2, "NATO—Exercises—Exercise Mainbrace, 1952," Volume 31163, RG24-D-1-c, Library and Archives Canada.

Norway.[138] The force refueled at sea on September 15 and then turned its attention to the Orange raider, the Canadian cruiser *Quebec*. The Canadian light cruiser left Narvik on September 14, and due to bad weather an air strike from the Carrier Striking Force failed to find the ship. However, a Blue surface force intercepted and destroyed *Quebec*. Between September 13 and 16, Orange submarines made six undetected attacks on the Blue task forces headed for northern Norway, while three submarines were sunk by the escorts and aircraft. As the Carrier Striking Force approached northern Norway, bad weather largely prevented the carriers from launching or landing aircraft. After conducting several shore bombardments, the Carrier Striking Force headed south toward Denmark. On September 21, the Hunter Killer Force escorting the Carrier Striking Force sank a submarine, but the British submarine *Sirdar* got inside the screen of the Hunter Killer Force and sank the force's only carrier, the American *Salerno Bay*. Later on September 21 another submarine made a long-range attack on another American carrier, the *Wright*.[139]

In the meantime, the Carrier Support Force (the dotted line on the map) escorted a convoy from Britain to Norway and then back again. Land-based patrol planes worked effectively in combination with the aircraft on the three carriers in the support force to keep the Orange submarines at bay until September 23, when an Orange submarine sank the British carrier *Theseus*. Aircraft from the *Magnificent* sank two submarines, and the support force escorts extracted revenge on the submarine that sank the *Theseus*.[140] More bad weather greeted the Carrier Striking Force in the North Sea, and air operations were severely limited as a result, though a second refueling at sea largely took place as planned. The exercise concluded on September 25.

The various commanders of the forces involved in Mainbrace gathered in Oslo, Norway, on September 27 to hold a conference critiquing the exercise. In addition to the senior exercise commanders, Admiral McCormick, SACLANT, and General Matthew Ridgway, SACEUR, also attended, as did King Haakon and Crown Prince Olav of Norway, along with the entire North Atlantic Council. This gathering of high-level dignitaries underscores the dual objectives of the exercise: to practice military operations and also to send a political message. The council's attendance was most likely a further effort to demonstrate the importance of the exercise to NATO members Denmark and Norway.[141]

The comments at the critique broadly established that the command and control organization currently in place worked effectively during the exercise and that SACLANT could provide rapid support for SACEUR. The exercise demonstrated that by and large the NATO navies could work together and that NATO's naval publications, ATP 1 in particular, provided an effective foundation for combined operations.[142] Several officers at the critique complained about the slow speed of the existing NATO system for encrypted communications.[143] As a result, messages often arrived at their destination far too late until Admiral Felix Stump, the Carrier Striking Force commander, ordered his ships to simply transmit their messages without encryption, "in the clear." The critique also revealed that several of the American officers did not feel that providing air support to ground forces represented the best use of their aircraft carriers. Rear Admiral Austin Doyle, one of the American carrier commanders, emphasized that "a Carrier Task Force is an offensive force and is not designed primarily for the type of operations carried out during this exercise. . . . We must not lose sight of the fact [that] carrier borne air should only be used in this role in a real emergency."[144] Admiral McCormick made this point more tactfully in his report to NATO's Standing Group by observing that in wartime the aircraft carriers would be required to perform a variety of other offensive tasks.[145] The commanders at the critique clearly avoided harshly criticizing each other's performance in order to promote a spirit of cooperation. However, internal Royal Navy reports told a different story.

The Royal Navy stationed liaison officers and observers on several of the American flagships for the duration of Mainbrace. Their reports praised the U.S. Navy's performance in several areas, notably air operations, but on the whole criticized the Americans for relying too heavily on their experience in the Pacific Theater during World War II. The officers on board the carrier *Midway* wrote of "the feeling that the U.S. Navy knows only one way of operating a carrier task force, the Pacific way."[146] At least four distinct features characterized this Pacific style of warfare: the offensive, flexible use of aircraft carriers; an almost nonexistent threat from enemy submarines; a significant threat of air attack; and weeks of operation at sea without returning to port. The actions of American commanders during Mainbrace often reflected the assumption that the Pacific style of warfare represented the best way to use aircraft carriers in a future war with the Soviet Union. This ap-

USS *Midway* off Firth of Clyde, Scotland, September 1952. *Source*: 80-G-K-13223, National Archives at College Park, College Park, MD.

proach shaped U.S. Navy operations throughout Mainbrace, which in turn led British observers to comment on differences between their two navies.

For example, at several points in the exercise the regional naval commander, commander in chief, East Atlantic, lacked information about the precise location of the Carrier Striking Force, which did not always keep higher headquarters informed of its movements. In the Pacific, American carrier groups often operated under conditions of radio silence, particular when conducting offensive operations, and they became used to infrequent communication with higher commands when in a combat area. The observers in *Midway* reported that the staff of the Carrier Striking Force felt that their group "was self-sufficient and therefore to a large extent independent of the East Atlantic Command," instead of properly coordinating their activities with other parts of the command.[147] In a similar vein, the British officers reported that the U.S. Navy appeared ill-suited to take advantage of the capabilities of allied forces. The *Midway* observers wrote of the "lack of interest displayed by the staff in the activities of any friendly forces" and an observer on the battleship *Wisconsin* noted that the fleet commander "had little idea of the operational characteristics of ships of the Royal Navy under their tactical command."[148] The British observers and the commander of the Home Fleet were also bothered by the lack of American interest in placing observers and liaison officers on their ships, which to the observers indicated a "deep rooted" inability to learn from other navies.[149]

The British found the American approach to antisubmarine warfare unimpressive on the whole. While U.S. Navy forces in the Pacific faced limited opposition from Japanese submarines, the Royal Navy spent most of World War II in the Atlantic and Mediterranean fending off German submarines. These diverging experiences led officers in each navy to place different levels of emphasis on antisubmarine warfare. The British felt the Americans incorrectly utilized the Hunter Killer Force to defend the replenishment ships rather than hunting submarines.[150] Furthermore, the staff in the Carrier Striking Force, composed largely of U.S. Navy aviators, showed insufficient interest in taking standard defensive measures against submarines, such as by zigzagging their course.[151] The Home Fleet's report described one of the fifteen successful submarine attacks on the carriers from inside their escorting screen, commenting how "once again the first indication of the presence of a submarine in the vicinity of a force was generally the explosion of a torpedo (represented by a green grenade)."[152]

Captain Michael Le Fanu felt so strongly that he wrote a "special report . . . not suitable for inclusion in the prescribed records of the exercise as it involves too many pungent strictures on the United States Navy."[153] Le Fanu criticized the American attitude toward defensive measures against submarines: "Zig-zagging and weaving were reluctantly introduced after six days of constant pressure by myself and the liaison officers." He felt that the American commander demonstrated a "completely passive attitude" toward submarines by failing to take advantage of information gained through radio warfare. When an Orange submarine sank the carrier in the Hunter Killer Force, the *Salerno Bay*, Le Fanu could not understand why twelve minutes passed before escorts were sent to hunt the submarine. The liaison officer on the *Salerno Bay* thought that "this incident was the most startling example of indecision and incompetence on the part of the Screen Commander—or any Screen Commander—I have ever witnessed."[154] Captain Le Fanu balanced his criticism by emphasizing his appreciation for the U.S. Navy:

I would not wish it to be thought that my complaints are the exaggerated out-pourings of one who dislikes the United States Navy. On the contrary, I have served 12 months in the American Navy and have a profound admiration for that service. They do many things superbly well and in this exercise we learned many things from them—but not about Anti-Submarine Warfare. I have indeed put these impressions on paper because I am an admirer and because I feel that if they appreciate their ignorance of ASW at a sufficiently high level, they are big enough and competent enough to put things right in short order.[155]

The U.S. Navy certainly warranted much of this criticism about its ap-proach to antisubmarine warfare. The demands of the Korean War meant that many American ships in Mainbrace operated with a reduced crew, which in turn resulted in decreased efficiency.[156] However, British officers commenting on the observer reports detected other influences at work. The head of naval aviation at the Admiralty, Captain Arthur S. Bolt, wrote that the authors of the *Midway* observers' report "judged what they saw solely in the light of British methods and techniques without fully understanding the American theories of modern naval warfare."[157] Captain Bolt, who recently had commanded the British carrier *Theseus* in the Korean War, thought the *Midway* report fit into a larger, troubling pattern in which an "adverse re-port" on the U.S. Navy was received in the Admiralty with "obvious reliabil-ity" in contrast to "the apathy we tend to show when confronted with some of their more progressive ideas."[158]

In contrast to their observations on U.S. Navy antisubmarine warfare, British observers praised the operations onboard American aircraft carriers. "One could not fail to be impressed by the efficient manner in which air-craft were operated," wrote the *Midway* observers.[159] British officers visiting American carriers throughout this period routinely praised the deck opera-tions as "of a very high standard."[160] British observers also found American aircraft, which were designed for operations at sea, superior to their naval versions of land-based aircraft.[161]

The reports also praised American skill in refueling and resupplying at sea, another holdover from the Pacific War. The U.S. Navy benefited from purpose-built oilers and supply ships capable of keeping up with the fleet and manned by naval crews. In comparison, the British utilized converted merchant ships manned by civilians under the control of the Royal Navy.

The American ships repeatedly performed better at refueling and resupplying than their British counterparts, a fact lamented by the British carrier commander at the Oslo critique.[162] Mainbrace did demonstrate that British and American ships could be refueled from each other's oilers, provided that each side had the proper adapters to connect the fueling hoses.[163]

Exercise Mainbrace largely fulfilled its political objectives by demonstrating that NATO could rapidly bring large forces into action in its northern regions.[164] The Canadian minister to Denmark reported that "the Danes were given tangible proof that they are not the Cinderella of the Organization."[165] Militarily, the units involved received a significant dose of advanced training while demonstrating that the existing command and control system largely worked. Mainbrace highlighted difficulties in encrypted communications as well as the differing strengths of the U.S. and Royal Navies in naval air operations and antisubmarine warfare, respectively. The exercise also illustrated the effectiveness of Allied Tactical Publication 1 as well as the combined communications books written by Canada, the United Kingdom, and the United States (CANUKUS) and used by NATO, though American units needed more experience using these books.[166]

Several of the themes brought out in the reports and critique of Exercise Mainbrace appeared again in an Anglo-American naval exercise that took place in March 1950 in the Western Pacific.[167] At a meeting in October 1949, Vice Admiral Russell S. Berkey, commander of the American Seventh Fleet, and Admiral Patrick Brind, commander in chief, Far East Station, agreed to hold a combined exercise with their forces in March the following spring.[168] The British agreed to use U.S. Navy signal and tactical books during the exercise.[169] The American force, commanded by Rear Admiral Walter Boone, comprised the aircraft carrier *Boxer* and the heavy cruiser *Toledo* plus escorts and logistics ships. Rear Admiral William Andrewes, flag officer, second-in-command, Far East, commanded the light carrier *Triumph*, two light cruisers, *Kenya* and *Jamaica*, and several escorts and logistic ships.

On the first day of the exercise, February 28, 1950, the British force left Hong Kong heading south, protecting a simulated convoy composed of two actual ships. The Americans left Subic Bay in the Philippines also on February 28 with the intention of attacking the British-guarded convoy. However, before any attacks could be launched, each side needed to find the other. Royal Air Force (RAF) flying boats and U.S. Navy patrol planes scoured the

HMS *Triumph* off Subic Bay, Philippines, during U.S. Navy–Royal Navy Exercise, March 8, 1950. *Source*: NH 97010, Naval History and Heritage Command, Washington, D.C.

South China Sea throughout the day, and before dark the Americans found the British convoy, although not the main British force, which had sailed separately. The RAF planes located the Americans but communications difficulties prevented Admiral Andrewes from maintaining contact with their movements. Similar communications difficulties prevented Admiral Boone from receiving solid information from the American patrol planes. At dawn on March 1, approximately 130 miles separated the two forces, and *Triumph* launched reconnaissance planes to search for *Boxer*. As a result of a solid report from an American submarine, *Boxer*'s planes found *Triumph* first. As *Boxer*'s planes approached, Andrewes chose to launch the strike planes waiting on *Triumph* even though he did not have clear information about *Boxer*'s location. Further communications difficulties combined with a navigational error prevented *Triumph*'s first strike from finding *Boxer*.[170]

Meanwhile, between 8 a.m. and 11 a.m., two American air strikes hit the British force. The second air strike from *Triumph* found *Boxer*, but defending American fighters intercepted the strike at a distance from the task force.

Admiral Boone later wrote to a friend that "we hung it on the British pretty badly, delivering two deck load attacks before they got off their first attack against us."[171] During the commotion, an American submarine penetrated the British escort screen undetected and fired on *Triumph* before the British destroyer *Cockade* pounced on the sub. Later, the two forces merged and came under Admiral Boone's tactical control, with the senior British destroyer captain in command of the screen. The British rapidly adopted American procedures and "did an excellent job" using U.S. Navy books according to the American exercise report, a clear indication that their personnel had spent time studying the American publications.[172] Admiral Boone reported that after the linkup, "the operations proceeded very much as though both forces had been from our own fleet," an indication of the progress made since 1945 in retaining Anglo-American naval interoperability.[173]

During the night of March 1–2, the British and American destroyers practiced night torpedo attacks on the cruisers and carriers while *Boxer* operated night fighters that intercepted a shore-based patrol plane. British commanders found the night fighter operations impressive.[174] After a final set of air strikes by *Boxer* and *Triumph* on Philippine shore bases on March 2, the combined force entered Subic Bay on the 3rd. Officers from both fleets gathered on Saturday, March 4, 1950, and held a critique to analyze the exercises. Both sides generally agreed that "no insurmountable obstacles existed to British and U.S. Forces operating together at short notice."[175] Carrier capabilities represented the greatest difference between the two forces as *Boxer*'s ninety-five aircraft overshadowed *Triumph*'s thirty-odd planes. In addition, *Boxer* could travel several knots faster than *Triumph*.[176] Admiral Boone later wrote that "the air operations of *Boxer* and her air group appeared to be superior to *Triumph* and her air group in all respects."[177] The Americans certainly had a more developed flight deck procedure, which resulted in faster takeoff and landing times, but British pilots demonstrated considerable skill, particularly in the air strikes.

After a weekend in Subic Bay "too fully occupied" with parties for Admiral Boone's taste, the two forces proceeded to sea for basic training exercises.[178] Five fighters from *Boxer* landed on *Triumph*, and eleven British aircraft flew to *Boxer*. Each side provided the other with a landing signal officer to guide their aircraft down to the deck as the two navies were still in the process of standardizing their landing signals. This cross-decking exercise demonstrated that British and American aircraft could, with a little preparation, use each other's ships as landing fields and could refuel, though rearming and stowing aircraft below deck would prove more challenging. The British pilots also noticed that *Boxer*'s arresting gear brought their aircraft to a halt more rapidly than their own gear, a result of the U.S. Navy's more rugged purpose-built carrier aircraft. Each carrier also took the opportunity to control the other side's aircraft, similar to the exchange in Caribex 50.[179]

In addition to practicing air operations, three U.S. submarines on March 6 performed basic sonar tracking drills with the British and American escorts, giving the escorts' crews valuable sonar practice. The next day, the American provided airborne targets on which ships could practice their antiaircraft gunnery. Several of the British ships had not practiced their antiaircraft crews with an airborne target in some time, and as a result the Americans' antiaircraft performance was better. On the 8th, each side practiced taking on fuel from the other side's logistics ships using adaptors to connect the fueling hose. After a final critique in Subic Bay, the two task forces went their separate ways on March 10.[180]

Both sides acknowledged that during the first few days of combined operations, their ships had to make some adjustments to the other's procedures, but none of the obstacles were insurmountable.[181] The exercises also revealed the specific strengths of each navy. The Americans excelled at naval air operations, especially flight deck operations, underway replenishment, and antiaircraft gunfire, due to superior equipment and more frequent training. British Admiral Brind wrote, "The two fleets attach different weight to the various aspects of tactical training, and it was evident that the American Fleet is as good as ever at flying operations, A/A firing, and replenishment at sea, to all of which subjects they have clearly given much attention."[182]

The British excelled in communications procedures, sharing of contact information, directing of aircraft, and individual ship handling. The American report noted that "individual ship handling on the part of the British was impressive and generally superior to our own." Despite the Royal Navy's generally inferior communications equipment compared to the U.S. Navy's, British "training, industry, and initiative produce better results."[183] Vice Admiral Berkey, the commander of Seventh Fleet, observed that "as occurred during the war, when Australian ships with British-trained radar crews oper-

ated with the Seventh Fleet, the individual performance of the radar operators of the British was above that of the USN operators."[184]

Commanders on both sides thought that the exercises provided valuable
experience and training, and they recommended more combined exercises
in the future. The exercises demonstrated that by 1950 the two navies could
work together at sea with little advance warning. Admiral Boone's exercise
report concluded with a comment about the future that proved to be pro-
phetic: "In as much as it is virtually a certainty that United States and British Navies would be acting in concert in any future war, it is considered that
combined exercises . . . should be held at appropriate intervals."[185]

Combined exercises such as Caribex 50, Mainbrace, and the March 1950
Pacific exercise provided opportunities for British, Canadian, and American naval officers to compare their respective strengths and weaknesses. For
the U.S. Navy, exercises with the British and Canadians occurred more frequently than with any other allied navy during this period. Commanders
and officers who participated in these combined exercises tended to find
them very useful and became advocates for more exercises and closer cooperation between the three navies. In addition, personal contacts and friendships grew out of these exercises, similar to the contacts made by British and
Canadian officers attending American military schools. Although difficult to
measure at the time, these personal relationships frequently proved valuable
later in an officer's career, forming a central part of overall relations between
the three navies.

By the early 1950s, a solid network connected the U.S. Navy to the British and
Canadian fleets. This network came into being as a temporary structure during World War II, but all three navies took steps in the early postwar years to
make the temporary permanent. The U.S. Navy did not retreat into nationalistic isolation after the war. War college exchanges, antisubmarine schools,
and combined exercises all played a role in making this network permanent
in at least four ways. First, officers from one navy who spent time with another tended to return to their own fleet as advocates of greater contact and
cooperation between the navies. Second, contact with another navy naturally
led officers to compare and contrast the doctrine, procedures, equipment,
and culture of the two organizations. This comparing and contrasting could
help officers see their own fleet through someone else's eyes, a valuable per-

spective in itself.[186] Third, contact with other navies allowed officers to build personal relationships that strengthened the ties between fleets. Fourth, the practices of holding combined exercises and exchanging officers for training and education made contact with British and Canadian officers a regular, routine part of U.S. Navy life. Furthermore, the contacts between these three navies were both deep and wide. Education and training exchanges allowed a smaller group of officers to spend extended periods of time as a part of another navy. Training visits and combined exercises gave a much larger number of officers a shorter experience of operating with another fleet. While some of these factors could apply to relations between any two navies, the frequency of American contact with the British and Canadians far exceeded contact with any other navy in the areas of education, training, and exercises.

While the strength of this American-Canadian-British naval network was unmatched, the U.S. Navy insisted that the network largely remain out of the public's eye. Concerns over the response of the American public to a functional peacetime alliance shaped U.S. Navy policy regarding relations with the British and Canadians. The American willingness to favor the British and Canadians was inversely proportional to the likelihood that the public or other nations might uncover the special treatment. In high-profile arenas such as war colleges, the U.S. Navy decided it would rather remove British and Canadian officers than explain why officers from other nations, France in particular, could not attend. In contrast, training visits and exchange officers at antisubmarine schools were much lower profile activities, and as a result the Americans proved much more willing to show favoritism. In terms of public access to information, exercises represented the arena most suited to tight controls. Reporters and naval officers could observe exercises only if the U.S. Navy allowed them to, and the exercises themselves took place at sea, out of sight of the prying eyes of the media. Allowing fleet commanders to arrange exercises with their counterparts on their own increased the ease and frequency of these training events while also reducing their publicity since national headquarters' permission was not required. Prior to World War II, combined exercises, officer exchanges, and shared training events were extremely rare for the U.S. Navy. By 1953 all three were commonplace with the Royal Navy and the Royal Canadian Navy.

7

The Korean Test

The first rays of sunlight had just begun to peek over the horizon of the Yellow Sea when the roar of aircraft engines broke the morning stillness on July 3, 1950. At a signal from the flight deck, a Seafire fighter catapulted off the British carrier *Triumph* and climbed into the sky. Over the next hour, fifty-seven planes took off from *Triumph* and the American carrier *Valley Forge* and headed northeast toward Korea. Twenty-one British aircraft attacked the airfield at Haeju, while a larger American force struck airfields and bridges near Pyongyang before returning to the carriers.[1] Certainly none of the pilots, British or American, had any inkling that these air strikes would inaugurate three years of combined naval warfare off the coasts of Korea.

The Korean War served as a test of the U.S. Navy's efforts to retain close relations with its closest World War II allies. The operations of American, British, Canadian, Australian, and other allied warships in Korean waters cemented a pattern of operating in multinational formations that reached back to World War II. In particular, Task Group 95.1's work off the Korean west coast demonstrated that ships from these four navies could effectively cooperate. The effort put into maintaining interoperability between 1945 and 1950 paid off in Korean waters. The war also created more advocates within the U.S. Navy for maintaining ties with the British, Canadians, and Australians, which in turn spurred additional standardization efforts. At the same time, however, relations among the various naval contingents remained susceptible to divisive personalities such as

Rear Admiral George Dyer. Still, most naval officers in Korea found interallied relations to be harmonious and cooperative.

Although the North Korean invasion of South Korea on June 25, 1950, surprised many Americans, the offensive represented a violent escalation of an ongoing struggle between Seoul and Pyongyang for control of the peninsula.[2] At the end of World War II, the Soviet Union and the United States divided Korea along the thirty-eighth parallel. By 1948, a civil war, fought primarily in southern Korea, consumed the attention of Seoul and Pyongyang, each of which claimed to be the rightful ruler of the entire Korean peninsula. The North Korean invasion spurred the United States to respond and by the end of June, President Harry Truman committed U.S. naval, air, and ground forces to the defense of South Korea. Washington then secured a United Nations (UN) resolution casting North Korea as the aggressor and calling on UN member states to contribute forces to the defense of South Korea. The U.S. avoided a Soviet veto since the Soviets were boycotting the UN over its refusal to give Communist China a seat on the Security Council.[3]

Undeterred by international reaction, North Korean forces continued their advance south, capturing the South Korean capital, Seoul, and dealing severe blows to the Republic of Korea (ROK) Army. Throughout July and August, South Korean and American forces fell back toward the southern port city of Pusan. A stubborn defense of southeastern Korea combined with an amphibious landing at Inchon on the Korean west coast on September 15, 1950, defeated the initial North Korean offensive.[4]

UN forces pursued the retreating North Korean Army north of the thirty-eighth parallel and pushed on toward the Yalu River—which separated North Korea from China—in an effort to unify Korea by force. Undaunted by Chinese warnings delivered through India that Beijing would not allow North Korea to be totally occupied, General of the Army Douglas MacArthur continued to press his U.S. Eighth Army ever closer to China. On October 26, 1950, the Chinese made good on their threat, launching a devastating series of attacks on overextended South Korean and American forces. Chinese offensives drove the Eighth Army back, and by Christmas 1950 the Chinese front line ran close to the thirty-eighth parallel, forcing naval evacuations from Wonson and Hungnam on the east coast and Chinamp'o on the west coast along the way.[5]

The Chinese renewed their offensive in early January 1951 and, supported by a reorganized North Korean Army, recaptured Seoul. UN counterattacks in late January and February ordered by Eighth Army's new commander, Lieutenant General Matthew Ridgway, turned the tide once again in favor of UN forces. After halting another Chinese attack in mid-to-late February, Ridgway resumed his offensive, pushing north of the thirty-eighth parallel by the end of April and recapturing Seoul.[6] A further Chinese attack in May followed by a UN counterattack in late May and early June left the front line once again north of the thirty-eighth parallel. In July 1951, armistice talks began between the Americans and the Chinese with South Korean and North Korean representatives present. Neither side knew at the time that the talks would drag on for two years until July 1953.[7]

NAVAL FORCES IN KOREA

After President Truman ordered U.S. forces to come to South Korea's aid, Britain and individual Commonwealth countries quickly promised naval and air support. On June 29, the Admiralty placed British warships in Japanese waters at the disposal of Admiral C. Turner Joy, Commander, Naval Forces, Far East (COMNAVFE), and by July 1, Canada, Australia, and New Zealand followed suit.[8] An Anglo-American carrier task force launched airstrikes into North Korea in early July. This multinational naval response foreshadowed the combined naval operations that characterized the sea war in Korea.[9]

Throughout the Korean War, the UN enjoyed naval superiority and UN naval forces performed a variety of missions to support land operations. Naval gunfire and air strikes provided fire support for Eighth Army while blockade and minesweeping kept the Korean coasts open for UN use and clear of communist naval craft. The amphibious landing at Inchon in September 1950 and the evacuations from northeast Korea in December 1950 highlighted the inherent flexibility of naval forces. After the front line stabilized in the summer of 1951, naval missions such as gunfire support and air strikes persisted, while new tasks such as defending small islands just off the North Korean coast placed additional demands on UN warships.[10]

Overall command of the naval forces carrying out these missions lay with commander, Naval Forces, Far East, who reported to the overall Commander in Chief, Far East (CINCFE), General MacArthur. MacArthur also served as head of the United Nations Command and reported to the U.S.

Senior British and American naval officers confer on USS *Rochester*, July 1, 1950.
Left to right: Captain Arthur D. Torlesse, RN, commanding officer, HMS *Triumph*;
Rear Admiral John M. Hoskins, USN, commander, Carrier Group, Seventh Fleet; Vice
Admiral Arthur D. Struble, USN, commander, Seventh Fleet; and Rear Admiral William
G. Andrewes, RN, flag officer, second in command, Far East. *Source*: 80-G-416423,
National Archives at College Park, College Park, MD.

Joint Chiefs. The other American naval force in the Western Pacific, the
Seventh Fleet, initially stood apart from COMNAVFE, but by April 1951, it
was also placed under COMNAVFE's control. UN naval forces reported to
COMNAVFE.[11]

In accordance with U.S. Navy procedure, COMNAVFE divided his forces
into a variety of task forces to carry out naval operations in Korean waters.
The two most important task forces were Task Force (TF) 77 and TF 95.
TF 77, the Fast Carrier Task Force, comprised the U.S. Navy's large fleet carriers, embarking ninety to one hundred aircraft each, escorted by several
cruisers and over a dozen destroyers. Almost all of the ships in TF 77 were

American, although a British or Commonwealth destroyer rotated in and out of the force at times.[12]

In contrast to TF 77's all-American flavor, TF 95, the UN Blockading and Escort Force, comprised ships from the United States, Britain, Canada, Australia, New Zealand, and South Korea, with periodic contributions from the Netherlands and Thailand. Command of TF 95 remained in American hands except for a brief period in the spring of 1951 when British Vice Admiral William Andrewes took charge. TF 95's missions included blockading both Korean coasts, providing escorts for cargo ships bringing material to Korea, and providing air support from the Yellow Sea off the Korean west coast. The task force divided its ships into several smaller task groups. Task Group (TG) 95.1, commanded by a British admiral, handled operations on the Korean west coast while Task Group 95.2, commanded by an American, covered the east coast. Throughout the war, the British commander of TG 95.1 was Flag Officer, Second in Command, Far East (FO2FE), who also reported to the senior British naval officer in the area, commander in chief, Far East Station, for purely Royal Navy matters.[13] Three officers held the positions of FO2FE and commander, Task Group 95.1, during the war:

Vice Admiral William Andrewes, RN	July 5, 1950–April 10, 1951
Rear Admiral Alan Scott-Moncrieff, RN	April 10, 1951–September 16, 1952
Rear Admiral Eric G. A. Clifford, RN	September 23, 1952–November 18, 1953.[14]

Off the Korean west coast, a series of British, American, and Australian carriers each took turns supporting the ground war as part of Task Group 95.1. At any given time, two carriers were required to maintain one carrier on station. The Royal Navy typically provided one of the west coast carriers, with one break courtesy of the Royal Australian Navy, and the U.S. Navy contributed the alternating carrier.[15] Figure 7.1 shows the deployments of carriers that operated with Task Group 95.1.

COMBAT OPERATIONS

UN naval forces routinely bombarded targets on shore and launched air strikes against enemy targets. Carrier-based aircraft flew several different types of missions during the war. Attacks on industrial facilities and trans-

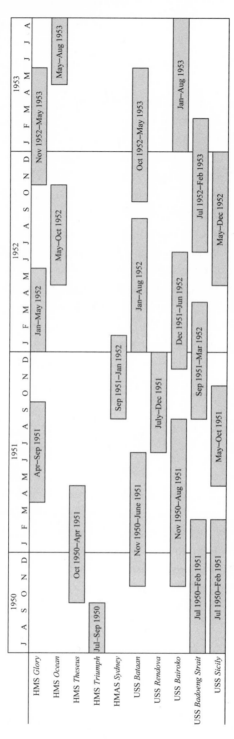

Figure 7.1 Task Force 95 Carrier Deployments. *Source:* David Hobbs, "British Commonwealth Carrier Operations in the Korean War," in *Coalition Air Warfare in the Korean War, 1950–1953*, ed. Jacob Neufeld and George M. Watson (Washington, D.C.: U.S. Air Force History and Museums Program, 2005) 142–157; Naval Historical Branch, "B.R. 1736 (54), Naval Staff History: British Commonwealth Naval Operations Korea, 1950–53," 304–305, September 1967, 319, Library, Sea Power Centre-Australia, Canberra; Roy Grossnick, *United States Naval Aviation, 1910–1995* (Washington, D.C.: Naval History and Heritage Command, 1997), appendix 25.

portation targets, especially bridges, were typically planned out in advance
and launched with specific targets in mind. In contrast, naval aircraft supporting ground troops attacked targets chosen by fire-support teams. Armed
reconnaissance missions sought out targets of opportunity behind communist lines with a particular emphasis on attacking transportation targets in
order to interdict supplies moving to the front lines.[16]

From the beginning of their involvement in Korea, UN naval commanders kept an eye on the Soviet Union's air and submarine forces stationed in
and around Vladivostok. Soviet naval intervention would pose a grave threat
to naval operations off Korea. As a result, UN carriers kept defensive patrols
in the air whenever on duty in Korean waters. These continuous patrols reduced the percentage of a carrier's aircraft that could be devoted to offensive
operations, a particular problem for the British, Australian, and U.S. carriers
in Task Force 95, which had smaller air groups than the fleet carriers on the
east coast.

Although British, American, and Australian aircraft carriers rotated duties on the Korean west coast, differences in equipment limited the ability
of British aircraft to attack targets deep inside Korea. The Seafire and Sea
Fury fighters and Firefly fighter-bombers operated by the British and Australian navies did not have the endurance or range enjoyed by American
Corsair fighters or Skyraider attack aircraft. When *Triumph* operated with
Valley Forge in July 1950, both carriers launched air strikes during the first
few days of operations. However, the Americans soon relegated the British
carrier's role to flying defensive Combat Air Patrol and antisubmarine missions, since these missions depended less on the range of the aircraft. Vice
Admiral Andrewes, the British naval commander, reported that this plan
"though galling for HMS *Triumph*, was entirely logical . . . [and] worked very
smoothly."[17] Still, the experience confirmed that British and American carriers could successfully operate together on short notice.[18]

During these initial operations in July 1950, the British ships switched
from Royal Navy to U.S. Navy publications and books. The transition occurred rapidly and smoothly, in large part because of the exercises held in
the South China Sea earlier in February and March 1950. Andrewes reported
that "it all seemed so familiar" and the British "were already getting back into
the easy use of American signal books."[19] The United Nations naval forces
deployed to Korea continued to use U.S. Navy books and publications until

the summer of 1952, when CANUKUS publications such as ATP 1 and ACP 175 came into use.

After the initial operations involving *Triumph* and *Valley Forge*, combined carrier operations became the exception rather than the rule. On the Korean east coast, the big U.S. Navy fleet carriers operated in their own formation, while on the west coast British, American, and Australian carriers took turns serving as the single carrier on duty. On those occasions when British and American carriers did operate together (listed below), the crews of each ship worked hard to try to outperform the other, especially in flight operations. For example, when the American *Bataan* and the British *Theseus* operated together in April 1951, the speed with which each carrier launched and recovered aircraft gradually increased. The British noted with pride that *Theseus* tended to launch aircraft more quickly than *Bataan*, even though the American carrier had two catapults to the British one.[20] A British pilot who flew from *Glory* in 1952 and 1953 later described the relationship as "rivalry, but real friendship . . . we had rivals with our opposite squadrons . . . there was rivalry, but friendly rivalry."[21]

Dates	Carriers Involved
July–August 1950	USS *Valley Forge*, HMS *Triumph*
April 1951	USS *Bataan*, HMS *Theseus*
May 1951	USS *Bataan*, HMS *Glory*
July 1951	USS *Sicily*, HMS *Glory*[22]

The Royal Navy viewed naval aviation as a particularly important arena of competition with the Americans, in part to counter the perception that U.S. naval aviation was superior. British aviators tended to feel, with some justification, that the U.S. Navy, especially American naval aviators, viewed the Royal Navy's Fleet Air Arm as second-class at best. In 1947, the American naval air attaché in London reported that British naval aviator pay "does not amount to much" but that in comparison with the U.S. Navy, "they have gotten about what they have paid for."[23] A senior British aviator noted in 1951 that "it is no secret that the USN has regarded RN aviation as amateur and weak."[24] Rear Admiral Arleigh Burke wrote to Vice Admiral Donald Duncan in 1952 that "the British do not believe in, nor do they know how to conduct, fast carrier task force operations."[25] British aviators resented this attitude held by elements of the U.S. naval aviation community, especially given British contributions to carrier aviation such as the angled flight deck and later the mirror landing system.

As a result, the British took particular pride in the relative performance of the British and American carriers in Task Group 95.1. The British repeatedly set records for numbers of sorties flown in a single day from a single light carrier. In September 1951 *Glory* reached 84 sorties in a single day, only to be surpassed by Australia's *Sydney* later in 1951 with 89 sorties. *Glory* then reached 105 sorties on March 17, 1952, but was later beaten by the British *Ocean* with an impressive 123 sorties. Each of these records proved unbeatable for the American escort carriers and light carriers deployed on the west coast.[26] The director of naval air warfare back in London commented approvingly on an earlier report of impressive performance that the Fleet Air Arm "can give as good as any in the USN."[27] One reason the British set records so frequently was their extensive practice in carrier flight deck operations while in transit to Korea. In contrast, American escort carriers did not go through this additional preparation.[28] The carrier operations on the Korean west coast demonstrated that British, Australian, and American carriers could successfully operate together. At the same time, British aviators sought to use the Korean War to demonstrate their skill and effectiveness to their American counterparts.

If competition as well as cooperation marked UN naval aviation in Korea, a search for consistency marked naval gunfire support. During the war, warships provided naval gunfire through two methods: observed and unobserved fire. Observed fire simply involved ground personnel or an aircraft watching the impact of the warship's shells and then radioing corrections to the warship, a process known as spotting. Unobserved fire, also known as harassment fire, did not benefit from the guidance of spotters. In 1948 the U.S. Navy and Royal Navy started to standardize their spotting procedures.[29] The two procedures did not differ radically from each other, they simply varied in terminology and phrasing. When the Korean War began the two procedures were still not standardized, in part because of the need to coordinate the procedures with both armies. To accelerate the process, UN navies in Korea adopted the American procedures with considerable success.[30]

Even so, warships often found that naval gunfire spotting methods varied depending on location and the forces involved. For example, the captain of the Canadian destroyer *Cayuga* noted that on the west coast aircraft spotted naval gunfire more frequently than on the east coast, which utilized more unobserved fire.[31] Captain Rudolph Johnson, commander of the carrier *Badoeng Strait*, found that British and Commonwealth ships lacked the up-to-date fire control equipment for shore bombardment that was found on American warships.[32]

By far, the most common complaint about naval gunfire in Korea involved American inconsistency in spotting procedures. Variations in procedure caused difficulties, especially when other UN ships came to Korea expecting to use American procedures. The Dutch frigate *Piet Hein* went through an intensive familiarization course at Hong Kong on American spotting methods before arriving in the Korean theater. Soon after arriving, the *Piet Hein* provided gunfire support observed by an American aircraft. The Dutch crew "was completely bewildered by the spotter's use of incorrect procedure," specifically the use of American slang and vernacular instead of the established terminology.[33] Fortunately, a British liaison officer assigned to *Piet Hein* provided translation services.[34] Rear Admiral Scott-Moncrieff vented his frustration in a September 1952 report, writing that "although the procedure is their own," U.S. Navy aircraft on both coasts and U.S. Air Force planes "seldom use the correct procedure and attach considerably less importance to this aspect than we do."[35] During the Inchon landings, an American officer observed both American and British pilots spotting naval gunfire and concluded that the British pilots "spotting procedure (not to mention their English) was more intelligible."[36] Ironically, British officers began giving lectures in American spotting procedure to American pilots on USN carriers operating on the west coast in an effort to bring about more consistency. This pattern of teaching newly arrived American ships and aircraft the U.S. Navy's own spotting procedures continued throughout the war. In January 1953, when the Seventh Fleet flagship, the battleship *Missouri*, visited the west coast, British pilots from the British carrier *Ocean* had to teach the American crew the correct U.S. Navy procedure before they could spot the battleship's gunfire.[37] However, spotting experience could also vary from ship to ship. The battleship *New Jersey* developed a reputation for accurate gunfire and adherence to procedure.[38] By common consent, the most competent ground spotting teams came from the U.S. Marine Corps.[39] Clearly, these inconsistencies highlighted variations within the U.S. Navy that made standardization across the fleet challenging.

Work on standardizing bombardment procedure continued throughout the Korean War, but agreement on a standard NATO procedure did not come until after the armistice.[40] The conflict did produce a renewed call for standardized procedures, particularly within the Royal Navy. The first six months of the war convinced Vice Admiral Andrewes that "the advantages of establishing mutual confidence" between the two countries overshadowed "the theoretical advantages of particular methods." Andrewes concluded that the procedure must be standardized regardless of which procedure proved to be superior since both were satisfactory.[41] Captain Patrick Brock served as the captain of the cruiser *Kenya* during the fall of 1950 and later as director of the Operations Division in the Admiralty. In an August 1951 memo, Brock wrote that he "strongly concurs in a policy of standardization at almost any price." He explained that while procedures were almost entirely standardized, the remaining differences caused unnecessary misunderstandings. Personnel in both navies would assume, wrongly, that the procedures were entirely standardized, leading to frustration and error when differences cropped up. Brock concluded that there would be less risk of misunderstandings if two completely different procedures were used since no one would assume matching methods. Paradoxically, 95 percent similarity could cause more problems than 10 percent similarity, a perceptive insight into naval standardization.[42]

The U.S. Navy's inconsistency in bombardment procedure demonstrated how U.S.-centric the fleet remained in its assumptions. Some American personnel assumed that they would operate with other American units and so variations from established bombardment procedure would not cause problems. This attitude did not take into account the impact of inconsistent procedure on foreign navies operating with the U.S. Navy. It is difficult to determine precisely what percentage of the American fleet in Korea held this perspective, but it appears to have been stronger on the east coast, where non-American warships were the exception rather than the rule. The largest American warships, battleships, cruisers, and large carriers operated primarily on the east coast, suggesting that this U.S.-centric assumption comprised a significant proportion of the U.S. Navy in Korea. As was true in other areas, the Korean War served as a learning experience for the U.S. Navy, specifically on how to operate routinely with allied navies.

In addition to inconsistencies in spotting procedure, the British and Commonwealth navies used unobserved fire to a far lesser extent than their American counterparts. The extensive, even excessive, American expenditure of ammunition featured prominently in British and certain Commonwealth Korean War reports. The British naval advisor in Tokyo wrote in August 1950 that in the U.S. Navy, "more weight is put on the number of rounds you fire than where they fall."[43] Andrewes observed in March 1951 that "the US Navy was prepared to fire a great deal more ammunition, much of it unobserved, than we considered necessary for the aim to be achieved and to regard the number of rounds fired as the criterion."[44]

Later that year, Admiral Guy Russell, the commander in chief of the Royal Navy's Far East Station, ruefully commented to the first sea lord that with the money the U.S. Navy wasted on ammunition, the British could buy a whole carrier task force. Russell also reported that the captain of the battleship *New Jersey* "is bitterly disappointed if he doesn't fire his whole ammunition outfit each time up the coast."[45] Commander James Plomer, the captain of the *Cayuga*, noted the American tendency to fire ammunition "without regard for cost."[46] The Australia captain of the *Warramunga*, Commander James Ramsay, described a visit to an American landing craft loaded with five thousand rockets fired from twenty launchers. The American captain told Ramsay that "he had to restrain himself from firing for too long because the rockets cost the taxpayers 50 bucks each." Ramsay concluded: "It is rare to find the USN practicing such self-restraint in bombardment."[47] U.S. Navy ammunition expenditure doubled from the first year of the Korean War to the second year, ending in June 1952.[48]

The U.S. Navy recognized this problem as early as September 1950, when COMNAVFE issued a warning against excessive unobserved fire.[49] However, the problem continued throughout the war. In 1952, internal U.S. Pacific Fleet reports commented on overly high ammunition expenditure, noting that this practice would eventually cost the navy money, which in turn would help the enemy.[50] By July 1952, Vice Admiral Robert Briscoe, COMNAVFE, and Vice Admiral Joseph Clark, commander, Seventh Fleet, were emphasizing to their subordinates that evaluation reports "would not depend on the amount of ammunition" fired.[51] This link between evaluation reports and ammunition expenditure stemmed from the tenure of Rear Admiral George Dyer, who proved to be a constant source of contention in U.S. Navy relations with the British, Canadian, and Australian navies in Korea.

Dyer had served as a senior intelligence officer for Admiral King during World War II and later spent time in several surface ships in the Pacific. On June 20, 1951, Dyer took command of Task Force 95, the United Nations Blockading and Escort Force, Korea, which included the warships on the Korean west coast.[52] Dyer entered his position with a firm conviction about the role of naval power in Korea. He believed that his force should fire more shells and drop more bombs onto the enemy than his predecessors "in an effort to keep up the pressure on the Communists at a high level," a reference by Dyer to the armistice talks. From his perspective, the UN negotiators were giving away too much and increasing the military pressure on the communists might lead them to be more accommodating in the talks.[53] Dyer's personal correspondence frequently touted the total number of bombs and shells expended by Task Force 95. For example, in an August 1951 letter he approvingly wrote that his ships were firing five hundred to one thousand shells and his planes were dropping ten to twenty-five tons of bombs each day.[54] Under his leadership, commanding officers who received fire from the shore and returned fire received top priority for awards and decorations. He told a friend in early 1952, "I believe that those who fight the war, in counter-distinction with those who are merely present while the fighting goes on about them, are deserving of some special recognition."[55]

Dyer's approach to naval bombardment grated the British, especially Rear Admiral Scott-Moncrieff, who complained about Dyer's practice through which "a ship's efficiency and aggressiveness has often been judged in proportion to the ammunition expended." The British admiral also deplored the "injunctions to 'get into the shooting war'" that came down from Dyer's flagship.[56] Scott-Moncrieff did not keep his feelings to himself. For example, he sent a message to one of the other senior officers in Task Force 95 describing an upcoming trip Dyer was taking to the west coast. In the message, he commented, "I hope he [Dyer] will cause no trouble," knowing full well that the message would be seen by junior officers in the task force. Captain James Plomer, commander, Canadian Destroyers Far East, reported that he had seen other examples of messages that brought Scott-Moncrieff and his staff's dislike of Dyer into the open. Plomer believed the situation was not helped by the "undercurrent of irritation with the Americans" and "frequent discouraging remarks and petty criticisms of the Americans and the American Navy" common on Scott-Moncrieff's staff. He further noted that the "rare exceptions" to this pattern of criticizing the U.S. Navy were officers "who have served in the United States," a further reminder that service with another navy often created advocates for closer cooperation or at least greater understanding. Plomer obliquely referred to Dyer as "the principal troublemaker," while Scott-Moncrieff's chief of staff, Captain R. A. Villiers, was "strongly anti-American in outlook."[57]

Part of the trouble between Dyer and the British was his approach to command, which reflected larger tendencies in the U.S. Navy's system of command and control. The U.S. Navy gave commanders at sea maximum flexibility and mobility by freeing them from administrative and logistical concerns that were handled by other organizations. In contrast, the British system of command combined operational, administrative, and logistical functions within a single command position located at a shore base.[58]

Due in part to his experience as a captain and then division commander in the Pacific, George Dyer believed that the best way to command Task Force 95, the UN Escort and Blockading Force, was to be at sea with the fleet as much as possible. Several months after taking command, Dyer wrote to a fellow admiral in Pearl Harbor: "The only way I can do my job adequately is to visit the areas where the fighting is going on."[59] He frequently took his staff to sea with him in the heavy cruiser *Toledo* to visit his forces on both coasts of Korea.[60] Although Task Force 95 commanders before and after Dyer also went to sea, Dyer did so far more often. This style of command caused two problems as far as Scott-Moncrieff and his staff were concerned. First, Dyer was frequently not present at his headquarters at Sasebo, which limited his day-to-day contact with liaison officers from the air force, army, intelligence, and other organizations. This reduction in day-to-day contact led to lower levels of cooperation between Task Force 95 and the various other organizations involved in fighting the Korean War. In the Central Pacific in World War II, the U.S. Navy largely ran the war as it saw fit with minimal contact with organizations not under the control of Admiral Nimitz at Pearl Harbor. Korea was different. Air support required constant coordination and communication with the army and air force, while raids and island defense missions needed to be coordinated with multiple intelligence organizations. Second, and more troubling for the British, Dyer's method upset the standing command arrangement in Task Force 95. Dyer's predecessor, Rear Admiral Allan Smith, and other previous Task Force 95 commanders concentrated their attention on east coast operations, giving flag officer, second in command, Far East, considerable autonomy over west coast operations. In contrast "a great deal of backseat driving" took place during Dyer's frequent trips to the west coast, according to Scott-Moncrieff. Dyer typically did not explain the rationale behind his issuing orders, as was customary in the Royal Navy. Furthermore, the British found that "any advice or question [upon receipt of Dyer's orders] appeared to be regarded as criticism or unwillingness."[61] Dyer's largely negative impact on relations within the command structure of Task Force 95 serves as a reminder of the important role of personality in military-to-military relations. Just as friendships and close relationships could smooth over differences, personal conflicts and organizational differences could easily sour relations.

On May 31, 1952, Rear Admiral John Gingrich relieved Dyer as commander, Task Force 95.[62] In contrast to Dyer, who spent roughly half his time at sea, Gingrich preferred to remain at Sasebo and let his east and west coast commanders run operations on their own. Scott-Moncrieff reported that "relations became far easier" since Gingrich returned to the pre-Dyer practice of remaining primarily at Sasebo. He concluded that Gingrich "has been most cooperative."[63] By mid-July, Vice Admiral Guy Russell, the British commander in chief, Far East Station, reported he was "happier than I have ever been about Anglo-American cooperation. . . . The departure of the rather ambitious and possibly anti-British Admiral Dyer has made a great difference all round."[64] Canadian officers such as Commander John Reed also thought highly of Gingrich. Reed wrote that the American was "an excellent administrator" and a "most pleasant and tactful personality."[65] In addition to reverting to the previous pattern of command, Gingrich took steps to reduce ammunition expenditure, precisely the action Scott-Moncrieff had been advocating. Soon after relinquishing command of Task Force 95, Gingrich told an audience at the Industrial College of the Armed Forces:

In the Korean action I was commander of Task Force 95 and I was worried about our heavy expenditure of ammunition. When I took over Task Force 95, I found that we were firing 37,000 rounds of 5-inch ammunition on the east coast of

Korea and 14,700 on the west coast of Korea. Much of this was unobserved fire. I gave instructions that I wanted air spots, shore fire-control spots, and director spots at the targets which were worth shooting at. I wanted to know specifically what damage was done, not that "great damage" was done. The result of this was that we cut down to 8,500 rounds on the east coast . . . on the west coast we cut down to 6,500 rounds.[66]

Scott-Moncrieff could not have said it better himself.

The combat operations of Task Force 95 in Korea revealed the significant progress made by the British, Canadian, Australian, and American navies in combined formations. Aircraft carriers could operate in the same task force in 1950, and by 1952 a standardized spotting procedure was in place, even if the Americans used it inconsistently. The operations in Korea also served to highlight important differences between the navies in their organization, command and control, equipment, and operating style. These differences did not spring out of thin air, but reflected the historical experience, national tradition, and culture unique to each service. British and Canadian naval officers did not share the all-encompassing experience of the U.S. Navy's war against Japan, just as the vast bulk of the U.S. Navy did not fend off U-boats for years in the North Atlantic. These differences in experience, tradition, and culture therefore influenced not only the way each navy approached combat in Korea, but also other tasks such as ship driving, communications procedures, and writing of operations orders.

COMBINED NAVIES IN KOREA

The combined operations in Korea provided significant numbers of officers and sailors from the UN navies opportunities to observe each other's practices and skills for an extended period. These observations revealed that U.S. Navy captains tended to be less skilled in their ship-handling abilities than captains in the British and Commonwealth navies. Communications also proved to be an ongoing challenge due to less advanced equipment on British-built warships and a small number of commonly held radio ciphers. Finally, the prodigious size of American operational orders illustrated important differences between the U.S. Navy and its allies. Even so, the UN navies found solutions that enabled operations to continue with minimal interference. Personal relationships at the working level helped smooth over differences.

Differences in ship handling in Korea served to illustrate different areas of emphasis within each navy. British and Canadian officers frequently commented on the generally lower ship-handling and piloting skill of American captains.[67] One Canadian officer wrote that American captains were "not quite as skillful at pilotage and ship handling" as their Commonwealth counterparts.[68] Admiral Russell reported that American ships "have to take pilots, even for the simplest harbors."[69] A British report from September 1952 identified one reason for generally superior British skill in ship handling: "It has been found that US ships are often reluctant to go into confined waters. This is attributed to the absence of specialist (N) [navigation] officers and the lack of practical pilotage training brought about by the custom of employing pilots when in pilotage waters to a far greater extent than is customary in the Royal Navy."[70]

British sailors later recalled that American heavy warships, such as battleships and cruisers, preferred to stay further from the coasts than their British counterparts.[71] Some Canadian officers with greater experience operating with the U.S. Navy noticed a difference in ships stationed in the United States compared to those in Korea. A Canadian officer, Michael Stirling, later remembered that when he operated with U.S. Navy destroyers off San Diego or Long Beach, he thought the RCN destroyers could "wipe their eye." However, when he went to the Korean theater, he found the American destroyers that had been operating for several months "hot as firecrackers."[72] However, after serving in Korea for several months, the captain of the Canadian *Athabaskan* still found that American destroyers were not well versed in the basic maneuvers required to screen and guard aircraft carriers.[73] The different levels of ship-handling skills also shaped the degree to which senior officers became involved in the details of operations. Geoffrey Habesch served on British logistics ships in Korea and remembered that "the British admiral never interfered. He said, 'I'd like you chaps to go bombard that. Alright, off you go.' Where the American admiral would then say, 'First, I want you to get your anchor up.'"[74]

American officers often willingly admitted that the British and Commonwealth navies demonstrated superior ship-driving abilities. Vice Admiral Gerald Miller, who commanded Task Force 77 from July 1950 to July 1951, later recalled, "The Brits are professional seamen. . . . They [the Royal Navy] are pros. They spent a lot more time in their ships than we do."[75] Rear Admiral Boone's report on the March 1950 South China Sea exercises noted that "individual ship handling on the part of the British was impressive and generally superior to our own."[76] The explanation for this difference lay primarily in the organization and training of the officer corps in each navy.

In the mid-twentieth-century Royal and Commonwealth navies, the officer corps comprised three broad categories: executive officers, engineering officers, and other specialty officers such as supply officers. During World War II and the Korean War, only executive officers could command warships and larger formations such as fleets. Engineering officers were not viewed as having equal status with executive officers.[77] Within the executive officer branch, most officers would specialize in fields such as gunnery, torpedo and antisubmarine, navigation, or communications, along with others. However, executive officers could also choose not to specialize. These nonspecialists were known as "salt horses." Executive officers benefited from extensive sea time early in their careers. As a whole, British, Canadian, and Australian executive officers received more training and experience in driving and maneuvering a ship at sea than their American counterparts.[78]

By comparison, U.S. Navy officers received more technical education than the British and Commonwealth navies provided their officers. The U.S. Naval Academy at Annapolis emphasized engineering education much more than the Royal Naval College, Dartmouth, which provided more time at sea for midshipmen. In contrast to the British specialization system, American officers were trained as generalists and could be rotated throughout a ship's divisions, from communications to navigation to engineering. The American focus on engineering education gave U.S. Navy officers a much stronger technical background than their British counterparts, but did not give the Americans as much experience in ship handling.[79]

While the U.S. Navy often came off second best in ship handling, the Royal Navy struggled to keep up with the volume of American communications in Korea. In general, U.S. Navy warships carried larger and more advanced sets of communications equipment than British and Australian ships, with the Canadians somewhere in between.[80] American warships also carried a larger complement of communications personnel than the British, Canadians, and Australians and as a result could handle more radio traffic.

Combat operations created far more message traffic than in peacetime. The sheer volume of radio messages being sent and received in the Korean theater at times threatened to overwhelm even American warships.[81] A British telegraphist who served on *Theseus* in Korea recalled that British warships often only had one radio operator on duty, while the Americans had two operators. He concluded that the communications aspect of Korea "really was horrendous."[82] Admiral Russell agreed, writing that "our friends and allies the Americans work on such lavish scales that it is hard to compete."[83] Certainly, the more plentiful American supply of personnel forced British communicators to work extra hard just to keep up.

The British also found their communications limited by their equipment. Throughout the war, the U.S. Navy gradually equipped more and more ships and aircraft with ultrahigh frequency (UHF) radios while the British still relied on very high frequency (VHF) radios. The Americans still carried VHF but preferred to use UHF when possible. In any event, the Americans used different radio crystals, which limited the number of VHF frequencies common to all sides.[84] Canadian warships carried UHF equipment, and Australian ships borrowed UHF radios from the U.S. Navy beginning in 1952.[85] Furthermore, American ships carried infrared signaling equipment, codenamed "Nancy," for use at night, which British ships did not carry, though Canadian ships did.[86] Vice Admiral Andrewes summarized the impact of superior American equipment on communications: "The USN will normally have more equipment and operators than ourselves and, having also more ships, can give their ships and operators longer rest periods and therefore work them harder when they are at sea. The natural tendency of US Communications Officers when a new requirement arises, is to open a new circuit for it. Within reasonable limits this tendency should be resisted."[87]

The British also discovered that their decryption equipment allowed them to decode messages sent in only certain American ciphers. Other coded messages could not be read unless the British could get the message retransmitted in a cipher they held.[88] Even when the British could decrypt communications, their personnel sometimes found that they were unfamiliar with certain American abbreviations. This particular problem eased over time for individual ships as their personnel gained experience, but the arrival of new ships and personnel meant the issue recurred frequently.[89]

From the British perspective, American reporting procedures, such as the need to order subordinates to comply, served to unnecessarily overload their already strained communications personnel and equipment. Throughout the 1940s, as the demands of naval communications steadily grew, the Royal Navy faced a choice: either expand the range of frequencies available in radio suites or exercise more radio discipline. In general, the British approach in communications was to exercise more discipline, turning necessity into a virtue, while the American solution was to upgrade their equipment.[90]

As a result of these different approaches to communications, radio discipline proved to be a major difference between the two sides. The British and Commonwealth navies repeatedly complained that U.S. pilots and ships talked far too much on their radios. Robert McCandless, who served as a Fleet Air Arm pilot in Korea, later recalled that while British pilots maintained silence over the front line in order to listen, "there were Americans yakking all the time about inconsequential stuff" such that "you couldn't get a word in edgewise." As a result, American ground liaison officers were frequently "delighted" to have British aircraft supporting them because the British kept their radio frequency clear for necessary messages.[91] Captain Reed of the *Athabaskan* complained of poor radio discipline after escorting the *Missouri* for a bombardment.[92] Paul Millett, another British pilot, reported that this problem extended to U.S. Air Force pilots, who "had nothing like our R/T [radio transmitter] discipline."[93] An internal U.S. Navy report from 1953 admitted as much, concluding that: "Considerable effort should be made by U.S. Fleet to reduce the amount of voice radio traffic. Our voice circuits are so cluttered up with routine checks and chatter that it is almost impossible to send an important message when required. Comparisons are odious, but we have much to learn in communications from the British."[94]

The difference in radio discipline stemmed in part from the importance each navy attached to using radio signals against the enemy, a discipline known at the time as "radio warfare." In the interwar years and in World War II, the British and Canadians placed considerable emphasis on operating under radio silence. Postwar combined exercises repeatedly revealed that the British and Canadians practiced radio warfare tactics considerably more than their American counterparts. Each navy's unique background shaped its communications policy and practices.[95]

Operations orders proved to be another aspect of communications in which many British and Commonwealth officers wished the U.S. Navy would learn from their experience. Complaints about the size of American operational orders went back to World War II. Captain Henry Burrell of the Australian destroyer *Bataan* reported receiving "a vast tome" of operations orders upon joining the Seventh Fleet in 1945.[96] Andrewes in his first Korean report attributed the large size of American operational orders to an overly rigid command system that gave less discretion to ships' captains:

Another product of this basic doctrine is the prodigious size of US operations orders and plans. These are superbly produced at very short notice but contain so much detail that some of the wood is inevitably lost in the trees. In communications orders for instance it is customary to print long extracts from US publications held by all ships and authorities concerned, and furthermore to duplicate or triplicate information . . . for instance the orders for air spotting for naval gunfire will appear in the air, gunnery, and communication sections.[97]

This duplication increased the time required to change orders. For instance, if the air-spotting orders required modification, the staff would need to issue the change for every appearance of the air-spotting orders within the overall plan. Even with this level of detail in operational orders, American commanders tended to issue regular reminders to perform basic tasks such as remaining alert for mines or enemy aircraft.[98] Andrewes's successor, Scott-Moncrieff, also blamed an overly rigid American command system for orders with excessive detail.[99]

However, some British and Commonwealth officers found American orders effectively formatted and quite useful. Despite joining the Inchon landing force with no notice and very little preparation, the captain of *Kenya* "found that the orders were so clear and comprehensive that in the course of a week's operations it was only necessary to ask one question."[100] Commander Plomer thought the Canadians were well positioned to take advantage of the fact "that the US format [for orders] combined with the British knack of using the chosen word produces a satisfactory directive."[101] For ships operating with an unfamiliar formation on short notice, detailed orders could help ease the transition. However, for ships accustomed to operating in long-standing formations—which tended to operate using less-detailed instructions—long operation orders could seem a burden.

Naval communications in Korea proved to be a perennial challenge, requiring constant work to mitigate technical and procedural differences, particularly between the U.S. Navy on the one hand and the British and Australians on the other. Superior American equipment, along with organizational differences, forced commanders to find ad hoc solutions in the short term while awaiting the arrival of new equipment and American-Canadian-British books such as ATP 1 and ACP 175. The conclusion of the Admiralty's director of Signal Division on Exercise Mainbrace equally applied to Korea. The director argued that the U.S. Navy tended to rely too much on its superior equipment, but did not make the most effective use of it. In contrast, the Royal Navy relied too heavily on its effective radio organization and was insufficiently flexible in using alternative radio circuits.[102]

EXCHANGES

In spite of the challenges discussed above, the UN navies proved quite capable of operating effectively and successfully together for extended periods of time. Exchanges of officers and crew between ships of different nationalities came to be an important part of this success. In 1950 and 1951 ships on the west coast frequently provided one or two liaison officers to one another. By the summer of 1952, the steady, relatively unchanging pace of operations in Korea created an opportunity for larger groups of personnel, typically under a dozen, to visit other ships for a couple days at a time. These exchanges served to familiarize personnel with the structure and organization of other ships while also building relationships between individual crew members.

An early example of these visits took place in October 1950 just after the Inchon landings. A UN force assigned to land X Corps at Wonson on the North Korean east coast found several minefields blocking access to the harbor. While waiting for minesweepers to arrive from Japan, Commander Robert Welland of the *Athabaskan* invited several captains from American destroyers also escorting the landing force to lunch. The American officers enjoyed the drinks available on Canadian warships, though Welland found them much less willing to drink when an American admiral was present. Several American captains reciprocated, which may well have been Welland's purpose all along, since he thought the Americans had much better food as well as ice cream, which was not available on *Athabaskan*.[103] These types of visits created personal connections between captains and allowed them to discuss the similar challenges they faced.

Visits and exchanges also served to help familiarize new ships with operating procedures and conditions in the Korean theater. By 1952 each carrier rotating off west coast duty would try to meet up with the replacement carrier to exchange "turnover notes." This exchange served both to give new ships the benefit of experience and to increase continuity in operations between carriers. Captain Almon Loomis of the light carrier *Sicily* found the turnover notes he received from the *Bataan* in September 1952 to be quite helpful as they included charts, working files, and "an excellent briefing." In addition to documents, the Task Group 95.1 staff in Sasebo and the *Ocean* each provided a British officer to answer questions and help acclimate the *Sicily* for the first part of the ship's patrol.[104] Captain Harry Horney of the carrier *Bataan* appreciated the opportunity to send four of his officers ahead of the ship to spend several days visiting ships on the west coast before the *Bataan*'s patrol since the "turnover period" with the *Badoeng Strait* was quite short.[105] In effect, these practices helped create stability in Task Force 95 methods.

Visits by Canadian Lieutenants John B. C. Carling and Robert A. Evans to the American destroyer *Higbee* in 1953 illustrate how such visits worked. Carling found the *Higbee* physically impressive, writing that "generally speaking all equipment worked well and the ship was generously endowed . . . boards in the CIC [Combat Information Center] were large, extremely well arranged, and contained a wealth of ready information." The *Higbee*'s internal layout was functional, well planned, and easy to keep clean, and the galley served excellent meals. Carling concluded that "with such a ship, her facilities and our Canadian way of doing things we would certainly approximate the ultimate."[106]

Evans also found the *Higbee*'s equipment impressive, though he found the bridge to be rather chaotic since the space was enclosed and had numerous personnel stationed there. He thought that the CIC was approximately twice the size of the comparable RCN space. Evans discovered that most of the crew and officers were reservists called up for the Korean War and "seem to be of an accord in their intention not to sign again once their present engagement is completed." Evans saved the second half of his report to praise American food:

Regarding the meals the only comment I can make to do justice is TERRIFIC [all caps original]. With large refrigerators to work with the Supply Officer is able to provide delicious meals even on prolonged patrols. Officers are on Wardroom messing and for it pay about 30 out of their allowed 48 dollars a month. However, they eat little better than the crew to whom steaks, chops, fried chicken, fresh frozen vegetables, etc., are the rule rather than the exception. Since the Captain likes Ice Cream, the Wardroom eats Ice Cream two meals out of three while the machine is in working order.[107] Lots of fresh fruit is also available to crew members and officers alike. Coffee: This liquid is even more vital aboard *Higbee* than fuel and is probably consumed in greater quantities. In every compartment and working space in the ship there is a hot plate with a pot of coffee ready 24 hours a day.[108]

With access to food like this, Canadian commanders preferred to draw food supplies from the U.S. Navy.[109] While British officers freely admitted that the food on their ships "wasn't all that much," they did find that the Americans enjoyed the alcohol available on British warships.[110]

These exchanges and visits also sometimes created connections between ships' crews. One natural pairing occurred between the Australian destroyer *Bataan* and the ship's American counterpart, the light carrier *Bataan*. The Australian *Bataan*'s Commander William Marks wrote of the first meeting between the two ships on February 21, 1951: "For some time past we had all been looking forward to the day when we would meet our namesake."[111] The two captains clearly enjoyed each other's company, and when the destroyer *Bataan* left the carrier *Bataan* after two days of operating together, Commander Marks signaled: "Consider the new firm Bataan & Son is a most happy and profitable team."[112] In April 1951, the two ships operated together for the last time, and the American *Bataan*'s Captain Edgar Neale signaled to Marks: "As usual yours is a very smart ship that reflects credit upon you. Let's hope our next meeting is soon and I suggest Sydney."[113]

Another relationship formed during the winter of 1952–1953 between the carriers *Badoeng Strait* and *Glory*. The two ships regularly exchanged officers over a period of months, both to familiarize the crews with each other's ships and to observe air operations. The officers tended to be junior officers, as the American ship could not spare others while on operations. Often, after observing operations for several days, the visiting officers would be flown

HMAS *Warramunga*, HMS *Charity*, HMAS *Bataan* moored at Yokosuka, Japan, January 26, 1951. *Source*: NH 90625, Naval History and Heritage Command, Washington, D.C.

back to Japan to rejoin their ship.[114] Captain Herman Ray of the *Badoeng Strait* thought that the exchanges were "interesting and [a] valuable source of training."[115]

Officer exchanges between carriers naturally led them to make comparisons. British Lieutenant Commander Robert McCandless spent nine days aboard the *Badoeng Strait* and decided that the British flight deck procedure allowed aircraft to land more rapidly. Conversations with American officers revealed that the ship's company had not practiced deck operations as extensively as the British had before deploying.[116] American officers on the *Glory* and the *Ocean* commented frequently on the high percentage of aircraft regularly available for service on the British carriers.[117] McCandless's conclusion succinctly summarizes perhaps one of the benefits of these exchanges: "It was just nice to be able to talk to people with similar problems and to see how they dealt with them."[118] In addition to forming connections,

USS *Badoeng Strait* in winter off Korea, November 30, 1950. *Source*: NH 97375, Naval History and Heritage Command, Washington, D.C.

Vice Admiral Harold Martin, commander, Seventh Fleet, thought that the exchanges improved operational effectiveness: "It is considered that the result obtained by visits, conferences, and assignment of liaison officers have been excellent. The personal contact achieved has permitted a much more detailed and timely approach to various problems than letters, dispatches, and reports would have accomplished. The free interchange of thought has facilitated parallel planning and operations against the enemy."[119]

EXERCISES

In addition to allowing personnel exchanges, the stalemate on land provided enough stability in operations to allow UN naval forces to train for antisubmarine operations in future conflicts. American and British commanders in Korean waters worried about the falling proficiency of their ships in antisubmarine warfare (ASW). The absence of an enemy submarine threat in

Korea slowly wore down the skills of sonar operators and captains in ASW tactics through lack of practice. A 1952 Pacific Fleet report summarized the problem: "Continuous ASW training is highly necessary in order to maintain satisfactory readiness. Air and surface units quickly show the deleterious effects of long lapses in training . . . training on a live submarine is absolutely necessary."[120]

While operating off the Korean coast early in the war, allied warships were simply too busy to practice ASW or train with friendly submarines. To address this problem, the U.S. Navy instituted a series of antisubmarine exercises beginning in July 1951.[121] American submarines played the part of enemy submarines while a hunter-killer group composed of an escort carrier and several destroyers hunted them. However, problems of time and distance appear to have precluded British and Commonwealth participation until after the armistice in July 1953. The Americans staged the exercises out of Yokosuka near Tokyo, almost six hundred miles from the British and Commonwealth base at Sasebo. Flag officer, second in command, Far East found that getting to Yokosuka and back took his ships out of service for too long. Until then, the British and Commonwealth made do with tabletop tactical games at Sasebo along with infrequent visits to Sasebo by Royal Navy submarines for ASW practice.[122]

When the British, Canadians, and Australians began to participate in these American exercises after the armistice, their experience underscored some of the realities of operating with the U.S. Navy in Korea, while also providing a window into Pacific Fleet ASW development and tactics. For example, the Australian destroyer *Tobruk* took part in a nine-day exercise in late August 1953 involving the carrier *Sicily*, eight American escorts, the British destroyer *Constance*, and two American submarines. The exercise involved basic skills practice as well as more advanced drills where the submarines could maneuver at will. The *Tobruk*'s captain, Commander Ian McDonald, thought the exercises "were most informative, and gave all personnel excellent practice in anti-submarine techniques, and general handling of destroyer screens." At the same time, the superiority of American radar, radio, and sonar equipment meant that neither of the Commonwealth ships was able to be as completely involved in the activities as the U.S. Navy destroyers. For example, neither ship could communicate with *Sicily*'s UHF-equipped aircraft and helicopters. McDonald thought the *Sicily*'s flight operations were of a high standard, especially the launches and landings at night, a reflection of American emphasis on carrier operations.[123]

A week after *Tobruk*'s exercise, the *Sicily* led another ASW exercise with the Canadian *Iroquois* and *Athabaskan*, seven USN escorts, and two submarines. The pattern of exercises mirrored the August set and was the first time some of the Canadian personnel worked with helicopters equipped with retractable sonar equipment, also known as dipping sonar. Helicopters promised a solution to a problem vexing the allied navies: how to successfully transfer contact with a submarine from orbiting aircraft to surface ships. Typically, aircraft, from either a carrier or a shore base, first made contact with a submarine at some distance from the escorts. However, in the early 1950s, aircraft did not have a weapon with which to effectively attack submarines underwater as air-dropping homing torpedoes were still being refined.

To attack the submarine, the aircraft maintained contact while guiding the surface ships to the submarine's location. As the surface ships approached the submarine, however, the noise from their propellers and engines began to drown out the noise from the submerged target picked up by the aircraft's passive sonobuoys. The escorts often approached the submarine's position at high speed in order to minimize the period during which they were most vulnerable to torpedoes. The noise from this high-speed run drowned out the submarine's noise, giving the submarine an opportunity to escape. In the September exercises, the American submarines successfully broke contact approximately half the time during the "handoff" from the aircraft to the escorts. The solution was a helicopter equipped with active sonar, which could maintain contact with the submarine even as the escorts approached since active sonar did not depend on hearing a submarine's noise. The Canadians found that with helicopter assistance, the process of "handing off" the submarine from the aircraft to the escorts without breaking contact succeeded every time. Captain William Landymore concluded that the use of helicopters was "the most significant advance in A/S (anti-submarine) operations since World War II."[124]

While the ASW exercises provided valuable experience operating in multinational formations, they served as more of an introduction to submarine hunting for American destroyers than as a refresher course as intended. Submarines frequently penetrated the screen during the exercises, and initial contact often came *after* the submarine fired its torpedoes.[125]

American submarine captains told an Australian officer that the escorts "were not very efficient A/S [antisubmarine] vessels" and did not present a serious threat to the submarines. The submarine captains identified "lack of constant practice" as the culprit.[126] A Pacific Fleet report noted that after taking part in the exercises, destroyer captains frequently said something to the effect of "This is the first time I've been on an ASW operation, it was very interesting, and I think I learned something."[127] The frequency of this kind of comment indicated the lack of training and experience among U.S. Navy destroyer crews in Korean waters in antisubmarine warfare.

The exchanges between west coast ships and the ASW exercises off Japan both provided opportunities for American personnel to meet their British, Canadian, and Australian counterparts. British and Commonwealth personnel often found American equipment impressive but doubted whether the U.S. Navy put its superior equipment to the best use. At the same time, the exchanges created connections and relationships between the four navies, connections that served as the bedrock of navy-to-navy relations. The exercises also provided valuable experience operating in American formations, particularly for the Canadians, who were beginning to exercise frequently with the U.S. Navy.

A NEW PATTERN OF COMBINED OPERATIONS

A significant number of officers serving in the Korean theater found the international nature of the fighting noteworthy. While several operations during World War II involved ships from multiple navies, many participants in the Korean War found that the number of different nations that were represented was remarkable. Despite the potential challenges, most observers agreed that the multinational navy off the Korean coast proved entirely capable of operating effectively. Many described the combination of ships from so many different nations operating together as "unique." Vice Admiral Andrewes opened his first report on Korean operations by noting that "the campaign was probably unique in that ships of seven nationalities were, with minor exceptions, operationally interchangeable, a state of affairs which was developed very quickly and harmoniously."[128] In June 1951, Rear Admiral Smith, commander, Task Force 95, wrote to the recently departed Admiral Dyer that ships from ten navies operating together "is unique in the world's history."[129] A month later, the British naval advisor to the embassy in Tokyo noted that Task Force 95 included ships from nine navies, making the unit "unique in the world's history."[130] Clearly, naval officers found the multinational UN force noteworthy.

Certainly, groups of warships from different nations had worked together prior to the Korean War. Almost all of the Allied naval operations in European waters in 1944 and 1945 involved warships from Britain, the United States, Canada, France, and sometimes other occupied European nations such Poland, Norway, and the Netherlands. The Royal Navy's Ninth Submarine Flotilla during World War II comprised British, Polish, Free French, Norwegian, and Dutch submarines. However, the Korean operations gave large sections of the U.S. Navy experience operating with several other navies. Furthermore, the number of navies operating together regularly created impressive international scenes. On April 8, 1951, two carriers, *Bataan* and *Theseus*, left Sasebo escorted by six destroyers, which included two American, one Australian, one British, and two Canadian ships. Almost a month later, on May 2, 1951, *Bataan* operated with *Glory*, both carriers being escorted by three Canadian, two Australian, one British, and two American destroyers for several days.[131] Rear Admiral Eric Clifford noted in July 1953 that formations with ships from four navies were "a common occurrence."[132] Captain Ignatius Galantin of the American oiler *Navasota* recorded in his memoir an incident where a British doctor from an Australian destroyer worked with an American doctor using British surgical gloves from a Canadian destroyer to remove the appendix of a South Korean corporal on board an American oiler.[133]

The overwhelming majority of comments on multinational naval operations in Korea emphasize the harmony, cooperation, and efficiency with which the operations were conducted. American, British, and Commonwealth officers praised the cooperation between their ships in operations "with a number of heterogeneous units," in the words of one overly technical American report.[134] Commander Marks of Australia's *Bataan* reported that for May 1951 the multinational screens for west coast carriers "operated in complete harmony." After a year of combined operations, Marks felt that the UN naval forces were "operating more and more as a composite force" due to growing "mutual confidence between ships of the various Navies." As a result of this confidence, "it is the rule and not the exception to operate ships drawn from the United States and British Commonwealth Navies together in units . . . with the certain knowledge that they will work as an efficient and happy team."[135]

Most of the American west coast carrier captains also concluded that the ships in Task Force 95 effectively worked together. Captain Miller of the carrier *Bataan* thought the combined carrier operations during May 1951 "went off remarkably well."[136] The commander of the *Badoeng Strait* praised the "almost universal knowledge and adoption of joint maneuvering, screening, communication, and replenishment evolutions by all units."[137] Captain William Schoech of the carrier *Sicily* thought "that the international character of the forces which comprise CTE [Carrier Task Element] 95.11 were no obstacle to smooth operation."[138] After his service in Korea, Canadian Commander Edward Madgwick wrote that "the combined naval efforts have been entirely successful and have achieved an extremely high degree of cooperation." He felt that one reason for this was that "the USN calls the tune in Korean waters and everybody else have to do their best to follow suit."[139]

The cooperation between navies in the Korean theater drew upon the experience of World War II combined naval operations. Admiral Martin commanded the Seventh Fleet from March 1951 to 1952 and felt that Korean War cooperation continued a pattern, noting that "as usual, the relationships between the British Navy and ours were cordial and no problem was too great to be settled by a brief discussion."[140] Captain Richard Peek of the *Tobruk* later recalled that operating with the U.S. Navy off Korea did not pose any problems because the RAN spent four years with the Americans in the Pacific theater.[141] When asked later in life about operating with the U.S. Navy in Korea, one British officer spoke for many when he replied that "one always regards them as being the same sort of things as ourselves."[142]

The experience of operating with foreign navies often made officers aware of the need for greater standardization between their fleets, particularly in the areas of procedures and communications. Miller, the captain of the carrier *Bataan*, thought that multinational operations "emphasized the benefits to be derived from the standardization of doctrine and operating techniques throughout the naval services of the United Nations" and recommended that "every opportunity be taken to train and operate these forces in company."[143] The Pacific Fleet's third evaluation report recommended that standardized documents such as ATP 1 and ACP 175 be made available to nations that did not currently receive them, a list that would include Colombia and Thailand.[144] Naval operations in Korea also led some officers to conclude that standardization was not proceeding rapidly enough. Commander Plomer, the senior Canadian naval officer in Korea in 1952, reported that "although nearly all naval components of the United Nations Forces looked eagerly forward to the introduction of ATP 1 and ACP 175, it did not occur. It is a great shame that the new Allied Maneuvering Instructions were not hurried into force in this theater for use by a truly United Nations Group."[145]

ATP 1 and ACP 175 did come into use in Korea in the summer of 1952, replacing the U.S. Navy publications used up to that point. The NATO navies, including Britain, Canada, and the U.S., received copies automatically, and the British made these documents available to Australia and New Zealand.[146] Rear Admiral Clifford reported in July 1953 that "no difficulty has been experienced in using ATP 1 and ACP 175 with American ships."[147] The use of ATP 1 and ACP 175 in Korea highlighted the importance of the CANUKUS organization. Although the two books were known as NATO books, the British, Canadian, and American navies retained ownership, which allowed them to use the material in non-NATO settings, such as during the Korean War.

Reports from British, Canadian, Australian, and American officers indicate that their ships effectively worked together in the Korean War. Relationships between officers played a central role in the success of multinational naval operations in Korea. Liaison officers, personnel exchanges, and visits between ships while in port all helped smooth over the inevitable differences and misunderstandings involved in bringing together ships from so many different navies. At the same time, some personnel such as the Royal Navy's Captain Villiers and the U.S. Navy's Admiral Dyer could create tension in navy-to-navy to relations. Still on the whole cooperation appears to have been more common than conflict. Small gestures and acts of kindness played a role as well. When the *Ocean* left Korea in 1953, the crew of the *Philippine Sea* gathered on the flight deck and stood at attention as the British carrier passed the American carrier. A U.S. Navy band played "God Save the Queen" as *Ocean* headed out to sea.[148] These kinds of gestures helped foster cooperative relations and worked in tandem with the relationships built between ship's personnel.

While UN naval forces overall cooperated effectively during the Korean War, the conflict also served as a reminder that basic differences between navies—

such as fleet and budget size as well as technical capabilities—could create potential problems that could undermine effective cooperation. Overcoming these problems required constant work by commanders, their staffs, and liaison officers. This work, in turn, depended on relationships that, while typically harmonious, remained vulnerable to divisive personalities, such as Admiral Dyer. Though personally pro-British, Dyer's command style and approach to operations damaged relations with Admiral Scott-Moncrieff and the British naval staff at Sasebo. Personalities also mattered at sea, though relations at sea were strengthened by the aid that ships regularly provided to each other, such as picking up downed pilots, providing meals for visiting personnel and liaison officers, and pooling medical personnel and chaplains.

The Korean War also provided a significant number of American officers with extensive experience operating with allied navies, primarily the British, Canadian, and Australian fleets. In Task Group 95.1, multinational formations with ships from three or four countries became as regular as the tide, while personnel in Task Force 77 regularly worked with a Commonwealth destroyer as a part of the carriers' screen. In contrast to exercises where a large number of officers gained relatively brief experience working with allied navies, the three years of the Korean War gave a large portion of a generation of American officers a deep background in multinational naval operations. The war served to cement a pattern of warfare begun during World War II that involved warships from different navies operating in combined formations.

In contrast to World War II, the American, British, Canadian, and Australian naval forces off Korea could draw upon the progress made in standardization. For example, the U.S. Navy and Royal Navy followed standardized procedures for underway replenishment and could manufacture adaptors for fueling lines on short notice. By the end of the war, allied navies in Korea also operated by using standardized communications and tactical books such as ATP 1 and ACP 175. Even in areas where common procedures were not yet in existence, the work of standardization increased the knowledge of other navy's procedures, typically British and Commonwealth awareness of American methods. For example, the work done to develop common signals for landing aircraft on carriers exposed the bulk of the Fleet Air Arm to American landing signals. Furthermore, the Korean experience increased awareness of the benefits of standardization and the work still to be done, particularly in the U.S. Navy, where awareness of the subject tended to rise and fall with the level of contact with foreign navies.

The Korean War also demonstrated that the U.S. Navy could effectively operate with the British, Canadians, and Australians on short notice. The units involved achieved this rapid integration through a combination of "when in Rome" solutions such as adopting American books, ad hoc work-arounds such as fueling adaptors, and personnel exchanges to smooth over inevitable misunderstandings. In particular, the success of liaison officers and exchange officers in American warships depended in large measure on the U.S. Navy's collective view of the trustworthiness of the navy being represented. The British, Canadian, and Australian navies fought alongside the U.S. Navy in World War II, and ties between the four fleets grew deeper through the exchanges and exercises of the next five years. By the time of the Korean War, American contact with these three fleets was regular and frequent, although more so with the British and Canadians than with the Australians. This level of contact clearly eased the work of integration in the early weeks and months of the Korean War.

Conclusion: Deep and Wide Naval Links

The U.S. Navy's early Cold War pursuit of closer ties with the British and Canadians and later the Australians represented a shift away from a largely independent past toward an ally-based future. No longer a temporary wartime expedient, combined naval operations now became a permanent part of the navy's experience. Within this American shift to ally-based operations, the British and Canadians played critical roles. The Canadians, in particular, proposed projects and agreements leading to closer relations more than the Americans did. These proposals and agreements included officer educational exchanges, sharing of training facilities, establishment of liaison offices, and combined training exercises. While the U.S. Navy's World War II experience provided some impetus for the postwar shift to ally-based warfare, the RN and RCN also pushed the Americans in that direction, forcing them to consider how best to achieve peacetime cooperation.

The Canadian and British efforts to establish liaison and exchange programs, to send officers to American schools, and to create formal channels for exchanging information frequently highlighted the U.S. Navy's relative inexperience in building peacetime ties with foreign navies. The U.S. Navy posted only a small number of officers to liaison positions and only intermittently sent observers to British naval exercises. While the British and Canadians sent high-caliber officers to American military schools, the U.S. Navy showed comparatively less interest in ensuring that USN officers filled slots offered by Britain and Canada. The Office of Naval Intelligence proved unable to achieve the easy flow of information with the RN and RCN desired by much of the USN, and the security walls around the Bureau of Aeronautics repeatedly stymied the British and Canadians. All of this underlines the fact that the U.S. Navy struggled to adopt the procedures and processes required to make international naval cooperation work. Simply put, the Americans were largely unprepared for the organizational and administrative challenges of close navy-to-navy relations. American naval officers, for the most part, knew they wanted close postwar ties with the RN and RCN, but had to learn how to build and maintain them.

However much the U.S. Navy wanted to grant the British and Canadians privileges not given to other nations, the Americans did not want to say so publicly or be seen to do so. Public and congressional opinion remained supportive of the United Nations in the initial years after World War II, and close peacetime relations with the British and Canadians would have been interpreted as undermining the UN. Navy leaders understood this political dynamic, which shaped their policies on Anglo-American and Canadian-American naval relations. This perspective supports Charles Brower's argument that in World War II U.S. military leaders, far from being apolitical, clearly understood and acted in light of domestic political concerns.[1]

When faced with a choice between open favoritism and elimination of British and Canadian special privileges, the U.S. Navy chose elimination over open favoritism. This American approach to international military relations was demonstrated in the decisions to kick the British naval staff in Washington out of their Pentagon offices in 1949 and no longer to allow British and Canadian officers to attend the Naval War College after 1950. In these decisions, the U.S. Navy acted in accordance with its perception of the politics of American society in the late 1940s.

The impact of these decisions on British and Canadian access to U.S. Navy information was mitigated by the web of links that the two navies maintained with the Americans. The web of liaison officers, combined training, officer exchanges, standardization programs, and the naval staffs in Washington provided numerous conduits through which information could flow.

The links between these four navies can be divided into two groups: deep links and wide links. Deep links involved immersing an officer within another navy for an extended period of time. Liaison officers, pilot and staff exchanges, naval attachés, and war college exchanges all fit into this category. Deep links provided a small number of officers with extensive knowledge of another navy through immersion. At the same time, officers in these positions served as ambassadors for their own navy and nation.

Wide links gave large numbers of personnel a briefer experience interacting with another navy. These links consisted of visits by ships and aircraft to ASW training facilities, combined exercises, and ship visits. Wide links gave a wide swathe of personnel a brief, more limited experience than the immersion involved in deep links. These wide links fostered familiarity with foreign capabilities and naval cultures and built confidence in the ability of foreign personnel to operate in combined formations. Exercises in particular created shared operational experiences, while visits provided opportunities to build relationships and therefore trust in allies' sailors.

Standardization programs such as the development of ATP 1 and ACP 175 began as deep links due to the detailed discussions conducted by a small group of officers involved in the program. If an agreement was reached, then the link became wide as the agreement was implemented across each fleet. Similarly, the Korean War provided deep links in that British, American, and Commonwealth ships operated together in Task Force 95 for extended periods. At the same time, the sheer number of personnel in Task Force 95 meant that a large number of officers and crew could interact with their foreign counterparts. By 1953 the U.S. Navy had both deep and wide links with the British and Canadian navies, and to a lesser degree the Australians.

Despite these institutional links, relations between the U.S. Navy and the British, Canadian, and Australian fleets were repeatedly influenced and affected by individual personalities and relationships. Bruce Fraser's ability to connect with American officers improved ties between Task Force 99 and the Home Fleet and later between the British Pacific Fleet and the U.S. Pacific Fleet. Ben Custer in Ottawa played a crucial role in the RCN's acquisition of USN Avengers, while Stephen Jurika played an equally significant role in Australia's loss of access to classified American data. Field Marshal Montgomery's interventions in Ottawa and Washington advanced the standardization agenda that he thought was so important. Rear Admiral Dyer's more aggressive approach to naval operations in Korea damaged relations with the Royal Navy, especially Rear Admiral Scott-Moncrieff. At the same time, the anti-American views of Scott-Moncrieff's chief of staff, Captain R. A. Villiers, infected Scott-Moncrieff's headquarters staff, negatively influencing relations with the American command in Sasebo. Personalities repeatedly and unpredictably thrust themselves into navy-to-navy relations.

In addition to links at the national level, the operating forces of these four fleets regularly interacted with one another. Coordination and cooperation occurred through fleet commanders and their staffs, such as war planning conferences between the U.S. Navy's Sixth Fleet and Britain's Mediterranean Fleet. The U.S. Navy in particular delegated authority and initiative to fleet commanders to coordinate with their British, Canadian, and Australian counterparts. This more decentralized approach to navy-to-navy relations helped reduce the influence of politics on day-to-day connections while also easing the process of coordination. In important ways the U.S. Navy began to view and relate to its closest partners as simply neighboring naval commands. Liaison, coordination, and shared exercises were all part of the day-to-day business of commands with shared or neighboring areas of responsibility. In this sense, the Ramsey-Collins and Radford-Collins agreements in the Pacific showed how the Pacific Fleet was viewing the Royal Australian Navy as similar to Far East Command, rather than as an entirely foreign entity. Delegating authority to coordinate also led to a growing number of combined exercises.

Beginning in 1946, the U.S. Navy regularly participated in combined exercises with the RN, RCN, and RAN, ranging from simple training exercises to massive wargames such as NATO's Exercise Mainbrace in 1952. As a result, U.S. Navy personnel became more comfortable working with these navies. In these exercises, the British and Canadian navies were reminded of the influence of the Pacific War on American operating patterns. The U.S. Navy practiced a Pacific style of warfare emphasizing mobile carrier operations over direct convoy defense. Thus, exercises both helped to build the trust, confidence, and familiarity required for effective combined naval operations and simultaneously highlighted the enduring differences between the fleets.

These exercises gave large numbers of personnel experience operating with foreign navies, while also revealing the need for common communications and tactical maneuvering books. Beginning in 1949, the CANUKUS ASW Working Group, a group of British, Canadian, and American officers whose existence was a poorly kept Washington secret, began writing a combined communications book and a tactical book for use by the three navies. These books went on to become the basis for combined naval operations by the navies of NATO.

Winston Churchill wrote to the foreign secretary, Ernest Bevin, in November 1945 that he hoped that the continuation of close military-to-military relations between Britain and America would result in "similarity and interchangeability of weapons, common manuals of instruction for the Armed Forces, inter-related plans for the war mobilization of industry, and finally interchange of officers at schools and colleges."[2] Churchill made a similar appeal publicly in his Iron Curtain speech in Missouri in March 1946. The thirty-fifth recommendation of the Canadian-American PJBD mirrored most of the military-to-military proposals in Churchill's Missouri speech. For the RN, RCN, and USN, significant progress toward accomplishing these goals had been made by 1953.

The U.S. Navy's experience in international naval cooperation reflected wider changes in American foreign policy and American society. World War II left the United States with a preponderance of power, and Pearl Harbor vividly demonstrated the importance of overseas affairs to American national security interests.[3] Many American officials concluded that the United States must play a more active role overseas in cooperation with like-minded allies, especially the British and the Commonwealth. At the same time, suspicion toward Britain was a long-standing tradition in American politics, as was a rejection of permanent alliances. The competition between these sets of ideas was best captured in the congressional debates over NATO that ended with the treaty's approval. Even before NATO was ratified in 1949, the U.S. Navy was creating a functional peacetime naval alliance in cooperation with the British and Canadians, a fundamental shift in American naval policy.

Despite the overall trend toward close relations, attitudes within the USN toward the RN and RCN varied. While American fleet commanders often welcomed the opportunity for combined training with British and Commonwealth formations, the Navy Department did not want to place major American warships under foreign operational control as had occurred during World War II. By 1953, the Strategic Plans Division in the Office of the

Chief of Naval Operations had an unwritten rule that "no heavy U.S. Navy forces should operate under a British admiral."[4] Attitudes also varied by community within the U.S. Navy. American naval aviators were quite willing to help the RCN establish its new naval aviation branch, but tended to feel that the U.S. Navy had little to learn about aircraft carrier operations from the British. While serving on SACLANT's staff in 1952, Captain Herbert Riley once told British Admiral Andrewes, "I don't think there's anything that the Royal Navy or the Fleet Air Arm can teach American naval aviators about operations in combat."[5] In this respect American naval aviators tended to act as the older brother who was happy to teach his younger brother how to tie his shoes but rarely considered that his sibling might have something to teach him. At the same time, some within the U.S. Navy's aviation community expressed admiration for British naval aviation, particularly technical developments such as the angled flight deck, the mirror landing system, and the steam catapult. In contrast, the U.S. Navy's ASW and submarine communities tended to consider the British to be a relatively equal partner, though one with a comparatively tighter budget.

In popular understanding, the "special relationship" between the United States and the United Kingdom conjures up images of two partners working together in total harmony. American relations with Canada and Australia are also sometimes labeled "special." In reality, American naval relations with the British, Canadians, and Australians in the years after World War II were hardly free of conflict. Segments of the American officer corps thought the Royal Navy had nothing to teach them about naval aviation, while many British officers resented being supplanted by the Americans as the world's largest, most powerful fleet. The Canadians were divided, according to an American admiral in 1945, between "one faction that favors intimate association" with the U.S. Navy while the other "demands [that] the Canadian Navy continue its old association with the Royal Navy."[6] The U.S. Navy played a prominent role in cutting Australia off from classified American information for two years, hardly a conflict-free relationship. However, as Nick Barr has shown in his recent study of Anglo-American army relations in World War II, the presence of conflict and friction is to be expected.[7] What is noteworthy is that the U.S. Navy, building on the experience of World War II, learned to operate with these three fleets in the years after the war. Sailing with allies became a normal part of the U.S. Navy's day-to-day operations during this period, establishing a pattern that had not been present prior to the war and that continues to the present. The Korean War allowed all four navies to demonstrate their ability to effectively operate together on short notice. Korea also demonstrated that members of all four navies could confidently claim that "we are still one fleet."[8]

Appendix: American, British, Canadian, and Australian Naval Leaders, 1945–1953

Position / Officer	Period
Chief of Naval Operations (U.S.)	
Fleet Admiral Ernest King	Mar 42–Dec 45
Fleet Admiral Chester Nimitz	Dec 45–Dec 47
Admiral Louis Denfeld	Dec 47–Nov 49
Admiral Forrest Sherman	Nov 49–Jul 51
Admiral William Fechteler	Aug 51–Aug 53
Admiral Robert Carney	Aug 53–Aug 55
Commander in Chief, U.S. Atlantic Fleet	
Admiral Jonas Ingram	Nov 44–Sep 46
Admiral Marc Mitscher	Sep 46–Feb 47
Admiral William Blandy	Feb 47–Feb 50
Admiral William Fechteler	Feb 50–Aug 51
Admiral Lynde McCormick	Aug 51–Apr 54
Commander in Chief, U.S. Pacific Fleet	
Fleet Admiral Chester Nimitz	Dec 41–Nov 45
Admiral Raymond Spruance	Nov 45–Feb 46
Admiral John Towers	Feb 46–Feb 47
Admiral Louis Denfeld	Feb–Dec 47
Admiral DeWitt Ramsey	Dec 47–Apr 49
Admiral Arthur Radford	Apr 49–Jul 53
Admiral Felix Stump	Jul 53–Jan 58

Appendix: Continued

	1945	1946	1947	1948	1949	1950	1951	1952	1953
Commander, U.S. Naval Forces Europe[a]									
Admiral Kent Hewitt	Aug 45–Sep 46								
Admiral Richard Conolly		Sep 46–Dec 50							
Admiral Robert Carney						Dec 50–Jun 52			
Admiral Jerauld Wright								Jun 52–Mar 54	
First Sea Lord (U.K.)									
Admiral of the Fleet Andrew Cunningham	Oct 43–May 46								
Admiral of the Fleet John Cunningham		May 46–Sep 48							
Admiral of the Fleet Bruce Fraser				Sep 48–Dec 51					
Admiral of the Fleet Rhoderick McGrigor							Dec 51–Apr 55		
Chief of Naval Staff (Canada)									
Vice Admiral George Jones	Jan 44–Feb 46								
Vice Admiral Howard Reid		Feb 46–Aug 47							
Vice Admiral Harold Grant			Sep 47–Dec 51						
Vice Admiral Edmond Mainguy							Dec 51–Jan 56		
Chief of Naval Staff (Australia)[b]									
Admiral Guy Royle	Jul 41–Jun 45								
Admiral Louis Hamilton	Jun 45–Feb 48								
Rear Admiral John Collins				Feb 48–Feb 55					

[a] Commander, U.S. Naval Forces Europe became commander, U.S. Naval Forces Eastern Atlantic and Mediterranean in November 1947.

[b] Admiral Guy Royle and Admiral Louis Hamilton were seconded to the Royal Australian Navy from the Royal Navy. Rear Admiral John Collins was an officer in the Royal Australian Navy. Collins was promoted to vice admiral in May 1950.

ARCHIVAL ABBREVIATIONS USED IN

NOTES AND BIBLIOGRAPHY

1946 CMD   Post January 1946 Command File, Naval History and Heritage
Command, Washington, D.C.

1946 RPT   Post January 1946 Reports File, Naval History and Heritage
Command, Washington, D.C.

Andrewes Papers   Papers of Admiral Sir William Andrewes, Imperial War
Museum, London

AR/131   Records of the Strategic Plans Division, AR/131, Naval History
and Heritage Command, Washington, D.C.

AWM   Australian War Memorial, Canberra

Burke Papers   Papers of Admiral Arleigh A. Burke, Naval History and Heritage
Command, Washington, D.C.

DDE   Dwight D. Eisenhower Presidential Library, Abilene, Kansas

DHH   Directorate of History and Heritage, Ottawa

Dyer Papers   George C. Dyer Papers, Library of Congress, Washington, D.C.

ECU   J. Y. Joyner Library, East Carolina University, Greenville, North
Carolina

Entry A1 202   Entry A1 202, CINCPACFLT Top Secret Administrative
Files, Red 62, 1944–1946, National Archives and Records
Administration, College Park, Maryland

Entry A1 204   Entry A1 204, CINCPACFLT Operation Files, Red 65, 1948,
National Archives and Records Administration, College Park,
Maryland

Entry A1 337A   Entry A1 337A, Operational, Tactical, and Instructional
Publications, 1947–1970, National Archives and Records
Administration, College Park, Maryland

Entry A1 1001B   Entry A1 1001B, Secret Naval Intelligence Reports, 1948, National
Archives and Records Administration, College Park, Maryland

Entry A1 1001D   Entry A1 1001D, Secret Naval Intelligence Reports, 1949, National
Archives and Records Administration, College Park, Maryland

Entry NM3 47E   Entry NM3 47E, Assistant Chief of Staff, G-2 (Intelligence),
Project Decimal Files, 1949–1950, National Archives and Records
Administration, College Park, Maryland

Entry NM84 421   Entry NM84 421, American-British Conversations
Correspondence Relating to Planning and Combat Operations,
1940–1948, National Archives and Records Administration,
College Park, Maryland

Entry P 3	Entry P 3, Korean War Interim Evaluation Reports, 1950–1953, National Archives and Records Administration, College Park, Maryland
Entry P 9	Entry P 9, CINCPACFLT, Restricted Admin Files, 1946–1948, National Archives and Records Administration, College Park, Maryland
Entry P 28	Entry P 28, General Administrative Correspondence, 1950, National Archives and Records Administration, College Park, Maryland
Entry P 111	Entry P 111, CINCLANT Secret and Top Secret Correspondence, 1941–1949, National Archives and Records Administration, College Park, Maryland
Entry P 1204	Entry P 1204, CNO/SecNav Security Classified General Correspondence, 1948–1951, National Archives and Records Administration, College Park, Maryland
Entry P 1208	Entry P 1208, Security Classified Chronological Files, 1948–1950, National Archives and Records Administration, College Park, Maryland
Entry P 1214	Entry P 1214, Formerly Classified OP34 Chronological Files (Serial Pinks), 1948–1950, National Archives and Records Administration, College Park, Maryland
Entry UD 3	Entry UD 3, Central Decimal Files, 1946–1947, National Archives and Records Administration, College Park, Maryland
Entry UD 5	Entry UD 5, Central Decimal Files, 1948–1950, National Archives and Records Administration, College Park, Maryland
Entry UD 7	Entry UD 7, Geographic Files, 1948–1950, National Archives and Records Administration, College Park, Maryland
Entry UD-09D 19	Entry UD-09D 19, World War II Command Files, 1918–1945, National Archives and Records Administration, College Park, Maryland
Entry UD-09D 20	Entry UD-09D 20, British Records & Publications, 1914–1955, National Archives and Records Administration, College Park, Maryland
Entry UD-09D 26	Entry UD-09D 26, Naval History and Heritage Command, Operations Division (OP-32), Subject Files, 1946–1950, National Archives and Records Administration, College Park, Maryland
Entry UD 10	Entry UD 10, Central Decimal Files, 1951–1953, National Archives and Records Administration, College Park, Maryland
Entry UD 16	Entry UD 16, Security Classified Correspondence, 1940–1947, National Archives and Records Administration, College Park, Maryland

Entry UD 17	Entry UD 17, Top Secret Correspondence, 1944–1947, National Archives and Records Administration, College Park, Maryland
Flatley Papers	James Flatley Papers, Patriots Point Naval & Maritime Museum, Charleston, South Carolina
FRUS	Foreign Relations of the United States
HIA	Hoover Institution Archives, Stanford, California
IWM	Imperial War Museum, London
Jurika Papers	Stephen J. Jurika Jr. Papers, Hoover Institution Archives, Stanford, California
LAC	Library and Archives Canada, Ottawa
Leahy Papers	William D. Leahy Papers, Library of Congress, Washington, D.C.
LOC	Naval History Collection, Manuscript Division, Library of Congress, Washington, D.C.
NAA	National Archives of Australia
NACP	National Archives at College Park, College Park, Maryland
NDL	U.S. Naval Institute Oral Histories, Navy Department Library, Washington, D.C.
NHHC	Naval History and Heritage Command, Washington, D.C.
NLA	National Library of Australia, Canberra
NMM	Caird Library, National Maritime Museum, London
OH-CU	Naval History Project, Oral History Research Office, Columbia University, New York City
PPM	Patriots Point Naval & Maritime Museum, Mount Pleasant, South Carolina
Radford Papers	Papers of Admiral Arthur W. Radford, Naval History and Heritage Command, Washington, D.C.
RG 38	Records of the Office of the Chief of Naval Operations, Record Group 38, National Archives and Records Administration, College Park, Maryland
RG 80	General Records of the Department of the Navy, Record Group 80, National Archives and Records Administration, College Park, Maryland
RG 165	Records of the War Department General and Special Staffs, Record Group 165, National Archives and Records Administration, College Park, Maryland
RG 218	Records of the U.S. Joint Chiefs of Staff, Record Group 218, National Archives and Records Administration, College Park, Maryland
RG 313	Records of Naval Operating Forces, Record Group 313, National Archives and Records Administration, College Park, Maryland

RG 319	Records of the Army Staff, Record Group 319, National Archives and Records Administration, College Park, Maryland
SPC-A	Sea Power Centre-Australia, Canberra
TNA	The National Archives of the UK, London
TS 1951	Top Secret Control Office Files, 1951, Naval History and Heritage Command, Washington, D.C.
USNA	Nimitz Library, United States Naval Academy, Annapolis, Maryland
USNI	U.S. Naval Institute Library, Annapolis, Maryland
USNWC	Naval Historical Collection, U.S. Naval War College, Newport, Rhode Island
UVL	Military History Oral History Collection, Special Collections, University of Victoria Library, British Columbia

INTRODUCTION

1 For weather data, see Meteorological Committee, "Monthly Weather Report of the Meteorological Office," December 1918, accessed January 17, 2019, https://www.metoffice.gov.uk/binaries/content/assets/mohippo/pdf/h/b/dec1918.pdf.

2 Jerry Jones, *U.S. Battleship Operations in World War I* (Annapolis, MD: Naval Institute Press, 1998), 74.

3 Craig Symonds, *World War II at Sea: A Global History* (New York: Oxford University Press, 2018).

4 David Hobbs, *The British Pacific Fleet: The Royal Navy's Most Powerful Strike Force* (Annapolis, MD: Naval Institute Press, 2011), 305.

5 In keeping with contemporary U.S. military doctrine, "combined" refers to multinational efforts and operations while "joint" refers to multiservice efforts and operations.

6 Lisle Rose, *Power at Sea: A Violent Peace, 1946–2006* (Columbia: University of Missouri Press, 2007), 3–5, 65–66.

7 Michael Isenberg, *Shield of the Republic: The United States Navy in an Era of Cold War and Violent Peace*, vol. 1, *1945–1962* (New York: St. Martin's Press, 1993), 140.

8 "Washington's Farewell Address 1796," Avalon Project, accessed March 25, 2018, http://avalon.law.yale.edu/18th_century/washing.asp.

9 A few scholars have hinted that Allied naval relations in World War II played a role in postwar naval relations without examining whether this was in fact the case. Mark Jones's work on World War II British naval liaison officers suggested a link between wartime and postwar cooperation while admitting that "the precise manner in which NATO benefited from the Royal Navy (RN) liaison system has yet to appear in the literature." See Mark C. Jones, "Experiment at Dundee: The Royal Navy's 9th Submarine Flotilla and Multinational Naval Cooperation during World War II," *Journal of Military History* 72, no. 4 (October 2008): 1179–1212; Mark C. Jones, "Friend and Advisor to the Allied Navies: The Royal Navy's Principal Liaison Officer and Multinational Naval Operations in World War II," *Journal of Military History* 77, no. 3 (July 2013): 1023. Steven Paget's recent book expertly analyzes American, British, and Australian naval cooperation in the Korean War, the Vietnam War, and the 2003 Iraq War, focusing on naval bombardment. Paget focuses on the operational experience of allied navies in these conflicts rather than the organizational links that developed in the late 1940s. See Steven Paget, *The Dynamics of Coalition Naval Warfare: The Special Relationship at Sea* (New York: Routledge, 2017). Joel Sokolsky and Sean Maloney examined the naval side of the North Atlantic Treaty

Organization (NATO) in the 1990s. Both their books used recently declassified records but lacked access to archival material opened since then. This material has shed new light on the importance of informal Anglo-American-Canadian naval ties outside of NATO as well as Australian-American naval relations. See Joel J. Sokolsky, *Seapower in the Nuclear Age: The United States Navy and NATO, 1949–80* (Annapolis, MD: Naval Institute Press, 1991); Sean Maloney, *Securing Command of the Sea: NATO Naval Planning, 1948–1954* (Annapolis, MD: Naval Institute Press, 1995). Richard Best's book on postwar Anglo-American security cooperation focuses on the national level rather than delving into organizational links between services. Jeffrey Engel's work on conflict in Anglo-American export policies highlights conflict in the field of aviation in the early Cold War. See Richard Best, *"Co-operation with Like-Minded Peoples," British Influences on American Security Policy, 1945–1949* (New York: Greenwood Press, 1986); Jeffrey Engel, *Cold War at 30,000 Feet: The Anglo-American Fight for Aviation Supremacy* (Cambridge, MA: Harvard University Press, 2007). Eric Grove and Geoffrey Till's 1989 article on postwar Anglo-American naval relations focuses on strategic concepts rather than organizational links. See Eric Grove and Geoffrey Till, "Anglo-American Maritime Strategy in the Era of Massive Retaliation, 1945–60," in *Maritime Strategy and the Balance of Power: Britain and America in the Twentieth Century,* by John Hattendorf and Robert Jordan (New York: St. Martin's Press, 1989), 271–303. Peter Nash's excellent book on Anglo-American naval logistics examines standardization efforts in refueling and resupplying at sea, while this work focuses on standardization of doctrine, communications, and sonobuoys. See Peter Nash, *The Development of Mobile Logistic Support in Anglo-American Naval Policy 1900–1953,* (Gainesville: University Press of Florida, 2009). A number of Canadian authors have examined U.S. Navy relations with the Royal Canadian Navy in the Cold War, though not with a detailed focus on the late 1940s. See Fred Crickard, "A Tale of Two Navies: United States Security and Canadian and Australian Naval Policy during the Cold War" (M.A., Dalhousie University, 1993); Marc Milner, *Canada's Navy: The First Century* (Toronto: University of Toronto Press, 1999); Nicholas Tracy, *A Two-Edged Sword: The Navy as an Instrument of Canadian Foreign Policy* (Montreal: McGill-Queen's University Press, 2012); Peter Haydon, "A Tale of Two Navies: Building the Canada–United States Cold War Naval Relationship," *Northern Mariner* 24, nos. 3 & 4 (2014): 176–194. David Zimmerman's recent book tackles the Royal Canadian Navy's links with the U.S. Navy on the Canadian West Coast using primarily Canadian records. See David Zimmerman, *Maritime Command Pacific: The Royal Canadian Navy's West Coast Fleet in the Early Cold War* (Victoria: University of British Columbia Press, 2015). U.S. Navy relations with the Royal Australian Navy have been examined by David Stevens and Tom Frame. See Tom Frame, *Pacific Partners: A History of Australian-American Naval Relations* (Sydney: Hodder & Stoughton, 1992); David Stevens, ed., *The Royal Australian Navy* (New York: Oxford University Press, 2001); Thomas-Durell Young was one of the first scholars to analyze the Radford-Collins Agreement, though the actual agreement has since been declassified. See Thomas-Durell Young, *Australian, New Zealand, and United States Security Relations, 1951–1986* (Boulder, CO: Westview Press, 1992).

10 For pre-December 1941 relations, see Theodore Wilson, *The First Summit: Roosevelt and Churchill at Placentia Bay 1941* (Boston: Houghton Mifflin, 1969); Patrick Abbazia, *Mr. Roosevelt's Navy: The Private War of the U.S. Atlantic Fleet, 1939–1942* (Annapolis, MD: Naval Institute Press, 1975); James Leutze, *Bargaining for Supremacy: Anglo-American Naval Collaboration, 1937–1941* (Chapel Hill: University of North Carolina Press, 1977); Christopher G. Thorne, *Allies of a Kind: The United States, Britain, and the War against Japan, 1941–1945* (New York: Oxford University Press, 1978); David Reynolds, *The Creation of the Anglo-American Alliance, 1937–1941: A Study in Competitive Co-Operation* (Chapel Hill: University of North Carolina Press, 1982); Malcolm H. Murfett, *Fool-Proof Relations: The Search for Anglo-American Naval Cooperation during the Chamberlain Years, 1937–1940* (Singapore: Singapore University Press, 1984); Waldo Heinrichs, *Threshold of War: Franklin D. Roosevelt and American Entry into World War II* (New York: Oxford University Press, 1988); Ian Cowman, *Dominion or Decline: Anglo-American Naval Relations in the Pacific, 1937–1941* (Oxford, U.K.: Berg, 1996); David Zimmerman, *Top Secret Exchange: The Tizard Mission and the Scientific War* (Montreal: McGill-Queen's University Press, 1996); Phillips Payson O'Brien, *British and American Naval Power, Politics and Policy, 1900–1936* (Westport, CT: Praeger, 1998); Greg Kennedy, *Anglo-American Strategic Relations and the Far East, 1933–1939: Imperial Crossroads* (London: Frank Cass, 2002); Michael Simpson, ed., *Anglo-American Naval Relations, 1919–1939* (Burlington, VT: Ashgate, 2010); William Johnsen, *The Origins of the Grand Alliance: Anglo-American Military Collaboration from the Panay Incident to Pearl Harbor* (Lexington: University Press of Kentucky, 2016); Stephen Roskill, *Naval Policy between the Wars*, vol. 1, *The Period of Anglo-American Antagonism, 1919–1929* (Barnsley, U.K.: Seaforth Publishing, 2016); Stephen Roskill, *Naval Policy between the Wars*, vol. 2, *The Period of Reluctant Rearmament, 1930–1939* (Barnsley, U.K.: Seaforth Publishing, 2016). For wartime naval relations see Marc Milner, *North Atlantic Run: The Royal Canadian Navy and the Battle for the Convoys* (Annapolis, MD: Naval Institute Press, 1985); Kevin Smith, *Conflict over Convoys: Anglo-American Logistics Diplomacy in the Second World War* (New York: Cambridge University Press, 1996); Allan Harris Bath, *Tracking the Axis Enemy: The Triumph of Anglo-American Naval Intelligence* (Lawrence: University Press of Kansas, 1998); Phyllis L. Soybel, *A Necessary Relationship: The Development of Anglo-American Cooperation in Naval Intelligence* (Westport, CT: Praeger, 2005); Peter Dean, *MacArthur's Co-*

alition: US and Australian Operations in the Southwest Pacific Area, 1942–1945 (Lawrence: University Press of Kansas, 2018).

11   Baylis says that close wartime links were dismantled in 1945 and 1946. See John Baylis, *Anglo-Americans Relations since 1939: The Enduring Alliance* (Manchester, U.K.: Manchester University Press, 1997), 38.

12   J. P. D. Dunbabin, *The Cold War: The Great Powers and Their Allies* (Harlow, U.K.: Pearson, 2008), chs. 3 and 4.

13   Matthew Muehlbauer and David Ulbrich, *Ways of War: American Military History from the Colonial Era to the Twenty-First Century* (New York: Routledge, 2014), 421–422.

14   Townsend Hoopes and Douglas Brinkley, *Driven Patriot: The Life and Times of James Forrestal* (Annapolis, MD: Naval Institute Press, 1992), 208, 212, 250, 265–269.

15   "Appendix III," enclosure to Captain Paul R. Heineman, USN, Chairman, Combined Canadian, United Kingdom, United States [CANUKUS] Anti-Submarine Working Group to Combined Canadian, United Kingdom, United States Anti-Submarine Warfare Committee, "Final Draft of Papers of the Combined Working Group—Forwarding Of," April 6, 1949, File 8100–5, vol. 35135, RG24-D-1-c, Library and Archives Canada [LAC].

16   Jeffrey Barlow, *From Hot War to Cold: The U.S. Navy and National Security Affairs, 1945–1955* (Stanford, CA: Stanford University Press, 2009), 49.

17   Bath, *Tracking the Axis Enemy*, 233.

18   Paul Kennedy, "History from the Middle: The Case of the Second World War," *Journal of Military History* 74, no. 1 (January 2010): 38. Kennedy developed this theme further in Paul Kennedy, *Engineers of Victory: The Problem Solvers Who Turned the Tide in the Second World War* (New York: Random House, 2013).

19   Wilfred G. D. Lund, "Vice-Admiral Harold Grant: Father of the Post-War Royal Canadian Navy," in *Warrior Chiefs: Perspectives on Senior Canadian Military Leaders*, ed. Bernd Horn and Stephen Harris (Toronto: Dundurn Press, 2001), 196.

20   Aaron Friedberg, *In the Shadow of the Garrison State: America's Anti-Statism and Its Cold War Grand Strategy* (Princeton, NJ: Princeton University Press, 2000), 37; Michael Sherry, *Preparing for the Next War: American Plans for Postwar Defense, 1941–1945* (New Haven, CT: Yale University Press, 1977).

CHAPTER 1. FROM WORLD WAR I TO THE COLD WAR

1   Donald Canney, *Africa Squadron: The U.S. Navy and the Slave Trade, 1842–1861* (Washington, D.C.: Potomac Books, 2006).

2   Kemp Tolley, *Yangtze Patrol: The U.S. Navy in China* (Annapolis, MD: Naval Institute Press, 1971), 17.

3   David Trask, "The Entry of the USA into the War and Its Effects," in *The Ox-*

ford Illustrated History of the First World War, ed. Hew Strachan (New York: Oxford University Press, 2016), 240–241.

4 William Still, *Crisis at Sea: The United States Navy in European Waters in World War I* (Gainesville: University Press of Florida, 2006), 70.

5 Still, *Crisis at Sea*, 70–72.

6 Jerry Jones, *U.S. Battleship Operations in World War I* (Annapolis, MD: Naval Institute Press, 1998), 52.

7 Still, *Crisis at Sea*, 200–203.

8 Jones, *U.S. Battleship Operations*, 54.

9 Jones, 28, 45.

10 Reminiscences of Eugene E. Wilson, interview by John T. Mason Jr., 1972, 134, Naval History Project, Oral History Archives at Columbia, Rare Book & Manuscript Library, Columbia University, New York City [OH-CU].

11 Reminiscences of Admiral Harry W. Hill, USN, interview by John T. Mason Jr., 1967, 232–233, OH-CU; Still, *Crisis at Sea*, 201.

12 Mike Farquharson-Roberts, *A History of the Royal Navy: World War I* (New York: Palgrave Macmillan, 2014), 189.

13 Michael Simpson, "Admiral William S. Sims, U.S. Navy and Admiral Sir Lewis Bayly, Royal Navy: An Unlikely Friendship and Anglo-American Cooperation, 1917–1919," *Naval War College Review* 41, no. 2 (Spring 1988): 69.

14 Simpson, "Admiral William S. Sims," 71.

15 Simpson, 72.

16 Reminiscences of Rear Admiral Charles J. Wheeler, USN, interview by Etta Belle Kitchen, 1970, 310, E.746.W48 A3 1970, U.S. Naval Institute Oral Histories, Special Collections & Archives Department, Nimitz Library, United States Naval Academy [USNA].

17 Still, *Crisis at Sea*, 478–504.

18 William Still, *Victory without Peace: The United States Navy in European Waters, 1919–1924* (Annapolis, MD: Naval Institute Press, 2018), 32–33, 245.

19 David Reynolds and David Dimbleby, *An Ocean Apart: The Relationship between Britain and America in the Twentieth Century* (New York: Random House, 1988), 85.

20 Reynolds and Dimbleby, *An Ocean Apart*, 87.

21 Michael Simpson, ed., *Anglo-American Naval Relations, 1919–1939* (Burlington, VT: Ashgate, 2010), 8.

22 Reynolds and Dimbleby, *An Ocean Apart*, 88–89.

23 Joseph Maiolo, "Naval Armaments Competition Between the Two World Wars," in *Arms Races in International Politics: From the Nineteenth to the Twenty-First Century*, ed. Thomas Mahnken, Joseph Maiolo, and David Stevenson (Oxford, UK: Oxford University Press, 2016), 98.

24 Reynolds and Dimbleby, *An Ocean Apart*, 91.

25   Greg Kennedy, *Anglo-American Strategic Relations and the Far East, 1933–1939: Imperial Crossroads* (London: Frank Cass, 2002), 18–19, 34.

26   Kennedy, *Anglo-American Strategic Relations*, 183.

27   Simpson, *Anglo-American Naval Relations*, 232–233.

28   David Zimmerman, *Top Secret Exchange: The Tizard Mission and the Scientific War* (Montreal: McGill-Queen's University Press, 1996), 30–31.

29   Simpson, *Anglo-American Naval Relations*, 250; Lawrence Pratt, "The Anglo-American Naval Conversations on the Far East of January 1938," *International Affairs* 44, no. 4 (October 1971): 745–763; Commodore Percy W. Welles, RCN, Chief of the Naval Staff, "Conversations Held in Washington, DC on the 19th and 20th January 1938" January 22, 1938, Folder RCN-USN Liaison—Correspondence & Documents [1 of 3], File 5, Box 111, 81/520/1550, Directorate of History and Heritage [DHH].

30   Reminiscences of Admiral Alan Goodrich Kirk, USN, interview by John T. Mason Jr., 1961, 1:133, OH-CU.

31   John H. Towers, "Entry for 20 March 1941," March 20, 1941, Folder 3, Box 1, John H. Towers Papers, Naval Historical Foundation Collection, Manuscript Division, Library of Congress, Washington, D.C. [LOC].

32   Reminiscences of Admiral James Fife, USN, interview by John T. Mason Jr., 1962, 93, 110, 129, 131, Microfiche E746.F54 A3 1972, USNA.

33   William Johnsen, *The Origins of the Grand Alliance: Anglo-American Military Collaboration from the Panay Incident to Pearl Harbor* (Lexington: University Press of Kentucky, 2016), 91–96; Commander, U.S. Naval Forces in Europe [COMNAVEU] to Director of Naval History [DNH], "Serial 0266, Administrative History, U.S. Naval Forces in Europe," June 11, 1946, pt. 1, chap. 1, 5–34, Folder Europe, Commander, Naval Forces—Administrative History, pts. 1–3, Box 281, Entry UD-09D 19, World War II Command Files, 1918–1945 [Entry UD-09D 19]; Records of the Office of the Chief of Naval Operations, Record Group 38 [RG 38], National Archives at College Park, College Park, MD [NACP].

34   Waldo Heinrichs, *Threshold of War: Franklin D. Roosevelt and American Entry into World War II* (New York: Oxford University Press, 1988).

35   Maurice Matloff and Edwin M. Snell, *Strategic Planning for Coalition Warfare, 1941–1942* (Washington, D.C.: Center of Military History, 1999), 32–33.

36   Rear Admiral Victor Danckwerts, RN, to Admiral of the Fleet Dudley Pound, RN, First Sea Lord [1SL], April 17, 1941, 2, CAB 122/294, National Archives of the UK [TNA].

37   Director of Naval Intelligence [DNI], Admiralty, "NID Report No. 18, United States Naval Efficiency," January 21, 1942, 1, ADM 205/19, TNA.

38   Captain G. D. Owen, RN, "Report, Torpedoes and Mining, 1941 to 1945," July 1946, 228, ADM 199/1236, TNA.

39   Patrick Uniacke Bayly, interview by Conrad Wood, August 11, 1992, Reel 2,

Sound Archive, Catalogue 12590, Imperial War Museum, London, United Kingdom [IWM].

40 Robert Dallek, *Franklin D. Roosevelt and American Foreign Policy, 1932–1945* (New York: Oxford University Press, 1995).

41 See footnote 10 in the introduction to this volume for a list.

42 Ronald Spector, *Eagle against the Sun: The American War with Japan* (New York: Free Press, 1985), 123–132.

43 Jeffrey Cox, *Rising Sun, Falling Skies: The Disastrous Java Sea Campaign of World War II* (New York: Osprey, 2014).

44 Tom Womack, *The Allied Defense of the Malay Barrier, 1941–1942* (Jefferson, NC: McFarland, 2016), 196–204.

45 George Hermon Gill, *Royal Australian Navy, 1942–1945* (Canberra: Australian War Memorial, 1968), 584.

46 Commander Henry Eccles, USN, Commanding Officer [CO], USS John D. Edwards to Commander, U.S. Naval Forces, Southwest Pacific [COM-NAVSWPAC], "DD216/A16–3/(CF 00020), Battle of Bawean Islands—Report of Action; Events Prior and Subsequent Thereto," March 4, 1942, accessed October 4, 2015, http://www.ibiblio.org/hyperwar/USN/ships/logs/DD/dd216 -Bawean.html.

47 Paul Dull, *A Battle History of the Japanese Navy, 1941–1945* (Annapolis, MD: Naval Institute Press, 1978), 78.

48 Eccles to COMNAVSWPAC, "Battle of Bawean Islands."

49 H. P. Willmott, *Empires in the Balance: Japanese and Allied Pacific Strategies to April 1942* (Annapolis, MD: Naval Institute Press, 2008), 294.

50 Cox, *Rising Sun*, 291; Gerhard Weinberg, *A World at Arms: A Global History of World War II* (New York: Cambridge University Press, 1994), 320.

51 Spector, *Eagle Against the Sun*, 134.

52 Richard Colbert, a junior officer on one of the American destroyers in the battle, later became a major advocate of international naval cooperation. Colbert is one of the few participants in the battle who did not criticize the ABDA Striking Force's communications arrangements. He believed that ship-to-ship communications functioned smoothly. Colbert's perspective is difficult to explain. He may have felt that the communications were not as difficult as they could have been, given the diversity in languages and communication procedures in the formation. See John Hattendorf, "International Naval Cooperation and Admiral Richard G. Colbert: The Intertwining of a Career with an Idea," in *Naval History and Maritime Strategy: Collected Essays* (Malabar, FL: Krieger Publishing, 2000), 165.

53 Rear Admiral Richard Hugh Leir, RCN (ret), My Navy Recollections, interview by Hal Lawrence, June 10, 1984, pt. 3, SC066_LRH_262, Military History Oral History Collection, Special Collections, University of Victoria Library, British Columbia [UVL]; Thomas John George Adams, interview by Conrad Wood,

1981, Reel 2, Sound Archive, Catalogue 5206, IWM; Gill, *Royal Australian Navy, 1942–1945*, 556; Eccles to COMNAVSWPAC, "Battle of Bawean Islands."

54 Office of Naval Intelligence, "The Java Sea Campaign" (U.S. Navy, 1943), 83, updated June 18, 2002, http://ibiblio.org/hyperwar/USN/USN-CN-Java/index .html.

55 Cornelius H. Bull, "First Seminar [with U.S. Correspondents]," November 6, 1942, Folder 9, Diary of Cornelius H. Bull, Box 6, MS Collection 37, Buell, Thomas/Whitehill, Walt; Naval Historical Collection, U.S. Naval War College, Newport, RI [USNWC].

56 W. A. B. Douglas, Roger Sarty, and Michael Whitby, *No Higher Purpose*, vol. 2, pt. 1, of *The Official Operational History of the Royal Canadian Navy in the Second World War, 1939–1943* (St. Catharines, Ontario: Vanwell Publishing, 2002), 217.

57 Douglas, Sarty, and Whitby, *No Higher Purpose*, 234–235; Marc Milner, *The Battle of the Atlantic* (New York: History Press, 2011), 66–67.

58 Milner, *The Battle of the* Atlantic, 78–79.

59 Robert C. Fisher, "'We'll Get Our Own': Canada and the Oil Shipping Crisis of 1942," *Northern Mariner* 3, no. 2 (April 1993): 34–36.

60 Milner, *The Battle of the Atlantic*, 91.

61 Still, *Crisis at Sea*, 355–356, 369–373.

62 Milner, *The Battle of the Atlantic*, 114.

63 Milner, 113–114.

64 Milner, 144–145; Robert W. Love Jr., *History of the U.S. Navy*, vol. 2, *1942–1991* (Harrisburg, PA: Stackpole Books, 1992), 108–111.

65 Milner, *The Battle of the Atlantic*, 153.

66 William T. Y'Blood, *Hunter-Killer: U.S. Escort Carriers in the Battle of the Atlantic* (Annapolis, MD: Naval Institute Press, 1983), 99.

67 Clay Blair, *Hitler's U-Boat War: The Hunters, 1939–1942* (New York: Random House, 1996), 758.

68 Reminiscences of Vice Admiral Charles Wellborn Jr., USN, interview by John T. Mason Jr., 1972, 154, U.S. Naval Institute Library, Annapolis, MD [USNI].

69 Reminiscences of Wellborn, 155.

70 Reminiscences of Hill, 229; Richard Humble, *Fraser of North Cape: The Life of Admiral of the Fleet Lord Fraser, 1988–1981* (London: Routledge, 1983), 167.

71 Entry for August 30, 1943, enclosure to Rear Admiral Tully Shelley, USN to Fraser, March 24, 1950, File 28/9, Box 10, MSS/83/158, Bruce Fraser Papers, Manuscripts Section, Caird Library, National Maritime Museum [NMM].

72 Chris Sheehy, "USS Robin: An Account of the HMS Victorious' First Mission to the Pacific" (MA thesis, University of New Brunswick, 1996), 79–90.

73 H. P. Willmott, *Grave of a Dozen Schemes: British Naval Planning and the War against Japan, 1943–1945* (Annapolis, MD: Naval Institute Press, 1996), 232–233.

74 John Fay, interview by Richard McDonough, August 11, 1992, Reel 2, Sound Archive, Catalogue 34023, IWM.

75 Rupert Clive Wilkinson, interview by Richard McDonough, May 11, 2006, Reel 2, Sound Archive, Catalogue 28936, IWM.

76 Chris Sheehy, "USS Robin," 116.

77 Sheehy, 119.

78 Sheehy, 121.

79 Clark G. Reynolds, "'Sara' in the East," *U.S. Naval Institute Proceedings* 87, no. 12 (December 1961): 75.

80 Willmott, *Grave of a Dozen Schemes.*

81 Michael Coles, "Ernest King and the British Pacific Fleet: The Conference at Quebec, 1944 ('Octagon')," *Journal of Military History* 65, no. 1 (January 2001): 105–129.

82 The British Pacific Fleet has been the subject of a number of works in recent years. See Nicholas Sarantakes, *Allies against the Rising Sun: The United States, the British Nations, and the Defeat of Imperial Japan* (Lawrence: University Press of Kansas, 2009); Jonathan Robb-Webb, *The British Pacific Fleet: Experience and Legacy, 1944–50* (Burlington, VT: Ashgate, 2013); David Hobbs, *The British Pacific Fleet: The Royal Navy's Most Powerful Strike Force* (Annapolis, MD: Naval Institute Press, 2011).

83 Humble, *Fraser of North Cape,* 249–250.

84 Edward Ashmore, interview by Nigel Tyrie, July 30, 2003, Reel 9, Sound Archive, Catalogue 25203, IWM.

85 Reminiscences of Wheeler, 310.

86 Lieutenant Commander Paul Bernard Kincade, USN (retired), "The Forgotten Few: A Yank with the British Pacific Fleet," 1998, 115–116, Library, Sea Power Centre - Australia, Canberra [SPC-A].

87 Kincade, "The Forgotten Few," 127.

88 Kincade, 109.

89 Kincade, 137.

90 "Information Bulletin No. 8," Enclosure A to Captain Charles J. Wheeler, USN, Senior U.S. Naval Liaison Officer, British Pacific Fleet [BPF] to Commander in Chief, U.S. Pacific Fleet and Pacific Ocean Areas [CINCPACFLT], "Monthly Report," September 3, 1945, 13, Folder Detached Enclosures #1–46 [3 of 6], Box 1, Entry A1 202, CINCPACFLT Top Secret Administrative Files, Red 62, 1944–1946 [Entry A1 202]; Records of Naval Operating Forces, Record Group 313 [RG 313], NACP, Wheeler to Fleet Admiral Chester Nimitz, USN, October 1, 1945, Folder 4, Box 2, Charles Julian Wheeler Papers, Hoover Institution Archives, Stanford, CA [HIA].

91 "Information Bulletin No. 9," Enclosure A to Wheeler to CINCPACFLT, "Monthly Report," October 1, 1945, 7, Folder Detached Enclosures #1–46 [4 of 6], Box 1, Entry A1 202, RG 313, NACP.

92   The following paragraphs are drawn from John Lewis Gaddis, *The Cold War: A New History* (New York: Penguin Press, 2005), 15–34; J. P. D. Dunbabin, *The Cold War: The Great Powers and Their Allies* (New York: Longman, 1994), 51–100.

93   Tony Judt, *Postwar: A History of Europe since 1945* (New York: Penguin Press, 2005), 160–162.

94   James Patterson, *Grand Expectations: The United States, 1945–1974* (New York: Oxford University Press, 1997), 126–133.

CHAPTER 2. POSTWAR PARTNERSHIPS

 1   *Selected Executive Session Hearings of the House Committee on Foreign Affairs* [HCFA], *1943–50*, vol. 6, *Military Assistance Programs Part 2*, 80th Cong., 1st sess. (1947), 524.

 2   "U.S.-Canada Security Plan Announced," *Los Angeles Times*, February 13, 1947, 1; Willard Edwards, "U.S. and Canada Continue Joint Military Work," *Chicago Daily Tribune*, February 13, 1947, 13.

 3   Richard Best, *"Co-Operation with Like-Minded Peoples": British Influences on American Security Policy, 1945–1949* (New York: Greenwood Press, 1986).

 4   "Washington's Farewell Address 1796," Avalon Project, accessed March 25, 2018, http://avalon.law.yale.edu/18th_century/washing.asp.

 5   Joint Chiefs of Staff, "Fundamental Military Factors in Relation to Discussions Concerning Territorial Trusteeships and Settlements," in *Foreign Relations of the United States* [*FRUS*], *1944*, vol. 1 (Washington, D.C.: Government Printing Office, 1966), 701–703.

 6   Julian Lewis, *Changing Direction: British Military Planning for Post-War Strategic Defense, 1942–1947* (London: Sherwood Press, 1987), 104; Michael Palmer, "The Influence of Naval Strategy on National Security Planning, 1945–1955," Naval History and Heritage Command, 1989, accessed June 3, 2018, https://www.history.navy.mil/research/library/online-reading-room/title-list-alphabetically/t/time-change.html.

 7   Stanley W. Dziuban, *Military Relations between the United States and Canada, 1939–1945* (Washington, D.C.: Center of Military History, 1959).

 8   Best, *Co-Operation with Like-Minded Peoples*, 54.

 9   CAB 122/1579, TNA cited in Best, *Co-Operation with Like-Minded Peoples*, 29.

10   Admiral Richard S. Edwards, USN, Vice Chief of Naval Operations [VCNO], to Fleet Admiral William D. Leahy, USN, Chief of Staff to the President, January 7, 1946, Folder 10, "Canada—1946," Box 2, Papers of William D. Leahy [Leahy Papers], Naval History and Heritage Command, Washington, D.C. [NHHC]; Keith Jeffery, *MI6: The History of the Secret Intelligence Service, 1909–1949* (London: Bloomsbury, 2010), 718; Philip White, *Our Supreme Task: How Winston Churchill's Iron Curtain Speech Defined the Cold War Alliance* (New York: Public Affairs, 2012), 206.

11 Brigadier General George A. Lincoln, "Status of the Combined Chiefs of Staff," February 8, 1946, 1, Folder ABC 381 United Nations [1-23-42], Sec. 7, Box 378, Entry NM84 421, American-British Conversations Correspondence Relating to Planning and Combat Operations, 1940–1948 [Entry NM84 421], Records of the War Department General and Special Staffs, Record Group 165 [RG 165], NACP.

12 Robert Hathaway, *Ambiguous Partnership: Britain and America, 1944–1947* (New York: Columbia University Press, 1981), 172–175.

13 Alan Harris Bath, *Tracking the Axis Enemy: The Triumph of Anglo-American Naval Intelligence* (Lawrence: University Press of Kansas, 1998), 239–230.

14 Michael Peterson, *Bourbon to Black Friday: The Allied Collaborative COMINT Effort against the Soviet Union, 1945–1948* (Ft. Meade, MD: Center for Cryptologic History, National Security Agency, 1995), 35–42.

15 Daniel W. B. Lomas, *Intelligence, Security and the Attlee Governments, 1945–51: An Uneasy Relationship?* (Manchester, U.K.: Manchester University Press, 2017), 150. For the text of the agreement (now known as the UKUSA Agreement), see National Security Agency, "UKUSA Agreement Release, 1940–1956," accessed December 16, 2019, https://www.nsa.gov/news-features/declassified-documents/ukusa/.

16 Rhodri Jeffrey-Jones, *In Spies We Trust: The Story of Western Intelligence* (Oxford, U.K.: Oxford University Press, 2013), 104.

17 Michael Simpson, "Somerville, Sir James Fownes (1882–1949)," *Oxford Dictionary of National Biography*, 2018, accessed April 28, 2018, https://doi-org.proxy.lib.ohio-state.edu/10.1093/ref:odnb/36191.

18 "History of the British Admiralty Delegation to U.S.A., 1941–1945, Section 4, Statistical Data," July 1946, 465, ADM 199/1236, TNA.

19 Michael Simpson, ed., *The Somerville Papers*, Publications of the Navy Records Society 134 (Aldershot, U.K.: Navy Records Society, 1995), 173; "Clark, A. Dayton: Papers, 1930–63," Dwight D. Eisenhower Presidential Library [DDE], accessed April 28, 2018, https://www.eisenhower.archives.gov/research/finding_aids/pdf/Clark_Dayton_Papers.pdf; Admiral of the Fleet Dudley Pound, RN, 1SL to Vice Admiral Robert L. Ghormley, USN, Special Naval Observer, "M.01309/42," February 1, 1942, and Paymaster Captain Alan W. Laybourne, RN, "Minute," February 6, 1942: both in ADM 205/19, TNA.

20 Simpson, *Somerville Papers*, 394.

21 Simpson, *Somerville Papers;* 444–445; Admiralty to British Admiralty Delegation Washington [BAD], "Msg, 0048B," July 12, 1942, ADM 116/4877, TNA.

22 Clark G. Reynolds, "'Sara' in the East," *U.S. Naval Institute Proceedings* 87, no. 12 (December 1961): 75–83.

23 Simpson, *Somerville Papers*, 537.

24 Simpson, 594n1, 607, 649, 651.

25 Simpson, 629.

26 Admiral James Somerville, RN, Head of BAD to Secretary of the Admiralty, "Comparison between British and American Ships and Equipment," July 3, 1945, 38–39, ADM 1/19308, TNA.

27 Somerville to Secretary, 38.

28 Second Sea Lord, "Minute," August 23, 1945, 36–37, ADM 1/19308, TNA.

29 British Joint Staff Mission in Washington [BJSM(W)], "MM (1) (45), 491st Meeting," October 25, 1945, CAB 122/548, TNA.

30 Office of the Chief of Naval Operations, "No. 16, Naval Communications" (Microfiche, 1946), Fiche 2, 116, U.S. Naval Administration in World War II, Microform Room, USNA.

31 Captain George A. Worth, RCN, to Chief of Naval Staff, "Signal Books and Procedures," October 16, 1945, File 1300–33, vol. 8135, RG24-D-1-c, LAC; Tactical and Staff Duties Division, "CB 3016/47, Progress in Tactics, 1947," October 17, 1947, 1, Box 12, Entry UD-09D 20, British Records & Publications, 1914–1955 [Entry UD-09D 20]; RG 38; NACP.

32 Worth to Chief of Naval Staff, October 16, 1945.

33 Admiral Henry Moore, RN, BAD, to Secretary of the Admiralty, "N.O. 27/45," December 19, 1945, 63, ADM 1/19308, TNA.

34 "Extract from the Interim Report of the Review of Admiralty Organisation Committee," April 1951, 124, ADM 1/19308, TNA.

35 William D. Leahy, "Entry for 17 December 1945," 196, Frame 259, Folder 1945, Box 6, reel 4, Leahy Papers, LOC.

36 Chiefs of Staff Committee, "COS (46) 3rd Meeting," January 7, 1946, 10, CAB 79/43/3, TNA.

37 Alan Bullock, *Ernest Bevin: Foreign Secretary, 1945–1951* (New York: W. W. Norton, 1983), 124.

38 Marshall Carter to George Marshall, August 19, 1948, in *FRUS, 1948* (Washington, D.C.: Government Printing Office, 1974), 3:644.

39 Best, *Co-Operation with Like-Minded Peoples*, 30–31.

40 Best, 28.

41 Edwards to Leahy, January 7, 1946; Jeffery, *MI6*, 718; White, *Our Supreme Task*, 206.

42 Best, *Co-Operation with Like-Minded Peoples*, 31–32; Nicholas Sarantakes, *Allies against the Rising Sun: The United States, the British Nations, and the Defeat of Imperial Japan* (Lawrence: University Press of Kansas, 2009), 357–359.

43 Walter Poole, "From Conciliation to Containment: The Joint Chiefs of Staff and the Coming of the Cold War, 1945–1946," *Military Affairs* 42, no. 1 (February 1978): 15; Mark Stoler, "FDR and the Origins of the National Security Establishment," in *FDR's World: War, Peace, Legacies*, ed. David Woolner, Warren Kimball, and David Reynolds (New York: Palgrave Macmillan, 2008), 77–78.

44 Joint Staff Mission (Washington) [JSM(W)] to Cabinet Office, "JSM 167," January 11, 1946, CAB 105/51, TNA.

45 William D. Puleston, "The Probable Effect on American National Defense of the United Nations and the Atomic Bomb," *U.S. Naval Institute Proceedings* 72, no. 8 (August 1946): 1022.

46 Eric Grove, "UN Armed Forces and the Military Staff Committee: A Look Back," *International Security* 17, no. 4 (Spring 1993): 172–182.

47 JSM(W) to Cabinet Office, "JSM 168"; January 11, 1946, 168, CAB 105/51, TNA.

48 JSM(W), "JSM 168"; Chiefs of Staff Committee, "COS (46) 10th Meeting," January 18, 1946, 2, CAB 79/43/10, TNA.

49 Lincoln, "Status of the Combined Chiefs of Staff"; Leahy, "Entry for 8 February 1946," Folder 1946, Box 7, reel 4, Leahy Papers, LOC; JSM(W) to Cabinet Office, February 9, 1946, U.K. Foreign and Commonwealth Office, *Documents on British Policy Overseas*, chap. 1, vol. 4, series 1; JSM(W) to Cabinet Office, "JSM 185," February 14, 1946, and JSM(W) to Cabinet Office, "JSM 186," February 14, 1946: both in CAB 105/51, TNA.

50 Winston S. Churchill, ed., *Never Give In! Winston Churchill's Speeches* (New York: Bloomsbury, 2013), 344.

51 American Presidency Project, "53-The President's News Conference," March 8, 1946, http://www.presidency.ucsb.edu/ws/?pid=12600; Jeremy Ward, "Winston Churchill and the 'Iron Curtain' Speech," *History Teacher* 1, no. 2 (January 1968): 8–9; Alan Dobson, "Churchill's Fulton Speech and the Context of Shared Values in a World of Dangers," in *Churchill and the Anglo-American Special Relationship*, ed. Alan Dobson and Steve Marsh (New York: Routledge, 2017), 45; David McCullough, *Truman* (New York: Simon & Schuster, 1992), 583.

52 Earl of Halifax to Ernest Bevin, "AN 656/1/45," March 10, 1946, U.K. Foreign and Commonwealth Office, *Documents on British Policy Overseas*, chap. 1, vol. 4, series 1; John Moser, *Twisting the Lion's Tail: Anglophobia in the United States, 1921–48* (London: Macmillan Press, 1999), 170, 177–179; Dobson, "Churchill's Fulton Speech," 44.

53 White, *Our Supreme Task*, 211.

54 "Armed Accord Proposal Draws Capital Dissent," *Atlanta Constitution*, March 6, 1946, 10; "Churchill Plea Is 'Shocking' to 3 Senators," *Washington Post*, March 7, 1946, 1.

55 "Fraternal Association," *Washington Post*, March 9, 1946.

56 Dobson, "Churchill's Fulton Speech," 59.

57 "The Quarter's Polls," *Public Opinion Quarterly* 10, no. 2 (Summer 1946): 264.

58 "The Quarter's Polls," 263.

59 William Scott and Stephen Withey, *The United States and the United Nations: The Public View, 1945–1955* (New York: Manhattan, 1958), 26.

60 Dennis Showalter, "Global Yet Not Total: The U.S. War Effort and Its Consequences," in *A World at Total War: Global Conflict and the Politics of Destruction, 1937–1945*, ed. Roger Chickering, Stig Förster, and Bernd Greiner (New York: Cambridge University Press, 2005), 132; Cees Wiebes and Bert Zeeman, "NATO

and the United States: An Essay in Kaplanesque History," in *The Romance of History: Essays in Honor of Lawrence S. Kaplan*, ed. Scott Bills and E. Timothy Smith (Kent, OH: Kent State University Press, 1997), 26.

61 George Kennan to Secretary of State James Byrnes, February 22, 1946 in *FRUS, 1946* (Washington, D.C.: Government Printing Office, 1969), 6:696–709.

62 Poole, "From Conciliation to Containment," 14.

63 Leahy, "Entry for 10 February 1946," 14, Frame 297; "Entry for 3 March 1946," 21, Frame 304; "Entry for 7 March 1946," 23, Frame 306: all in Folder 1946, Box 7, reel 4, Leahy Papers, LOC.

64 Joint Strategic Survey Committee to Joint Chiefs of Staff [JCS], "SM-5242," March 13, 1946, 3, Folder CCS 334, Combined Chiefs of Staff (2-9-46), Sec. 1, Box 81, Entry UD 10, Central Decimal Files, 1951–1953 [Entry UD 10], Records of the U.S. Joint Chiefs of Staff, Record Group 218 [RG 218], NACP.

65 *FRUS, 1940* (Washington, D.C.: Government Printing Office, 1958), 3:146; Galen Perras, *Franklin Roosevelt and the Origins of the Canadian-American Security Alliance, 1933–1945* (Westport, CT: Praeger, 1998), 76–66; Fred Pollock, "Roosevelt, the Ogdensburg Agreement, and the British Fleet: All Done with Mirrors," *Diplomatic History* 5, no. 3 (Summer 1981): 203–219; David R. Murray, ed., *Documents on Canadian External Relations, 1939–1941*, pt. 2, vol. 8 (Ottawa: Department of External Affairs, 1976), 134–140.

66 H. L. Keenleyside, "The Canada-United States Permanent Joint Board on Defence, 1940–1945," *International Journal: Canada's Journal of Global Policy Analysis* 16, no. 1 (1961): 53–55.

67 Joseph Jockel, *No Boundaries Upstairs: Canada, the United States, and the Origins of North American Air Defence, 1945–1958* (Vancouver: University of British Columbia Press, 1987), 11–12.

68 Richard Best, "Approach to Alliance: British and American Defense Strategies, 1945–1948" (Ph.D. diss., Georgetown University, 1983), 63.

69 Dwight David Eisenhower, "Document 1221," in *The Papers of Dwight David Eisenhower*, ed. Louis Galambos (Baltimore, MD: Johns Hopkins University Press, 1978), 8:1417; Dziuban, *Military Relations*, 122, 336.

70 Sean Maloney, *Learning to Love the Bomb: Canada's Nuclear Weapons during the Cold War* (Washington, D.C.: Potomac Books, 2007), 4–5.

71 Jockel, *No Boundaries Upstairs*, 15.

72 Jockel, 16–17.

73 Eisenhower, "Document 1471," 8:1688–1689.

74 *Selected Executive Session Hearings of the HCFA*, 80th Cong., 1st sess. (1947), 520.

75 Permanent Joint Board on Defense [PJBD], American Section, "Thirty-Fourth Recommendation," May 6, 1946, Folder CNO TS 1946 A14–5/EF13(39), Box 43, Entry UD 17, Top Secret Correspondence, 1944–1947 [Entry UD 17], General Records of the Department of the Navy, Record Group 80 [RG 80], NACP; Dziuban, *Military Relations*, 337–338; Jockel, *No Boundaries Upstairs*, 17.

76 Denford W. Middlemiss and Joel J. Sokolsky, *Canada's Defence: Decisions and Determinants* (Toronto: Harcourt Brace Jovanovich Canada, 1989), 19; Nicholas Tracy, *A Two-Edged Sword: The Navy as an Instrument of Canadian Foreign Policy* (Montreal: McGill-Queen's University Press, 2012).

77 Jockel, *No Boundaries Upstairs*, 23–25.

78 Robert Bothwell, "Review of The Reagan Reversal," *International Journal* 53, no. 2 (Spring 1998): 239.

79 Pierre Trudeau, speech at Washington Press Club, March 25, 1969, http://www.cbc.ca/archives/entry/trudeaus-washington-press-club-speech.

80 Douglas Bland, ed., *Canada's National Defence* (Kingston, ON: School of Policy Studies, Queen's University, 1997), 1:20; Middlemiss and Sokolsky, *Canada's Defence*, 16–17.

81 Best, "Approach to Alliance," 66.

82 Jockel, *No Boundaries Upstairs*, 29; Marc Milner, "A Canadian Perspective on Canadian and American Naval Relations Since 1945," in *Fifty Years of Canada–United States Defense Cooperation: The Road from Ogdensburg* (Lewiston, NY: E. Mellen Press, 1992), 149–150; Dziuban, *Military Relations*, 338.

83 Willard Edwards, "U.S. and Canada Continue Joint Military Work," 13; "U.S.-Canada Security Plan Announced," 1.

84 The committee became the State-Army-Navy-Air Force Coordinating Committee (SANACC) in 1947 when the Department of the Air Force was created.

85 Alvin F. Richardson, Harold W. Moseley, and Charles W. McCarthy, "The State-War-Navy Coordinating Committee," *Department of State Bulletin* 13, no. 333 (November 11, 1945): 745.

86 Robert F. Kolterman, "Interagency Coordination: Past Lessons, Current Issues, and Future Necessities," U.S. Army War College, March 2006, accessed March 20, 2020, https://apps.dtic.mil/dtic/tr/fulltext/u2/a448331.pdf.

87 Richardson, Moseley, and McCarthy, "The State-War-Navy," 745–747.

88 The Joint Chiefs initiated the request for guidance. See "State-Defense Military Information Control Committee (S-DMICC)," June 27, 1962, accessed May 30, 2018, https://www.cia.gov/library/readingroom/docs/CIA-RDP80B01676R003100200011-6.pdf.

89 David Frost, *Classified: A History of Secrecy in the United States Government* (Jefferson, NC: McFarland, 2017), 170.

90 "SWNCC 206/16," May 23, 1946, 66–74, Folder CCS 350.05 (3–16–44) Sec. 8, Box 76, Entry UD 3, Central Decimal Files, 1946–1947 [Entry UD 3], RG 218, NACP.

91 Jeffrey Dorwart, *The Office of Naval Intelligence: The Birth of America's First Intelligence Agency, 1865–1918* (Annapolis, MD: Naval Institute Press, 1979); Wyman Packard, *A Century of U.S. Naval Intelligence* (Washington, D.C.: Office of Naval Intelligence and Naval History and Heritage Command, 1996).

92 Captain Charles J. Moore, USN, Deputy Secretary, to Joint Intelligence Com-

mittee [JIC], "SM-6117, Comments on SWNCC 206/16," May 23, 1946, Folder CCS 350.05 (3–16–44), Sec. 8, Box 76, Entry UD 3, RG 218, NACP.

93 Secretary, State-War-Navy Coordinating Committee [SWNCC], to Secretary, JCS, "Comments on SWNCC 206/16," June 24, 1946; Colonel Andrew J. McFarland, USA to JIC, "SM-6355," July 23, 1946; JIC to Secretary, JCS, "Disclosure of Classified Military Information to Foreign Governments and Their Nationals," July 23, 1946: all in Folder CCS 350.05 (3–16–44) Sec. 8, Box 76, Entry UD 3, RG 218, NACP.

94 Enclosure and Appendix to Joint Intelligence Staff, "JIS 196/3," July 24, 1946, and Joint Intelligence Staff, "JIC 265/24," July 29, 1946, 2: both in Folder CCS 350.05 (3–16–44) Sec. 8, Box 76, Entry UD 3, RG 218, NACP.

95 Joint Intelligence Staff, "JIC 265/27," September 5, 1946, 199, Folder CCS 350.05 (3–16–44), Sec. 9, Box 76, Entry UD 3, RG 218, NACP.

96 Allen Weinstein and Alexander Vassiliev, *The Haunted Wood: Soviet Espionage in America—The Stalin Era* (New York: Random House, 1999), 291; Jeffrey-Jones, *In Spies We Trust*, 105.

97 JIC, "JCS 927/38," September 9, 1946, 232, Folder CCS 350.05 (3–16–44), Sec. 9, Box 76, Entry UD 3, RG 218, NACP.

98 Enclosure to Joint Intelligence Staff, "JIS 196/2," July 17, 1946, 1, Folder CCS 350.05 (3–16–44), Sec. 8, Box 76, Entry UD, RG 218, NACP.

99 JIC, "JCS 927/38," 232.

100 JCS, "Decision Amending JCS 927/38," October 26, 1946; SWNCC, "SWNCC 206/27," October 29, 1946; SWNCC, "SWNCC 206/29," November 13, 1946; JCS, "JCS 927/40," November 16, 1946: all in Folder CCS 350.05 (3–16–44), Sec. 9, Box 76, Entry UD 3, RG 218, NACP.

101 Secretary, Chiefs of Staff Committee, to Secretary, Joint Communications Committee, "Combined Communications Board," May 22, 1946, 1–2, File CSC 1415.1, pt. 1, vol. 21161, RG24-B-1, LAC.

102 Christopher Sterling, ed., *Military Communications: From Ancient Times to the 21st Century* (Santa Barbara, CA: ABC Clio, 2008), 294; National Archives and Records Administration, *Federal Records of World War II*, vol. 2, *Military Agencies* (Washington, D.C.: Government Printing Office, 1951), 5.

103 Alan Burnett, Thomas-Durell Young, and Christine Wilson, eds., *The ANZUS Documents* (Canberra: Australian National University, 1991), 66.

104 Secretary, Chiefs of Staff Committee, to Secretary, Joint Communications Committee, "Combined Communications Board," May 22, 1946, 2.

105 "Facts Bearing on the Problem and Discussion," Enclosure B to Joint Communications-Electronics Committee [JCEC], "JCEC 275/18," December 28, 1949, 3–4, Folder CCS 334 CCB (6–25–42), Sec. 15, Box 105, Entry UD 5, RG 218, NACP.

106 British Joint Communications Board, "C.O.S. (46) 222, Combined Co-Ordination of Post War Radio Planning," August 30, 1946, 1, CAB 80/102, TNA.

107 General of the Army Dwight D. Eisenhower, USA, "JCS 1732/13," January 31,

1947, and JCS to Representatives of the British Chiefs of Staff, "CCS 962/1," February 17, 1947: both in Folder CCS 334 CCB (6–25–42), Sec. 7, Box 62, Entry UD 3, RG 218, NACP.

108 Lloyd Norman, "Year after V-J, U.S.-British War Link-Up Remains," *Chicago Daily Tribune*, August 18, 1946, 8; Frank Holeman, "British Rule U.S. Fleet Cruising Mediterranean," *Chicago Daily Tribune*, September 9, 1946, 5; Chesly Manly, "Monty Seeking U.S.-British War Alliance," *Chicago Daily Tribune*, September 16, 1946, 1; "A Scheme to Starve America," *Chicago Daily Tribune*, September 16, 1946, 18.

109 Bernard Law Montgomery, *The Memoirs of Field-Marshal the Viscount Montgomery of Alamein, K.G.* (London: Collins, 1958), 443.

110 Sidney Shalett, "Montgomery to Install Methods of U.S. Staff in British Army," *New York Times*, September 12, 1946, 8.

111 American Presidency Project, "216-The President's News Conference," September 12, 1946, accessed February 8, 2018, http://www.presidency.ucsb.edu/ws /?pid=12508.

112 "A Scheme to Starve America," 18.

113 "A Wartime Relic," *Daily Boston Globe*, October 11, 1946, 18.

114 Admiral Henry Moore, RN, Chairman, BJSM(W), to Chiefs of Staff, "N.0.01/46(3)," May 27, 1947, PREM 8/953, TNA.

115 Commander Vere Alison Wight-Boycott, RN, to Mother, August 27, 1949, Folder 1949, Documents.6854, Private Papers of Captain VA Wight-Boycott [Wight-Boycott Papers], IWM.

116 Jeffrey Engel, *Cold War at 30,000 Feet: The Anglo-American Fight for Aviation Supremacy* (Cambridge, MA: Harvard University Press, 2007), 75–77.

117 Daniel W. B. Lomas, *Intelligence, Security and the Attlee Governments, 1945–51: An Uneasy Relationship?* (Manchester, U.K.: Manchester University Press, 2017), 149.

118 Chiefs of Staff Committee, "CoS (47) 70th Meeting," June 4, 1947, 1, DEFE 4/4/70, TNA.

119 Group Captain Deryck Stapleton, RAF, "CoS (47) 124 (o)," June 9, 1947, DEFE 5/4/124; Chiefs of Staff Committee, "CoS (47) 74th Meeting," June 11, 1947, 7–8, DEFE 4/4/74: both in TNA.

120 Minister of Defence Albert V. Alexander to Prime Minister Clement Attlee, November 12, 1947, 2, PREM 8/953, TNA; Stapleton, "CoS (47) 124 (o)."

121 Alexander to Attlee, "The Future of the Combined Chiefs of Staff," May 5, 1947, PREM 8/953, TNA.

122 Acheson to Hickerson in *FRUS, 1949* (Washington, D.C.: Government Printing Office, 1975), 4:294.

123 George Catlett Marshall, "283," in *The Papers of George Catlett Marshall*, ed. Larry Bland and Mark Stoler (Baltimore, MD: Johns Hopkins University Press, 2013), 6:523.

124 Office of Congressional Directory, *Official Congressional Directory, 79th Congress, 2nd Session* (Washington, D.C.: Government Printing Office, 1946), 326–327; Office of Congressional Directory, *Official Congressional Directory, 80th Congress, 1st Session* (Washington, D.C.: Government Printing Office, 1947), 315; Office of Congressional Directory, *Official Congressional Directory, 80th Congress, 2nd Session* (Washington, D.C.: Government Printing Office, 1947), 315; Office of Congressional Directory, *Official Congressional Directory, 81st Congress, 1st Session* (Washington, D.C.: Government Printing Office, 1949), 316; Office of Congressional Directory, *Official Congressional Directory, 81st Congress, 2nd Session* (Washington, D.C.: Government Printing Office, 1950).

125 JIC, "JCS 1698/4," November 20, 1948, 28, Folder CCS 300 (1–25–42), Sec. 13, Box 65, Entry UD 5, RG 218, NACP.

126 JIC, 21, 27.

127 John Young, *France, the Cold War, and the Western Alliance, 1944–49: French Foreign Policy and Post-War Europe* (New York: St. Martin's Press, 1990), 170–171.

128 Pierre Melandri, "The Troubled Friendship: France and the United States, 1945–1989," in *No End to Alliance: The United States and Western Europe: Past, Present, and Future*, ed. Geir Lundestad (New York: St. Martin's Press, 1998), 118–119.

129 Thomas Robb and Michael Seibold, "Spying on Friends: British Assessments of French Security, 1945–50," *International History Review* 36, no. 1 (2014): 117, 127.

130 Christopher Andrew and Vasili Mitrokhin, *The Sword and the Shield: The Mitrokhin Archive and the Secret History of the KGB* (New York: Basic Books, 1999), 150–154.

131 Irwin Wall, *The United States and the Making of Postwar France, 1945–1954* (New York: Cambridge University Press, 1991), 46; Susan McCall Perlman, "Contesting France: French Informants and American Intelligence in the Dawning Cold War," *Cold War History* 17, no. 1 (2017): 96.

132 Hickerson to Acheson in *FRUS, 1949* (Washington, D.C.: Government Printing Office, 1975), 4:120–121.

133 David Chuter, *Humanity's Soldier: France and International Security, 1919–2001* (Providence, RI: Berghahn Books, 1996), 238–239.

134 L. H. Landon, "Liaison with the French Army," *Army Quarterly and Defense Journal* 99 (October 1969): 82.

135 David McKnight, "The Moscow-Canberra Cables: How Soviet Intelligence Obtained British Secrets through the Back Door," *Intelligence and National Security* 13, no. 2 (1998): 159–170; Brigadier General Hugh F. Hester, USA, to Colonel Riley F. Ennis, USA, Intelligence Division, January 26, 1949, Folder Australia 311, 1 Jan 49 thru 31 Dec 50, Box 88, Entry NM3 47E, Assistant Chief of Staff, G-2 (Intelligence), Project Decimal Files, 1949–1950 [NM3 47E], Records of the Army Staff, Record Group 319 [RG 319], NACP; Commander Stephen Jurika,

U.S. Naval Attaché, Australia, "4-S-48, Australia—Communism in Australia," August 6, 1948, Folder Melbourne (S) 1–6, 191 1948, Box 18, Entry A1 1001-B, Secret Naval Intelligence Reports, 1948 [Entry A1 1001B], RG 38, NACP.

136 JCS, "JCS 60/7," March 22, 1948, 7, and JCS, "CCS 89/7," March 23, 1948: both in Folder CCS 334 CCB (6–25–42), Sec. 9, Box 63, Entry UD 3, RG 218, NACP.

137 "Minutes, Chiefs of Staff Committee 444th Meeting," April 5, 1949, 1, File CSC 1415.1, pt. 1, vol. 21161, RG24-B-1, LAC.

138 Minutes of SANAC-Military Information Control Subcommittee meetings on SANACC 206/57, in Martin P. Claussen, ed., *State-War-Navy Coordinating Committee Policy Files, 1944–1947* (Wilmington, DE: Scholarly Resources, 1977), reel 18.

139 Enclosure A to JCEC, "JCEC 275/6," November 17, 1948, 3, Folder CCS 334 CCB (6–25–42), Sec. 10, Box 104, Entry UD 5, RG 218, NACP.

140 Chiefs of Staff, "Extract from Confidential Annex to COS (49) 38th Meeting, Minute 1," March 7, 1949, 1, AIR 20/2559, TNA.

141 Captain Richard D. Coleridge, RN, to General Alfred Gruenther, USA, Director, Joint Staff, "RDC 5/72," March 15, 1949, 72, Folder CCS 334 Combined Chiefs of Staff (2–9-46), Sec. 1, Box 81, Entry UD 10, RG 218, NACP.

142 Commander Michael G. Stirling, RCN, Director of Naval Communications to Vice Chief of the Naval Staff, July 6, 1949, 3, File 1225-DN-COM, pt. 2, vol. 31106, RG24-D-1-c, LAC.

143 Combined Communications Board [CCB], "CCB 1/4," April 22, 1949, Folder CCS 334 CCB (6–25–42), Sec. 12, Box 104, Entry UD 5, RG 218, NACP; BJSM(W) to Minister of Defense, "JSM 603," September 22, 1949, PREM 8/953, TNA.

144 Combined Chiefs of Staff, "CCS 89/9, Charter, Combined Communications Board," April 1, 1949, AIR 20/2559, TNA.

145 Director General of Signals to Air Chief Marshal Arthur Sanders, RAF, Vice Chief of the Air Staff, "COS (49) 382, Replacement for Combined Communications Board," November 10, 1949, 1, AIR 20/2559, TNA.

146 Enclosure B to JCEC, "JCEC 275/18," 6.

147 Director General to Sanders, "COS (49) 382," November 10, 1949, 2.

148 Charles E. Bohlen to Acheson in *FRUS, 1949*, 4:256.

149 Eisenhower described a 1942 debate about Allied planning for the North Africa landings as a "great transatlantic essay contest." See Niall Barr, *Eisenhower's Armies: The American-British Alliance during World War II* (New York: Pegasus Books, 2015), 202.

150 Coleridge to Gruenther, "RDC 5/82," April 27, 1949, Folder CCS 334 Combined Chiefs of Staff (2–9-46), Sec. 1, Box 81, Entry UD 10, RG 218, NACP.

151 JSM(W) to Cabinet Office, February 9, 1946; Coleridge to Gruenther, "RDC 5/72," March 15, 1949, 72.

152 British officers reviewed this question in January 1946, February 1946, June 1947, and July 1949. See Joint Planning Staff, "J.P. (46) 13 (Final)," enclosure to

Chiefs of Staff Committee, "COS (46) 10th Meeting"; JSM(W) to Cabinet Office, February 9, 1946; Stapleton, "CoS (47) 124 (0)"; Joint Planning Staff, "J.P. (49) 81 (Final)," enclosure to Chiefs of Staff Committee, "COS (49) 108th Meeting," July 28, 1949, DEFE 4/23/108, TNA.

153 Hathaway, *Ambiguous Partnership*, 5.

154 Commodore Valentine S. Godfrey, RCN, Chairman, Canadian Joint Staff (Washington) [CJS(W)], to Chairman, BJSM(W), "CJS/1–2, Composition of the Combined Communications Board," April 27, 1949, File CSC 1415.1, pt. 1, vol. 21161, RG24-B-1, LAC; "Minutes, Chiefs of Staff Committee 444th Meeting," 2.

155 Godfrey to Captain William G. Lalor, USN, Secretary, JCS, "Combined Communications Board," April 27, 1949, File CSC 1415.1, pt. 1, vol. 21161, RG24-B-1, LAC.

156 JCS to Representatives of the British Chiefs of Staff, "SM-926–49, Future Status of the Combined Chiefs of Staff," May 20, 1949, Folder CCS 334 Combined Chiefs of Staff (2–9-46), Sec. 1, Box 81, Entry UD 10, RG 218, NACP.

157 Coleridge to General Omar Bradley, USA, "RDC 5/94," June 3, 1949, Folder CCS 334 Combined Chiefs of Staff (2–9-46), Sec. 1, Box 81, Entry UD 10, RG 218, NACP.

158 Admiral Frederick Dalrymple-Hamilton, RN, Chairman, BJSM, to Godfrey, "No. 22/48, Composition of the Combined Communications Board," May 20, 1949, and Secretary, JCEC to Canadian Representative, CCB, "CECM-788," May 23, 1949: both in File CSC 1415.1, pt. 1, vol. 21161, RG24-B-1, LAC.

159 Escott Reid, *Radical Mandarin: The Memoirs of Escott Reid* (Toronto: University of Toronto Press, 1989), 159.

160 "Minutes, Chiefs of Staff Committee 449th Meeting," June 27, 1949, File CSC 1415.1, pt. 1,vol. 21161, RG24-B-1, LAC.

161 "Minutes, Chiefs of Staff Committee 450th Meeting," July 19, 1949, File CSC 1415.1, pt. 1, vol. 21161, RG24-B-1, LAC.

162 Godfrey to Lalor, "CJS/1–2, Composition of the Combined Communications Board," July 11, 1949, Folder CCS 334 CCB (6–25–42), Sec. 14, Box 105; "Meeting of the Board, Edmonton, Alberta, 22–23 Jun 1949," Enclosure to PJBD, "JCS Info Memo 668," August 12, 1949, 9, Folder CCS 334 PJBD (10–1-45), Sec. 7, Box 122: both in Entry UD 5, RG 218, NACP; Godfrey to Lalor, April 27, 1949; Rear Admiral Walter F. Boone, USN, Assistant Chief of Naval Operations (Strategic Plans), "Serial 000360P30, A Revised Charter for the Combined Communications Board," July 15, 1949, 1–2, Folder F3, Singed Spindles 1949 (2 of 2), Box 70, Records of the Strategic Plans Division, AR/131 [AR/131], NHHC.

163 Chiefs of Staff Committee, "COS (49) 113th Meeting," August 3, 1949, 2, DEFE 4/23/113, TNA.

164 Lieutenant Colonel George M. Seignious to Brigadier General Edwin H. J.

Carns, Secretary, JCS, November 10, 1954, 1, Folder CCS 334 Combined Chiefs of Staff (2-9-46), Sec. 2, Box 81, Entry UD 10, RG 218, NACP; BJSM(W) to Minister of Defense, "JSM 603."

165 Steven Rearden, *Council of War: A History of the Joint Chiefs of Staff, 1942–1991* (Washington, D.C.: National Defense University Press, 2012), 17; "Sequence of Events Regarding the Dissolution of the Combined Chiefs of Staff" (c.1950s), and JCS, "Memorandum for Information No. 687: Dissolution of the Combined Chiefs of Staff Organization," October 14, 1949: both in Folder CCS 334 Combined Chiefs of Staff (2-9-46), Sec. 1, Box 81, Entry UD 10, RG 218, NACP.

166 Chiefs of Staff Committee, "COS (49) 104th Meeting," July 20, 1949, 3, DEFE 4/23/104, TNA; Chiefs of Staff Committee, "COS (49) 108th Meeting," 4.

167 Joint Planning Staff, "JP (49) 133 (Final), Visit of the United Kingdom Joint Planning Staff to Washington—September—October, 1949," October 14, 1949, DEFE 4/25, TNA.

168 Captain Jack R. Allfrey, RN, to Admiral of the Fleet Bruce Fraser, RN, 1SL, "Notes on Meeting between First Sea Lord and Chief of Naval Operations on 24th March 1950 at 1700," April 1950, 2, and Admiral Forrest Sherman, USN, CNO, "Memorandum of a Meeting between the Chief of Naval Operations and the First Sea Lord on Friday, 24 March 1950," April 3, 1950, 3–4: both in Folder F7, A19, Box 72, AR/131, NHHC.

169 JCS, "SM-2661-50, Minutes of U.S.-U.K. Chiefs of Staff Meeting," October 23, 1950, 24, Folder CCS 337 (7–22–48), Sec. 2, Box 132, Entry UD 5, RG 218, NACP.

170 CCB, "CCB 134th Meeting, Minutes," October 7, 1949, 2, Folder CCS 334 CCB (6-25-46), Box 61, Entry UD 3, RG 218, NACP.

171 Enclosure B to CCB, "CCB 286/4," September 28, 1949, Folder CCS 334 CCB (6-25-42), Sec. 14, Box 105, Entry UD 5, RG 218, NACP.

172 Director General to Sanders, "COS (49) 382," November 10, 1949, 1.

173 JCEC, "JCEC 587," November 1, 1949, Folder CCS 334 CCB (6-25-42), Sec. 14, Box 105, Entry UD 5, RG 218, NACP.

174 United Kingdom JCEC (Washington), "CCB 286/5," November 17, 1949, Folder CCS 334 CCB (6–25–42), Sec. 15, Box 105, Entry UD 5, RG 218, NACP; BJSM to JCS, "RDC 1/29," November 18, 1949, Enclosure C to JCEC, "JCEC 275/18."

175 Enclosure A to JCEC, "JCEC 275/18"; Coleridge to Lalor, "RDC 1/47," February 16, 1950, 47, Folder CCS 334 CCB (6-25-42), Sec. 15, Box 105, Entry UD 5, RG 218, NACP.

176 Group Captain Alick Foord-Kelcey, RAF, to Secretary, CJS(W), "Replacement for Combined Communications Board," March 27, 1950, File CSC 1415.1, pt. 1, vol. 21161, RG24-B-1, LAC; Air Vice Marshal Hugh Campbell, RCAF, Chairman, CJS(W) to Secretary, Chiefs of Staff Committee, "Msg, CJS 182, 142245Z," April 14, 1950, File CSC 1415.1, pt. 1, vol. 21161, RG24-B-1, LAC.

177 Group Captain Edward A. D. Hutton, RCAF, Chairman, Joint Telecommunications Committee [JTC] to Secretary, Chiefs of Staff Committee, "JTC 2–1,

Replacement for Combined Communications Board," April 17, 1950, File CSC 1415.1, pt. 1, vol. 21161, RG24-B-1, LAC.

178 Campbell to Secretary, Chiefs of Staff Committee, "Msg, CJS 178, 132145Z," April 13, 1950, File CSC 1415.1, pt. 1, vol. 21161, RG24-B-1, LAC; Campbell to Secretary, Chiefs of Staff Committee, "Msg, CJS 182, 142245Z."

179 Hutton to Secretary, Chiefs of Staff Committee, "JTC 2–1."

180 "Minutes, Chiefs of Staff Committee 463rd Meeting," May 16, 1950, File CSC 1415.1, pt. 1, vol. 21161, RG24-B-1; Vice Admiral Harold Grant, RCN, Chief of the Naval Staff to Admiral of the Fleet Bruce Fraser, RN, 1SL, May 30, 1950, File ACS 1300-1, vol. 11146, RG24-D-10: both in LAC.

181 Canadian Joint Staff (London) to Secretary, Chiefs of Staff Committee, "Msg, CJS (L) 116, 241615A," May 24, 1950, and Brigadier J. D. B. Smith, Secretary, Chiefs of Staff Committee, "CSC 2–4–5, Replacement for Combined Communications Board," May 26, 1950: both in File CSC 1415.1, pt. 1, vol. 21161, RG24-B-1, LAC.

182 "Extract from Minutes of Special Meeting of CSC," July 18, 1950, File JTC 15-13-4, vol. 20898, and "Minutes, Chiefs of Staff Committee Meeting," July 18, 1950, File CSC 1415.1, pt. 1, vol. 21161: both in RG24-B-1, LAC.

183 Campbell to Secretary, JCS, "CJS 202–13, Canadian Participation in Combined Telecommunication Agency," July 13, 1950, File CSC 1415.1, pt. 1, vol. 21161, RG24-B-1, LAC.

184 JCEC, "JCEC 275/20," July 19, 1950, and JCEC, "JCS 60/15," August 25, 1950: both in Folder CCS 334 CCB (6–25–42), Sec. 16, Box 105, Entry UD 5, RG 218, NACP.

185 Hutton to Secretary, Chiefs of Staff Committee, "Canadian Participation in Combined Telecommunications Agency," November 2, 1950, File JTC 15-13-4, vol. 20898, RG24-B-1, LAC.

186 JTC, "Minutes, 38/50 Meeting," October 18, 1950, File JTC 15-13-4, vol. 20898, and "Minutes, Chiefs of Staff Committee Special Meeting," November 14, 1950, File CSC 1415.1, pt. 1, vol. 21161: both in RG24-B-1, LAC.

187 Canadian Chiefs of Staff to Secretary, JCS, "CJS 202–13," December 4, 1950, Folder CCS 334 CCB (6-25-42), Sec. 17, and JCEC, "Third Addendum to JCEC 275/21," December 7, 1950, Folder CCS 334 CCB (6-25-42), Sec. 16: both in Box 105, Entry UD 5, RG 218, NACP; Wing Commander K. C. Cameron, RCAF, to Secretary, JTC, "Canadian Participation in Combined Telecommunications Agency," January 4, 1951, File JTC 15-13-4, vol. 20898, RG24-B-1, LAC.

188 Campbell to General Charles Foulkes, Chairman, Chiefs of Staff Committee, "US-UK-Canada Telecommunications Relationship," February 5, 1951, File CSC 1415.1, pt. 1, vol. 21161, RG24-B-1, LAC.

189 United Kingdom JCEC (Washington), "BDS(W)/800/2/2," September 20, 1961, 2, File CSC 2203:5, pt. 1, vol. 21763, RG24-B-1, LAC.

190 George Orwell, *Animal Farm* (New York: Signet Classics, 1996), 134.

CHAPTER 3. GLOBAL NAVAL PLANNING

1 Edward Miller, *War Plan Orange: The U.S. Strategy to Defeat Japan, 1897–1945* (Annapolis, MD: Naval Institute Press, 1991).

2 Vincent Davis, *Postwar Defense Policy and the U.S. Navy, 1943–1946* (Chapel Hill: University of North Carolina Press, 1962), 24.

3 Kathleen Burk, *Old World, New World: Great Britain and America from the Beginning* (New York: Atlantic Monthly Press, 2008), 461–464; Phillips Payson O'Brien, *British and American Naval Power, Politics and Policy, 1900–1936* (Westport, CN: Praeger, 1998), 5.

4 Davis, *Postwar*, 7–8.

5 Davis, 27; Michael Palmer, *Origins of the Maritime Strategy: The Development of American Naval Strategy, 1945–1955* (Annapolis, MD: Naval Institute Press, 1990), 9.

6 Waldo Heinrichs, *Threshold of War: Franklin D. Roosevelt and American Entry into World War II* (New York: Oxford University Press, 1988), 44.

7 Jeffrey Barlow, *From Hot War to Cold: The U.S. Navy and National Security Affairs, 1945–1955* (Stanford, CA: Stanford University Press, 2009), 46.

8 Frank Blazich, "Neptune's Oracle: Admiral Harry E. Yarnell's Wartime Planning, 1918–20 and 1943–44," *Naval War College Review* 73, no. 1 (2020):123; Davis, *Postwar*, 35.

9 Blazich, "Neptune's Oracle," 124–125.

10 Davis, *Postwar*, 95.

11 Palmer, *Origins*, 8.

12 Palmer, 12.

13 Mark Stoler, *Allies and Adversaries: The Joint Chiefs of Staff, the Grand Alliance, and U.S. Strategy in World War II* (Chapel Hill: University of North Carolina Press, 2000), 215.

14 Julian Lewis, *Changing Direction: British Military Planning for Post-War Strategic Defense, 1942–1947* (London: Sherwood Press, 1987), 104.

15 Michael Palmer, "The Influence of Naval Strategy on National Security Planning, 1945–1955," Naval History and Heritage Command, 1989, accessed June 3, 2018, https://www.history.navy.mil/research/library/online-reading-room/title-list-alphabetically/t/time-change.html; Walter Poole, "From Conciliation to Containment: The Joint Chiefs of Staff and the Coming of the Cold War, 1945–1946," *Military Affairs* 42, no. 1 (February 1978): 15.

16 Palmer, "The Influence of Naval Strategy"; Davis, *Postwar*, 263–264.

17 Peter Swartz, *Sea Changes: Transforming U.S. Navy Deployment Strategy: 1775–2002* (Alexandria, VA: Center for Naval Analyses, 2002), 46–51.

18 James Forrestal, *Annual Report of the Secretary of the Navy* (Washington, D.C.: Government Printing Office, 1947), 22.

19 David Edgerton, *The Rise and Fall of the British Nation: A Twentieth-Century History* (London: Allen Lane, 2018), 148–150.

20 Malcolm Murfett, *In Jeopardy: The Royal Navy and British Far Eastern Defence Policy, 1945–1951* (Kuala Lumpur: Oxford University Press, 1995), 7.

21 Randall Bennett Woods and Howard Jones, *Dawning of the Cold War: The United States' Quest for Order* (Athens: University of Georgia Press, 1991), 75.

22 Christopher Chantrill, "Time Series Chart of Public Spending," U.K. Public Spending, accessed July 6, 2018, https://ukpublicspending.co.uk/spending_chart_1900_2020UKp_XXc11i111tcn_Got; Michael Neiberg, *Potsdam: The End of World War II and the Remaking of Europe* (New York: Basic Books, 2015), 74.

23 Peter Clarke, *The Last Thousand Days of the British Empire: Churchill, Roosevelt, and the Birth of Pax Americana* (New York: Bloomsbury Press, 2008), 402.

24 Malcolm Murfett, ed., *The First Sea Lords: From Fisher to Mountbatten* (Westport, CT: Praeger, 1995), 220–221.

25 B. R. Mitchell, *British Historical Statistics* (Cambridge: Cambridge University Press, 1988), "Historical Tables," table 6–1.

26 Murfett, *In Jeopardy*, 29.

27 Murfett, *In Jeopardy*, 33.

28 Woods and Jones, *Dawning*, 148.

29 Murfett, *The First Sea Lords*, 218; U.K., Central Statistical Office, *Annual Abstract of Statistics No. 90* (London: Her Majesty's Stationery Office, 1953), 95.

30 Fleet Admiral Chester W. Nimitz, USN, to Secretary of the Navy James Forrestal, July 23, 1946, Folder Russia (5 of 8), Box 15, Clark M. Clifford Papers, Harry S. Truman Presidential Library.

31 "An Estimate of Soviet Submarine Potential, June 1950," Enclosure C to Captain Paul R. Heineman, USN, Chairman, Combined CANUKUS Anti-Submarine Working Group, "Final Draft of Papers of the Combined Working Group—Forwarding Of," April 21, 1949, III-4, File 8100-5, vol. 35135, RG24-D-1-c, LAC.

32 Derek Waller, "The Surrender of the U-Boats in 1945," *Argonauta* 35, no. 2 (Spring 2018): 5–26.

33 Barlow, *From Hot War to Cold*, 163; Palmer, *Origins*, 39.

34 Samuel Eliot Morison, *History of United States Naval Operations in World War II*, vol. 10, *The Atlantic Battle Won, May 1943–May 1945* (Edison, NJ: Castle Books, 2001), 362; Eric Grove, ed., *The Defeat of the Enemy Attack on Shipping, 1939–1945*, vol. 137 (Aldershot, U.K.: Ashgate, 1957), 228–231.

35 Palmer, *Origins*, 27–35.

36 Enclosure A to CNO, "Serial 00012P34, Proceedings of Anti-Submarine Warfare Conference, 17 June 1946—Forwarding Of," June 25, 1946, 1–2, Series: Conferences, Anti-Submarine Warfare, 1946–1948, Box 325A, Post January 1946 Command File [1946 CMD], NHHC; Forrestal, *Annual Report*, 9.

37 Palmer, *Origins*, 39.

38 Palmer, "The Influence of Naval Strategy"; Barlow, *From Hot War to Cold*, 165.

39 Palmer, *Origins*, 39.

40 Jeffrey Barlow, *Revolt of the Admirals: The Fight for Naval Aviation, 1945–1950* (Washington, D.C.: Naval Historical Center, 1994).

41 Malcolm Llewellyn-Jones, *The Royal Navy and Anti-Submarine Warfare, 1917–1949* (New York: Routledge, 2006), 175–176.

42 Llewellyn-Jones, *The Royal Navy*, 149–150; Ian Speller, "Defence or Deterrence? The Royal Navy and the Cold War, 1945–1955," in *Cold War Britain, 1945–1964: New Perspectives*, ed. Michael Hopkins, Michael Kandiah, and Gillian Staerck (Basingstoke, U.K.: Palgrave Macmillan, 2003), 109–110.

43 Llewellyn-Jones, *The Royal Navy*, 2–3.

44 Eric Grove and Geoffrey Till, "Anglo-American Maritime Strategy in the Era of Massive Retaliation, 1945–60," in *Maritime Strategy and the Balance of Power: Britain and America in the Twentieth Century*, ed. John B. Hattendorf and Robert Jordan (New York: St. Martin's Press, 1989), 286.

45 Grove, *From Vanguard to Trident*, 56.

46 Enclosure A to CNO, "Serial 00012P34," June 25, 1946, 8.

47 CNO to Forrestal, "Serial 008P03, Anti-Submarine Warfare Situation," July 23, 1946, Folder CNO TS 1946 A8–3, Box 42, Entry UD 17, RG 80, NACP.

48 CNO to Forrestal, "Serial 007P31, Bilateral Exchange of Military Information with Royal Canadian Navy," September 18, 1946, Folder CNO TS 1946 A8–3, Box 42, Entry UD 17, RG 80, NACP.

49 Julian Zelizer, *Arsenal of Democracy: The Politics of National Security—From World War II to the War on Terrorism* (New York: Basic Books, 2012), 64.

50 John Moser, *Twisting the Lion's Tail: Anglophobia in the United States, 1921–48* (London: Macmillan Press, 1999), 175–179.

51 "'Good Will' Label Taken Off U.S. Navy In Mediterranean," *Washington Post*, October 1, 1946.

52 Rear Admiral Jules James, USN, Commander, U.S. Naval Forces, Mediterranean, to Vice Admiral Louis Denfeld, USN, Chief of Naval Personnel, January 15, 1946, Folder B, Correspondence, January 1946–March 1946, Box 3, Jules James Papers (#223), Special Collections Department, J. Y. Joyner Library, East Carolina University, Greenville, North Carolina [ECU].

53 CNO, "Serial 0023P30, Canadian-United States Military Cooperation," February 26, 1947, Folder A16-1 Jacket #1 (1-10/47) (3 of 3), 1947 Secret, Box 166, Entry P 111, CINCLANT Secret and Top Secret Correspondence, 1941–1949 [Entry P 111], RG 313, NACP.

54 Memo, Rear Admiral Cato D. Glover, USN, to CNO, November 12, 1946 in Naval Historical Center, *The Records of the Strategic Plans Division: Office of the Chief of Naval Operations and Predecessor Organizations* (Wilmington, DE: Scholarly Resources, 1974), reel 19, frames 1016–1018.

55 Stephen Ross, *American War Plans, 1945–1950* (Portland, OR: Frank Cass, 1996).

56 "Record of Fourteenth Meeting," November 22, 1946, Enclosure to Com-

mander Anthony H.G. Storrs, RCN, Deputy Director of Naval Plans, to Captain Horatio N. Lay, RCN, Director of Naval Plans and Intelligence [DNPI], "Tripartite Discussions on Standardization and Strategic Problems—Washington, November 1946," December 7, 1946, File 1272–35, vol. 8087, RG24-D-1-c, LAC.

57 "Record of Eighth Meeting," November 19, 1946, Enclosure to Storrs to Lay, 2.

58 "Situation in 1956 in Respect of the Development of New Weapons and Its Effect on War," Enclosure 2 to Storrs to Lay, 9.

59 Sean Maloney, *Learning to Love the Bomb: Canada's Nuclear Weapons during the Cold War* (Washington, D.C.: Potomac Books, 2007), 7.

60 Rear Admiral Charles W. Styer, USN, Chairman, Submarine Conference to CNO, "Submarine Conference on 8 January 1947, Report Of," January 9, 1947, 4–5, Folder A19, Jacket 1, 1947, Box 10, Entry P 9, CINCPACFLT, Restricted Admin Files, 1946–1948 [Entry P 9], RG 313, NACP.

61 Enclosure A to CNO, "Serial 003P31, Report of Coordinator of Undersea Warfare and Assistants' Visit to British Naval Activities, Jan. 19–Feb. 12, 1947—Forwarding Of," April 30, 1947, 1, Folder A16-3(1) ASW (2-6/47) (1 of 2), 1947, Secret, Box 168, Entry P 111, RG 313, NACP.

62 "Underwater Weapons—Coordination of Effort with the USA," Enclosure M to CNO, "Serial 003P31," 1.

63 Enclosure B to CNO, "Minutes of Inter-Fleet Discussions on Anti-Submarine Warfare, Forwarding Of," June 26, 1947, 49, Folder A16–3(1) (6-12/47) (4 of 4), 1947, Secret, Box 168, Entry P 111, RG 313, NACP.

64 Vice Admiral Howard E. Reid, RCN, Chief of the Naval Staff to Minister of National Defense, January 28, 1947, File 4425–27, pt, 1, vol. 34238, RG24-D-1-c, LAC.

65 CNO to Commander in Chief, U.S. Atlantic Fleet [CINCLANTFLT], "101945Z," June 10, 1947, Folder EF 13–39 Canada, 1946–1947, Box 30, Entry UD-09D 26, Naval History and Heritage Command, Operations Division (OP-32), Subject Files, 1946–1950 [Entry UD-09D 26], RG 38, NACP.

66 CNO to Commander Destroyers, U.S. Atlantic Fleet, "171438Z," July 16, 1947, Folder EF 13–39 Canada, 1946–1947, Box 30, Entry UD-09D 26, RG 38, NACP.

67 CNO to CINCLANTFLT, "291501Z," July 29, 1947, Folder EF 13–39 Canada, 1946–1947, Box 30, Entry UD-09D 26, RG 38, NACP.

68 Sean Maloney, *Securing Command of the Sea: NATO Naval Planning, 1948–1954* (Annapolis, MD: Naval Institute Press, 1995), 44–46.

69 Ross, *War Plans*, 25–45.

70 Maloney, *Securing Command*, 64.

71 Maloney, *Securing Command*, 73.

72 Admiral Rhoderick R. McGrigor, RN, Commander in Chief, Home Fleet [CINCHF], to Admiral of the Fleet Fraser, RN, 1SL, November 24, 1948, ADM 205/70, TNA.

73 Vice Admiral Arthur D. Struble, USN, Deputy Chief of Naval Operations (Operations), "Serial 000473P30, Naval Command in the Atlantic Ocean," November 9, 1948, Folder A3–1, Jacket #5 (9–11/48) (3 of 4), 1948, T.S., Box 175, Entry P 111, RG 313, NACP.

74 Atomic Energy Act of 1946, Pub. L. 79–585, *U.S. Statutes at Large* 60 (1947), 755; Robert Hathaway, *Ambiguous Partnership: Britain and America, 1944–1947* (New York: Columbia University Press, 1981), 262.

75 Reminiscences of Vice Admiral Herbert D. Riley, USN, interview by John T. Mason Jr., 2004, 297, USNI.

76 Admiral William Blandy, USN, CINCLANTFLT, to CNO, "Serial 00042, Anti-Submarine Operations, Determination of Operational Assistance Required from the Other Services of the Military Establishment For," April 29, 1949, 3, Folder A16–3(1) (1–6/49), 1949, T.S., Box 216, Entry P 111, RG 313, NACP.

77 Maloney, *Securing Command*, 93–94.

78 Maloney, *Securing Command*, 116–117.

79 Alan Dobson and Steve Marsh, "Churchill at the Summit: SACLANT and the Tone of Anglo-American Relations in January 1952," *International History Review* 32, no. 2 (June 2010): 213.

80 Steve Marsh, "Churchill, SACLANT, and the Politics of Opposition," *Contemporary British History* 27, no. 4 (2013): 446.

81 Dobson and Marsh, "Churchill at the Summit," 224.

82 Dobson and Marsh, 217–218.

83 Marsh, "Churchill, SACLANT," 456.

84 Dobson and Marsh, "Churchill at the Summit," 219.

85 Dobson and Marsh, 216.

86 Maloney, *Securing Command*, 136.

87 Maloney, *Securing Command*, 109–111, 172–173.

88 Maloney, *Securing Command*, 178–186.

89 Maloney, *Securing Command*, 109–111.

90 Philip Ziegler, *Mountbatten* (New York: Harper & Row, 1985), 216.

91 Ziegler, *Mountbatten*, 517; Maloney, *Securing Command of the Sea*, 194–195.

92 Philip Alphonse Dur, "The Sixth Fleet: A Case Study of Institutionalized Naval Presence, 1946–1968" (PhD diss., Harvard University, 1975), 37–54; Admiral Robert B. Carney, USN, Commander in Chief, U.S. Naval Forces Eastern Atlantic and Mediterranean [CINCNELM], to Admiral Forrest Sherman, USN, CNO, "Serial 00053, Durable II Conference at Malta; Subsidiary Agenda," February 7, 1951, Folder F4, A-1(2), Box 77 (OF), AR/131, NHHC; Office of the Chief of Naval Operations, "USF 1, Principles and Applications of Naval Warfare," May 1, 1947, 1, Box 269, Entry UD-09D 19, RG 38, NACP.

93 Trevor Reese, *Australia, New Zealand, and the United States: A Survey of International Relations, 1941–1968* (London: Oxford University Press, 1969), 60; Peter Dean, *MacArthur's Coalition: US and Australian Operations in the*

Southwest Pacific Area, 1942–1945 (Lawrence: University Press of Kansas, 2018), 371.

94 Stuart Macintyre, *A Concise History of Australia* (Cambridge: Cambridge University Press, 2004), 209; Dean, *MacArthur's Coalition*, 371; Stephen Frühling, *A History of Australian Strategic Policy since 1945* (Canberra, Australia: Defence Publishing Service, 2009), 11–12.

95 David Horner, *Defense Supremo: Sir Frederick Shedden and the Making of Australian Defense Policy* (Sydney: Allen & Unwin, 2000), 236.

96 Murfett, *In Jeopardy*, 18, 33.

97 Hal Friedman, *Creating an American Lake: United States Imperialism and Strategic Security in the Pacific Basin, 1945–1947* (Westport, CT: Greenwood Press, 2001).

98 Supreme Commander for the Allied Powers, *Reports of General MacArthur, prepared by his General Staff*, ed. Charles A. Willoughby, vol. 1 supp., *MacArthur in Japan: The Occupation: Military Phase* (Washington, D.C.: Government Printing Office, 1966), 82.

99 Edward J. Drea, *History of the Unified Command Plan, 1946–2012* (Washington, D.C.: Joint History Office, Office of the Chairman of the Joint Chiefs of Staff, 2013), 113; Allan Millett, *The War for Korea, 1950–1951: They Came from the North* (Lawrence: University Press of Kansas, 2010), 33.

100 Greg Kennedy, *Anglo-American Strategic Relations and the Far East, 1933–1939: Imperial Crossroads* (London: Frank Cass, 2002), 18, 34; Franco David Macri, *Clash of Empires in South China: The Allied Nations' Proxy War With Japan, 1935–1941* (Lawrence: University Press of Kansas, 2012), 13.

101 Kennedy, *Anglo-American Strategic Relations*, 34.

102 Joseph M. Worthington, "Admiral Royal E. Ingersoll, U.S. Navy" (1979), reel 1, 53, Dudley Knox Library, Naval Postgraduate School, Monterey, CA; Admiral Thomas C. Hart, USN, Commander in Chief, U.S. Asiatic Fleet, to Commander in Chief, U.S. Fleet, "Narrative of Events, Asiatic Fleet Leading Up to War and From 8 December 1941 to 15 February 1942," June 11, 1942, 1–36, Admiral Thomas C Hart (CINCAF), A, World War II War Diaries, Fold3.com, https://www.fold3.com/image/251/267940695.

103 Michael Simpson, *A Life of Admiral of the Fleet Andrew Cunningham: A Twentieth Century Naval Leader* (New York: Routledge, 2004), 205; Arthur Marder, Mark Jacobsen, and John Horsfield, *Old Friends, New Enemies: The Royal Navy and the Imperial Japanese Navy*, vol. 2, *The Pacific War, 1942–1945* (New York: Clarendon Press, 1990), 363; Jonathan Robb-Webb, *The British Pacific Fleet: Experience and Legacy, 1944–50* (Burlington, VT: Ashgate, 2013), 73.

104 Fraser to Vice Admiral Edward Neville Syfret, RN, Vice Chief of Naval Staff, "Msg, 221417Z," September 23, 1945, ADM 1/17759, TNA.

105 Secretary, Admiralty, "C.E. 62875/45," March 11, 1948, ADM 1/17759, TNA.

106 David Hobbs, *The British Pacific Fleet: The Royal Navy's Most Powerful Strike Force* (Annapolis, MD: Naval Institute Press, 2011), 364.

107 Vice Admiral Robert M. Griffin, USN, Commander, Naval Forces Far East [COMNAVFE], to Admiral Louis Denfeld, USN, CINCPACFLT, June 5, 1947, 3, Folder A1 Jacket #1, Box 1, Entry A1 202, RG 313, NACP; Rear Admiral Charles H. L. Woodhouse, RN, "No 98/5/2, Orders for Blue Force in Exercise 13th August, 1947," August 10, 1947, and Griffin to CNO, "Joint Navy-Air Force and Inter Task Force Exercises," August 22, 1947: both in Folder A16–3(1)-(16), Box 2877, Entry UD 16, Security Classified Correspondence, 1940–1947 [Entry UD 16], RG 80, NACP.

108 Murfett, *In Jeopardy*, 74; Hobbs, *The British Pacific Fleet*, 371.

109 Paul Orders, *Britain, Australia, New Zealand and the Challenge of the United States, 1939–46: A Study in International History* (New York: Palgrave Macmillan, 2003), 157.

110 Anthony Clayton, "'Deceptive Might': Imperial Defence and Security, 1900–1968," in *Oxford History of the British Empire*, vol. 4, *The Twentieth Century*, ed. Judith Brown (New York: Oxford University Press, 1999), 294.

111 Orders, *Challenge of the United States*, 161–162.

112 Orders, 163.

113 Orders, 163–170.

114 Orders, 171–173.

115 Glen Barclay, *Friends in High Places: Australian-American Diplomatic Relations since 1945* (New York: Oxford University Press, 1985), 24.

116 Orders, *Challenge of the United States*, 184–185.

117 Orders, 185.

118 Friedman, *Creating an American Lake*, 66.

119 Frederick G. Shedden, Secretary, Department of Defense, "Note of Secraphone Conversation with the Chief of the Naval Staff," June 9, 1947, 1445/6, A5954, National Archives of Australia [NAA].

120 "Interview with Admiral Denfeld, USN," June 10, 1947, Enclosure to Admiral Louis Hamilton, RN, Chief of Naval Staff (Australia), to Shedden, June 12, 1947, 1, 1445/6, A5954, NAA; Hamilton to Shedden, June 12, 1947, 12/2, Discussions CNS ADM Denfeld USN; Record Group 11, SPC-A.

121 Friedman, *Creating an American Lake*, 37.

122 "Estimate of Soviet Objectives and Capabilities in the Pacific," Enclosure A to Denfeld, "Serial 00037, Estimate; Forwarding Of," October 27, 1947, I-E-2, VI-B-5b, Folder A7-A8, Box 51, Entry UD 17, RG 80, NACP.

123 "U.S.S. Valley Forge World Cruise, 1947–48" (1948), 32, 1948; USS Valley Forge (CV-45); V; Navy Cruise Books, 1918–2009, Fold3.com, https://www.fold3 .com/image/1/301476460.

124 Shedden to Minister for the Navy William Riordan, MP, "Australian-American Co-Operation—Staff Talks with United States Officers," September 8, 1948, 1, 1445/6, A5954, NAA; Harold M. Martin, *The Naval Career of Harold M. Martin*, Tennessee Regional Oral History Collection, pt. 1, no. 6. Glen Rock, NJ: Micro-

filming Corporation of America, 1977 (Glen Rock, NJ: Microfilming Corporation of America, 1977), 114–115.

125   Admiral Dewitt C. Ramsey, USN, CINCPACFLT to CNO, "Information Discussions with First Sea Lord of the Royal Australian Navy—Comments On," April 9, 1948, 3, Folder A8-3/A-FF12, Box 195, Entry P 1204 CNO/SecNav Security Classified General Correspondence, 1948–1951 [Entry P 1204], RG 38, NACP.

126   Peter Jones, "Collins, Sir John Augustine (1899–1989)," *Australian Dictionary of Biography* (2007), accessed July 23, 2018,http://adb.anu.edu.au/biography/collins-sir-john-augustine-12335; Vice Admiral John Collins, *As Luck Would Have It: The Reminiscences of an Australian Sailor* (Sydney: Angus and Robertson, 1965).

127   Collins, *As Luck Would Have It*, 133–135; Vice Admiral John Collins, interview by Mel Pratt, August 27, 1975, 728011, Mel Pratt Collection, National Library of Australia [NLA], http://nla.gov.au/nla.oh-vn728011.

128   "Note on Defense Cooperation with the United States of America in the Post-War Period," December 1950, 1, 2317/22, A5954, NAA.

129   Commander Stephen Jurika, U.S. Naval Attaché, Australia, to Captain Paul D. Stroop, USN, July 10, 1948, and Jurika to Ramsey, September 27, 1948: both in Folder June-1948-December, Box 3, Stephen Jurika Jr. Papers [Jurika Papers], Hoover Institution Archives [HIA].

130   Jurika to Ramsey, September 27, 1948; Alastair Cooper, "The Development of an Independent Navy for Australia: Correspondence between the First Naval Member and the First Sea Lord, 1947–59," in *The Naval Miscellany*. vol. 7, ed. Susan Rose (London: George Allen & Unwin, 2008), 547.

131   "Plans Summary," Enclosure A to CINCPACFLT to DNH, "Semi-Annual Summary of CinCPacFlt Command Narrative for the Period 1 October 1948–31 March 1949," June 17, 1949, Folder CINCPACFLT Summary 1 October 1948–31 March 1949, Box 672, 1946 CMD, NHHC.

132   Appendix D to "Plans Summary," Enclosure A to CINCPACFLT to DNH.

133   Arthur Dudden, *The American Pacific: From the Old China Trade to the Present* (New York: Oxford University Press, 1992), 207; Roger Thompson, *The Pacific Basin since 1945: A History of the Foreign Relations of the Asian, Australasia, and American Rim States and the Pacific Islands* (London: Longman, 1994), 15.

134   Orders, *Challenge of the United States*, 188.

135   Hector Donohue, *From Empire Defence to the Long Haul: Post-War Defence Policy and Its Impact on Naval Force Structure Planning, 1945–1955*, Papers in Australian Maritime Affairs 1 (Canberra: Sea Power Centre - Australia, 1996), 20–21.

136   Ian McGibbon, "ANZAM," in *The Oxford Companion to New Zealand Military History* (Auckland, NZ: Oxford University Press, 2000), 30.

137 Edgerton, *The Rise and Fall*, 77.

138 Donohue, *From Empire Defence*, 77–78.

139 Anthony Farrar-Hockley, "The Post-War Army, 1945–1963," in *The Oxford History of the British Army*, ed. David Chandler and Ian Beckett (Oxford, U.K.: Oxford University Press, 1994), 318.

140 W. David McIntyre, *Background to the ANZUS Pact: Policy-Making, Strategy, and Diplomacy, 1945–55* (Christchurch, NZ: Canterbury University Press, 1995), 317, 325, 330, 352.

141 Captain Charles R. Calhoun, USN, "Report of a Lecture," April 7, 1950, 3, Folder F13, P11, Box 73, AR/131, NHHC.

142 Tom Frame, *Pacific Partners: A History of Australian-American Naval Relations* (Sydney: Hodder & Stoughton, 1992), 85.

143 Director, Strategic Plans, to Deputy Chief of Naval Operations (Operations), "Serial 000543P30, Visit of Prime Minister Menzies of Australia; Items for Discussion in Connection With," July 17, 1950, 1–2, Folder F7, A19, Box 72, AR/131, NHHC.

144 General Omar Bradley, Chairman, JCS, to Secretary of Defense Louis Johnson, July 31, 1950, Folder CCS 337 Australia (7–12–50) Sec. 1, Box 10, Entry UD 7, Geographic Files, 1948–1950 [Entry UD 7], RG 218, NACP.

145 *History of the Joint Chiefs of Staff: The Joint Chiefs of Staff and the First Indochina War, 1947–1954* (Washington, D.C.: Office of Joint History, Office of the Chairman of the Joint Chiefs of Staff, 2004), 77.

146 Vice Admiral John Collins, RAN, Chief of the Naval Staff, to Shedden, September 5, 1950, 1445/1, A5954, NAA.

147 "Note on Defense Cooperation," 1; "American Visitor," *Age*, May 1, 1950, 5; "Radford Delayed," *Daily Mercury* (Mackay, Qld.: 1906–1954), May 10, 1950, 1, accessed December 19, 2019, http://nla.gov.au/nla.news-article172317336.

148 Stephen Jurika, ed., *From Pearl Harbor to Vietnam: The Memoirs of Admiral Arthur W. Radford* (Stanford, CA: Hoover Institution Press, 1980); John K. Lohl, "Out-Spoken—Arthur William Radford (1896–1973)," in *Nineteen-Gun Salute: Case Studies of Operational, Strategic, and Diplomatic Naval Leadership during the 20th and Early 21st Centuries*, ed. John B. Hattendorf and Bruce A. Elleman (Newport, RI: Naval War College Press, 2010), 107–116.

149 "U.S. Admiral's Flying Visit to Canberra," *Canberra Times*, May 4, 1950, 1; Reminiscences of Rear Admiral Charles Adair, USN, interview by John T. Mason Jr., 1977, 515, Navy Department Library, Washington, D.C. [NDL]

150 Reminiscences of Adair, 515–516.

151 Collins to Shedden, September 5, 1950.

152 JCS, "SM-2661-50, Minutes of U.S.-U.K. Chiefs of Staff Meeting," October 23, 1950, 21–22, Folder CCS 337 (7–22–48), Sec. 2, Box 132, Entry UD 5, Central Decimal Files, 1948–1950 [Entry UD 5], RG 218, NACP.

153 Collins to Shedden, February 2, 1951, 1, 1445/1, A5954, NAA.

154 Collins to Secretary, Defense Committee, "Progress of Planning between AN-ZAM and C-in-C PAC Fleet," May 5, 1952, 2, 97/1952, A5799, NAA.

155 "Report of the Radford-Collins Conference," Enclosure to Admiral Arthur Radford, USN, CINCPACFLT to Sherman, "Serial 00012, Radford-Collins Conference on ANZAM Boundaries—26 Feb to 2 Mar 10951," March 9, 1951, Folder 000276–000300, Box 81, Top Secret Control Office Files, 1951 [TS 1951], NHHC. Copy also available in Australian records, see "Report of the Radford-Collins Conference Held at Pearl Harbor, T.H., 26 Feb.–2 Mar. 1951" (March 2, 1951), AWM 123/614, Australian War Memorial [AWM].

156 Collins, interview, NLA; Vice Admiral Alan McNicoll, RAN, interview by Frances McNicoll and Suzanne Lunney, 1977, 3:2/91–3:2/92, ORAL TRC 534, Oral History & Folklore Branch, NLA.

157 "Excerpts from CNS: First Sea Lord Correspondence," *Journal of Australian Naval History* 6, no. 1 (March 2009): 121.

158 David Stevens, *A Critical Vulnerability: The Impact of the Submarine Threat on Australia's Maritime Defence, 1915–1954* (Canberra, Australia: Sea Power Centre, 2005), 292–296.

159 CNO, "Serial 0079P30, Organization for World-Wide Anti-Submarine Warfare," October 13, 1947, 11, Folder A16-3(1) (6-12/47) (3 of 4), 1947 Secret, Box 168, Entry P 111, RG 313, NACP; Denfeld to CINCPACFLT and CINCLANT-FLT, "Anti-Submarine Warfare and Shipping Control Responsibilities, Assignment Of," June 10, 1949, File 8740-800-2, vol. 35282, RG24-D-1-c, LAC.

CHAPTER 4. PERSONNEL

1 Based on Lieutenant Raymond D. Lygo, RN, to Staff Officer (Air), BJSM(W), Washington, "Exchange Duty—Final Report," March 19, 1951, ADM 1/23063, TNA; Admiral Raymond Derek Lygo, RN (ret), interview by Richard Mc-Donough, May 8, 2006, reel 10, Sound Archive, Catalogue 28776, IWM; Roy Grossnick, *Dictionary of American Naval Aviation Squadrons*, vol. 1 (Washington, D.C.: Naval History and Heritage Command, 1995), 243.

2 The first U.S. Navy attaché was assigned to London in 1882. The United States and Canada first exchanged military, air, and naval attachés in 1940. Australia and the U.S. first exchanged naval attachés in 1941. See Wyman Packard, *A Century of U.S. Naval Intelligence* (Washington, D.C.: Office of Naval Intelligence and Naval History and Heritage Command, 1996), 58, 73; Stanley W. Dziuban, *Military Relations between the United States and Canada, 1939–1945* (Washington, D.C.: Center of Military History, 1959), 71–72; "U.S. Naval Attaché for Australia," *Sydney Morning Herald,* February 22, 1941, 12.

3 "CoS (47) 124—Future of Combined Chiefs of Staff" (1947), DEFE 5/4, and Chiefs of Staff Committee, "CoS (47) 74th Meeting," June 11, 1947, 7, DEFE 4/4/74: both in TNA.

4   W. G. Mills, Deputy Minister, to Mr. Fraser (Peterborough West), "RCN-USN Liaison," January 29, 1943, 1, Folder 1 of 3, File 5, Box 111, 81/520/1550, DHH.

5   No. 26, Telegram, JSM(W) to Cabinet Office, February 9, 1946, in U.K. Foreign and Commonwealth Office, *Documents on British Policy Overseas,* series 1, vol. 4, *Britain and America: Atomic Energy, Bases and Food, 12 December 1945–31 July 1946* (London: Her Majesty's Stationery Office, 1987), 93–96.

6   Dziuban, *Military Relations,* 72–75.

7   Isabel Campbell, "A Brave New World, 1945–1960," in *The Naval Service of Canada, 1910–2010: The Centennial Story* (Toronto: Dundurn Press, 2009), 128–130.

8   Air Vice Marshal Wilfred A. Curtis, RCAF, Acting Chief of the Air Staff, "Memo, Canadian Joint Staff Washington, S.15–9–52," November 29, 1945, Folder 1 of 3, File 5, Box 111, 81/520/1550, DHH.

9   Norman Harper, *A Great and Powerful Friend: A Study of Australian-American Relations between 1900–1975* (New York: University of Queensland Press, 1986), 84; Carl Bridge, "Allies of a Kind: Three Wartime Australian Ministers to the United States, 1940–46," in *Australia Goes to Washington: 75 Years of Australian Representation in the United States, 1940–2015,* ed. David Lowe, David Lee, and Carl Bridge (Acton, ACT: Australian National University Press, 2016), 23–25.

10 Joint Secretariat, "Note to Holders of JCS 1981," October 1948, 1, Folder CCS 334 Australian Joint Services Staff (9–8–48), Box 103, Entry UD 5, RG 218, NACP.

11 Admiral Louis Denfeld, USN, CNO, to JCS, "JCS 1981, Establishment of an Australian Joint Services Staff," February 15, 1949, and Major General John A. Chapman, Australian Military Mission to Foreign Liaison Office, U.S. Army, July 21, 1949: both in Folder CCS 334 Australian Joint Services Staff (9–8–48), Box 103, Entry UD 5, RG 218, NACP.

12 Rear Admiral Carl F. Espe, USN, Deputy Director of Naval Intelligence, to Director of Joint Staff, "New Chief of Australian Joint Service Staff in Washington," August 19, 1949, Folder CCS 334 Australian Joint Services Staff (9–8–48), Box 103, Entry UD 5, RG 218, NACP.

13 Joint Strategic Survey Committee, "JCS 1981/2," December 21, 1950, 11–13, Folder CCS 334 Australian Joint Services Staff (9–8–48), Box 103, Entry UD 5, RG 218, NACP.

14 "HMCS Niagara: Duties and Responsibilities of Washington Staff Steadily Growing," *Crowsnest,* November 1953, 1, Folder 73/1223 Series 5, File 2535B, File 1, HMCS Niagara (Base) General, 1940–1966, Box 338, 81/520/8000, DHH; Mills to Under-Secretary of State for External Affairs, October 26, 1948, File 28–6-10, vol. 5274, RG24-E-1-b, LAC.

15 Rear Admiral John Alexander Charles, RCN (ret), My Navy Recollections, interview by William S. Thackray, July 17, 1980, pt. 9, SC104_CJA_206, UVL.

16 Charles, pt. 9; Rear Admiral Michael Grote Stirling, RCN (ret), My Navy Recol-

lections, interview by William S. Thackray, June 1980, pt. 6, SC104_SMG_189, UVL.

17   Bureau of Aeronautics [BuAir], "Correspondence Designations and Directory Information," October 1, 1945, 42, Folder 1, Oct 1945; BuAir, "Correspondence Designations and Directory Information for Bureau of Aeronautics," May 1, 1946, 2, Folder 1 May 1946; BuAir, "Bureau of Aeronautics Directory," September 1949, 22, Folder 1949: all in Box 88, Aviation History Branch, NHHC; BuAir, "Bureau of Aeronautics Directory," August 15, 1950, 22, Folder 1950; BuAir, "Bureau of Aeronautics Directory," August 15, 1951, 30, Folder 1951; BuAir, "Bureau of Aeronautics Directory," November 15, 1952, 31, Folder 1952: all in Box 89, Aviation History Branch, NHHC.

18   Rear Admiral Edmund Nicholas Poland, RN (ret), interview by Nigel de Lee, April 8, 1991, reel 17, Sound Archive, Catalogue 11951, IWM.

19   BJSM(W), "MM(S) 47 6th Meeting, Minutes," March 25, 1947, 2, CAB 138/8, TNA; Henry M. Wilson, *Eight Years Overseas, 1939–1947* (London: Hutchinson, 1948), 262.

20   BJSM(W), "MM(S) (48) 5th Meeting, Minutes," April 5, 1948, 1, CAB 138/8, TNA.

21   Joint Planning Staff, "JP (49) 133 (Final), Visit of the United Kingdom Joint Planning Staff to Washington—September–October, 1949," October 14, 1949, DEFE 4/25, TNA.

22   Vice Admiral Cecil Charles Hughes-Hallett, RN, BJSM(W), to Admiral Rhoderick R. McGrigor, RN, 1SL, November 3, 1952, ADM 205/86, TNA.

23   Hughes-Hallett to McGrigor, "BNS 0036/52," December 1, 1952, 3, ADM 205/86, TNA.

24   Poland, interview, reel 18.

25   Poland, reel 17.

26   Packard, *A Century of U.S. Naval Intelligence*, 310–311.

27   Captain Thomas M. Brownrigg, RN, Director of Plans [DoP], to DNI, Admiralty, "Discussions with DNI US Navy," October 13, 1949, 1, ADM 205/72, TNA.

28   "Air," Appendix 4 to Commodore Horatio N. Lay, RCN, Naval Member, Canadian Joint Staff (Washington) [NMCJS(W)], to Naval Secretary, "HMCS Niagara Report of Proceedings for November 1950," December 15, 1950, 3, File 3, Box 338, 81/520/8000, DHH.

29   Commodore Morson A. Medland, RCN, NMCJS(W), to Naval Secretary, "HMCS Niagara Report of Proceedings for November 1952," December 3, 1952, 1, File 5, Box 338, 81/520/8000, DHH.

30   "Ordnance," Appendix 6 to Medland to Naval Secretary, "November 1952."

31   Rear Admiral Tully Shelley, USN, U.S. Naval Attaché, London, to Chief of Naval Intelligence, "Serial 00531, Reorganization of Naval Intelligence Division," November 15, 1947, 2, Folder A3-A3-1/Secret-1947, Box 2848, Entry UD 16, RG 80, NACP.

32 Office of Naval Intelligence, "Information Exchange Projects, Annex B-1," July 1950, and Tripartite Ad Hoc Committee on Standardization Objectives, "Report to Chief of Naval Staff, Royal Navy; Chief of Naval Staff, Royal Canadian Navy; Chief of Naval Operations, United States Navy," May 11, 1950: both in File 1961-23, pt. 1, vol. 34091, RG24-D-1-c, LAC.

33 Director of Standardization Division [DStand], Admiralty, "Naval Tripartite Standardization Program, Progress Report—Six Months Ending 31st December 1950" (March 1951), pt. I, ADM 1/22428, TNA.

34 "Information Exchange Projects," Appendix 7 to Lay to Naval Secretary, "HMCS Niagara Report of Proceedings for April 1952," May 2, 1952, File 5, Box 338, 81/520/8000, DHH; NMCJS(W) to Naval Secretary, "Cancellation of IEP ABC-9," October 15, 1957, File 1961-34-1, vol. 34094, RG24-D-1-c, LAC.

35 "Ordnance," Appendix 6 to Medland to Naval Secretary, "HMCS Niagara Report of Proceedings for March 1953," April 9, 1953, 1–2, File 6, Box 338, 81/520/8000, DHH.

36 Medland to Naval Secretary, "HMCS Niagara Report of Proceedings for December 1952," January 1953, File 5, and Medland to Naval Secretary, "HMCS Niagara Report of Proceedings for April 1953," May 11, 1953, File 6: both in Box 338, 81/520/8000, DHH.

37 CJS(W) to Chiefs of Staff, "JS 113, Interchange of Officers between United States and Canadian Armed Forces," October 15, 1945, File 4425-27, pt. 1, vol. 34238, RG24-D-1-c, LAC.

38 Captain Horatio N. Lay, RCN, DNPI, "Interchange of Officers with USN," April 26, 1946, 2, File 4425–27, pt. 1, vol. 34238, RG24-D-1-c, LAC.

39 Director, Naval Air Division [DNAD], "Minute," May 27, 1946, File 4425–27, pt. 1, vol. 34238, RG24-D-1-c, LAC.

40 DGS(A) to Chief of the General Staff, "Interchange of Officers with U.S. Army," February 18, 1946, 1, and "Memo, Interchange of Officers with U.S. Forces," July 16, 1948, 1: both in File 4425–27, pt. 1, vol. 34238, RG24-D-1-c, LAC

41 CNO to NMCJS(W), "Serial 58P31, Exchange of Officers with U.S. Navy," May 24, 1948, File 4425–27, pt. 1, vol. 34238, RG24-D-1-c, LAC; "Memo, Interchange of Officers," July 16, 1948, 3.

42 Chief of Naval Staff, "Confidential Naval General Order 30.74/9, Integrated United States Naval Officers in the Royal Canadian Navy," April 22, 1949, 1–2, File 4425-27, pt. 2, vol. 34238, RG24-D-1-c, LAC.

43 CANAVUS to CANAVHED, "261245Z," May 26, 1953, File 4425-27, pt. 3, vol. 34238, RG24-D-1-c, LAC.

44 CNO to NMCJS(W), "Serial 58P31"; "Memo, Interchange of Officers," July 16, 1948, 3; Naval Secretary to Commander Fred Janney, USN, Naval Attaché, Ottawa, "Lieutenant Max. C. Gunn, USN," August 26, 1948, File 4425–27, pt. 1, vol. 34238, RG24-D-1-c, LAC.

45 Rear Admiral Robert Waught Murdoch, RCN (ret), My Navy Recollections, interview by Chris Main, September 21, 1978, reel 3, SC104_MRW_197, UVL.

46 Rear Admiral Edmund R. Mainguy, RCN, Flag Officer Pacific Coast [FOPC], to Naval Secretary, "U.S. Tactical Doctrines," July 9, 1948, 1, File ACS 1300–33, vol. 11147, RG24-D-10, LAC.

47 Commodore John C. I. Edwards, RCN, CO HMCS Naden, to FOPC, June 22, 1948, Enclosure A to Mainguy to Naval Secretary, 2.

48 Captain James C. Hibbard, RCN, CO HMCS Ontario, to FOPC, May 13, 1948, Enclosure B to Mainguy to Naval Secretary, 2.

49 Naval Secretary to NMCJS(W), "U.S.N. Officers' Appointments," August 15, 1949, and Naval Secretary to U.S. Naval Attaché, Ottawa, January 17, 1952: both in File 4425–27, pt. 2, vol. 34238, RG24-D-1-c, LAC.

50 Medland to Naval Secretary, "Loan of Officers from the United States Navy," February 9, 1953, File 4425–27, pt. 3, vol. 34238, RG24-D-1-c, LAC.

51 Lay to Naval Secretary, "HMCS Niagara Report of Proceedings for March 1951," April 10, 1951, 1, File 4, Box 338, 81/520/8000, DHH.

52 "Torpedo Anti-Submarine," Appendix 9 to Lay to Naval Secretary, "HMCS Niagara Report of Proceedings for July 1951," August 6, 1951, 2, File 4, Box 338, 81/520/8000, DHH.

53 "Torpedo Anti-Submarine," Appendix 10 to Lay to Naval Secretary, "HMCS Niagara Report of Proceedings for December 1951," January 8, 1952, File 4, Box 338, 81/520/8000, DHH.

54 "Air," Appendix 4 to Lay to Naval Secretary, "HMCS Niagara Report of Proceedings for August 1951," September 10, 1951, 2, File 4, Box 338, 81/520/8000, DHH.

55 Lay to Naval Secretary, "HMCS Niagara Report of Proceedings for November 1951," December 13, 1951, 1, File 4, Box 338, 81/520/8000, DHH.

56 "Engineering," Appendix 7 to Lay to Naval Secretary, "July 1951."

57 "Air," Appendix 4 to Lay to Naval Secretary, "December 1951."

58 "North of the Border with the RCN," Naval Aviation News, June 1954, 11, Aviation History Branch, NHHC.

59 "Air," Appendix 4 to Lay to Naval Secretary, "April 1952"; "Air," Appendix 4 to Lay to Naval Secretary, "HMCS Niagara Report of Proceedings for July 1952," August 5, 1952, File 5, Box 338, 81/520/8000, DHH.

60 Medland to Naval Secretary, "Loan of USN Officer Specialized in Naval Aviation," February 6, 1953, File 4425–27, pt. 3, and NMCJS(W) to Naval Secretary, "Exchange of Officers between the U.S. Navy and the Royal Canadian Navy," December 17, 1948, File 4425–27, pt. 1: both in vol. 34238, RG24-D-1-c, LAC.

61 "Air," Appendix 4 and "Communications," Appendix 7 to Medland to Naval Secretary, "HMCS Niagara Report of Proceedings for September 1952," October 7, 1952, File 5, Box 338, 81/520/8000, DHH.

62 "Air," Appendix 4 to Medland to Naval Secretary, "HMCS Niagara Report of

Proceedings for October 1952," November 1952, File 5, Box 338, 81/520/8000, DHH.

63 Rear Admiral Ruthven E. Libby, USN, PJBD, to Commodore Valentine S. Godfrey, RCN, NMCJS(W), "Serial 09–49," January 12, 1949, File 4425–27, pt. 2, vol. 34238, RG24-D-1-c, LAC; Mark B. Watson, *Sea Logistics: Keeping the Navy Ready Aye Ready* (St. Catharines, Ontario: Vanwell, 2004), 82–88; Captain Mark B. Watson, RCN, "A View from the Great White North," *Navy Supply Corps Newsletter*, March 2010, 24–25.

64 "Supply Liaison and Logistics," Appendix 14 to Medland to Naval Secretary, "HMCS Niagara Report of Proceedings for July 1953," August 11, 1953, File 6, Box 338, 81/520/8000, DHH.

65 U.S. Department of State, *Foreign Service List, January 1, 1948* (Washington, D.C.: Government Printing Office, 1948), 2; U.S. Department of State, *Foreign Service List, January 1, 1950* (Washington, D.C.: Government Printing Office, 1950), 2.

66 "Appendix C," enclosure to SANACC, "Information Memorandum 113," January 21, 1948, 14, Folder CCS 334 SANACC (12-19-44)(1) Sec. 3, Box 74, Entry UD 3, RG 218, NACP.

67 Captain Stanley Herbert King Spurgeon, RAN, Naval Attaché, Washington, to Jurika, May 29, 1947, Folder 1949, Box 4, Jurika Papers, HIA; Reminiscences of Captain Stephen Jurika, Jr., interview by Captain Paul B. Ryan, USN (Ret.), 1979, 2:728, USNI.

68 Reminiscences of Jurika, 2:728.

69 Reminiscences of Jurika, 2:750.

70 Jurika to Captain Murray Jones Tichenor, USN, October 29, 1947, Folder 1947, Box 4, Jurika Papers, HIA.

71 Jurika to Captain Paul D. Stroop, USN, June 16, 1948, and Jurika to Stroop, July 10, 1948: both in Folder June-1948-December, Box 3; Jurika to Rear Admiral Stuart H. Ingersoll, USN, Deputy CINCPACFLT, February 16, 1949, Folder 1949, Box 4: all in Jurika Papers, HIA.

72 Jurika to Captain Benjamin F. Tompkins, USN, and Isabel Tompkins, July 11, 1947, Folder 1947, Box 4, Jurika Papers, HIA.

73 Geoffrey Blainey, *A Shorter History of Australia* (Sydney: Vintage Books, 2009), 222–227.

74 D. B. Waterson, "Chifley, Joseph Benedict," *Australian Dictionary of Biography*, vol. 13, 1993, http://adb.anu.edu.au/biography/chifley-joseph-benedict-ben-9738.

75 Jurika to Tichenor, October 29, 1947, 2.

76 Jurika to Rear Admiral Ernest W. Litch, USN, September 19, 1948, 2, Folder June-1948-December, Box 3, Jurika Papers, HIA.

77 Jurika to Office of Naval Intelligence, "3-S-49, Australia—New Security Setup in Australia," March 3, 1949, Folder Melbourne (S) 1–13,53 1949; Box 23; En-

try A1 1001D, Secret Naval Intelligence Reports, 1949 [Entry A1 1001D]; RG 38, NACP.

78 Medland to Naval Secretary, "HMCS Niagara Report of Proceedings for October 1953," November 4, 1953, 3, File 6, Box 338, 81/520/8000, DHH.

79 David Horner, *Defense Supremo: Sir Frederick Shedden and the Making of Australian Defense Policy* (Sydney: Allen & Unwin, 2000), 278; Christopher Andrew, "The Growth of the Australian Intelligence Community and the Anglo-American Connection," *Intelligence and National Security* 4, no. 2 (1989): 228–229.

80 Allen Weinstein and Alexander Vassiliev, *The Haunted Wood: Soviet Espionage in America—The Stalin Era* (New York: Random House, 1999), 291.

81 Richard Rhodes, *Dark Sun: The Making of the Hydrogen Bomb* (New York: Simon & Schuster, 1995), 183–186.

82 Horner, *Defense Supremo*, 266–267.

83 Horner, 265–266.

84 Julian Zelizer, *Arsenal of Democracy: The Politics of National Security—From World War II to the War on Terrorism* (New York: Basic Books, 2012), 67.

85 Horner, *Defense Supremo*, 271; "Note on Exchange of Classified Military Information between the United States and Australia," ca. 1952, 2317/2, A5954, NAA; "Disclosure of U.S. Classified Military Information to Australia," Enclosure to Serial 260, SANACC 206/60, July 27, 1948, in Martin P. Claussen, ed., *State-War-Navy Coordinating Committee Policy Files, 1944–1947* (Wilmington, DE: Scholarly Resources, 1977), reel 18.

86 BJSM(W), "MM(S) 47 12th Meeting, Minutes," June 27, 1947, 4, CAB 138/8, TNA; "Policy for the Control of the Disclosure of Classified Military Information to Foreign Governments," Enclosure A to Elmer T. Cummins, Chairman Subcommittee for Military Information Control, March 10, 1948 in Claussen, *State-War-Navy*, reel 18.

87 Spurgeon to Commander George C. Oldham, RAN, DNI, May 19, 1948; Spurgeon to Captain Patrick W. W. Wootten, RN, Naval Attaché, Washington, May 13, 1948; Spurgeon to Collins, April 12, 1948: all in 4/159, AWM124, Australian War Memorial [AWM].

88 Minutes of SANAC-Military Information Control Subcommittee meetings on SANACC 206/57, in Claussen, *State-War-Navy*, reel 18.

89 Horner, *Defense Supremo*, 279; David Lowe, *Menzies and the Great World Struggle: Australia's Cold War, 1948–1954* (Sydney: University of New South Wales Press, 1999), 40.

90 David Horner, *The Spy Catchers: The Official History of ASIO, 1949–1963* (Melbourne: Allen & Unwin, 2014).

91 Jurika to Office of Naval Intelligence, "2-S-49, Australia—Australian Policy Re Dutch," February 7, 1949, 1, Folder Melbourne (S) 1–13,53 1949, Box 23, Entry A1 1001D, RG 38, NACP.

92 Jurika to Office of Naval Intelligence, "3-S-49," March 3, 1949, 1.

93 Horner, *Defense Supremo*, 278–282.

94 "Note on Defense Cooperation," December 1950, 2317/22, A5954, NAA.

95 Jurika's role in better known in Australian works than in the United States. See Horner, *Defense Supremo*, 279; Frank Cain, "Venona in Australia and Its Long-Term Ramifications," *Journal of Contemporary History* 35, no. 2 (April 2002): 235–236; Stuart Macintyre, *Australia's Boldest Experiment: War and Reconstruction in the 1940s* (Sydney: Newsouth Publishing, 2015), 451–452.

96 Thanks to Michael Whitby for making this point.

97 Captain Owen C. S. Robertson, RCN, Senior Canadian Naval Liaison Officer, London, to Naval Secretary, "Meeting between First Sea Lord and Chief of Naval Staff, RCN," May 13, 1949, 1–2, File NUKC 1270–1, pt. 3, vol. 11279, RG24-D-13, LAC.

98 Lieutenant Vincent J. Murphy, RCN, to Commodore, Halifax, Nova Scotia, "Naval Air Anti-Submarine Warfare," July 27, 1949, File ACS 8100–1 Sub. 1, vol. 11182, RG24-D-1-10, LAC.

99 Lieutenant Commander W. E. Widdows, RCN, "Staff Officer (Air) Report of Proceedings," enclosure to Lay to Naval Secretary, "HMCS Niagara Report of Proceedings for August 1949," September 7, 1949, and Commander Ernest H. Russell, RCN, Chief of Staff to Naval Member to NMCJS(W), "0–64350," October 5, 1949, 2: both in File 2, Box 338, 81/520/8000, DHH.

100 U.S. Department of State, *Foreign Service List, October 1, 1948* (Washington, D.C.: Government Printing Office, 1949), 8; U.S. Department of State, *Foreign Service List, January 1, 1951* (Washington, D.C.: Government Printing Office, 1951), 7.

101 Reminiscences of Admiral Ben Scott Custer, USN, interview by John T. Mason Jr., July 1965, 967–968, E746.C87 A3 1968, USNA. The following section relies heavily on Custer's oral history, done fifteen years after the events described.

102 Reminiscences of Custer, 984.

103 Reminiscences of Custer, 973–974; Stuart Soward, "Canadian Naval Aviation, 1915–69," in *The RCN in Retrospect, 1910–1968*, ed. James A. Boutilier (Vancouver: University of British Columbia Press, 1982), 277.

104 "A Review of the Liaison Work of the Naval Staff—Washington, 31st March 1950—31st March 1951," Appendix 1 to Lay to Naval Secretary, "HMCS Niagara Report of Proceedings for March 1951."

105 "Procurement," Appendix 7 to Lay to Naval Secretary, "HMCS Niagara Report of Proceedings for March 1950," April 7, 1950, File 3, Box 338, 81/520/8000, DHH; Wilfred G. D. Lund, "Vice-Admiral Harold Grant: Father of the Post-War Royal Canadian Navy," in *Warrior Chiefs: Perspectives on Senior Canadian Military Leaders*, ed. Bernd Horn and Stephen Harris (Toronto: Dundurn Press, 2001), 208; Jerry Proc, "Canadian Avenger AS3 A/S Aircraft," September 25, 2012, https://web.archive.org/web/20150316142633/http://jproc.ca/rrp/rrp3/avenger.html; Leo Pettipas, *The Grumman Avenger in the Royal Canadian Navy* (Winnipeg: Canadian Naval Air Group, 1988), 2.

106 Reminiscences of Custer, 978–979.

107 Lay to Naval Secretary, "HMCS Niagara Report of Proceedings for January 1952," February 16, 1952, 1, File 5, Box 338, 81/520/8000, DHH.

108 Commodore Charles L. Keighley-Peach, RN, "Transcript of an Address Given by the Assistant Chief of Naval Staff (Air) to the Ninth Meeting of Senior Officers," March 17, 1952, iii, File ACS 1279–9, vol. 11141, RG24-D-10, LAC.

109 "Stephen Jurika Jr., 82, Officer and a Scholar," *New York Times*, July 24, 1993; "Vice Admiral John Augustine Collins," Australian War Memorial, accessed September 2, 2018, https://web.archive.org/save/https://www.awm.gov.au/peo ple/P10676561/; Jurika to Ramsey, September 27, 1948, Folder June-1948-December, Box 3, Jurika Papers, HIA.

110 Collins to Jurika, June 11, 1948, Folder June-1948-December, Box 3, Jurika Papers, HIA.

111 "Procedure for Obtaining Clearances for Visits," Enclosure A to CNO, "Serial 0020P33, Instructions Concerning Visits by U.S. Naval Vessels to Foreign Countries," April 2, 1947, 2–3, Folder A4–3 (2–12/47), 1947 Secret, Box 160, Entry P 111, RG 313, NACP.

112 "Professional Notes: Collaboration with Other Navies," *U.S. Naval Institute Proceedings* 74, no. 1 (April 1948): 511.

113 Captain Wilfred Harrington, RAN, to Secretary, Australian Commonwealth Naval Board [ACNB], "Report on Visit to Pearl Harbour," February 17, 1948, 3, 1968/2/722, MP1049/5, NAA.

114 Harrington to Secretary, 4–5.

115 Commander N. A. MacKinnon, RAN, "Some Miscellaneous Observations," in "Report on Communication Aspects," Appendix D to Harrington to Secretary, February 17, 1948.

116 Hector Donohue, *From Empire Defence to the Long Haul: Post-War Defence Policy and Its Impact on Naval Force Structure Planning, 1945–1955* (Canberra, Australia: Sea Power Centre, 1996), 52–62; David Stevens, ed., *The Royal Australian Navy* (New York: Oxford University Press, 2001), 160–161.

117 "Note on Defense Cooperation," 1.

118 Harold M. Martin, *The Naval Career of Harold M. Martin*, Tennessee Regional Oral History Collection, pt. 1, no. 6 (Glen Rock, NJ: Microfilming Corporation of America, 1977), 115.

119 Jurika to Litch, USN, September 19, 1948.

120 Naval History and Heritage Command, "Valley Forge (CV-45), 1946–1970," *Dictionary of American Naval Fighting Ships*, March 29, 2004, http://www .history.navy.mil/research/histories/ship-histories/danfs/v/valley-forge-cv-45 .html.

121 Reminiscences of Admiral Arthur D. Struble, USN, interview by John T. Mason Jr., 2011, 109–110, USNI.

CHAPTER 5. STANDARDIZATION

1 Ian Ballantyne, *Warships of the Royal Navy: Warspite* (Annapolis, MD: Naval Institute Press, 2001), 138–140.

2 Captain J. H. Breaks, RN, British Advisory Repair Mission, "Report, Engineering, 1941 to 1945," July 1946, 218, ADM 199/1236, TNA.

3 "DCOS/117/45" November 24, 1945, 45, CAB 21/2066, TNA.

4 Controller, "Standardization of Equipment as between the United Kingdom, Canada, and the United States," January 8, 1946, Enclosure I, CAB 21/2066, TNA.

5 Chiefs of Staff, "DO (46) 73," May 30, 1946, CAB 21/2066, TNA.

6 Minute, Foreign Secretary Ernest Bevin for Prime Minister Clement Attlee, February 13, 1946, in U.K. Foreign and Commonwealth Office, *Documents on British Policy Overseas*, series 1, vol. 4, 114.

7 Deputy Chiefs of Staff Committee, "DCOS (46) 33" March 2, 1946, Annex I & II, CAB 21/2066, TNA.

8 Chiefs of Staff, "DO (46) 73."

9 Julian Lewis, *Changing Direction: British Military Planning for Post-War Strategic Defense, 1942–1947* (London: Sherwood Press, 1987), 265.

10 General Leslie Hollis, Secretary, "Standardization, Integration and Control of Armaments," September 1946, CAB 21/2066, TNA.

11 Hollis, "Standardization, Integration."

12 James Eayrs, *In Defence of Canada: Peacemaking and Deterrence* (Toronto: University of Toronto Press, 1972), 322.

13 PJBD, "Thirty-Fifth Recommendation," May 6, 1946, Folder CNO TS 1946 A14-5/EF13(39), Box 43, Entry UD 17, RG 80, NACP.

14 Dean Acheson for President Truman, October 1, 1946, in U.S. Department of State, *FRUS, 1946* (Washington, D.C.: Government Printing Office, 1969), 5:55–56.

15 Ambassador Ray Atherton for Secretary of State James Byrnes, August 28, 1946, in *FRUS, 1946*, 5:53–55.

16 C. P. Stacey, *Canada and the Age of Conflict*, vol. 2, *1921–1948, The Mackenzie King Era* (Toronto: University of Toronto Press, 1981), 406–411.

17. Atherton for Byrnes, August 28, 1946.

18 Truman for Mackenzie King, enclosure to memo, Acheson for Truman, October 26, 1946, in *FRUS, 1946*, 5:57–61; Eayrs, *In Defence of Canada*, 347–348.

19 Nigel Hamilton, *Monty: Final Years of the Field-Marshal, 1944–1976* (New York: McGraw-Hill, 1986), 641–655.

20 Bill Jackson and Dwin Bramall, *The Chiefs: The Story of the United Kingdom Chiefs of Staff* (London: Brassey's, 1992), 274.

21 Minister of National Defense Douglas Abbott, "Notes Re Conversation at Laurier House," September 9, 1946, C166968-69, and Lieutenant General Charles Foulkes, "Notes on Conference, Prime Minister—Field Marshal Montgom-

ery," September 9, 1946, C166971: both in Microfilm H-1478, vol. 249, MG26-J4, William Lyon Mackenzie King Papers, LAC.

22   Hamilton, *Monty*, 654–659.

23   Addison, Commonwealth Relations Office to Attlee, July 14, 1947, CAB 21/2067, TNA.

24   Jackson and Bramall, *The Chiefs*, 272–275.

25   Memo, J. Graham Parsons, October 31, 1946, in *FRUS, 1946*, 5:61–63.

26   "DCOS (46) 32nd Meeting, Deputy Chiefs of Staff Committee," October 22, 1946, 32, and Deputy Chiefs of Staff Committee, "DCOS (46) 214, Report," October 26, 1946: both in CAB 21/2066, TNA.

27   Commander Anthony H. G. Storrs, RCN, Deputy Director of Naval Plans, to Captain Horatio N. Lay, RCN, DNPI, "Tripartite Discussions on Standardization and Strategic Problems—Washington, November 1946," December 7, 1946, File 1272–35, vol. 8087, RG24-D-1-c, LAC.

28   "Record of Eighth Meeting, 1000 hours, November 19, 1946," enclosure to Storrs to Lay, 1–2.

29   "Record of Twelfth Meeting, 1000 hours, November 21, 1946," enclosure to Storrs to Lay, 1.

30   "Record of Fourteenth Meeting, 1500 hours, November 22, 1946," enclosure to Storrs to Lay, 1.

31   Joint Planning Staff, "JP (46) 224, Standardization of Equipment between United Kingdom, United States, and Canada," December 13, 1946, CAB 21/2067, TNA.

32   The following paragraphs rely on the RCN's copy of the report cited in the following footnote.

33   "Appendix A, British-Canadian-United States Standardization, Pertinent Facts and Considerations Bearing on the Problem," November 22, 1946, enclosure to Storrs to Lay, 4.

34   "Appendix B," enclosure to Storrs to Lay, 5.

35   "Appendix B," enclosure to Captain Philip H. E. Welby-Everard, RN, DStand, "Admiralty Standardization Memo No. 16, Naval Tripartite Standardization Program," July 9, 1951, 7–8, ADM 1/22477, TNA.

36   Rear Admiral Edmund Nicholas Poland, RN (ret), interview by Nigel de Lee, April 8, 1991, reel 18, Sound Archive, Catalogue 11951, IWM.

37   "Appendix B," enclosure to Storrs to Lay, 7–10.

38   "Record of First Meeting, 1400 hours, Nov. 12, 1946," enclosure to Storrs to Lay, 2.

39   Joint Logistics Committee, "JLC 419/5 (2nd revision), Coordination of Matters Pertaining to Standardization with Other Countries," enclosure to CNO, "Coordination of Matters Pertaining to Standardization with Other Countries," December 3, 1947, 25, Folder A16-1-A16-1(EF), Box 2876, Entry UD 16, RG 80, NACP.

40 DoP (Q) to Director of Tactical and Staff Duties Division [DTSD], "Standardization RN/USN," June 3, 1948, Appendix C to DTSD to Assistant Chief of Naval Staff, "Standardization RN/USN, T.S.D. 4581/48," July 14, 1948, 1, ADM 1/22428, TNA.

41 Chiefs of Staff Committee, "COS (46) 184th Meeting, Confidential Annex," December 18, 1946, 2, CAB 21/2067, TNA.

42 "Minute," January 10, 1947, DO 35/2336, TNA.

43 Addison to Attlee, July 14, 1947; Elisabeth Barker, *The British between the Superpowers, 1945–50* (Toronto: University of Toronto Press, 1983), 72.

44 "Minute," January 22, 1947, DO 35/2336; Hollis to Field Marshal Henry M. Wilson, "TOO 031715Z," February 3, 1947, CAB 21/2067: both in TNA.

45 Chiefs of Staff Committee, "COS (47) 113, Standardization," May 29, 1947, DEFE 5/4, TNA.

46 Wilson to Hollis, "TOO 062345Z," February 6, 1947, 062345, CAB 21/2067, TNA.

47 Wilson to Hollis, "TOO 062345Z"; BJSM(W), "MM(S) 47 14th Meeting, Minutes," July 29, 1947, CAB 138/8, TNA.

48 Russell Mason, "The Evolution of Airborne Antisubmarine Warfare," March 9, 1970, 24, Author's personal collection, provided by Dr. Owen R. Cote.

49 Mason, "The Evolution of Airborne Antisubmarine Warfare," 10.

50 Russell Mason, "Sonobuoys—Part I: Historical Development thru WWII," *IEEE Aerospace & Electronic Systems Society Newsletter*, September 1984, 19.

51 Mason, "Airborne Antisubmarine Warfare," 23–25; Roger Holler, Arthur Horbach, and James McEachern, *The Ears of Air ASW: A History of U.S. Navy Sonobuoys* (Warminster, PA: Navmar Applied Sciences Corporation, 2008), 35.

52 Roger Holler, "The Evolution of the Sonobuoy from World War II to the Cold War," *U.S. Navy Journal of Underwater Acoustics*, January 2014, 330.

53 Mason, "Airborne Antisubmarine Warfare," 29.

54 Mason, 30.

55 Holler, Horbach, and McEachern, *Ears of Air ASW*, 43–44.

56 Russell Mason, "Sonobuoys—Part II: After WW II," *IEEE Aerospace & Electronic Systems Society Newsletter*, October 1984, 1.

57 "Report of Underwater Sonar," Enclosure E to CNO, "Serial 0062P31, Report of Visit of Undersea Warfare Weapons Group to British Isles during August–September 1947," October 31, 1947, 65, Folder A16–3(1) (6–12/47) (3 of 4), 1947 Secret, Box 168, Entry P 111, RG 313, NACP.

58 Enclosure E to CNO, 78.

59 Enclosure E to CNO, 65.

60 Commander James M. Robb, RN, and Wing Commander Anthony Gadd, RAF, "Sonobuoy Development Program, Sub-SAWC I/5/49," April 9, 1949, File 1270–78, pt. 2, vol. 8071, RG24-D-1-c, LAC.

61 "Joint Sea/Air Warfare Committee, Minutes of the Seventh Meeting of the Tac-

tical and Training Subcommittee," Enclosure B to ALUSNA London, "300-S-48, Great Britain—Navy ASW Doctrine," November 1, 1948, 1, Folder A16-3(1) ASW-Jacket #3 (10-12/48) (2 of 3), 1948 Secret, Box 191, Entry P 111, RG 313, NACP.

62 Air Commodore Geoffrey W. Tuttle, RAF, Director of Operational Requirements, "Report on Sonobuoys—British/American Standardization, Sub SAWC II/54/48," August 4, 1948, File 1270–78, pt. 1, vol. 8071, RG24-D-1-c, LAC.

63 Tuttle, "Report."

64 Robb and Gadd, "Sonobuoy Development," Appendix B.

65 Directors, Joint A/S School, Londonderry [JASS], "53/2, Progress Report—Summer Term, 1951," August 31, 1951, 11, AIR 20/6833, TNA.

66 "Air," Appendix 4 to Lay to Naval Secretary, "HMCS Niagara Report of Proceedings for August 1952," September 5, 1952, 1, File 5, Box 338, 81/520/8000, DHH.

67 Commander Hunter Killer Force, U.S. Atlantic Fleet to CINCLANTFLT, "Report of Hunter Killer Operations Conducted by Task Force 81 during the Period 9 June 1952 to 7 November 1952," November 6, 1952, 4, Folder A16–4-A16–6, Confidential, 1952, Box 35, Entry P 80, Confidential & Restricted General Administrative Files, 1946–1956–Commander, 2nd Fleet [Entry P 80]; RG 313; NACP.

68 CINCLANTFLT to CNO, "Report of Hunter Killer Operations Conducted by Task Force 81 during the Period 9 June 1952 to 7 November 1952," December 23, 1952, 8, Folder A16-4–A16-6, Confidential, 1952, Box 35, Entry P 80, RG 313, NACP; Mason, "Airborne Antisubmarine Warfare," 39–40; Holler, "Evolution of the Sonobuoy," 331.

69 Mason, "Airborne Antisubmarine Warfare," 38–39.

70 Poland, interview, reel 17.

71 Joint Secretaries, "Minutes of the Eighteenth Meeting of the Technical Investigation Subcommittee," October 17, 1950, 1, File 1270–78, pt. 3, vol. 8071, RG24-D-1-c, LAC.

72 Tuttle, "Report on Sonobuoys," August 4, 1948.

73 Robb and Gadd, "Sonobuoy Development," 1; Joint Secretaries, "Minutes of the Eighteenth Meeting," 3.

74 "Air," Appendix 4 to Lay to Naval Secretary, "HMCS Niagara Report of Proceedings for December 1950," January 9, 1951, 1, File 3, Box 338, 81/520/8000, DHH.

75 Group Captain Clare L. Annis, RCAF, "RCAF Anti-Submarine Policy," January 20, 1950, 1–3, File 28-1-1, pt. 1, vol. 5269, RG24-E-1-b, LAC.

76 "Air," Appendix 4 to Lay to Naval Secretary, "December 1950."

77 Appendix 4 to Lay to Naval Secretary, 2.

78 Commander Malcolm C. Morris, RN, and Wing Commander R. E. Jay, RAF, "Minutes of the Twenty-First Meeting of the Policy and Plans Subcommittee,

Sub SAWC 1/21/51," December 14, 1951, File 1270–78, pt. 4, vol. 8071, RG24-D-1-c, LAC.

79 Squadron Leader Reginald R. Ingrams, RCAF, "Notes Taken during an Informal Discussion of Maritime Warfare Tactics and Equipment with Dr. J. W. Abrams—21 May 1951," May 23, 1951, 2, File 28–1-1, pt. 3, vol. 5270, RG24-E-1-b, LAC.

80 Morris and Jay, "Minutes of the Twenty First Meeting"; Lay to Naval Secretary, "HMCS Niagara Report of Proceedings for October 1951," November 7, 1951, 1, File 4, Box 338, 81/520/8000, DHH.

81 Secretary, Naval Board (Canada), "Minutes of 271st Meeting of the Naval Board." December 15, 1948, 3, Folder 3 or 4, File 1, Box 56, 81/520/1000–100/2, DHH.

82 Lieutenant (P) Frederic G. Townsend, RCN, "Suggested Equipment Standard for RCN Avenger Aircraft," Enclosure C to Commodore Kenneth F. Adams, RCN, CO, HMCS Magnificent, to Naval Secretary, "A/S Training in the USN," November 23, 1950, 2, File ACC 1225–1, vol. 11189, RG24-D-10, LAC.

83 Ingrams, "Notes Taken," 1; "Air," Appendix 4 to Lay to Naval Secretary, "HMCS Niagara Report of Proceedings for December 1951," January 8, 1952, File 4, Box 338, 81/520/8000, DHH.

84 Holler, Horbach, and McEachern, *Ears of Air ASW*, 55.

85 Lieutenant P. C. H. Cooke, RCN, Secretary, "Minutes of the First Meeting of the Subcommittee, Tactics and Training, of the Sea/Air Warfare Committee," April 6, 1950, 2, File ACS 8100–1 F.D.1, vol. 11182, RG24-D-10, LAC.

86 Holler, Horbach, and McEachern, *Ears of Air ASW*, 55.

87 Rear Admiral Ruthven E. Libby, USN, Director, General Planning Group, to DStand, Admiralty, and DStand, Canadian Naval Staff, "Serial 237P001, Naval Tripartite Standardization Program, Minutes of a Conference Held in Washington, D.C. during the Period 17–21 August 1950," August 22, 1950, 5, File 1961–23, pt. 1, vol. 34091, RG24-D-1-c, LAC.

88 Rear Admiral Donald R. Osborn Jr., USN, to Joint Logistics Plans Committee, "Standardization of Equipment, Operational Procedures and Organization with the Military Department of the Canadian and British Governments within the Navy Department," December 31, 1948, 2, Folder Secret (00500–00572) 1948, Box 795, Entry P 1208, Formerly Classified OP34 Chronological Files (Serial Pinks), 1948–1950 [Entry P 1208], RG 38, NACP.

89 Rear Admiral Thomas B. Inglis, USN, Chief of Naval Intelligence, to Commodore Valentine S. Godfrey, RCN, NMCJS(W), December 31, 1948, File 8100–5, vol. 35135, RG24-D-1-c, LAC.

90 Naval Secretary, "Anti-Submarine Tactical Papers" February 3, 1949, File 1270–78, pt. 2, vol. 8071, RG24-D-1-c, LAC.

91 Captain Paul R. Heineman, USN, Chairman, Combined CANUKUS Anti-Submarine Working Group, "Final Draft of Papers of the Combined Work-

ing Group—Forwarding of," April 21, 1949, File 8100–5, vol. 35135, RG24-D-1-c, LAC.

92 "Recommended 'Common Doctrine for the Conduct of ASW on the High Seas,'" Enclosure A to CNO, "Serial 00130P31, Common Doctrine for the Conduct of Anti-Submarine Warfare on the High Seas," April 22, 1949, Folder A16-3(1) ASW (1-12/49) (3 of 3), 1949 Secret, Box 216; "Command Structure and Relations Involved in the Conduct of Anti-Submarine Warfare," October 9, 1947, Enclosure A to CNO, "Serial 0079P30, Organization for World-Wide Anti-Submarine Warfare," October 13, 1947, Folder A16-3(1) (6-12/47) (3 of 4), 1947 Secret, Box 168: both in Entry P 111, RG 313, NACP.

93 "Common Doctrine for the Conduct of Anti-Submarine Warfare on the High Seas," Enclosure B to Heineman to Combined CANUKUS ASW Committee, "Final Draft of Papers of the Combined Working Group—Forwarding of," April 6, 1949, 1–2, File 8100-5, vol. 35135, RG24-D-1-c, LAC.

94 "Common Doctrine," Enclosure A to CNO, "Serial 00130P31."

95 Rear Admiral Brian B. Schofield, RN, Chief of Staff, BJSM, to Secretary of the Admiralty, "BNS 1865/48," June 13, 1949, File 8100–5, vol. 35135, RG24-D-1-c, LAC.

96 Admiral Royal E. Ingersoll, USN, CINCLANTFLT, "Carrier Anti-Submarine Operations—Letter of Instructions," August 24, 1944, 1, File 7–6-2, vol. 11022, RG24-D-10, LAC.

97 Marc Milner, *North Atlantic Run: The Royal Canadian Navy and the Battle for the Convoys* (Annapolis, MD: Naval Institute Press, 1985), 9, 59–61, 102, 181–182. Thanks to Michael Whitby for this insight.

98 "ASW Operational and Tactical Report," Enclosure A to CNO, "Serial 0062P31," October 31, 1947, 7.

99 Commander James R. Pratt, RCN, "Memo" January 27, 1951, File 8100-5, vol. 35135, RG24-D-1-c, LAC.

100 RCN-RCAF Representatives to Chairman, Combined CANUKUS ASW Working Group, May 25, 1949, File 8100–5, vol. 35135, RG24-D-1-c, LAC.

101 "Status of Anti-Submarine Warfare," Enclosure C to CNO, "Fourth Anti-Submarine Conference," August 18, 1949, 43, File 8100–5, vol. 35135, RG24-D-1-c, LAC.

102 Lieutenant Commander Thomas C. Mackay, RCN, Staff Officer (Communications) to Lay, "0–8530," August 31, 1949, File 2, Box 338, 81/520/8000, DHH.

103 Mackay to Lay, "W. 0–44540," October 5, 1949, 1, File 2, Box 338, 81/520/8000, DHH.

104 Malcolm Llewellyn-Jones, *The Royal Navy and Anti-Submarine Warfare, 1917– 1949* (New York: Routledge, 2006), 148, 154.

105 Schofield to Chairman, "BNS 1865/48/1," December 27, 1949; Lay to Chairman, "CANUKUS ASW Working Group Papers," January 12, 1950; Rear Admiral Charles B. Momsen, USN, to CNO, "Serial 0028P31, Combined Canadian,

United States, United Kingdom, Anti-Submarine Committee Papers, Forwarding of," February 12, 1950: all in File 8100-5, vol. 35135, RG24-D-1-c, LAC.

106 "Minutes of the 10th Meeting of the Working Group," Enclosure C to Major
R. F. Walker, Secretary, CJS(W), to Chiefs of Staff Committee, "CANUKUS
Anti-Submarine Warfare Working Group," November 22, 1949, File 28-6-10,
vol. 5274, RG24-E-1-b, LAC.

107 Admiralty, "Draft Reply to BJSM," August 1949, File 8100-5, vol. 35135, RG24-
D-1-c, LAC; Mackay to Lay, "NMW 0-44540," November 8, 1949, and Lieuten-
ant Commander W. E. Widdows, Staff Officer (Air) to Lay, "NMW 0–77865,"
November 3, 1949: both in File 2, Box 338, 81/520/8000, DHH.

108 W. A. B. Douglas, Roger Sarty, and Michael Whitby, A Blue Water Navy, vol.
2, part 2 of The Official Operational History of the Royal Canadian Navy in the
Second World War, 1943–1945 (St. Catharines, ONT: Vanwell, 2007), 93–94.

109 Enclosure C to Walker to Chiefs of Staff Committee.

110 Ingrams, "Report of a Visit to MGP HQ, 28 Jan to 1 Feb Inclusive," February 5,
1951, 4, File 28–1-1, pt. 2, vol. 5269, RG24-E-1-b, LAC.

111 Walker to Chiefs of Staff Committee, 2.

112 Mackay to Lay, "W. 0–44540"; Lay to Naval Secretary, "Combined Signal
Book," September 27, 1949, File ACS 1300–1, vol. 11146, RG24-D-10, LAC.

113 Walker to Chiefs of Staff Committee, 2.

114 Richard Humble, Fraser of North Cape: The Life of Admiral of the Fleet Lord Fraser, 1888–1981 (London: Routledge & Kegan Paul, 1983), 283; Captain Charles
J. Wheeler, USN, Senior U.S. Naval Liaison Officer, BPF, to Nimitz, "Monthly
Report," October 1, 1945, Folder Detached Enclosures #1–46 [4 of 6], Box 1, Entry A1 202, RG 313, NACP.

115 Edward Ashmore, interview by Nigel Tyrie, July 30, 2003, reel 11, Sound Archive, Catalogue 25203, IWM; Eric Grove, ed., The Battle and the Breeze: The
Naval Reminiscences of Admiral of the Fleet Sir Edward Ashmore (Gloucestershire, U.K.: Sutton, 1997), 71–72; Vice Controller to Assistant Chief of Naval
Staff, June 9, 1948, 3, ADM 1/26858, TNA.

116 Director of Gunnery & Anti-Aircraft Warfare, Director of Torpedo, Anti-
Submarine and Mine Warfare [DTASW], and Director of Naval Air Warfare
[DAW], "G.D. 2116/48, Standardization," June 30, 1948, pt. 2, ADM 1/22428,
TNA.

117 Rear Admiral Jerauld Wright, USN, Director of Operational Readiness to Rear
Admiral Patrick W. B. Brooking, RN, BAD, January 26, 1948, Folder Secret 1948
001-00221, Box 795, Entry P 1208, RG 38, NACP.

118 Joint War Production Staff, "Standardization," 3.

119 Lay to Naval Secretary, "Combined Signal Book."

120 Mackay to Lay, "W. 0–44540," 1; Lay to Naval Secretary, "HMCS Niagara Report of Proceedings for September 1949," October 10, 1949, 1, File 2, Box 338,
81/520/8000, DHH.

121 Naval Secretary to Lay, "Combined Signal Book," October 26, 1949, File ACS 1300-1, vol. 11146, RG24-D-10, LAC.

122 Canada, *House of Commons Debates* (August 19, 1946), 5021 (Hon. Douglas Abbott, Minister of National Defense).

123 Rear Admiral John Alexander Charles, RCN (ret), My Navy Recollections, interview by Hal Lawrence, June 10, 1983, SC066_CJA_256; Rear Admiral John Alexander Charles, My Navy Recollections, interview by William Thackray, July 17, 1980, SC104_CJA_206: both in UVL.

124 "Minutes of Meetings Held on 2nd and 3rd October to Discuss the Implications of Changing to American Communication and Tactical Doctrine," October 8, 1946, 1, File 1300-33, vol. 8135, RG24-D-1-c, LAC.

125 Charles, Navy Recollections, June 10, 1983.

126 Wilfred G. D. Lund, "Vice-Admiral Harold Grant: Father of the Post-War Royal Canadian Navy," in *Warrior Chiefs: Perspectives on Senior Canadian Military Leaders*, ed. Bernd Horn and Stephen Harris (Toronto: Dundurn Press, 2001), 197; Wilfred G. D. Lund, "Vice-Admiral Howard Emmerson Reid and Vice Admiral Harold Taylor Wood Grant: Forging the New 'Canadian' Navy," in *The Admirals: Canada's Senior Naval Leadership in the Twentieth Century*, ed. Michael Whitby, Richard H. Gimblett, and Peter Haydon (Toronto: Dundurn Press, 2006), 164.

127 Naval Secretary, "Minutes of Fourth Meeting of Senior Officers," November 26, 1947, 8, File ACS 1279–1, vol. 11141, RG24-D-10, LAC.

128 Rear Admiral John R. Redman, USN, Chief of Naval Communications, to Lay, "Serial 0463P20," October 28, 1949, File ACS 1300-1, vol. 11146, RG24-D-10, LAC.

129 "Staff Study," enclosure to Redman to Lay, 1.

130 "Staff Study," enclosure to Redman to Lay, 2–3.

131 Lay to Naval Secretary, "Combined Naval Signal Books," November 17, 1949, File ACS 1300–1, vol. 11146, RG24-D-10, LAC.

132 Lay to Naval Secretary, "Combined Naval Signal Books," December 30, 1949, File ACS 1300–1, vol. 11146, RG24-D-10, LAC.

133 Lay to Naval Secretary, November 17, 1949; Naval Secretary to Lay, "Combined Naval Signal Books," December 7, 1949, and Commander Michael G. Stirling, RCN, Director of Naval Communications, "Allied Signal and Tactical Publications," April 14, 1950, 1: both in File ACS 1300–1, vol. 11146, RG24-D-10, LAC.

134 "Communications," Appendix 4 to Lay to Naval Secretary, "HMCS Niagara Report of Proceedings for January 1950," February 8, 1950, File 3, Box 338, 81/520/8000, DHH.

135 Lay to Naval Secretary, "Allied Signal and Tactical Publications," March 30, 1950, 1–2, File ACS 1300–1, vol. 11146, RG24-D-10, LAC.

136 Captain Jack R. Allfrey, RN, Secretary to Fraser, "Notes on Meeting between First Sea Lord and Chief of Naval Operations on 24th March 1950 at 1700,"

April 1950, 2, and Admiral Forrest Sherman, USN, CNO, "Memorandum of a Meeting between the Chief of Naval Operations and the First Sea Lord on Friday, 24 March 1950," April 3, 1950, 2: both in Folder F7, A19; Box 72, AR/131, NHHC.

137 "Communications," Appendix 7 to Lay to Naval Secretary, "HMCS Niagara Report of Proceedings for April 1950," May 12, 1950, File 3, Box 338, 81/520/8000, DHH.

138 Lay to Naval Secretary, "Allied Naval Signal Book," May 15, 1950, File ACS 1300–1, vol. 11146, RG24-D-10, LAC.

139 CANAVUS to CANAVHED, "061936Z," June 6, 1950, File ACS 1300–1, vol. 11146, RG24-D-10, LAC.

140 Allfrey to Fraser, "Notes on Meeting," 2; Sherman, "Memorandum of a Meeting," April 3, 1950, 3–4.

141 "Allied Naval Maneuvering Instructions, ATP 1," June 1951, IX, Folder ATP 1 Change 1, Jan. 1952, Conf, Box 3, Entry A1 337A, Operational, Tactical, and Instructional Publications, 1947–1970 [Entry A1 337A], RG 38, NACP.

142 CNO, "Serial 0834P31, Original Draft of Chapters 1 through 8 of 'Allied Naval Maneuvering Instructions,'" September 13, 1950, 31, Folder A4-3–A4-3(1)(d), Confidential, 1950, Box 26, Entry P 80, RG 313, NACP.

143 "A Review of the Liaison Work of the Naval Staff—Washington, 31 March 1950–31 March 1951," Appendix 1 to Lay to Naval Secretary, "HMCS Niagara Report of Proceedings for March 1951," April 10, 1951, File 4, Box 338, 81/520/8000, DHH.

144 "Memorandum for Reviewers of Subject Draft," Enclosure A to CNO, "Serial 0834P31," September 13, 1950, 1.

145 Captain Lamar P. Carver, USN, Air Operations, Second Fleet, to Captain John Sylvester, USN, "Comments on ATP 1," October 2, 1950, Folder A4–3-A4–3(1)(d), Confidential, 1950, Box 26, Entry P 80, RG 313, NACP.

146 Commander Second Fleet to CNO, "Original Draft of Chapters 1 through 8 of 'Allied Naval Maneuvering Instructions,'" October 6, 1950, 1, Folder A4-3–A4-3(1)(d), Confidential, 1950, Box 26, Entry P 80, RG 313, NACP.

147 "Communications and Tactics," Appendix 9 to Lay to Naval Secretary, "HMCS Niagara Report of Proceedings for October 1950," November 10, 1950, File 3, Box 338, 81/520/8000, DHH.

148 Humble, *Fraser of North Cape*, 34.

149 "Communications and Tactics," Appendix 5 to Lay to Naval Secretary, "HMCS Niagara Report of Proceedings for April 1951," May 8, 1951, File 4, Box 338, 81/520/8000, DHH.

150 "Communications," Appendix 6 to Lay to Naval Secretary, "HMCS Niagara Report of Proceedings for January 1952" and "Communications," Appendix 6 to Lay to Naval Secretary, "HMCS Niagara Report of Proceedings for March 1952," April 2, 1952: both in File 5, Box 338, 81/520/8000, DHH.

151 "Communications," Appendix 10 to Lay to Naval Secretary, "March 1951."

152 "Communications and Tactics," Appendix 5 to Lay to Naval Secretary, "HMCS Niagara Report of Proceedings for August 1951," September 10, 1951, File 4, Box 338, 81/520/8000, DHH.

153 Lieutenant Commander Philip S. Booth, RCN, Director, Joint Maritime Warfare School [JMWS], to Director of Weapons & Tactics [DWS], "Air A/S Homing Procedure," October 15, 1951, File 1270–78, pt. 4, vol. 8071, RG24-D-1-c, LAC.

154 "Report of Surface Operations," Enclosure A to CINCNELM to CNO, "Report of Operations and Condition of Command, 1 July 1951 to 14 June 1952," June 14, 1952, 2, Folder CINCNELM Annual Report 1 Jul 51–14 Jun 52, Box 727A, 1946 CMD, NHHC.

155 Reminiscences of Rear Admiral Thomas Howard Morton, USN, interview by John T. Mason Jr., 1975, 273–274, 330–333, NDL.

156 Commander Hunter Killer Force, U.S. Atlantic Fleet, to CINCLANT, "Report of Hunter Killer Operations," 4; "Serial 0105, Longstep Exercise, Report of Participation in NATO Training in the Mediterranean Area," November 21, 1952, II-8, II-9, Folder CARDIV 18, Serial 0105, Nov. 21, 1952, Box 221, 1946 RPT, NHHC.

157 "TAS," Appendix 11 to Medland to Naval Secretary, "HMCS Niagara Report of Proceedings for April 1953," May 11, 1953, File 6, Box 338, 81/520/8000, DHH.

158 "Communications," Appendix 9 to Medland to Naval Secretary, "HMCS Niagara Report of Proceedings for June 1953," July 6, 1953, File 6, Box 338, 81/520/8000, DHH.

159 Canadian JCEC (Washington), "CJT 1–1: A Discussion of the CAN-UK JCECS and US MCEB Organization and Procedure," April 25, 1962, 18, File CSC 2203:5, pt. 1, vol. 21763, RG24-B-1, LAC.

160 "Communications," Appendix 9 to Medland to Naval Secretary, "HMCS Niagara Report of Proceedings for March 1953," April 9, 1953, File 6, Box 338, 81/520/8000, DHH.

161 Rear Admiral Willard K. Goodney, USN, Deputy Chief of Staff, SACLANT, "Minutes of a Conference Convened by SACLANT at 1030 (R), 26 April 1954, at Norfolk, Virginia, to Discuss a Proposed NCSX for 1954," May 11, 1954, 28, File 1640–21 pt. 7, vol. 33770, RG24-D-1-c, LAC.

162 Naval Secretary to Senior Naval Liaison Officer (UK), "Standardization with U.S. Navy Communications," August 25, 1949, File 1300–33, vol. 8135, RG24-D-1-c, LAC.

163 Commodore Charles L. Keighley-Peach, RN, Assistant Chief of Naval Staff (Air), "A Summary of Minutes, Naval Aviation Conference" (December 1952), 8–9, File NUKC 1270–1, pt. 3, vol. 11279, RG24-D-13, LAC.

164 "BAD 1687/47, R.N./U.S.N. Standardization," May 28, 1948, enclosure to Vice Controller to Assistant Chief of Naval Staff, June 9, 1948, 8.

165 Rear Admiral Robert Waught Murdoch, RCN (ret), My Navy Recollections, interview by Chris Main, September 21, 1978, pt. 4, SC104_MRW_197, UVL.

CHAPTER 6. TRAINING AND EDUCATION

1 Commander William Hynd Norrie Martin, RN, "Typescript Memoir" (1986), 69–70, 98/1/1, Private Papers of Commander W. H. N. Martin, RN, Documents.7695, IWM.

2 John Whiteclay Chambers II, ed., *The Oxford Companion to American Military History* (New York: Oxford University Press, 1999), 638–639.

3 Secretary to Admiral of the Fleet John Cunningham, RN, 1SL, "U.S. Joint Operations Staff College: Vacancies for British Officers," September 2, 1946, ADM 205/68, TNA.

4 Reminiscences of Admiral Harry W. Hill, USN, interview by John T. Mason Jr., 1967, 901–990, OH-CU.

5 John B. Hattendorf, Mitchell Simpson, and John R. Wadleigh, *Sailors and Scholars: The Centennial History of the U.S. Naval War College* (Newport, RI: Naval War College Press, 1984), 173–174.

6 John Hattendorf, "Note: A Special Relationship: The Royal Navy and the U.S. Naval War College," *Mariner's Mirror* 72, no. 2 (1986): 200.

7 Admiral Raymond Spruance, USN, President, Naval War College, to Nimitz, June 19, 1946, Folder 31, Box 2, Records of the Immediate Office of the Chief of Naval Operations, Double Zero Files 1942–1947, NHHC.

8 Hattendorf, "A Special Relationship," 200.

9 For a list of officers who attended during this period see Hattendorf, 200; United States Naval War College, "Register of Officers, 1884–1979," July 11, 1975, 86–97, accessed September 3, 2018, https://web.archive.org/web/20150911223408 /https://www.usnwc.edu/getattachment/de2da848-af41–42d1-b715-ad -b3dfdbb834/NWC-Students—Faculty1884to1979.aspx.

10 Commander Ernest H. Russell, RCN, Secretary, CJS(W), to Secretary, Chiefs of Staff Committee, "Attendance of Indian and Pakistani Officers at Staff Colleges," August 31, 1949, File 4902–5, vol. 34412, RG24-D-1-c, LAC.

11 Rear Admiral James C. Hibbard, RCN (ret), My Navy Recollections, interview by Chris Main, August 2, 1979, reel 14, SC104_HJC_208, UVL.

12 Admiral John Fitzroy Duyland Bush, interview by Nigel Tyrie, 2005, reel 3, Sound Archive, Catalogue 28352, IWM; British Admiralty Delegation, "BAD 331/46," June 25, 1947, ADM 1/19822, TNA.

13 Admiral Philip Vian, RN, Deputy Chief of Naval Staff, "Minute," January 13, 1947, 1, ADM 1/19822, TNA.

14 Vian, "Minute."

15 Naval Secretary, "Minute," January 14, 1947, ADM 1/19822; BJSM(W), "MM(S) 47 6th Meeting, Minutes," 2, CAB 138/8: both in TNA.

16 Captain Philip H. E. Welby-Everard, RN, Lieutenant Colonel William P. Care-

less, and Major W. J. C. Hayward, "The United States Industrial College of the Armed Forces, Preliminary Report," November 19, 1946, 7–8, ADM 1/20663, TNA.

17 Welby-Everard, Careless, and Hayward, 6.

18 Welby-Everard, Careless, and Hayward, "The United States Industrial College of the Armed Forces," June 26, 1947, ADM 1/20663, TNA.

19 Commander T. V. Briggs, RN, "Second Report on the U.S. Naval War College," March 1, 1947, enclosure to BAD, "BAD 331/46," May 19, 1947, 6, ADM 1/19822, TNA.

20 Briggs, "Report on the U.S. Naval War College," October 1, 1946, enclosure to BAD, "BAD 331/46," November 13, 1946, 3, ADM 1/19822, TNA.

21 Welby-Everard, Careless, and Hayward, June 26, 1947.

22 Welby-Everard, Careless, and Hayward, November 19, 1946, 7.

23 Briggs, "Third and Final Report on the U.S. Naval War College," June 3, 1947, enclosure to BAD, "BAD 331/46," June 25, 1947, 4.

24 Martin, "Typescript Memoir," 69.

25 Reminiscences of Hill, 945.

26 Reminiscences of Rear Admiral Elliot B. Strauss, USN, interview by Paul Stillwell, 1989, 299, USNI.

27 Medland to Naval Secretary, "Report on Visit of Naval Member to Naval War College, Newport, Rhode Island," May 1, 1953, 3–4, File 1225-193-139, pt. 3, vol. 33487, RG24-D-1-c, LAC.

28 Assistant Chief of Naval Operations (Strategic Plans) to DNI, "Serial o6P30, Classification of Papers, Review Of," January 24, 1950, Folder F1, A5, Box 71, AR/131, NHHC.

29 Reminiscences of Vice Admiral Truman J. Hedding, USN, interview by Etta Belle Kitchen, 1972, 163, NDL.

30 "Eighth Senior Officers' Meeting, 29 Jan–2 Feb 1951," February 29, 1951, 5, File ACS 1279–1, vol. 11141, RG24-D-10, LAC.

31 "Attendance of British and American Officers in Military Schools in Each Other's Countries," appendix to Chiefs of Staff Committee, "COS (50) 327," August 25, 1950, DEFE 5/23, TNA.

32 British Naval Staff (Washington) to Admiralty, "041647Z," June 4, 1951, ADM 1/22762, TNA; Hibbard, Navy Recollections, reel 15.

33 Chiefs of Staff Committee, "COS (51) 95th Meeting," June 8, 1951, 6, DEFE 6/8; DTSD, "Minute" (June 21, 1951), ADM 1/22762: both in TNA.

34 J. P. L. Thomas to Anthony Eden, May 30, 1952, ADM 1/24626, TNA.

35 "Minute" (May 29, 1952), ADM 1/24626, TNA; Academic Plans Section to Heads of Departments, "British Naval Officer Students at Naval War College," October 15, 1953, Folder Foreign Officers (NCC), Record Group 27, USNWC.

36 Richard G. Hewlett and Oscar Anderson, *The New World, 1939–1946*, vol. 1, *A History of the United States Atomic Energy Commission* (University Park: Penn-

sylvania State University Press, 1962), 408–532; Commander John A. Tyree Jr., USN, "Information Obtained during Visit to Washington," July 13, 1949, 2, Folder A3–2(1), Memoranda (5–11/49), 1949 TS, Box 202, Entry P 111, RG 313, NACP.

37 Oliver Franks to William Strang, June 13, 1952, ADM 1/24626, TNA.

38 The commander of the Royal Navy's Far East Station complained to the first sea lord in December 1951, "The French are so very sensitive and so damned insecure." Vice Admiral Guy Russell, RN, Commander in Chief, Far East Station [CINCFE] to Admiral Rhoderick R. McGrigor, RN, 1SL, "D/005," December 17, 1951, ADM 205/86, TNA.

39 See also Rear Admiral George C. Dyer, USN, to Lieutenant General Harold R. Bull, USA, July 31, 1951, Folder 9, Box 1, George C. Dyer Papers [Dyer Papers], LOC.

40 Malcolm Llewellyn-Jones, *The Royal Navy and Anti-Submarine Warfare, 1917–1949* (New York: Routledge, 2006), 131–133; Doug McLean, "Muddling Through: Canadian Anti-Submarine Doctrine and Practice, 1942–1945," in *A Nation's Navy: In Quest of Canadian Naval Identity*, ed. Michael Hadley, Rob Huebert, and Fred Crickard (Montreal: McGill-Queen's University Press, 1996), 178.

41 Captain John Sinkankas, USN, CO, Patrol Squadron 34, to Commander Fleet Air Wing 5, "Information on Course of Instruction at Joint Anti-Submarine School, Londonderry, Northern Ireland, U.K.," May 6, 1949, 2, Folder 6, Admiral's Personal File, Box 8, Robert F. Hickey Papers, HIA.

42 "Londonderry Staff Memo 1," enclosure to Office of Directors, JASS, "Londonderry Joint Air/Sea Training Orders," c. 1947–1948, File 4973–30, pt. 1, vol. 34443, RG24-D-1-c, LAC.

43 Canadian Naval Mission Overseas, London, to Naval Secretary, "Joint A/S School, Londonderry," November 26, 1946, 1, File 4973–30, pt. 1, vol. 34443, RG24-D-1-c, LAC.

44 Malcolm Llewellyn-Jones, "The Pursuit of Realism: British Anti-Submarine Tactics and Training to Counter the Fast Submarine, 1944–52," in *The Face of Naval Battle: The Human Experience of Modern War at Sea*, ed. John Reeve and David Stevens (Crows Nest, NSW: Allen & Unwin, 2003), 231–232.

45 Roger Sarty, "Canada and Submarine Warfare, 1909–1950," in *The Maritime Defence of Canada* (Toronto: Canadian Institute of Strategic Studies, 1996), 183–216; Chief of Naval Staff, "RCN/RCAF Maritime Warfare School, Halifax, NS—Organization and Functions," October 12, 1951, 1, File 1700–178/1, pt. 1, vol. 33858, RG24-D-1-c, LAC; Wing Commander Reginald R. Ingrams, RCAF, "Report of a Visit to Stn Greenwood 24 and 25 Sept 51 and to MGP HQ and MWS 26 and 27 Sept 51," September 28, 1951, 5, File 28-1-1, pt. 3, vol. 5270, RG24-E-1-b, LAC.

46 Douglas S. Thomas, "'In Cooperation Lies Success': The Early Years of the Mar-

itime Warfare School, 1944–1964," in *People, Policy and Programmes: Proceedings of the 7th Maritime Command (MARCOM) Historical Conference (2005)*, ed. Rich Gimblett (Ottawa: Canadian Naval Heritage Team, 2008), 135–136.

47 Flag Officer Atlantic Coast [FOAC], Assistant Chief of Staff, "Minute," December 24, 1952, in Commander Frederick N. Russell, USN, Staff Officer, Submarines, JMWS, to FOAC, "Visit of Staff Officer, Submarines to JASS Londonderry and Flag Officer, Submarines," December 16, 1952, File ACC 1225–1, vol. 11189, RG24-D-10, LAC; Michael Whitby to Corbin Williamson, September 25, 2015.

48 Ingrams, "Report of a Visit," 4.

49 Donald James Goodspeed, *A History of the Defence Research Board of Canada* (Ottawa: Queen's Printer, 1958), 170.

50 Lay to Naval Secretary, "RCN Liaison Officer at USN Base, Key West," June 5, 1951, File 4973–1, pt. 2, vol. 34440, RG24-D-1-c, LAC.

51 CNO to Forrestal, "Serial 008P03, Anti-Submarine Warfare Situation," July 23, 1946, Folder CNO TS 1946 A8–3, Box 42, Entry UD 17, RG 80, NACP; Norman Friedman, *U.S. Submarines since 1945: An Illustrated Design History* (Annapolis, MD: Naval Institute Press, 1994), 8.

52 CNO, "Second Anti-Submarine Conference," October 1947, 46, 159, Folder A16–3(1) (6–12/47) (2 of 4), 1947 Secret, Box 168, Entry P 111, RG 313, NACP; CNO, "Fourth Anti-Submarine Conference," August 18, 1949, File 8100–5, vol. 35135, RG24-D-1-c, LAC.

53 Vice Admiral Forrest Sherman, USN DCNO, (Operations), "Serial 0012P34, Proceedings of Anti-Submarine Warfare Conference, 17 June 1946—Forwarding Of," June 25, 1946, 8, 30, Folder CNO TS 1946 A16-3(17), Box 45, Entry UD 17,RG 80, NACP.

54 CNO to Forrestal, July 23, 1946.

55 CNO to Forrestal, "Serial 007P31, Bilateral Exchange of Military Information with Royal Canadian Navy," September 18, 1946, Folder CNO TS 1946 A8–3, Box 42, and Captain Charles E. Weakley, USN to DNI, "Attached Top Secret Letter from Naval Member, Canadian Joint Staff," November 15, 1946, Folder CNO TS 1946 A16-3(17), Box 45: both in Entry UD 17; RG 80, NACP.

56 Enclosure B to CNO, "Minutes of Inter-Fleet Discussions on Anti-Submarine Warfare, Forwarding Of," June 26, 1947, 49, Folder A16-3(1) (6-12/47) (4 of 4), 1947 Secret, Box 168, Entry P 111, RG 313, NACP.

57 Jeffrey Barlow, *From Hot War to Cold: The U.S. Navy and National Security Affairs, 1945–1955* (Stanford, CA: Stanford University Press, 2009), 164.

58 Enclosure A to CNO, "Serial 003P31, Report of Coordinator of Undersea Warfare and Assistants' Visit to British Naval Activities, Jan. 19—Feb. 12, 1947—Forwarding Of," April 30, 1947, 2, Folder A16-3(1) ASW (2-6/47) (1 of 2), 1947 Secret, Box 168, Entry P 111, RG 313, NACP.

59 CNO, "Serial 003P31," 6.

60 Reminiscences of Rear Admiral Roy S. Benson, USN, interview by John T. Mason Jr., 1984, 358–359, NDL.

61 Reminiscences of Rear Admiral Robert W. McNitt, USN, interview by Paul Stillwell, 2002, 345, USNI.

62 Enclosure A to CNO, "Serial 0062P31, Report of Visit of Undersea Warfare Weapons Group to British Isles during August–September 1947," October 31, 1947, 13, Folder A16-3(1) (6-12/47) (3 of 4), 1947 Secret, Box 168, Entry P 111, RG 313, NACP.

63 Enclosure X to CNO, 163, 166.

64 Rear Admiral Charles B. Momsen, USN, Assistant Chief of Naval Operations (Undersea Warfare), "Serial 00266P31, Highlights in USW Progress, 15 May— 15 June 1949," June 15, 1949, 7, Folder A16–3 Warfare Operations—Jacket #1 (1-5/49)(1 of 3), 1949 Secret, Box 215, Entry P 111, RG 313, NACP; Directors, JASS, "JASS/S.53/Air/49, Progress Report—Spring Term, 1949 (17 January—9 April)," April 23, 1949, 8; DTASW, "TASW 148/49, Minutes of Meeting Held at Air Ministry on 7.12.48 to Discuss the Joint A/S School Unit Training Courses," May 10, 1949: both in AIR 20/6831, TNA.

65 CINCPACFLT to CNO, "Serial 00181, ASW Training," July 12, 1948, 4–5, Folder A 16-3(1) Jacket #1 (1-7/48) (1 of 3), 1948 Secret, Box 190, Entry P 111, RG 313, NACP.

66 Admiral Richard Conolly, USN, CINCNELM, to Cunningham, June 17, 1948, ADM 205/70, TNA.

67 Rear Admiral Donald R. Osborn Jr., USN, to Joint Logistics Plans Committee, "Standardization of Equipment, Operational Procedures and Organization with the Military Department of the Canadian and British Governments within the Navy Department," October 4, 1948, Folder Secret (00400) 1948, Box 795, Entry P 1208, RG 38, NACP.

68 See the reports of JASS for 1948 to 1953 in AIR 20/6831, AIR 20/6832, and AIR 20/6833: all in TNA.

69 Directors, JASS, "156/1, Progress Report Summer Term, 1950 (7 May–29 July)," August 17, 1950, 3, and Directors, JASS, "53/1, Progress Report—Spring Term, 1951 (15 January–21 March)," April 19, 1951, 17: both in AIR 20/6832, TNA.

70 Lieutenant Commander Ernest H. Leggett, USN, "Report of Tour of Duty as Exchange Pilot with the Royal Navy Fleet Air Arm," August 22, 1951, 2, ADM 1/23063, TNA.

71 Sinkankas to Commander Fleet Air Wing 5, May 6, 1949.

72 Sinkankas to Commander Fleet Air Wing 5, 1.

73 Captain George P. Unmacht, USN, CO, USS Waldron, to CINCNELM, "Serial 08," October 12, 1949, enclosure to CINCNELM to CNO (Op-31), "Serial 00238, Operational Reports of Rothesay, Scotland and Londonderry, North Ireland Exercises Conducted by USS Waldron (DD-699) and USS Borie (DD-704)—Forwarding of, FF7/A5," November 22, 1949, 4, Folder CINCNELM, Serial 00238, 22 Nov 1949, Box 44, 1946 RPT, NHHC.

74 Directors, JASS, "JASS/7/3/AIR/49, Progress Report—Autumn Term, 1948 (13 September–10 December)," December 29, 1948, 7, AIR 20/6831, TNA.

75 DDTG, "Minute, Attachment of USN Aircraft to Joint Anti Submarine School," July 8, 1949, AIR 20/6831, TNA; Directors, JASS, "156/1."

76 Rear Admiral James Fife, USN, COMSUBLANT, to CNO, "U.S.S. Trumpet-fish (SS425), Operations with Royal Naval Forces off Londonderry, May–June 1948," July 22, 1948, Folder A16-3(1) War Operations-Jacket#4 (11-12/48) (2 of 2), 1948 TS, Box 190, Entry P 111, RG 313, NACP.

77 "Progress at Londonderry during the Last Twelve Months," by Captain Anthony F. Pugsley, RN, in Group Captain Zebulon L. "Lewie" Leigh, RCAF, "Minutes of Royal Navy Ninth TAS Liaison Meeting," April 5, 1951, 138, File 28–1-1, pt. 2, vol. 5269, RG24-E-1-b, LAC.

78 DTASW, "TASW 9/131/47, Minutes of the Meeting to Discuss the Expansion of the Joint A/S School to Meet Air Ministry Requirements," February 16, 1951, 3, AIR 20/6832, and DDTG, "JUC Courses—Joint Anti-Submarine School," June 1, 1949, AIR 20/6831: both in TNA.

79 Directors, JASS, "JASS/S.53/Air/49," 7.

80 Enclosure 1 to Rear Admiral Ira E. Hobbs, USN, Commander Carrier Division [COMCARDIV] Eighteen, to Rear Admiral Frank Ward, USN, Commander Hunter Killer Force, Atlantic Fleet, "Serial 058, Combined ASW Operations with the Royal Navy in the Londonderry North Ireland Area; Report On," June 23, 1953, 2, File 4903-4, vol. 34414, RG24-D-1-c, LAC.

81 Captain James H. Flatley, USN, CO USS Block Island, to Ward, May 14, 1953, 1, 2005.801.125, James Flatley Papers [Flatley Papers], Patriots Point Naval & Maritime Museum [PPM].

82 Captain Donald H. Connell-Fuller, RN, Director, JASS, to DTASW and DAW, "No 81/6, Report on Visit of U.S. Hunter/Killer Group to Londonderry," June 17, 1953, 2, File 4903–4, vol. 34414, RG24-D-1-c, LAC.

83 Connell-Fuller to DTASW and DAW, 2–6.

84 Flatley to Radford, May 14, 1953, 1, 2005.801.125, Flatley Papers, PPM; Steve Ewing, *Reaper Leader: The Life of Jimmy Flatley* (Annapolis, MD: Naval Institute Press, 2002), 293–294.

85 Hobbs to Ward, "Serial 058," 1–2; "Analysis of USN vs. RN Communications," Enclosure 5 to Hobbs to Ward, 1–2.

86 Hobbs to Ward, 1.

87 "Analysis of USN vs. RN Concept of ASW Operations," Enclosure 2 to Hobbs to Ward, 2.

88 Lieutenant Commander R. S. Walker, RN, and Mr. F. Ward, Director of Anti-Submarine Warfare (Washington), "Report, Anti-Submarine Warfare, 1942 to 1945," 1945, 285–287, ADM 199/1236, TNA.

89 Lay to Naval Secretary, "Visit to USN Establishments, Key West, Florida, by

CANAVUS Staff Officers," May 30, 1952, File 1225–193–139, pt. 2, vol. 33487, RG24-D-1-c, LAC.

90 Friedman, *U.S. Submarines since 1945*, 23.

91 "BAD Secret Letter No. 23/47," November 24, 1947, Enclosure A to CNO to CINCLANTFLT, "Serial 0001P31, Visit of H.M. Ships Battleaxe and Crossbow to Key West, Florida," March 12, 1948, Folder A4–3 (1–12/48), 1948, T.S., Box 177, Entry P 111, RG 313, NACP.

92 CNO to CINCLANTFLT, 1; Commander, Key West Force, to CINCLANTFLT, "Serial 0013, Visit of HMS Battleaxe and HMS Crossbow to Key West," August 10, 1948, Folder A4-3 Employment of Vessels (1–12/48), 1948, TS, Box 177, Entry P 111, RG 313, NACP.

93 Enclosure A to CNO, "Serial 003P31," 8; Vice Admiral William Tennant, RN, Commander-in-Chief, America and West Indies Station, to Admiralty, "Exercises with USS Coral Sea," May 22, 1948, File 4903–4, Pt. 1, vol. 34413, RG24-D-1-c, LAC.

94 Air Vice Marshal Somerled D. MacDonald, RAF, Assistant Chief of Air Staff (Training), to BJSM(W), May 20, 1949, and Air Ministry to BJSM(W), "AX 3947," July 5, 1949: both in AIR 20/6831, TNA.

95 "Status of Anti-Submarine Warfare," Enclosure C to CNO, "Fourth Anti-Submarine Conference," 40; Thomas Keppel Edge-Partington, "A Short Life History," c. 1990s, 2–13, 09/161/1, Documents.16709, IWM.

96 DTASW, "TASW 0168/48, US/UK Joint Anti-Submarine School," December 10, 1948, 3–4, AIR 20/6831, TNA; Appendix A to "Visit of CNS to the Admiralty," April 8, 1949, 1, File 1225-CNS, vol. 31101, RG24-D-1-c, LAC; Op-301E to Op-30, "Brief of Progress in Planning a Combined U.S./U.K. Joint A/S Training Organization and Proposals for Future Planning," August 24, 1950, 1, Folder F3, A16–3 (1 of 2), Box 72, AR/131, NHHC.

97 "Ordnance," Appendix 6 to Lay to Naval Secretary, "HMCS Niagara Report of Proceedings for February 1951," March 13, 1951, File 4, Box 338, 81/520/8000, DHH; "Report of Visit to the Fleet Sonar School, Key West, Florida," Appendix E to Lay to Naval Secretary, May 30, 1952.

98 Lieutenant James R. Coulter, RCN, to Officer in Charge, HMC Torpedo Anti-Submarine School, "Report of Proceedings A/S Training Classes, 19 February to 19 March, 1948," April 3, 1948, and Vice Admiral Harold Grant, RCN, Chief of the Naval Staff to Admiral Louis Denfeld, USN, CNO, June 16, 1948: both in File 4903–4, Pt. 1, vol. 34413, RG24-D-1-c, LAC.

99 "Air," Appendix 4 to Lay to Naval Secretary, "HMCS Niagara Report of Proceedings for December 1951," January 8, 1952, File 4, and "Air," Appendix 4 to Lay to Naval Secretary, "HMCS Niagara Report of Proceedings for April 1952," May 2, 1952, File 5: both in Box 338, 81/520/8000, DHH.

100 Appendix E to Lay to Naval Secretary, May 30, 1952.

101 Medland to Naval Secretary, "TAS Exchange and Liaison Officers," May 4, 1953, File 4425–27, pt. 3, vol. 34238, RG24-D-1-c, LAC.

102 "Procurement," Appendix 7 to Lay to Naval Secretary, "HMCS Niagara Report of Proceedings for March 1950," April 7, 1950, File 3, Box 338, 81/520/8000, DHH.

103 Lieutenant (O) J. A. Shee, RCN, "A Summary of a Report by Lt. (C) J. Steel, RCN on an Anti-Submarine Course given by the U.S. Navy," October 1951, 1, File 4973-1, pt. 2, vol. 34440, RG24-D-1-c, LAC.

104 Enclosure to Lay to Naval Secretary, "Report of a Visit to NAS Norfolk by Staff Officer (Air)," April 30, 1952, 1, 3, File 1225–193–139, pt. 2, vol. 33487, RG24-D-1-c, LAC.

105 Shee, "Summary," 2.

106 Shee, "Summary," 3.

107 Shee, "Summary," 3.

108 Lieutenant (P) Frederic G. Townsend, RCN, "Report," Enclosure A to Commodore Kenneth F. Adams, RCN, CO HMCS Magnificent, to Naval Secretary, "A/S Training in the USN," November 23, 1950, 1, File ACC 1225-1, vol. 11189, RG24-D-10; Enclosure to NMCJS(W) to Naval Secretary, "Visit to NAS Norfolk—CANAVUS Staff Officer (Air)," April 27, 1951, 3, File 1225–193–139, pt. 1, vol. 33487, RG24-D-1-c: both in LAC.

109 Enclosure A to Adams to Naval Secretary, November 23, 1950.

110 Shee, "Summary," 4.

111 Captain Duncan L. Raymond, RCN, to FOAC, "Unit Course No. 38 at Joint Anti-Submarine School Londonderry," May 14, 1952, 1, File ACC 1225-1, vol. 11189, RG24-D-10, LAC; Adams to Naval Secretary, November 23, 1950, 1.

112 Shee, "Summary," 3.

113 Commander Malcolm C. Morris, RN, and Wing Commander R. E. Jay, RAF, "NATO Sea Air Training Establishment, Sub SAWC II/7/51," October 29, 1951, 2, File 1270–78, Pt. 4, vol. 8071, RG24-D-1-c, LAC.

114 Albert Nofi, *To Train the Fleet for War: The U.S. Navy Fleet Problems, 1923–1940* (Newport, RI: Naval War College Press, 2010).

115 Joint War Production Staff, "Standardization," February 10, 1948, 3, CAB 21/2067, TNA; Rear Admiral M. Bledsoe, USN, Commander Support Group, Naval Forces, Far East to CNO, "Serial 0116, Joint Exercises with Units of the British and Australian Navies—Report Of," December 3, 1947, and Rear Admiral Robert D. Oliver, RN, Flag Officer Commanding Fifth Cruiser Squadron, to Admiral Denis W. Boyd, RN, Commander in Chief, British Pacific Fleet, "CS5/T2/2009, Joint Exercises with Americans—25th and 26th November, 1947," December 14, 1947: both in 622/202/4240, MP981/1, NAA.

116 PJBD, "Journal of Discussions and Decisions," November 21, 1947, 10, Folder A16-3(1) Jacket #2 (6-12/47) (1 of 2), 1947, T.S., Box 167, Entry P 111, RG 313,

NACP; Naval Secretary, "Minutes of Fourth Meeting of Senior Officers," November 26, 1947, 9, File ACS 1279-1, vol. 11141, RG24-D-10, LAC.

117 "Plans Summary, Future Plans Section," Enclosure A to Vice Admiral John L. McCrea, USN, Deputy CINCPACFLT, to DNH, "Semi-Annual Summary of CinCPacFlt Command Narrative for the Period 1 April—30 September 1948," October 30, 1948, Folder Command Narrative (1 of 3), Box 4, Entry A1 204, CINCPACFLT Operation Files, Red 65, 1948 [Entry A1 204]; CNO to CINCLANTFLT, "Serial 00020P33, Combined Exercises with the British Royal Navy," June 5, 1948, Folder A4-3 (1-12/48), 1948, T.S., Box 177, Entry P 111: both in RG 313, NACP.

118 CNO, "Serial 00020P33."

119 COMNAVEU, "Narrative of U.S. Naval Forces, Europe," December 30, 1946, 35, Folder COMNAVEU 1 September 1945 to 1 October 1946 (1 of 2), Box 727, 1946, CMD, NHHC.

120 Commanding Officer, Atlantic Coast, to Chief of Naval Staff, "301355/7/47," July 30, 1947, 47, File 4903-4, Pt. 1, vol. 34413, RG24-D-1-c, LAC; COMSUBLANT to Submarine Force, U.S. Atlantic Fleet, "Serial 0033, Minor Combined Exercises with Units of the British and Royal Canadian Navies; Publicity and Security Regarding," August 13, 1948, 1, Folder A4-3 (3–12/48), 1948, Secret, Box 177, Entry P 111, RG 313, NACP.

121 W. G. Mills, Deputy Minister of National Defence for Naval Services, to Under-Secretary of State for External Affairs, October 26, 1948, File 28-6-10, vol. 5274, RG24-E-1-b, LAC.

122 Admiral Arthur Power, RN, Commander in Chief, Mediterranean Fleet, to Admiral Bruce Fraser, RN, 1SL, "SP/A7/1389," May 9, 1949, 7, ADM 205/72, TNA.

123 CNO, "Serial 0031P33,"May 4, 1950, enclosure to CNO to CINCPACFLT, "Serial 00100, Combined Naval Exercises with Nations of the North Atlantic Treaty Organization—Instructions Concerning," May 26, 1950, Folder A16–3 Jacket #1, Box 6, Entry P 28, General Administrative Correspondence, 1950 [Entry P 28], RG 313, NACP.

124 Canadian Ambassador to the United States to Secretary of State for External Affairs, "Proposed Press Release," February 16, 1950, File 28-6-10, vol. 5274, RG24-E-1-b, LAC; Admiral William F. Fechteler, USN, CINCLANTFLT, "Report of the Commander in Chief U.S. Atlantic Fleet for Period 1 February to 30 June 1950," August 28, 1950, 19, Folder CINCLANTFLT Annual Report FY1950, Box 648, 1946 CMD, NHHC.

125 Stuart Soward, *Hands to Flying Stations: A Recollective History of Canadian Naval Aviation*, vol. 1, *1945–1954* (Victoria, BC: Neptune Developments, 1984), 169–170.

126 "Discussion of Second Fleet Exercises (Caribex Fifty) March 1950," Enclosure A to Commander Second Fleet to CINCLANTFLT, "Remarks of Commander

Second Fleet at Type Commanders Conference, 8 May 1950," May 16, 1950, 3, Folder A3–1-A4–1(2), Confidential, 1950, Box 26, Entry P 80, RG 313, NACP.

127   Adams to FOAC, April 17, 1950, 4.

128   Adams to FOAC, 4.

129   Enclosure A to Commander Second Fleet to CINCLANTFLT, May 16, 1950, 2–4.

130   Fechteler, August 28, 1950, 19.

131   Commander Bruce S. McEwen, RN, Commander (Air), HMCS Magnificent, to Adams, "Air Report of Proceedings for the Spring Cruise," April 12, 1950, 3, Folder QQ-12, File 250, 79/246, DHH.

132   Fechteler, August 28, 1950, 19; Enclosure A to Commander Second Fleet to CINCLANTFLT, May 16, 1950, 4.

133   Sean Maloney, *Securing Command of the Sea: NATO Naval Planning, 1948–1954* (Annapolis, MD: Naval Institute Press, 1995), ch. 3.

134   Hanson Baldwin, "Navies Meet the Test in Operation Mainbrace," *New York Times*, September 28, 1952.

135   Maloney, *Securing Command*, 155–157.

136   Edgar D'Arcy McGreet, Canadian Minister to Denmark, to Secretary of State for External Affairs, "Exercise Mainbrace," October 28, 1952, File 1640–21–14, pt. 1, vol. 31163, RG24-D-1-c, LAC; "Press Release No. 2797," September 10, 1952; "NATO, Operation Mainbrace," *Time*, September 22, 1952: both in Folder 42, Box 115, 81/520/1650, DHH.

137   DTSD, "Brief Outline Exercise Mainbrace (Revised Edition)" (August 14, 1952), File 1640–21–14, pt. 2, vol. 31163, RG24-D-1-c, LAC; SACLANT, "Mainbrace Booklet," September 1952, Folder Miscellaneous (1), Box 8, Lynde Dupuy McCormick Papers, LOC.

138   The following narrative of Exercise Mainbrace draws heavily on the remarks at the Oslo critique given by Admiral Patrick Brind, RN. "Combined Narrative Given at Critique," Enclosure 2 to Captain Harold V. W. Groos, RCN, Naval Member, Canadian Joint Staff (London), to Naval Secretary, "Exercise Main Brace—Critique," November 15, 1952, 1–13, File 1640-21-14, pt. 1, vol. 31163, RG24-D-1-c, LAC.

139   Lieutenant Junior Grade Arthur P. Miller, USNR, "SACLANT: Guardian of the Atlantic," *All Hands*, October 1952, 30.

140   Captain Kenneth L. Dyer, RCN, CO, HMCS Magnificent, to CINCHF, "Program for HMCS Magnificent before and after Exercise Mainbrace," August 14, 1952, File NUKS 1660–1, vol. 11288, RG24-D-13, LAC.

141   Permanent Representative of Canada to North Atlantic Council to Secretary of State for External Affairs, "Exercise Mainbrace Critique," October 3, 1952, File 1640–21–14, pt. 1, vol. 31163, RG24-D-1-c, LAC.

142   DTSD, "M 03031/52, Summary of Remarks on Exercise Mainbrace," April 1, 1953, 2, ADM 116/6438, PRO Documents, DHH.

143 SACLANT to Secretary, Standing Group, "Serial 763," November 6, 1952, File 1640–21, pt. 3, vol. 33769, RG24-D-1-c, LAC; Enclosures 1, 2, and 3 to Groos to Naval Secretary, November 15, 1952.

144 Enclosure 3 to Groos to Naval Secretary, 3.

145 SACLANT, "Serial 763," November 6, 1952, 2–3.

146 Lieutenant Commander Robin Buller, RN, and Lieutenant Commander David Seely, RN, to CINCHF, "Report on Experiences in Exercise Mainbrace," October 6, 1952, 2, ADM 1/23452, TNA.

147 Buller and Seely to CINCHF, October 6, 1952, 1.

148 Buller and Seely, 1; Lieutenant Commander John O. Coote, RN, to Captain (S/M), HMS Montclare, "Report," October 8, 1952, 1, ADM 116/6438, PRO Documents, DHH.

149 Enclosure 2 to CINCHF, "HF/EA 1299/0265/2/95, Report on Exercise Mainbrace," November 12, 1952, ADM 116/6438, PRO Documents, DHH; "General," Annex A to Buller and Seely to CINCHF, 1.

150 "Comments on Exercise," Enclosure 1 to CINCHF, "HF/EA 1299/0265/2/95," November 12, 1952, 2.

151 Buller and Seely to CINCHF, October 6, 1952, 1; Appendix Baker to Coote to Captain (S/M), October 8, 1952, 1.

152 Enclosure 2 to CINCHF, "HF/EA 1299/0265/2/95," November 12, 1952.

153 Captain Michael Le Fanu, RN, Captain (D) of Third Training Squadron, HMS Relentless, "Conduct of A/S Operations by the United States Navy," enclosure to Vice Admiral Cecil Charles Hughes-Hallett, RN, BJSM(W), to Admiral Rhoderick R. McGrigor, RN, 1SL, "Participation of U.S. Naval Forces in F.O. S/M's—Summer War 1953," November 21, 1952, 1, ADM 205/86, TNA; Alastair Wilson, *A Biographical Dictionary of the Twentieth Century Royal Navy*, vol. 1, *Admirals of the Fleet and Admirals* (Barnsley, U.K.: Seaforth, 2013), 843.

154 Enclosure to Hughes-Hallett to McGrigor, November 21, 1952, 1.

155 Enclosure to Hughes-Hallett to McGrigor, 2.

156 Enclosure 2 to CINCHF, "HF/EA 1299/0265/2/95," November 12, 1952.

157 Director of Naval Air Organization and Training, "Minute," March 11, 1953, ADM 116/6438, PRO Documents, DHH.

158 Director of Naval Air Organization and Training, "Minute."

159 Annex F to Buller and Seely to CINCHF, October 6, 1952, 1.

160 Commander Victor Browne, RCN, Director, JMWS, to FOAC, "Report of Visit of Lieutenant P. J. Edwards, RN to USS Siboney, June 1953," October 21, 1953, 8, File 4903–4, Pt. 4, vol. 34414, RG24-D-1-c, LAC; "Monthly Intelligence Report No. 16," April 1947, 50, Box 6, Entry UD-09D, RG 38, NACP.

161 David Wright, interview by Richard McDonough, October 3, 2005, reel 4, Sound Archive, Catalogue 28498; Admiral Raymond Derek Lygo, RN (ret), interview by Richard McDonough, May 8, 2006, reel 10, Sound Archive, Catalogue 28776: both in IWM; Browne to FOAC, "Report of Visit," 9.

162 "Review of Replenishment at Sea," ADM 116/6439, PRO Documents, DHH; Enclosure 3 to Groos to Naval Secretary, November 15, 1952, 5; Enclosure 2 to SACLANT, "Serial 763," 11.

163 Appendix Able to Coote to Captain (S/M), October 8, 1952, 4; Enclosure 2 to SACLANT, "Serial 763," November 6, 1952, 11.

164 Permanent Representative of Canada to North Atlantic Council to Secretary of State for External Affairs, "Exercise Mainbrace Critique," October 3, 1952, 2, File 1640–21–14, pt. 1, vol. 31163, RG24-D-1-c, LAC.

165 McGreet to Secretary of State for External Affairs, October 28, 1952, 3.

166 DTSD, "M 03031/52," 2; Enclosure 2 to SACLANT, "Serial 763," 9–10.

167 Barlow, *From Hot War to Cold*, 256.

168 Vice Admiral Russell Berkey, USN, Commander Seventh Fleet [COM7THFLT], to Radford, "Report of Combined Exercises with British Far East Fleet during the Period 28 February—19 March 1950," March 30, 1950, Folder CINCPAC-FLT, Serial 0332, 30 Apr 1950, Box 22, 1946 RPT, NHHC.

169 Rear Admiral William Andrewes, RN, Flag Officer Second-in-Command, Far East [FO2FE], to Admiral Patrick Brind, RN, CINCFE, "Fo2FE/2263/22, Combined Exercises with United States Navy—March, 1950," March 12, 1950, 3, ADM 1/21868, TNA.

170 Andrewes to Brind, 4; Rear Admiral Walter F. Boone, USN, COMCARDIV Five, to Berkey, "Report of Combined Exercises with British Far East Fleet during the Period 28 February—19 March 1950," March 21, 1950, 1, Folder CINCPACFLT, Serial 0332, 30 Apr 1950, Box 22, 1946 RPT, NHHC.

171 Boone to Vice Admiral Thomas L. Sprague, USN, COMAIRPAC, March 11, 1950, 1–2, Folder BO, Box 29, Papers of Admiral Arthur W. Radford [Radford Papers], NHHC.

172 Boone to Berkey, 4.

173 Andrewes to Brind, 4; Boone to Sprague, 2.

174 Andrewes to Brind, 5.

175 Andrewes to Brind, 8.

176 Andrewes to Brind, 6.

177 Boone to Berkey, 2.

178 Boone to Sprague, 2.

179 Boone to Berkey, 2; Andrewes to Brind, 9.

180 Andrewes to Brind, 10–12; Boone to Sprague, 3; Boone to Berkey, 3; Berkey to Radford, 2.

181 Commander Charles P. Coke, RN, "United States Navy Report of Exercises with the British Fleet in the Far East," June 12, 1950, ADM 1/21868, TNA.

182 Brind to Secretary of the Admiralty, "363/FES/263/1, Combined Exercises with United States Navy, March 1950," May 15, 1950, ADM 1/21868, TNA.

183 Boone to Berkey, 5.

184 Berkey to Radford, 2.

185 Boone to Berkey, 7.

186 Captain William Kaye Edden, RN, a director in the Admiralty approvingly wrote a line from "To a Louse," a poem by eighteenth-century noted Scottish poet Robert Burns, on a report by a U.S. Navy exchange pilot who served with a British naval air squadron: "O wad some Power the giftie gie us, To see oursels as others see us! It wad frae many a blunder free us, and foolish notion." See Captain William K. Edden, RN, DTSD, "Minute," November 5, 1951, ADM 1/23063, TNA. The English translation is "And would some Power give us the gift, to see ourselves as others see us! It would from many a blunder free us, and foolish notion."

CHAPTER 7. THE KOREAN TEST

1 Norman Polmar, *Aircraft Carriers: A History of Carrier Aviation and Its Influence on World Events*, vol. 2, 1946–2006 (Washington, D.C.: Potomac Books, 2008), 57; Warren E. Thompson, *Naval Aviation in the Korean War* (Barnsley, U.K.: Pen & Sword Aviation, 2012), 16.

2 For a review of the literature on the Korean War, see Donald Boose and James Matray, eds., *The Ashgate Research Companion to the Korean War* (Farnham, U.K.: Ashgate, 2014); Lester Brune, ed., *The Korean War: Handbook of the Literature and Research* (Westport, CT: Greenwood Press, 1996); Allan Millett, *The Korean War* (Washington, D.C.: Potomac Books, 2007). For the naval war in Korea, selected standard works include Malcolm Cagle, *The Sea War in Korea* (Annapolis, MD: Naval Institute Press, 1957); James Field, *History of United States Naval Operations, Korea* (Washington, D.C.: Naval Historical Center, 1962); Edward Marolda, ed., *The U.S. Navy in the Korean War* (Annapolis, MD: Naval Institute Press, 2007); John Lansdown, *With the Carriers in Korea: The Fleet Air Arm Story, 1950–1953* (Cheshire, U.K.: Crecy, 1997).

3 Allan Millett, *The War for Korea, 1950–1951: They Came From the North* (Lawrence: University Press of Kansas, 2010), 120–217.

4 Millett, *The War for Korea*, 239–254.

5 Millett, 301, 317, 350.

6 Millett, 385, 404–405.

7 Millett, 449.

8 Rear Admiral Sir William Andrewes, RN, FO2FE, to Admiral Patrick Brind, RN, CINCFE, "FO2FE/2960/11, Korean War—Second Report of Proceedings, 1st to 5th July, 1950," July 7, 1950, 3, Naval Ops in Korea I–IV, DS/Misc/12, Microfilm reel 1, Papers of Admiral Sir William Andrewes [Andrewes Papers], IWM.

9 Steven Paget's recent book examines coalition naval warfare in Korea through the lens of naval gunfire support. See Steven Paget, *The Dynamics of Coalition Naval Warfare: The Special Relationship at Sea* (New York: Routledge, 2017).

10 Jeffrey Barlow, "The U.S. Navy's Air Interdiction Effort during the Korean

War," in *Coalition Air Warfare in the Korean War, 1950–1953*, ed. Jacob Neufeld and George M. Watson (Washington, D.C.: U.S. Air Force History and Museums Program, 2005), 135–141.

11 Cagle, *The Sea War in Korea*, 30–33.

12 Cagle, 30–37.

13 Cagle, 293–96.

14 Naval Historical Branch, "B.R. 1736 (54), Naval Staff History: British Commonwealth Naval Operations Korea, 1950–53," September 1967, 319, Library, Sea Power Centre - Australia, Canberra.

15 Thompson, *Naval Aviation in the Korean War*, 154.

16 Richard P. Hallion, *The Naval Air War in Korea* (Tuscaloosa: University of Alabama Press, 2011).

17 Andrewes, "Report of Experience in Korean Operations, July–December 1950," March 31, 1951, pt. 3, sec. 1, ADM 116/6230, TNA.

18 Andrewes, "July–December 1950," pt. 3, sec. 1.

19 Andrewes to Brind, "1st to 5th July, 1950," July 10, 1950, 2.

20 Ray Sturtivant, *British Naval Aviation: The Fleet Air Arm, 1917–1990* (Annapolis, MD: Naval Institute Press, 1990), 167–68.

21 Lieutenant Commander Robert McCandless, RN (ret), interview by Richard McDonough, December 18, 2004, reel 17, Sound Archive, Catalogue 27344, IWM.

22 Richard P. Hallion, *The Naval Air War in Korea* (Tuscaloosa: University of Alabama Press, 2011), 154–155; David Hobbs, *The British Carrier Strike Fleet after 1945* (Annapolis, MD: Naval Institute Press, 2015), 37–44; Lansdown, *With the Carriers*, 110, 136, 157.

23 Captain Robert F. Hickey, USN, Assistant U.S. Naval Attaché, United Kingdom, to Rear Admiral Joseph F. Bolger, USN, DCNO (Air), March 17, 1947, 1, Folder 9, Box 3, Hickey Papers, HIA.

24 Director of Naval Air Organization and Training to Head of Military Branch, "D/143/51," December 10, 1951, ADM 116/6231, TNA.

25 Rear Admiral Arleigh Burke, USN, Strategic Plans Division, to Vice Admiral Donald B. Duncan, USN, VCNO, "Comments on SGM 2538-52," November 15, 1952, 2, #46, Personal Files, Papers of Admiral Arleigh A. Burke [Burke Papers], NHHC.

26 Hobbs, *The British Carrier Strike Fleet after 1945*, 44, 47, 51–53, 59.

27 DAW, "Minute" (July 23, 1951), ADM 116/6230, TNA.

28 McCandless, interview, reel 17.

29 "Minutes of the Second Meeting of the Committee Investigating USN and RN Tactical and Communication Books," November 22, 1948, 1, File 1279-59, vol. 8092, RG24-D-1-c, LAC.

30 Andrewes, "July–December 1950," pt. 3, sec. 3-4.

31 Commander James Plomer, RCN, Commander Canadian Destroyers, Far East

[CANCOMDESFE], "Korea War Report, Part One," 1952, 21, File 2, Box 144, 81/520/1650-239/187, DHH.

32 Captain Rudolph Lee "Roy" Johnson, USN, CO USS Badoeng Strait, to CNO, "Action Report 7 January–16 January 1952 and 25 January–6 February 1952, A12/OF30," March 17, 1952, 16, Aviation History Branch, NHHC.

33 CINCPACFLT, "Chapter 5 Surface Operations, Interim Evaluation Report No. 4" (1952), 5–63, Folder Chapter 5; Box 7; Entry P 3, Korean War Interim Evaluation Reports, 1950–53 [Entry P 3]; RG 38, NACP.

34 Rear Admiral Alan K. Scott-Moncrieff, RN, FO2FE, "Report of Experience in Korean Operations, July 1951–June 1952," September 15, 1952, pt. 3, sec. 3, File 1926-102/11, Pt. 2, vol. 8204, RG24-D-1-c, LAC.

35 Scott-Moncrieff, "July 1951–June 1952."

36 Lansdown, *With the Carriers*, 37.

37 Lieutenant-Commander Paul Millett, RN (ret), interview by Rodney William Giesler, May 21, 1997, reel 1, Sound Archive, Catalogue 17572, and Alan Leahy, interview by Richard McDonough, September 28, 2010, reel 9, Sound Archive, Catalogue 32843: both in IWM; McCandless, interview, reel 17.

38 Australian Naval Aviation Museum, *Flying Stations: A Story of Australian Naval Aviation* (Sydney: Allen & Unwin, 1998), 88.

39 Scott-Moncrieff, "July 1951–June 1952," pt. 3, sec. 3.

40 Captain Cromwell F. J. L. Davies, RN, DStand, "Minute," October 12, 1951, ADM 116/6230, TNA; "Gunnery," Appendix 12 to Lay to Naval Secretary, "HMCS Niagara Report of Proceedings for February 1952," March 7, 1952, File 5, Box 338, 81/520/8000, DHH; Rear Admiral Eric G. A. Clifford, RN, FO2FE, "Report of Experience in Korean Operations, July 1952–April 1953," July 15, 1953, pt. 3, sec. 3, File 1926-102/11, Pt. 2, vol. 8204, RG24-D-1-c, LAC.

41 Andrewes, "July–December 1950," pt. 3, sec. 3.

42 Captain Patrick W. Brock, RN, Director of Operations Division [DOD], "Minute," August 15, 1951, ADM 116/6230, TNA.

43 Commander J. M. D. Gray, RN, Naval Advisor Tokyo, to CINCFE, "NA 41/792/50," August 9, 1950, 7, ADM 116/6227, TNA.

44 Andrewes, "July–December 1950," pt. 3, sec. 3.

45 Admiral Guy Russell, RN, CINCFE, to Fraser, October 23, 1951, 4–5, ADM 205/76, TNA.

46 Plomer, "Korea War Report, Part One," 21, 26.

47 Commander James M. Ramsay, RAN, CO HMAS Warramunga, to Captain (D), 10th Destroyer Flotilla, HMAS Bataan, March 1, 1952, 358/3, AWM78, AWM.

48 "US Navy—Items of General Interest," Appendix 1 to Medland to Naval Secretary, "HMCS Niagara Report of Proceedings for November 1952," December 3, 1952, 2, File 5, 1952, Box 338, 81/520/8000, DHH.

49 Gray to CINCFE, "NA 41/912/50, Third Report of Proceedings," September 28, 1950, 1, ADM 116/6227, TNA.

50 CINCPACFLT, "Report No. 4," 5–64.
51 Russell to Admiral Rhoderick R. McGrigor, RN, 1SL, "D/010," July 12, 1952, 5, ADM 205/86, TNA.
52 Rear Admiral George C. Dyer, USN to Mrs. E. Bacon, July 16, 1951, Folder 9, Box 1, George C. Dyer Papers [Dyer Papers], LOC.
53 Dyer to Lieutenant Commander David R. Sword, USN, December 20, 1951, Folder 1, Box 2, Dyer Papers, LOC.
54 Dyer to Bacon, August 22, 1951, Folder 9, Box 1, Dyer Papers, LOC.
55 Dyer to Rear Admiral Clarence L. C. Atkeson Jr., USN, January 4, 1952, Folder 2, Box 2, Dyer Papers, LOC.
56 Scott-Moncrieff, "July 1951–June 1952," pt. 3, sec. 3.
57 Plomer, "Korea War Report, Part Two" (1952), sec. 1, File 3, Box 144, 81/520/1650 -239/187, DHH.
58 Scott-Moncrieff, "Report of Experience in Korean Operations, January–June 1951," July 27, 1951, pt. 2, ADM 116/6230, TNA.
59 Dyer to Rear Admiral John W. Roper, USN, October 28, 1951, Folder 1, Box 2, Dyer Papers, LOC.
60 Dyer to Rear Admiral Allan E. Smith, USN, July 24, 1951, Folder 9, Box 1, Dyer Papers, LOC; Dyer to Bacon, July 16, 1951.
61 Scott-Moncrieff, "July 1951–June 1952," pt. 2.
62 Dyer to Lieutenant Command Joseph Raymond Tenanty, USN, February 12, 1952, Folder 2, Box 2, Dyer Papers, LOC.
63 Scott-Moncrieff, "July 1951–June 1952," pt. 2.
64 Russell to McGrigor, "D/010," July 12, 1952, 3.
65 Commander John C. Reed, RCN, to CANCOMDESFE, "Report of Proceedings, February 1953," March 17, 1953, 1, File 1926-355/31, pt. 2, vol. 11374, RG24-D-22, LAC.
66 Vice Admiral John E. Gingrich, USN. "Publication No. 154-54, Military Procurement." Industrial College of the Armed Forces, November 18, 1953, 3, February 23, 2004, https://web.archive.org/web/20040223004723/http://www.ndu.edu/library/ic2/L54-054.pdf.
67 Piloting involves maneuvering a ship in dangerous, confined waters such as a harbor or river mouth.
68 Plomer, "Korea War Report, Part Two," 27.
69 Russell to McGrigor, "D/010," July 12, 1952, 3.
70 Scott-Moncrieff, "July 1951–June 1952," pt. 3, sec. 5.
71 William Russell Smith, interview by Conrad Wood, October 25, 1990, reel 2, Sound Archive, Catalogue 11618, and Leonard Alfred Dunn, interview by Conrad Wood, August 2, 2000, reel 6, Sound Archive, Catalogue 20473: both in IWM.
72 Rear Admiral Michael Grote Stirling, RCN (ret), My Navy Recollections, interview by Hal Lawrence, December 6, 1984, pt. 4, SC066_SMG_265, UVL.

73 Appendix B to Reed to CANCOMDESFE, "Report of Proceedings, September 1953," September 30, 1953, 2–3, File 1926-355/31, Part 2, vol. 11374, RG24-D-22, LAC.

74 Geoffrey David Habesch, interview by Conrad Wood, July 29, 1988, reel 4, Sound Archive, Catalogue 10304, IWM.

75 Reminiscences of Vice Admiral Gerald E. Miller, USN, interview by Paul Stillwell, 1983, 131–133, USNI.

76 Boone to Berkey, "Report of Combined Exercises," March 21, 1950, 6, Folder CINCPACFLT, Serial 0332, 30 Apr 1950, Box 22, 1946 RPT, NHHC.

77 Conversation with Dr. W. J. R. Gardner, Historian and Deputy Head, Naval Historical Branch Portsmouth, on January 1, 2015, at H.M. Naval Base, Portsmouth, UK; Mike Farquharson-Roberts, *Royal Navy Officers from War to War, 1918–1939* (New York: Palgrave Macmillan, 2015), 85, 90, 122.

78 Lieutenant Commander J. Stewart, RN, "The Officers of the Royal Navy," *U.S. Naval Institute Proceedings* 85, no. 3 (March 1959): 48–55; Ian Sumner, *The Royal Navy 1939–45* (Oxford, U.K.: Osprey, 2001), 41; J. R. Hill, "The Realities of Medium Power, 1946 to the Present," in *The Oxford Illustrated History of the Royal Navy*, ed. J. R. Hill (New York: Oxford University Press, 1995), 406.

79 Conversation with Dr. W. J. R. Gardner on January 1, 2015. See also Donald Chisolm, *Waiting for Dead Men's Shoes: Origins and Development of the U.S. Navy's Officer Personnel System, 1793–1941* (Stanford, CA: Stanford University Press, 2001), 699.

80 Naval Historical Branch, "B.R. 1736 (54), Naval Staff History: British Commonwealth Naval Operations Korea, 1950–53," September 1967, 284, Library, SPC-A.

81 Enclosure 1 to Captain William Miller, USN, CO USS Bataan, to CNO, "Serial 051, Action Report; Period 12 May 1951–13 June 1951, Submission Of," June 15, 1951, Aviation History Branch, NHHC.

82 Ken Taylor, RN (ret), interview by Peter M. Hart, May 2004, reel 13, Sound Archive, Catalogue 26562, IWM.

83 Russell to Fraser, August 7, 1951, ADM 205/76, TNA.

84 Enclosure 1 to Miller to CNO, June 15, 1951, VI–3.

85 Lieutenant Commander John H. Bovey, RCN, CO HMCS Crusader, "HMCS Crusader's Report on Operation in Korean Waters, 18 June, 1952 to 19 June, 1953," June 19, 1953, Appendix 14, File DCRS1926, vol. 11421, RG24-D-22, LAC; COMNAVFE to ACNB, "N58/29," March 29, 1952, 4276/104/56, MP926/1, NAA.

86 Plomer, "Korea War Report, Part One," 45; Johnson to CNO, March 17, 1952, 15.

87 Andrewes, "July–December 1950," pt. 3, sec. 2.

88 Commander Frederick C. Frewer, RCN, February 23, 1953, 3, File 1926-102/11 Pt. 2, vol. 8204, RG24-D-1-c, LAC.

89 Clifford, "July 1952–April 1953," pt. 3, sec. 2.

90 Conversation with Dr. W. J. R. Gardner on January 1, 2015.

91 McCandless, interview, reel 17.

92 Reed to CANCOMDESFE, March 17, 1953, 2.

93 Millett, interview, reel 1.

94 CINCPACFLT, "Report No. 6," 1953, 5–113; Box 8; Entry P 3; RG 38, NACP.

95 Annex D to Buller and Seely to CINCHF, October 6, 1952, 1, ADM 1/23452, TNA; Le Fanu, "Exercise Mainbrace," enclosure to Hughes-Hallett to Mc-Grigor, November 21, 1952, 1, ADM 205/86, TNA.

96 Henry Burrell, *Mermaids Do Exist: The Autobiography of Vice-Admiral Sir Henry Burrell, RAN* (Melbourne: Macmillan, 1986), 168.

97 Andrewes, "July–December 1950," pt. 3, sec. 2.

98 Andrewes, "July–December 1950," pt. 5.

99 Scott-Moncrieff, "January–June 1951," pt. 2.

100 Brock, "Minute," August 15, 1951.

101 Plomer, "Korea War Report, Part One," 54.

102 Director of Signal Division [DSD], "Minute," January 16, 1953, ADM 116/6438, PRO Documents, DHH.

103 Rear Admiral Robert P. Welland, RCN (ret), My Navy Recollections, interview by Hal Lawrence, May 24, 1983, pt. 4, SC066_WRP_268, UVL.

104 Captain Almon E. Loomis, USN, CO USS Sicily, to CNO, "Serial 001, Action Report for the Period of 4 September through 13 September 1952, CVE118/A16-13," November 13, 1952, 11, Aviation History Branch, NHHC.

105 Captain Harry Ray Horney, USN, CO USS Bataan, to CNO, "Serial 051, Action Report 15 February through 26 February 1953, CVL29, A12," March 9, 1953, 15, Aviation History Branch, NHHC.

106 Lieutenant John B. C. Carling, RCN, "Report," Enclosure A to Reed to Naval Secretary, "Report of Visit to USS Higbee," May 4, 1953, File ACC 1225-1, vol. 11189, RG24-D-10, LAC.

107 "Wardroom" is shorthand for the officers who ate in the wardroom.

108 Lieutenant Robert A. Evans, RCN, "Report," Enclosure B to Reed to Naval Secretary, May 4, 1953.

109 Bovey, "18 June, 1952 to 19 June, 1953," Appendix 6.

110 Sid Gandey, interview by Richard McDonough, n.d., reel 3, Sound Archive, Catalogue 33301; Commander Daniel Patrick Norman, RN (ret), interview by Conrad Wood, November 24, 1994, reel 3, Sound Archive, Catalogue 14796: both in IWM.

111 Commander William Marks, RAN, CO HMAS Bataan, to Flag Officer Commanding, HMA Fleet, "Report of Proceedings–February, 1951," March 7, 1951, 4, 58/2, AWM78, AWM.

112 Marks, "Report of Proceedings–March, 1951," April 1, 1951, 2, 58/2, AWM78, AWM.

113 Marks, "Report of Proceedings–April, 1951," May 5, 1951, 2, 58/2, AWM78, AWM.

114 Captain Herman Lamar Ray, USN, CO USS Badoeng Strait, to CNO, "Action Report 19 November through 29 November 1952," January 4, 1953, 2a; Ray to CNO, "Action Report 7 December through 17 December 1952, A16-13/30," January 20, 1953, 3; Ray to CNO, "Action Report 11 January 1953 through 21 January 1953, A16-13/30," February 20, 1953, 5, 11: all in Aviation History Branch, NHHC.

115 Ray to CNO, "Action Report 26 December 1952 through 5 January 1953, A16-13/30," January 27, 1953, 26, Aviation History Branch, NHHC.

116 McCandless, interview, reel 17.

117 Clifford, "July 1952–April 1953," 1.

118 McCandless, interview, reel 17.

119 Vice Admiral Harold Martin, USN, COM7THFLT, to CNO, "Serial 0038, Report of Operations of U.S. Seventh Fleet, 28 March 1951 to 3 March 1951," February 11, 1952, 27, Box 38, 1946 RPT, NHHC.

120 CINCPACFLT, "Report No. 4," 5–40.

121 Scott-Moncrieff, "January–June 1951," pt. 3, sec. 6.

122 Clifford, "July 1952–April 1953," pt. 3, sec. 4.

123 Commander Ian H. McDonald, RAN, CO HMAS Tobruk, to FO2FE, "Report of Proceedings—HMAS Tobruk—Month of August, 1953," August 31, 1953, 343/2, AWM78, AWM.

124 Appendix B to Reed to CANCOMDESFE, "Report of Proceedings, September 1953," 2; Frewer, "Report of Hunter/Killer Exercise," October 28, 1953, and Captain William M. Landymore, RCN, CANCOMDESFE, to Naval Secretary, "Report of Hunter Killer Exercise," October 1, 1953: both in File 4903-4, Pt. 4, vol. 34414, RG24-D-1-c, LAC.

125 CINCPACFLT, "Report No. 4," 5–39; Landymore to Naval Secretary, "Report of Hunter Killer Exercise," October 1, 1953, 2.

126 Lieutenant Commander A. W. Savage, RAN, CO HMAS Murchison, to FO2FE, "Report on A/S Exercises Carried Out in Sagami Wan off Yokosuka on 16th, 17th, and 18th December, 1953," December 22, 1953, 3, 4283/112/32, MP926/1, NAA.

127 CINCPACFLT, "Report No. 6," 5–163.

128 FO2FE/21176/1, March 31, 1951, enclosure to Andrewes, "July–December 1950," 1.

129 CTF 95, "200004Z," June 20, 1951, Folder 7, Box 6, Dyer Papers, LOC.

130 Captain Hugh W. S. Browning, RN, Naval Advisor, Tokyo, to CINCFE, "NA 41/611/51, Twelfth Report of Proceedings," July 1, 1951, 3, ADM 116/6227, TNA.

131 Enclosure 1 to Miller to CNO, "Serial 050, Action Report; Period 8 April 1951–11 May 1951, CVL29, A16-13," June 12, 1951, I–1, I–5, NHHC.

132 Clifford, "July 1952–April 1953," 1.

133 Ignatius J. Galantin, *Submarine Admiral: From Battlewagons to Ballistic Missiles* (Urbana: University of Illinois Press, 1995), 175–176.

134 Loomis to CNO, November 13, 1952, 11.

135 Marks to Flag Officer Commanding, HMA Fleet, "HMAS Bataan—Report of Proceedings—May 1951," June 1, 1951, 1, 58/2, AWM78, AWM.

136 Enclosure 1 to Miller to CNO, June 12, 1951, I–5.

137 Johnson to CNO, March 17, 1952, 16.

138 Captain William A. Schoech, USN, CO USS Sicily, to CNO, "Serial 075, Action Report—13 June 1951 through 16 September 1951, CVE118/A9," March 28, 1952, 19, NHHC.

139 Commander Edward T. G. Madgwick, RCN, Director of Manning and Personnel Statistics, "Minute," May 22, 1952, File 1926-102/11 Pt. 2, vol. 8204, RG24-D-1-c, LAC.

140 Harold M. Martin, *The Naval Career of Harold M. Martin*, Tennessee Regional Oral History Collection, part 1, no. 6 (Glen Rock, NJ: Microfilming Corporation of America, 1977), 155.

141 Vice Admiral Richard Innes Peek, RAN, S02797, interview by Colonel David Chinn, August 15, 2002, 55:00, S02797, Oral History Collection, AWM.

142 Jocelyn Stuart Cambridge Salter, interview by Conrad Wood, June 5, 1986, reel 3, Sound Archive, Catalogue 9304, IWM.

143 Enclosure 1 to Miller to CNO, June 12, 1951, VI-1-VI–2.

144 CINCPACFLT, "Report No. 3," 11–35.

145 Plomer, "Korea War Report, Part One," 45.

146 Scott-Moncrieff, "July 1951–June 1952," pt. 3, sec. 2.

147 Clifford, "July 1952–April 1953," pt. 3, sec. 2.

148 John Shoebridge, interview by Nick Haslam, reel 8, Sound Archive, Catalogue 31408, IWM.

CONCLUSION: DEEP AND WIDE NAVAL LINKS

1 Charles F. Brower, *Defeating Japan: The Joint Chiefs of Staff and Strategy in the Pacific War, 1943–1945* (New York: Palgrave Macmillan, 2012).

2 Document 102, Winston Churchill to Ernest Bevin, "FO 800/512," November 13, 1945, 316–318, chap. 3, vol. 3, series 1, *Documents on British Policy Overseas.*

3 Melvyn Leffler, *A Preponderance of Power: National Security, the Truman Administration, and the Cold War* (Stanford, CA: Stanford University Press, 1992).

4 Rear Admiral Arleigh Burke, USN, "Talk to Op-30," Personal Files, Burke Papers, NHHC.

5 Reminiscences of Vice Admiral Herbert D. Riley, USN, interview by John T. Mason Jr., 2004, 295–297, USNI.

6 Admiral Richard S. Edwards, USN, Vice Chief of Naval Operations to Fleet Admiral William D. Leahy, USN, Chief of Staff to the President, January 7, 1946, Folder 10, "Canada—1946," Box 2, Leahy Papers, NHHC.

7 Niall Barr, *Yanks and Limeys: Alliance Warfare in the Second World War* (London: Jonathan Cape, 2015).

8 "Monthly Intelligence Report No. 16," April 1 1947, 51, Box 6, Entry UD-09020, RG 38, NACP.

BIBLIOGRAPHY

ARCHIVAL SOURCES (AUSTRALIA)
Australian War Memorial, Canberra
  AWM78, Reports of Proceedings, HMA Ships and Establishments
  AWM123, Special Collection II Defence Committee Records
  AWM124, Naval Historical Collection
National Archives of Australia, Canberra
  A5799, Defence Committee agenda, annual single number series
  A5954, Shedden Collection, two-number series
National Archives of Australia, Melbourne
  MP926/1, Confidential and restricted correspondence files, multiple number
    series (101 series)
  MP981/1, Correspondence files, multiple number series (201 series)
  MP1049/5, Correspondence files (general)
  MP1049/6, Correspondence files (general)
National Library of Australia, Canberra
  Trove Newspaper database
Sea Power Centre—Australia, Canberra
  Library
  Record Group 11

ARCHIVAL SOURCES (CANADA)
Directorate of History and Heritage, Ottawa
  79/246, Naval Policy Coordinating Committee Fonds
  81/520, Royal Canadian Navy Historical Section Fonds
  PRO Documents
Library and Archives Canada, Ottawa
  MG26-J4, William Lyon Mackenzie King Papers
  RG24-B-1, Joint Staff and Chiefs of Staff Committee Textual Records
  RG24-D-1-c, Royal Canadian Navy Third Central Registry
  RG24-D-10, Captain (D) Halifax Textual Records
  RG24-D-13, Senior Canadian Naval Liaison Officer London Textual Records
  RG24-D-22, Royal Canadian Navy Ships' Files
  RG24-E-1-b, Royal Canadian Air Force Second Central Registry

ARCHIVAL SOURCES (UNITED KINGDOM)
Imperial War Museum
  Papers of Admiral Sir William Andrewes
  Papers of Thomas Keppel Edge-Partington, Documents.16709

Private Papers of Commander W. H. N. Martin, Documents.7695
Private Papers of Captain Vere Alison Wight-Boycott, Documents.6854
National Archives of the U.K., London
    ADM 1, Correspondence and Papers
    ADM 116, Record Office: Cases
    ADM 199, War History Cases and Papers, Second World War
    ADM 205, Office of the First Sea Lord, later First Sea Lord and Chief of the
        Naval Staff
    AIR 20, Papers accumulated by the Air Historical Branch
    CAB 21, Cabinet Office Registered Files
    CAB 79, Chiefs of Staff Committee: Minutes
    CAB 80, Chiefs of Staff Committee: Memoranda
    CAB 105, War Cabinet: Telegrams
    CAB 122, British Joint Staff Mission: Washington Office Records
    CAB 138, British Joint Staff Mission: Minutes and Memoranda
    DEFE 4, Chiefs of Staff Committee: Minutes
    DEFE 5, Chiefs of Staff Committee: Memoranda
    DEFE 6, Reports of the Joint Planning Staff
    DO 35, Dominions Office: Original Correspondence
    PREM 8, Prime Minister's Office: Correspondence and Papers
National Maritime Museum, London, Caird Library, Manuscripts Section
    Bruce Fraser Papers, MSS/83/158

ARCHIVAL SOURCES (UNITED STATES)
Dwight David Eisenhower Presidential Library, Abilene, Kansas
    A. Dayton Clark Papers
J. Y. Joyner Library, Special Collections Department, East Carolina University,
    Greenville, North Carolina
    Jules James Papers (#233)
Hoover Institution Archives, Stanford, California
    Robert F. Hickey Papers
    Stephen Jurika Jr. Papers
    Charles Julian Wheeler Papers
Dudley Knox Library, Naval Postgraduate School, Monterey, California
    Joseph Worthington biography of Admiral Royal E. Ingersoll
Library of Congress, Manuscript Division, Washington, D.C.
    George C. Dyer Papers
    William D. Leahy Papers
    Lynde Dupuy McCormick Papers
    John H. Towers Papers
National Archives at College Park, College Park, Maryland
    Record Group 38, Records of the Office of the Chief of Naval Operations

Record Group 80, General Records of the Department of the Navy
Record Group 165, Records of the War Department General and Special Staffs
Record Group 218, Records of the U.S. Joint Chiefs of Staff
Record Group 313, Records of Naval Operating Forces
Record Group 319, Records of the Army Staff
Naval Historical Collection, U.S. Naval War College, Newport, Rhode Island
    MS Collection 37, Buell, Thomas/Whitehill, Walt
    Record Group 27, General Subjects
Naval History and Heritage Command, Washington, D.C.
    Archives Branch
        Records of the Immediate Office of the Chief of Naval Operations
        Records of the Strategic Plans Division
        Papers of William D. Leahy
        Papers of Admiral Arleigh Burke
        Papers of Arthur W. Radford
        Post January 1946 Command File
        Post January 1946 Reports File
        Top Secret Office Control Files, 1951
    Aviation History Branch
        Korean War Action Reports
        Telephone Directories
        Naval Aviation News
Nimitz Library, Microform Room, United States Naval Academy, Annapolis,
    Maryland
    U.S. Naval Administration in World War II
Patriots Point Naval & Maritime Museum, Charleston, South Carolina
    James Flatley Papers
Harry S. Truman Presidential Library, Independence, Missouri
    Clark M. Clifford Papers

ORAL HISTORIES
Military History Oral History Collection, Special Collections, University of Victoria
    Library, British Columbia
    John Alexander Charles, SC104_CJA_206 and SC066_CJA_256
    James C. Hibbard, SC104_HJC_208
    Richard Hugh Leir, SC-66_LRH_262
    Robert Waught Murdoch, SC104_MRW_197
    Michael Grote Stirling, SC104_SMG_189 and SC066_SMG-265
    Robert P. Welland, SC066_WRP_268
Naval Institute Library, Annapolis, Maryland
    George C. Dyer
    Stephen Jurika Jr.

Jerome H. King Jr.
Robert W. McNitt
Gerald E. Miller
Herbert D. Riley
Elliot B. Strauss
Arthur D. Struble
John S. Thatch
Charles Wellborn Jr.
Naval Institute Oral Histories, Navy Department Library, Naval History and
    Heritage Command, Washington, D.C.
Charles Adair
Roy S. Benson
Truman J. Hedding
Donald J. MacDonald
Thomas Howard Morton
Oral History & Folklore Branch, National Library of Australia, Canberra
John Collins, 728011
Alan McNicoll, 2131438
Oral History Archives, Rare Book & Manuscript Library, Columbia University,
    New York
Alan Goodrich Kirk
Harry W. Hill
Eugene W. Wilson
Oral History Collection, Australian War Memorial, Canberra
Richard Innes Peek, S02797
Sound Archive, Imperial War Museum, London
    Thomas John George Adams, Catalogue 5206
    Edward Ashmore, Catalogue 25203
    Patrick Uniacke Bayly, Catalogue 12590
    John Fitzroy Duyland Bush, Catalogue 28352
    Leonard Alfred Dunn, Catalogue 20473
    John Fay, Catalogue 34023
    Sid Gandey, Catalogue 33301
    Frank Edward Goldsworthy, Catalogue 11245
    Geoffrey David Habesch, Catalogue 10304
    Alan Leahy, Catalogue 32843
    Raymond Derek Lygo, Catalogue 28776
    Robert McCandless, Catalogue 27344
    Paul Millett, Catalogue 17572
    Daniel Patrick Norman, Catalogue 14796
    Edmund Nicholas Poland, Catalogue 11951
    Jocelyn Stuart Cambridge Salter, Catalogue 9304

John Shoebridge, Catalogue 31408
William Russell Smith, Catalogue 11618
Ken Taylor, Catalogue 26562
Rupert Clive Wilkinson, Catalogue 28936
David Wright, Catalogue 28498
Special Collections & Archives Department, Nimitz Library, United States Naval
    Academy, Annapolis, Maryland
Arthur Ben Scott Custer
James Fife
Charles J. Wheeler

NEWSPAPERS
Age (Melbourne)
Atlanta Constitution
Canberra Times
Chicago Daily Tribune
Daily Boston Globe
Daily Mercury (Mackay, Queensland)
Herald (Melbourne)
Los Angeles Times
New York Times
Sydney Morning Herald
West Australian (Perth)
Washington Post

PUBLISHED PRIMARY SOURCES
Burnett, Alan, Thomas-Durell Young, and Christine Wilson, eds. *The ANZUS Docu-
ments*. Canberra: Australian National University, 1991.
Canada. *House of Commons Debates*.
Canada Department of External Affairs. *Documents on Canadian External Relations*.
Claussen, Martin P., ed. *State-War-Navy Coordinating Committee Policy Files, 1944–
1947*. Wilmington, DE: Scholarly Resources, 1977.
Eisenhower, Dwight David. *The Papers of Dwight David Eisenhower*. Edited by Louis
Galambos. Baltimore, MD: Johns Hopkins University Press, 1978.
Fold 3.com. World War II War Diaries.
———. Navy Cruise Books, 1918–2009.
Marshall, George Catlett. *The Papers of George Catlett Marshall*. Edited by Larry
Bland and Mark Stoler. Baltimore, MD: Johns Hopkins University Press,
2013.
Martin, Harold M. *The Naval Career of Harold M. Martin*. Tennessee Regional Oral
History Collection. Part 1, no. 6. Glen Rock, NJ: Microfilming Corporation of
America, 1977.

Naval Historical Center. *The Records of the Strategic Plans Division: Office of the Chief of Naval Operations and Predecessor Organizations.* Wilmington, DE: Scholarly Resources, 1974.

Simpson, Michael, ed. *Anglo-American Naval Relations, 1919–1939.* Publications of the Navy Records Society 155. Burlington, VT: Ashgate, 2010.

———— ed. *The Somerville Papers.* Publications of the Navy Records Society 134. Aldershot, U.K.: Navy Records Society, 1995.

U.K. Foreign and Commonwealth Office. *Documents on British Policy Overseas.*

U.S. Department of State. *Department of State Bulletin.*

————. *Foreign Relations of the United States.*

————. *Foreign Service List.*

PUBLISHED WORKS

Abbazia, Patrick. *Mr. Roosevelt's Navy: The Private War of the U.S. Atlantic Fleet, 1939–1942.* Annapolis, MD: Naval Institute Press, 1975.

Andrew, Christopher. "The Growth of the Australian Intelligence Community and the Anglo-American Connection." *Intelligence and National Security* 4, no. 2 (1989): 213–256.

Andrew, Christopher, and Vasili Mitrokhin. *The Sword and the Shield: The Mitrokhin Archive and the Secret History of the KGB.* New York: Basic Books, 1999.

Australian Naval Aviation Museum. *Flying Stations: A Story of Australian Naval Aviation.* Sydney: Allen & Unwin, 1998.

Ballantyne, Ian. *Warships of the Royal Navy: Warspite.* Annapolis, MD: Naval Institute Press, 2001.

Barclay, Glen. *Friends in High Places: Australian-American Diplomatic Relations since 1945.* New York: Oxford University Press, 1985.

Barker, Elisabeth. *The British between the Superpowers, 1945–50.* Toronto: University of Toronto Press, 1983.

Barlow, Jeffrey. *From Hot War to Cold: The U.S. Navy and National Security Affairs, 1945–1955.* Stanford, CA: Stanford University Press, 2009.

————. *Revolt of the Admirals: The Fight for Naval Aviation, 1945–1950.* Washington, D.C.: Naval Historical Center, 1994.

————. "The U.S. Navy's Air Interdiction Effort during the Korean War." In *Coalition Air Warfare in the Korean War, 1950–1953,* edited by Jacob Neufeld and George M. Watson, 135–141. Washington, D.C.: U.S. Air Force History and Museums Program, 2005.

Barr, Niall. *Eisenhower's Armies: The American-British Alliance during World War II.* New York: Pegasus Books, 2015.

————. *Yanks and Limeys: Alliance Warfare in the Second World War.* London: Jonathan Cape, 2015.

Bartlett, Merrill, and Robert Love. "Anglo-American Naval Diplomacy and the British Pacific Fleet, 1942–1945." *American Neptune* 42, no. 3 (July 1982): 203–216.

Bath, Alan Harris. *Tracking the Axis Enemy: The Triumph of Anglo-American Naval Intelligence*. Lawrence: University Press of Kansas, 1998.

Baylis, John. *Anglo-Americans Relations since 1939: The Enduring Alliance*. Manchester, U.K.: Manchester University Press, 1997.

Bell, Christopher. "Air Power and the Battle of the Atlantic: Very Long Range Aircraft and the Delay in the Atlantic 'Air Gap.'" *Journal of Military History* 79, no. 3 (July 2015): 691–719.

Best, Richard. "*Co-operation with Like-Minded Peoples*," *British Influences on American Security Policy, 1945–1949*. New York: Greenwood Press, 1986.

Blainey, Geoffrey. *A Shorter History of Australia*. Sydney, Australia: Vintage Books, 2009.

Blair, Clay. *Hitler's U-Boat War: The Hunters, 1939–1942*. New York: Random House, 1996.

Bland, Douglas, ed. *Canada's National Defence*. Vol. 1, *Defence Policy*. Kingston, ON: School of Policy Studies, Queen's University, 1997.

Blazich, Frank. "Neptune's Oracle: Admiral Harry E. Yarnell's Wartime Planning, 1918–20 and 1943–44." *Naval War College Review* 73, no. 1 (2020): 107–134.

Boose, Donald, and James Matray, eds. *The Ashgate Research Companion to the Korean War*. Farnham, U.K.: Ashgate, 2014.

Bothwell, Robert. "Review of The Reagan Reversal." *International Journal* 53, no. 2 (Spring 1998): 363–364.

Bridge, Carl. "Allies of a Kind: Three Wartime Australian Ministers to the United States, 1940–46." In *Australia Goes to Washington: 75 Years of Australian Representation in the United States, 1940–2015*, edited by David Lowe, David Lee, and Carl Bridge, 23–37. Acton, ACT: Australian National University Press, 2016.

Brower, Charles F. *Defeating Japan: The Joint Chiefs of Staff and Strategy in the Pacific War, 1943–1945*. New York: Palgrave Macmillan, 2012.

Brune, Lester, ed. *The Korean War: Handbook of the Literature and Research*. Westport, CT: Greenwood Press, 1996.

Bullock, Alan. *Ernest Bevin: Foreign Secretary, 1945–1951*. New York: W. W. Norton, 1983.

Burk, Kathleen. *Old World, New World: Great Britain and America from the Beginning*. New York: Atlantic Monthly Press, 2008.

Burrell, Sir Henry. *Mermaids Do Exist: The Autobiography of Vice-Admiral Sir Henry Burrell, RAN*. Melbourne: Macmillan, 1986.

Cagle, Malcolm. *The Sea War in Korea*. Annapolis, MD: Naval Institute Press, 1957.

Cain, Frank. "Venona in Australia and Its Long-Term Ramifications." *Journal of Contemporary History* 35, no. 2 (April 2002): 231–248.

Campbell, Isabel. "A Brave New World, 1945–1960." In *The Naval Service of Canada, 1910–2010: The Centennial Story*, 123–137. Toronto: Dundurn Press, 2009.

Canney, Donald. *Africa Squadron: The U.S. Navy and the Slave Trade, 1842–1861*. Washington, D.C.: Potomac Books, 2006.

Chambers, John Whiteclay II, ed. *The Oxford Companion to American Military History*. New York: Oxford University Press, 1999.

Chandler, David, and Ian Beckett, eds. *The Oxford History of the British Army*. Oxford, U.K.: Oxford University Press, 1994.

Chisolm, Donald. *Waiting for Dead Men's Shoes: Origins and Development of the U.S. Navy's Officer Personnel System, 1793–1941*. Stanford, CA: Stanford University Press, 2001.

Churchill, Winston S., ed. *Never Give In! Winston Churchill's Speeches*. New York: Bloomsbury, 2013.

Chuter, David. *Humanity's Soldier: France and International Security, 1919–2001*. Providence, RI: Berghahn Books, 1996.

Clarke, Peter. *The Last Thousand Days of the British Empire: Churchill, Roosevelt, and the Birth of Pax Americana*. New York: Bloomsbury Press, 2008.

Clayton, Anthony. "'Deceptive Might': Imperial Defence and Security, 1900–1968." In *Oxford History of the British Empire*. Vol. 4, *The Twentieth Century*, edited by Judith Brown, 280–305. New York: Oxford University Press, 1999.

Coles, Michael. "Ernest King and the British Pacific Fleet: The Conference at Quebec, 1944 ('Octagon')." *Journal of Military History* 65, no. 1 (January 2001): 105–129.

Collins, John. *As Luck Would Have It: The Reminiscences of an Australian Sailor*. Sydney: Angus and Robertson, 1965.

Cooper, Alastair. "The Development of an Independent Navy for Australia: Correspondence between the First Naval Member and the First Sea Lord, 1947–59." In *The Naval Miscellany*. Vol. 7, edited by Susan Rose, 511–670. London: George Allen & Unwin, 2008.

Cowman, Ian. *Dominion or Decline: Anglo-American Naval Relations in the Pacific, 1937–1941*. Oxford, U.K.: Berg, 1996.

Cox, Jeffrey. *Rising Sun, Falling Skies: The Disastrous Java Sea Campaign of World War II*. New York: Osprey, 2014.

Dallek, Robert. *Franklin D. Roosevelt and American Foreign Policy, 1932–1945*. New York: Oxford University Press, 1995.

Davis, Vincent. *Postwar Defense Policy and the U.S. Navy, 1943–1946*. Chapel Hill: University of North Carolina Press, 1962.

Dean, Peter. *MacArthur's Coalition: US and Australian Operations in the Southwest Pacific Area, 1942–1945*. Lawrence: University Press of Kansas, 2018.

Dobson, Alan. "Churchill's Fulton Speech and the Context of Shared Values in a World of Dangers." In *Churchill and the Anglo-American Special Relationship*, edited by Alan Dobson and Steve Marsh, 43–63. New York: Routledge, 2017.

Dobson, Alan, and Steve Marsh. "Churchill at the Summit: SACLANT and the Tone of Anglo-American Relations in January 1952." *International History Review* 32, no. 2 (June 2010): 211–228.

Donohue, Hector. *From Empire Defence to the Long Haul: Post-War Defence Policy and Its Impact on Naval Force Structure Planning, 1945–1955.* Papers in Australian Maritime Affairs 1. Canberra: Sea Power Centre-Australia, 1996.

Dorwart, Jeffrey. *The Office of Naval Intelligence: The Birth of America's First Intelligence Agency, 1865–1918.* Annapolis, MD: Naval Institute Press, 1979.

Douglas, W. A. B., Roger Sarty, and Michael Whitby. *A Blue Water Navy.* Vol. 2, part 2, of *The Official Operational History of the Royal Canadian Navy in the Second World War, 1943–1945.* St. Catharines, ON: Vanwell, 2007.

———. *No Higher Purpose.* Vol. 2, part 1, of *The Official Operational History of the Royal Canadian Navy in the Second World War, 1939–1943.* St. Catharines, ON: Vanwell, 2002.

Drea, Edward J. *History of the Unified Command Plan, 1946–2012.* Washington, D.C.: Joint History Office, Office of the Chairman of the Joint Chiefs of Staff, 2013.

Dudden, Arthur. *The American Pacific: From the Old China Trade to the Present.* New York: Oxford University Press, 1992.

Dull, Paul. *A Battle History of the Japanese Navy, 1941–1945.* Annapolis, MD: Naval Institute Press, 1978.

Dunbabin, J. P. D. *The Cold War: The Great Powers and Their Allies.* New York: Longman, 1994.

Dziuban, Stanley W. *Military Relations between the United States and Canada, 1939–1945.* Washington, D.C.: Center of Military History, 1959.

Eayrs, James. *In Defence of Canada: Peacemaking and Deterrence.* Toronto: University of Toronto Press, 1972.

Edgerton, David. *The Rise and Fall of the British Nation: A Twentieth-Century History.* London: Allen Lane, 2018.

———. *Warfare State: Britain, 1920–1970.* New York: Cambridge University Press, 2006.

Engel, Jeffrey. *Cold War at 30,000 Feet: The Anglo-American Fight for Aviation Supremacy.* Cambridge, MA: Harvard University Press, 2007.

Ewing, Steve. *Reaper Leader: The Life of Jimmy Flatley.* Annapolis, MD: Naval Institute Press, 2002.

"Excerpts from CNS: First Sea Lord Correspondence." *Journal of Australian Naval History* 6, no. 1 (March 2009): 119–124.

Farquharson-Roberts, Mike. *A History of the Royal Navy: World War I.* New York: Palgrave Macmillan, 2014.

———. *Royal Navy Officers from War to War, 1918–1939.* New York: Palgrave Macmillan, 2015.

Field, James. *History of United States Naval Operations, Korea.* Washington, D.C.: Naval Historical Center, 1962.

Fisher, Robert C. "'We'll Get Our Own': Canada and the Oil Shipping Crisis of 1942." *Northern Mariner* 3, no. 2 (April 1993): 33–39.

Forrestal, James. *Annual Report of the Secretary of the Navy.* Washington, D.C.: Government Printing Office, 1947.

Frame, Tom. *Pacific Partners: A History of Australian-American Naval Relations*. Sydney: Hodder & Stoughton, 1992.

Friedberg, Aaron. *In the Shadow of the Garrison State: America's Anti-Statism and Its Cold War Grand Strategy*. Princeton, NJ: Princeton University Press, 2000.

Friedman, Hal. *Creating an American Lake: United States Imperialism and Strategic Security in the Pacific Basin, 1945–1947*. Westport, CT: Greenwood Press, 2001.

Friedman, Norman. *U.S. Submarines since 1945: An Illustrated Design History*. Annapolis, MD: Naval Institute Press, 1994.

Frost, David. *Classified: A History of Secrecy in the United States Government*. Jefferson, NC: McFarland, 2017.

Frühling, Stephen. *A History of Australian Strategic Policy Since 1945*. Canberra, Australia: Defence Publishing Service, 2009.

Gaddis, John Lewis. *The Cold War: A New History*. New York: Penguin Press, 2005.

Galantin, Ignatius J. *Submarine Admiral: From Battlewagons to Ballistic Missiles*. Urbana: University of Illinois Press, 1995.

Gill, G. Hermon. *Royal Australian Navy, 1942–1945*. Canberra: Australian War Memorial, 1968.

Goodspeed, Donald James. *A History of the Defence Research Board of Canada*. Ottawa: Queen's Printer, 1958.

Granatstein, Jack. "The American Influence on the Canadian Military, 1939–1963." *Canadian Military History* 2, no. 1 (1993): 63–73.

Grossnick, Roy. *Dictionary of American Naval Aviation Squadrons*. Vol. 1. Washington, D.C.: Naval History and Heritage Command, 1995.

Grove, Eric, ed. *The Battle and the Breeze: The Naval Reminiscences of Admiral of the Fleet Sir Edward Ashmore*. Gloucestershire, U.K.: Sutton, 1997.

———— ed. *The Defeat of the Enemy Attack on Shipping, 1939–1945*. Vol. 137. Aldershot, U.K.: Ashgate, 1957.

———. *From Vanguard to Trident: British Naval Policy Since World War II*. Annapolis, MD: Naval Institute Press, 1987.

———. "UN Armed Forces and the Military Staff Committee: A Look Back." *International Security* 17, no. 4 (Spring 1993): 172–182.

Grove, Eric and Geoffrey Till. "Anglo-American Maritime Strategy in the Era of Massive Retaliation, 1945–60." In *Maritime Strategy and the Balance of Power: Britain and America in the Twentieth Century*, edited by John Hattendorf and Robert Jordan, 271–303. New York: St. Martin's Press, 1989.

Hallion, Richard P. *The Naval Air War in Korea*. Tuscaloosa: University of Alabama Press, 2011.

Hamilton, Nigel. *Monty: Final Years of the Field-Marshal, 1944–1976*. New York: McGraw-Hill, 1986.

Harper, Norman. *A Great and Powerful Friend: A Study of Australian-American Relations between 1900–1975*. New York: University of Queensland Press, 1986.

Hathaway, Robert. *Ambiguous Partnership: Britain and America, 1944–1947.* New York: Columbia University Press, 1981.

Hattendorf, John B. "International Naval Cooperation and Admiral Richard G. Colbert: The Intertwining of a Career with an Idea." In *Naval History and Maritime Strategy: Collected Essays,* 161–186. Malabar, FL: Krieger, 2000.

———. "Note: A Special Relationship: The Royal Navy and the U.S. Naval War College." *Mariner's Mirror* 72, no. 2 (1986): 200–201.

Hattendorf, John B., Mitchell Simpson, and John R. Wadleigh. *Sailors and Scholars: The Centennial History of the U.S. Naval War College.* Newport, RI: Naval War College Press, 1984.

Haydon, Peter. "A Tale of Two Navies: Building the Canada–United States Cold War Naval Relationship." *Northern Mariner* 24, nos. 3 & 4 (2014): 176–194.

Heinrichs, Waldo. *Threshold of War: Franklin D. Roosevelt and American Entry into World War II.* New York: Oxford University Press, 1988.

Hewlett, Richard G., and Oscar Anderson. *The New World, 1939–1946.* Vol. 1, *A History of the United States Atomic Energy Commission.* University Park: Pennsylvania State University Press, 1962.

Hill, J. R., ed. *The Oxford Illustrated History of the Royal Navy.* New York: Oxford University Press, 1995.

History of the Joint Chiefs of Staff: The Joint Chiefs of Staff and the First Indochina War, 1947–1954. Washington, D.C.: Office of Joint History, Office of the Chairman of the Joint Chiefs of Staff, 2004.

Hobbs, David. *The British Pacific Fleet: The Royal Navy's Most Powerful Strike Force.* Annapolis, MD: Naval Institute Press, 2011.

———. "Inter-Allied Communication during the Korean War." In *Naval Networks: The Dominance of Communications in Maritime Operations,* edited by David Stevens, 169–185. Canberra: Sea Power Centre-Australia, 2012.

Holler, Roger. "The Evolution of the Sonobuoy from World War II to the Cold War." *U.S. Navy Journal of Underwater Acoustics* 62, no. 2 (January 2014): 322–346.

Holler, Roger, Arthur Horbach, and James McEachern. *The Ears of Air ASW: A History of U.S. Navy Sonobuoys.* Warminster, PA: Navmar Applied Sciences Corporation, 2008.

Hoopes, Townsend, and Douglas Brinkley. *Driven Patriot: The Life and Times of James Forrestal.* Annapolis, MD: Naval Institute Press, 1992.

Horn, Bernd, and Stephen Harris, eds. *Warrior Chiefs: Perspectives on Senior Canadian Military Leaders.* Toronto: Dundurn Press, 2001.

Horner, David. *Defense Supremo: Sir Frederick Shedden and the Making of Australian Defense Policy.* Sydney: Allen & Unwin, 2000.

———. *The Spy Catchers: The Official History of ASIO, 1949–1963.* Melbourne: Allen & Unwin, 2014.

Humble, Richard. *Fraser of North Cape: The Life of Admiral of the Fleet Lord Fraser, 1888–1981*. London: Routledge & Kegan Paul, 1983.

Isenberg, Michael. *Shield of the Republic: The United States Navy in an Era of Cold War and Violent Peace*. Vol. 1, *1945–1962*. New York: St. Martin's Press, 1993.

Jackson, Bill, and Dwin Bramall. *The Chiefs: The Story of the United Kingdom Chiefs of Staff*. London: Brassey's, 1992.

Jeffery, Keith. *MI6: The History of the Secret Intelligence Service, 1909–1949*. London: Bloomsbury, 2010.

Jeffrey-Jones, Rhodri. *In Spies We Trust: The Story of Western Intelligence*. Oxford, U.K.: Oxford University Press, 2013.

Jockel, Joseph. *No Boundaries Upstairs: Canada, the United States, and the Origins of North American Air Defence, 1945–1958*. Vancouver: University of British Columbia Press, 1987.

Johnsen, William. *The Origins of the Grand Alliance: Anglo-American Military Collaboration from the Panay Incident to Pearl Harbor*. Lexington: University Press of Kentucky, 2016.

Jones, Jerry. *U.S. Battleship Operations in World War I*. Annapolis, MD: Naval Institute Press, 1998.

Jones, Mark C. "Experiment at Dundee: The Royal Navy's 9th Submarine Flotilla and Multinational Naval Cooperation during World War II." *Journal of Military History* 72, no. 4 (October 2008): 1179–1212.

———. "Friend and Advisor to the Allied Navies: The Royal Navy's Principal Liaison Officer and Multinational Naval Operations in World War II." *Journal of Military History* 77, no. 3 (July 2013): 991–1023.

———. "Not Just Along for the Ride: The Role of Royal Navy Liaison Personnel in Multinational Naval Operations during World War II." *Journal of Military History* 76, no. 1 (January 2012): 127–158.

Judt, Tony. *Postwar: A History of Europe since 1945*. New York: Penguin Press, 2005.

Jurika, Stephen, ed. *From Pearl Harbor to Vietnam: The Memoirs of Admiral Arthur W. Radford*. Stanford, CA: Hoover Institution Press, 1980.

Keenleyside, H. L. "The Canada-United States Permanent Joint Board on Defence, 1940–1945." *International Journal: Canada's Journal of Global Policy Analysis* 16, no. 1 (1961): 50–77.

Kennedy, Greg. *Anglo-American Strategic Relations and the Far East, 1933–1939: Imperial Crossroads*. London: Frank Cass, 2002.

Kennedy, Paul. *Engineers of Victory: The Problem Solvers Who Turned the Tide in the Second World War*. New York: Random House, 2013.

———. "History from the Middle: The Case of the Second World War." *Journal of Military History* 74, no. 1 (January 2010): 35–51.

Key, David. *Admiral Jerauld Wright: Warrior among Diplomats*. Manhattan, KS: Sunflower University Press, 2001.

Landon, L. H. "Liaison with the French Army." *Army Quarterly and Defense Journal* 99 (October 1969): 76–84.

Lansdown, John. *With the Carriers in Korea: The Fleet Air Arm Story, 1950–1953.* Cheshire, U.K.: Crecy, 1997.

Leffler, Melvyn. *A Preponderance of Power: National Security, the Truman Administration, and the Cold War.* Stanford, CA: Stanford University Press, 1992.

Leutze, James. *Bargaining for Supremacy: Anglo-American Naval Collaboration, 1937–1941.* Chapel Hill: University of North Carolina Press, 1977.

Lewis, Julian. *Changing Direction: British Military Planning for Post-War Strategic Defense, 1942–1947.* London: Sherwood Press, 1987.

Llewellyn-Jones, Malcolm. *The Royal Navy and Anti-Submarine Warfare, 1917–1949.* New York: Routledge, 2006.

———. "The Pursuit of Realism: British Anti-Submarine Tactics and Training to Counter the Fast Submarine, 1944–52." In *The Face of Naval Battle: The Human Experience of Modern War at Sea,* edited by John Reeve and David Stevens, 219–239. Crows Nest, NSW: Allen & Unwin, 2003.

Lohl, John K. "Out-Spoken—Arthur William Radford (1896–1973)." In *Nineteen-Gun Salute: Case Studies of Operational, Strategic, and Diplomatic Naval Leadership during the 20th and Early 21st Centuries,* edited by John B. Hattendorf and Bruce A. Elleman, 107–116. Newport, RI: Naval War College Press, 2010.

Lomas, Daniel W. B. *Intelligence, Security and the Attlee Governments, 1945–51: An Uneasy Relationship?* Manchester, U.K.: Manchester University Press, 2017.

Love, Robert W. Jr. *History of the U.S. Navy.* Vol. 2, *1942–1991.* Harrisburg, PA: Stackpole Books, 1992.

Lowe, David. *Menzies and the Great World Struggle: Australia's Cold War, 1948–1954.* Sydney: University of New South Wales Press, 1999.

Lund, Wilfred G. D. "Vice-Admiral Harold Grant: Father of the Post-War Royal Canadian Navy," In *Warrior Chiefs: Perspectives on Senior Canadian Military Leaders,* edited by Bernd Horn and Stephen Harris, 193–218. Toronto: Dundurn Press, 2001.

———. "Vice-Admiral Howard Emmerson Reid and Vice Admiral Harold Taylor Wood Grant: Forging the New 'Canadian' Navy." In *The Admirals: Canada's Senior Naval Leadership in the Twentieth Century,* edited by Michael Whitby, Richard H. Gimblett, and Peter Haydon, 157–186. Toronto: Dundurn Press, 2006.

Macintyre, Stuart. *Australia's Boldest Experiment: War and Reconstruction in the 1940s.* Sydney: Newsouth, 2015.

———. *A Concise History of Australia.* Cambridge: Cambridge University Press, 2004.

Macri, Franco David. *Clash of Empires in South China: The Allied Nations' Proxy War with Japan, 1935–1941.* Lawrence: University Press of Kansas, 2012.

Maiolo, Joseph. "Naval Armaments Competition between the Two World Wars." In *Arms Races in International Politics: From the Nineteenth to the Twenty-First Cen-*

tury, edited by Thomas Mahnken, Joseph Maiolo, and David Stevenson, 93–114. Oxford, U.K.: Oxford University Press, 2016.

Maloney, Sean. *Learning to Love the Bomb: Canada's Nuclear Weapons during the Cold War*. Washington, D.C.: Potomac Books, 2007.

———. *Securing Command of the Sea: NATO Naval Planning, 1948–1954*. Annapolis, MD: Naval Institute Press, 1995.

Marder, Arthur, Mark Jacobsen, and John Horsfield. *Old Friends, New Enemies: The Royal Navy and the Imperial Japanese Navy*. Vol. 2, *The Pacific War, 1942–1945*. New York: Clarendon Press, 1990.

Marolda, Edward, ed. *The U.S. Navy in the Korean War*. Annapolis, MD: Naval Institute Press, 2007.

Marsh, Steve. "Churchill, SACLANT, and the Politics of Opposition." *Contemporary British History* 27, no. 4 (2013): 445–465.

Mason, Russell. "Sonobuoys—Part I: Historical Development Thru WWII." *IEEE Aerospace & Electronic Systems Society Newsletter*, September 1984.

———. "Sonobuoys—Part II: After WW II." *IEEE Aerospace & Electronic Systems Society Newsletter*, October 1984.

Matloff, Maurice, and Edwin M. Snell. *Strategic Planning for Coalition Warfare, 1941–1942*. Washington, D.C.: Center of Military History, 1999.

McCullough, David. *Truman*. New York: Simon & Schuster, 1992.

McGibbon, Ian, ed. *The Oxford Companion to New Zealand Military History*. Auckland, NZ: Oxford University Press, 2000.

McGuffie, Mitch. "A Rude Awakening." *U.S. Naval Institute Proceedings* 135, no. 1 (January 2009): 56–61.

McIntyre, W. David. *Background to the ANZUS Pact: Policy-Making, Strategy, and Diplomacy, 1945–55*. Christchurch, NZ: Canterbury University Press, 1995.

McKnight, David. "The Moscow-Canberra Cables: How Soviet Intelligence Obtained British Secrets through the Back Door." *Intelligence and National Security* 13, no. 2 (1998): 159–170.

McLean, Doug. "Muddling Through: Canadian Anti-Submarine Doctrine and Practice, 1942–1945." In *A Nation's Navy: In Quest of Canadian Naval Identity*, edited by Michael Hadley, Rob Huebert, and Fred Crickard, 173–189. Montreal: McGill-Queen's University Press, 1996.

Melandri, Pierre. "The Troubled Friendship: France and the United States, 1945–1989." In *No End to Alliance: The United States and Western Europe: Past, Present, and Future*, edited by Geir Lundestad, 112–133. New York: St. Martin's Press, 1998.

Middlemiss, Denford W., and Joel J. Sokolsky. *Canada's Defence: Decisions and Determinants*. Toronto: Harcourt Brace Jovanovich Canada, 1989.

Miller, Edward. *War Plan Orange: The U.S. Strategy to Defeat Japan, 1897–1945*. Annapolis, MD: Naval Institute Press, 1991.

Millett, Allan. *The Korean War*. Washington, D.C.: Potomac Books, 2007.

———. *The War for Korea, 1950–1951: They Came from the North*. Lawrence: University Press of Kansas, 2010.

Milner, Marc. *The Battle of the Atlantic*. New York: History Press, 2011.

———. *Canada's Navy: The First Century*. Toronto: University of Toronto Press, 1999.

———. "A Canadian Perspective on Canadian and American Naval Relations since 1945." In *Fifty Years of Canada–United States Defense Cooperation: The Road from Ogdensburg*, 145–174. Lewiston, NY: E. Mellen Press, 1992.

———. *North Atlantic Run: The Royal Canadian Navy and the Battle for the Convoys*. Annapolis, MD: Naval Institute Press, 1985.

Mitchell, B. R. *British Historical Statistics*. Cambridge: Cambridge University Press, 1988.

Montgomery, Bernard Law. *The Memoirs of Field-Marshal the Viscount Montgomery of Alamein, K.G.* London: Collins, 1958.

Morison, Samuel Eliot. *History of United States Naval Operations in World War II*. Vol. 10, *The Atlantic Battle Won, May 1943–May 1945*. Edison, NJ: Castle Books, 2001.

Moser, John. *Twisting the Lion's Tail: Anglophobia in the United States, 1921–48*. London: Macmillan Press, 1999.

Muehlbauer, Matthew, and David Ulbrich. *Ways of War: American Military History from the Colonial Era to the Twenty-First Century*. New York: Routledge, 2014.

Murfett, Malcolm H., ed. *The First Sea Lords: From Fisher to Mountbatten*. Westport, CT: Praeger, 1995.

———. *Fool-Proof Relations: The Search for Anglo-American Naval Cooperation during the Chamberlain Years, 1937–1940*. Singapore: Singapore University Press, 1984.

———. *In Jeopardy: The Royal Navy and British Far Eastern Defence Policy, 1945–1951*. Kuala Lumpur: Oxford University Press, 1995.

Nash, Peter. *The Development of Mobile Logistic Support in Anglo-American Naval Policy, 1900–1953*. Gainesville: University Press of Florida, 2009.

National Archives and Records Administration. *Federal Records of World War II*. Vol. 2, *Military Agencies*. Washington, D.C.: Government Printing Office, 1951.

Neiberg, Michael. *Potsdam: The End of World War II and the Remaking of Europe*. New York: Basic Books, 2015.

Nofi, Albert. *To Train the Fleet for War: The U.S. Navy Fleet Problems, 1923–1940*. Newport, RI: Naval War College Press, 2010.

O'Brien, Phillips Payson. *British and American Naval Power, Politics and Policy, 1900–1936*. Westport, CT: Praeger, 1998.

Orders, Paul. *Britain, Australia, New Zealand and the Challenge of the United States, 1939–46: A Study in International History*. New York: Palgrave Macmillan, 2003.

Orwell, George. *Animal Farm*. New York: Signet Classics, 1996.

Packard, Wyman. *A Century of U.S. Naval Intelligence.* Washington, D.C.: Office of Naval Intelligence and Naval History and Heritage Command, 1996.

Paget, Steven. *The Dynamics of Coalition Naval Warfare: The Special Relationship at Sea.* New York: Routledge, 2017.

Palmer, Michael. *Origins of the Maritime Strategy: The Development of American Naval Strategy, 1945–1955.* Annapolis, MD: Naval Institute Press, 1990.

Patterson, James. *Grand Expectations: The United States, 1945–1974.* New York: Oxford University Press, 1997.

Perlman, Susan McCall. "Contesting France: French Informants and American Intelligence in the Dawning Cold War." *Cold War History* 17, no. 1 (2017): 81–98.

Perras, Galen. *Franklin Roosevelt and the Origins of the Canadian-American Security Alliance, 1933–1945.* Westport, CT: Praeger, 1998.

Peterson, Michael. *Bourbon to Black Friday: The Allied Collaborative COMINT Effort against the Soviet Union, 1945–1948.* Fort Meade, MD: Center for Cryptologic History, National Security Agency, 1995.

Pettipas, Leo. *The Grumman Avenger in the Royal Canadian Navy.* Winnipeg: Canadian Naval Air Group, 1988.

Pfennigwerth, Ian. *The Royal Australian Navy and MacArthur.* Sydney: Rosenberg, 2009.

Pollock, Fred. "Roosevelt, the Ogdensburg Agreement, and the British Fleet: All Done with Mirrors." *Diplomatic History* 5, no. 3 (Summer 1981): 203–219.

Polmar, Norman. *Aircraft Carriers: A History of Carrier Aviation and Its Influence on World Events.* Vol. 2, *1946–2006.* Washington, D.C.: Potomac Books, 2008.

Poole, Walter. "From Conciliation to Containment: The Joint Chiefs of Staff and the Coming of the Cold War, 1945–1946." *Military Affairs* 42, no. 1 (February 1978): 12–16.

Pratt, Lawrence. "The Anglo-American Naval Conversations on the Far East of January 1938." *International Affairs* 44, no. 4 (October 1971): 745–763.

"Professional Notes: Collaboration with Other Navies." *U.S. Naval Institute Proceedings* 74, no. 1 (April 1948): 511.

Puleston, William D. "The Probable Effect on American National Defense of the United Nations and the Atomic Bomb." *U.S. Naval Institute Proceedings* 72, no. 8 (August 1946): 1017–1029.

"The Quarter's Polls." *Public Opinion Quarterly* 10, no. 2 (Summer 1946): 246–287.

Rearden, Steven. *Council of War: A History of the Joint Chiefs of Staff, 1942–1991.* Washington, D.C.: National Defense University Press, 2012.

Reese, Trevor. *Australia, New Zealand, and the United States: A Survey of International Relations, 1941–1968.* London: Oxford University Press, 1969.

Reid, Escott. *Radical Mandarin: The Memoirs of Escott Reid.* Toronto: University of Toronto Press, 1989.

Reynolds, Clark G.. "'Sara' in the East." *U.S. Naval Institute Proceedings* 87, no. 12 (December 1961): 75–83.

Reynolds, David. *The Creation of the Anglo-American Alliance, 1937–1941: A Study in Competitive Co-Operation*. Chapel Hill: University of North Carolina Press, 1982.

Reynolds, David, and David Dimbleby. *An Ocean Apart: The Relationship between Britain and America in the Twentieth Century*. New York: Random House, 1988.

Rhodes, Richard. *Dark Sun: The Making of the Hydrogen Bomb*. New York: Simon & Schuster, 1995.

Robb, Thomas, and Michael Seibold. "Spying on Friends: British Assessments of French Security, 1945–50." *International History Review* 36, no. 1 (2014): 112–141.

Robb-Webb, Jonathan. *The British Pacific Fleet: Experience and Legacy, 1944–50*. Burlington, VT: Ashgate, 2013.

Rose, Lisle. *Power at Sea: A Violent Peace, 1946–2006*. Columbia: University of Missouri Press, 2007.

Roskill, Stephen. *Naval Policy between the Wars*. Vol. 1, *The Period of Anglo-American Antagonism, 1919–1929*. Barnsley, U.K.: Seaforth, 2016.

———. *Naval Policy between the Wars*. Vol. 2, *The Period of Reluctant Rearmament, 1930–1939*. Barnsley, U.K.: Seaforth, 2016.

Ross, Stephen. *American War Plans, 1945–1950*. Portland, OR: Frank Cass, 1996.

Sarantakes, Nicholas. *Allies against the Rising Sun: The United States, the British Nations, and the Defeat of Imperial Japan*. Lawrence: University Press of Kansas, 2009.

Scott, William, and Stephen Withey. *The United States and the United Nations: The Public View, 1945–1955*. New York: Manhattan, 1958.

Sherry, Michael. *Preparing for the Next War: American Plans for Postwar Defense, 1941–1945*. New Haven, CT: Yale University Press, 1977.

Showalter, Dennis. "Global Yet Not Total: The U.S. War Effort and Its Consequences." In *A World at Total War: Global Conflict and the Politics of Destruction, 1937–1945*, edited by Roger Chickering, Stig Förster, and Bernd Greiner, 109–133. New York: Cambridge University Press, 2005.

Simpson, Michael. "Admiral William S. Sims, U.S. Navy and Admiral Sir Lewis Bayly, Royal Navy: An Unlikely Friendship and Anglo-American Cooperation, 1917–1919." *Naval War College Review* 41, no. 2 (Spring 1988): 66–80.

———. *A Life of Admiral of the Fleet Andrew Cunningham: A Twentieth Century Naval Leader*. New York: Routledge, 2004.

Smith, Kevin. *Conflict over Convoys: Anglo-American Logistics Diplomacy in the Second World War*. New York: Cambridge University Press, 1996.

Smith, Peter Charles. *Task Force 57: The British Pacific Fleet, 1944–1945*. London: Kimber, 1969.

Sokolsky, Joel J. *Seapower in the Nuclear Age: The United States Navy and NATO, 1949–80*. Annapolis, MD: Naval Institute Press, 1991.

Soward, Stuart. "Canadian Naval Aviation, 1915–69." In *The RCN in Retrospect, 1910–1968*, edited by James A. Boutilier, 271–285. Vancouver: University of British Columbia Press, 1982.

―――. *Hands to Flying Stations: A Recollective History of Canadian Naval Aviation*. Vol. 1, *1945–1954*. Victoria, BC: Neptune Developments, 1984.

Soybel, Phyllis L. *A Necessary Relationship: The Development of Anglo-American Cooperation in Naval Intelligence*. Westport, CT: Praeger, 2005.

Spector, Ronald. *Eagle against the Sun: The American War with Japan*. New York: Free Press, 1985.

Speller, Ian. "Defence or Deterrence? The Royal Navy and the Cold War, 1945–1955." In *Cold War Britain, 1945–1964: New Perspectives*, edited by Michael Hopkins, Michael Kandiah, and Gillian Staerck, 97–110. Basingstoke, U.K.: Palgrave Macmillan, 2003.

Stacey, C. P. *Canada and the Age of Conflict*. Vol. 2, *1921–1948, The Mackenzie King Era*. Toronto: University of Toronto Press, 1981.

Stein, Harold. *American Civil-Military Decisions*. Birmingham: University of Alabama Press, 1963.

Sterling, Christopher, ed. *Military Communications: From Ancient Times to the 21st Century*. Santa Barbara, CA: ABC Clio, 2008.

Stevens, David. *A Critical Vulnerability: The Impact of the Submarine Threat on Australia's Maritime Defence, 1915–1954*. Canberra: Sea Power Centre-Australia, 2005.

―――, ed. *The Royal Australian Navy*. New York: Oxford University Press, 2001.

―――. *The Royal Australian Navy in World War II*. Crows Nest, NSW: Allen & Unwin, 2005.

Stewart, J. "The Officers of the Royal Navy." *U.S. Naval Institute Proceedings* 85, no. 3 (March 1959): 48–55.

Still, William. *Crisis at Sea: The United States Navy in European Waters in World War I*. Gainesville: University Press of Florida, 2006.

―――. *Victory without Peace: The United States Navy in European Waters, 1919–1924*. Annapolis, MD: Naval Institute Press, 2018.

Stoler, Mark. *Allies and Adversaries: The Joint Chiefs of Staff, the Grand Alliance, and U.S. Strategy in World War II*. Chapel Hill: University of North Carolina Press, 2000.

―――. *Allies in War: Britain and America against the Axis Powers, 1940–1945*. London: Hodder Arnold, 2005.

―――. "FDR and the Origins of the National Security Establishment." In *FDR's World: War, Peace, Legacies*, edited by David Woolner, Warren Kimball, and David Reynolds, 63–90. New York: Palgrave Macmillan, 2008.

Strachan, Hew, ed. *The Oxford Illustrated History of the First World War*. New York: Oxford University Press, 2016.

Stueck, William. *The Korean War: An International History*. Princeton, NJ: Princeton University Press, 1997.

Sturtivant, Ray. *British Naval Aviation: The Fleet Air Arm, 1917–1990*. Annapolis, MD: Naval Institute Press, 1990.

Sumner, Ian. *The Royal Navy, 1939–45*. Oxford, U.K.: Osprey, 2001.

Supreme Commander for the Allied Powers. *Reports of General MacArthur, prepared by his General Staff*. Edited by Charles A. Willoughby. Vol. 1 supp., *MacArthur in Japan: The Occupation: Military Phase*. Washington, D.C.: Government Printing Office, 1966.

Swartz, Peter. *Sea Changes: Transforming U.S. Navy Deployment Strategy: 1775–2002*. Alexandria, VA: Center for Naval Analyses, 2002.

Symonds, Craig. *World War II at Sea: A Global History*. New York: Oxford University Press, 2018.

Thomas, Douglas S. "'In Cooperation Lies Success': The Early Years of the Maritime Warfare School, 1944–1964." In *People, Policy and Programmes: Proceedings of the 7th Maritime Command (MARCOM) Historical Conference (2005)*, edited by Rich Gimblett, 131–142. Ottawa: Canadian Naval Heritage Team, 2008.

Thompson, Roger. *The Pacific Basin since 1945: A History of the Foreign Relations of the Asian, Australasia, and American Rim States and the Pacific Islands*. London: Longman, 1994.

Thompson, Warren E. *Naval Aviation in the Korean War*. Barnsley, U.K.: Pen & Sword Aviation, 2012.

Thorne, Christopher G. *Allies of a Kind: The United States, Britain, and the War against Japan, 1941–1945*. New York: Oxford University Press, 1978.

Tolley, Kemp. *Yangtze Patrol: The U.S. Navy in China*. Annapolis, MD: Naval Institute Press, 1971.

Tracy, Nicholas. *A Two-Edged Sword: The Navy as an Instrument of Canadian Foreign Policy*. Montreal: McGill-Queen's University Press, 2012.

Trask, David. "The Entry of the USA into the War and Its Effects." In *The Oxford Illustrated History of the First World War*, edited by Hew Strachan, 240–241. New York: Oxford University Press, 2016.

U.K. Central Statistical Office. *Annual Abstract of Statistics No. 90*. London: Her Majesty's Stationery Office, 1953.

Wall, Irwin. *The United States and the Making of Postwar France, 1945–1954*. New York: Cambridge University Press, 1991.

Waller, Derek. "The Surrender of the U-Boats in 1945." *Argonauta* 35, no. 2 (Spring 2018): 5–26.

Ward, Jeremy. "Winston Churchill and the 'Iron Curtain' Speech." *History Teacher* 1, no. 2 (January 1968): 5–13, 57–63.

Watson, Mark B. *Sea Logistics: Keeping the Navy Ready Aye Ready*. St. Catharines, ON: Vanwell, 2004.

Weinberg, Gerhard. *A World at Arms: A Global History of World War II*. New York: Cambridge University Press, 1994.

Weinstein, Allen, and Alexander Vassiliev. *The Haunted Wood: Soviet Espionage in America—The Stalin Era*. New York: Random House, 1999.

Weir, Gary. *You Cannot Surge Trust: Combined Naval Operations of the Royal Austra-*

lian Navy, Canadian Navy, Royal Navy, and United States Navy, 1991–2003. Edited by Sandra Doyle. Washington, D.C.: Naval History & Heritage Command, 2013.

White, Philip. *Our Supreme Task: How Winston Churchill's Iron Curtain Speech Defined the Cold War Alliance*. New York: Public Affairs, 2012.

Wiebes, Cees, and Bert Zeeman. "NATO and the United States: An Essay in Kaplanesque History." in *The Romance of History: Essays in Honor of Lawrence S. Kaplan*, edited by Scott Bills and E. Timothy Smith, 15–31. Kent, OH: Kent State University Press, 1997.

Williamson, Corbin. "Industrial-Grade Generosity: British Warship Repair and Lend-Lease in 1941." *Diplomatic History* 36, no. 4 (September 2015): 745–772.

———. "Repair Work and Naval Musical Chairs: Conflict and Cooperation in Anglo-American Naval Relations in 1941." *International Journal of Naval History* 12, no. 2 (July 2015), http://www.ijnhonline.org/2015/07/21/repair-work-and-naval-musical-chairs-conflict-and-cooperation-in-anglo-american-naval-relations-in-1941-2/.

Willmott, H. P. *Empires in the Balance: Japanese and Allied Pacific Strategies to April 1942*. Annapolis, MD: Naval Institute Press, 2008.

———. *Grave of a Dozen Schemes: British Naval Planning and the War against Japan, 1943–1945*. Annapolis, MD: Naval Institute Press, 1996.

Wilson, Alastair. *A Biographical Dictionary of the Twentieth Century Royal Navy*. Vol. 1, *Admirals of the Fleet and Admirals*. Barnsley, U.K.: Seaforth, 2013.

Wilson, Henry M. *Eight Years Overseas, 1939–1947*. London: Hutchinson, 1948.

Wilson, Theodore. *The First Summit: Roosevelt and Churchill at Placentia Bay 1941*. Boston: Houghton Mifflin, 1969.

Winton, John. *The Forgotten Fleet: The British Navy in the Pacific, 1944–1945*. New York: Coward-McCann, 1970.

Womack, Tom. *The Allied Defense of the Malay Barrier, 1941–1942*. Jefferson, NC: McFarland, 2016.

Woods, Randall Bennett, and Howard Jones. *Dawning of the Cold War: The United States' Quest for Order*. Athens: University of Georgia Press, 1991.

Y'Blood, William T. *Hunter-Killer: U.S. Escort Carriers in the Battle of the Atlantic*. Annapolis, MD: Naval Institute Press, 1983.

Young, John. *France, the Cold War, and the Western Alliance, 1944–49: French Foreign Policy and Post-War Europe*. New York: St. Martin's Press, 1990.

Young, Thomas-Durell. *Australian, New Zealand, and United States Security Relations, 1951–1986*. Boulder, CO: Westview Press, 1992.

Zelizer, Julian. *Arsenal of Democracy: The Politics of National Security—From World War II to the War on Terrorism*. New York: Basic Books, 2012.

Ziegler, Philip. *Mountbatten*. New York: Harper & Row, 1985.

Zimmerman, David. *Maritime Command Pacific: The Royal Canadian Navy's West Coast Fleet in the Early Cold War*. Victoria: University of British Columbia Press, 2015.

————. *Top Secret Exchange: The Tizard Mission and the Scientific War.* Montreal: McGill-Queen's University Press, 1996.

THESES, DISSERTATIONS, AND OTHER WORKS

Best, Richard. "Approach to Alliance: British and American Defense Strategies, 1945–1948." PhD diss., Georgetown University, 1983.

Crickard, Fred. "A Tale of Two Navies: United States Security and Canadian and Australian Naval Policy during the Cold War." MA thesis, Dalhousie University, 1993.

Dur, Philip Alphonse. "The Sixth Fleet: A Case Study of Institutionalized Naval Presence, 1946–1968." PhD diss., Harvard University, 1975.

Mason, Russell. "The Evolution of Airborne Antisubmarine Warfare." March 9, 1970. Author's personal collection. Provided by Dr. Owen Cote.

Sheehy, Chris. "USS Robin: An Account of the HMS Victorious' First Mission to the Pacific." MA thesis, University of New Brunswick, 1996.

Willmot, H. P. "Just Being There: An Examination of the Record, Problems and Achievements of the British Pacific Fleet in the Course of Its Operations in the Indian and Pacific Oceans between November 1944 and September 1945." PhD diss., King's College, London, 1986.

INTERNET RESOURCES

Arlington National Cemetery Website. http://www.arlingtoncemetery.net.

Australian Dictionary of Biography. Accessed July 23, 2018. http://adb.anu.edu.au.

Australian War Memorial. "Vice Admiral John Augustine Collins." https://web.archive.org/save/https://www.awm.gov.au/people/P10676561/.

Central Intelligence Agency, Freedom of Information Act Electronic Reading Room. "State-Defense Military Information Control Committee (S-DMICC)," June 27, 1962. https://www.cia.gov/library/readingroom/docs/CIA-RDP80B01676R00310 0200011–6.pdf.

Chantrill, Christopher. *UK Public Spending.* Accessed July 6, 2018. https://www.uk publicspending.co.uk/.

Gingrich, John E., Vice Admiral USN, Chief of Naval Material. "Publication No. 154–54, Military Procurement." Industrial College of the Armed Forces, November 18, 1953. https://web.archive.org/web/20040223004723/http://www.ndu.edu /library/ic2/L54–054.pdf.

Kolterman, Robert F. "Interagency Coordination: Past Lessons, Current Issues, and Future Necessities." U.S. Army War College, March 2006. https://apps.dtic.mil /dtic/tr/fulltext/u2/a448331.pdf.

Meteorological Committee. "Monthly Weather Report of the Meteorological Office," December 1918. https://www.metoffice.gov.uk/binaries/content/assets/mo -hippo/pdf/h/b/dec1918.pdf.

National Security Agency. "UKUSA Agreement Release, 1940–1956." Accessed December 16, 2019. https://www.nsa.gov/news-features/declassified-documents/uk usa/.

National Security Archive. https://nsarchive.gwu.edu/.

Naval History and Heritage Command. Dictionary of American Naval Fighting Ships. http://www.history.navy.mil/research/histories/ship-histories/danfs.html.

Office of Naval Intelligence. "The Java Sea Campaign." U.S. Navy, 1943. Updated June 18, 2002. http://ibiblio.org/hyperwar/USN/USN-CN-Java/index.html.

Oxford Dictionary of National Biography. https://www.oxforddnb.com/.

Palmer, Michael. "The Influence of Naval Strategy on National Security Planning, 1945–1955." Naval History and Heritage Command, 1989. Accessed June 3, 2018. https://www.history.navy.mil/research/library/online-reading-room/title-list -alphabetically/t/time-change.html.

Proc, Jerry. "Canadian Avenger AS3 A/S Aircraft." https://web.archive.org/web/2015 0316142633/http://jproc.ca/rrp/rrp3/avenger.html.

Trudeau, Pierre Elliott. "Pierre Trudeau's Washington Press Club Speech." March 25, 1969. http://www.cbc.ca/archives/entry/trudeaus-washington-press-club-speech.

United States Naval War College. "Register of Officers, 1884–1979," July 11, 1975. https://web.archive.org/web/20150911223408/https://www.usnwc.edu/getat tachment/de2da848-af41–42d1-b715-adb3dfdbb834/NWC-Students—Facul ty1884to1979.aspx.

University of California, Santa Barbara, American Presidency Project. https://www .presidency.ucsb.edu/.

INDEX

Abbott, Douglas, 124, 136
ABDA. *See* American, British, Dutch,
　　Australian Command
Admiralty, British
　　British Admiralty Delegation, 36, 38, 54
　　and the British Pacific Fleet, 28, 90
　　in the Korean War, 201, 209, 220
　　and Somerville initiatives, 38–41
　　and standardization, 144–145, 149, 153
　　and training and education, 166, 171, 192
　　in World War I, 14–15
　　See also Royal Navy
Africa, 22, 30, 56, 101, 162
　　Northern Africa, 30, 56, 101
　　South Africa, 48–50, 133
AFSOUTH. *See* Allied Forces Southern
　　Europe
aircraft
　　antiaircraft, 24–25, 196
　　antisubmarine, 123–124, 173
　　Avenger, 25, 123–126, 175, 179
　　Banshee fighter, 103, 117
　　Firefly fighters, 123, 205
　　and global naval planning, 75–76, 82, 89, 98
　　and Korean War, 199, 202, 205–208, 217–
　　　219, 223, 226
　　patrol planes, 82, 188, 193–194
　　and personnel, 103–104, 123–125
　　and postwar partnerships, 39
　　and Scapa Flow, 24–26
　　and standardization, 135, 143, 146–148
　　and training and education, 170–171, 173–
　　　176, 184–186, 188–189, 192–196
　　See also aircraft carriers
aircraft carriers, 82, 171, 207
　　Anglo-American exchange of, 24–25
　　and antisubmarine schools, 171, 175–176
　　and antisubmarine warfare, 75
　　and Benjamin Custer, 123–124
　　and combined exercises, 184–196
　　and cross-decking, 25, 195
　　escort carriers, 22, 150, 207
　　flight deck operations, 195–196, 199, 207,
　　　223, 238

flight operations, 123, 206, 225
and global naval planning, 85
and the Korean War, 202–208, 214–215,
　　221–223, 226, 228–231
landing equipment, 39, 111
mirror landing system, 207, 238
and nuclear weapons, 81–82
operations, 77, 113, 127, 206–207, 236, 238
and training exercises, 175, 189, 192–193,
　　238
air force. *See specific national air forces*
air support, 186, 189, 201, 203, 212
alliances, 3–8, 233, 237, 239
and global naval planning, 68–71, 78, 82,
　　92, 100
and the Korean War, 199, 210, 214, 225–
　　226, 231
and personnel, 104, 106, 108, 120
post–World War II, 32–33, 37, 44, 58–59
and standardization, 132, 135, 153, 159–162
and training, 164, 181, 185–186, 197–198
See also North Atlantic Treaty
　　Organization
Allied Communications Publication 175,
　　159–160, 206, 220, 229–231, 235
Allied Forces Mediterranean, 85–86
Allied Forces Southern Europe, 85
*Allied Naval Maneuvering Instructions Allied
　　Tactical Publication I*, 38, 158–160, 162,
　　189, 193
and the Korean War, 229–230, 235
Allies, World War II
and the Cold War, 30
and the Combined Chiefs of Staff, 42, 51
and postwar relations, 33, 51–52, 247n9
and Scapa Flow, 10, 13
ambassadors, 104, 127, 235
American, 120, 122, 136
Australian, 106
British, 15, 169
French, 55
American, British, Dutch, Australian
　　Command, 19–21, 253n52
Combined Striking Force, 20–21